FROM OLD TIMES TO NEW EUROPE

To Hund and HDD

From Old Times to New Europe
The Polish Struggle for Democracy and Constitutionalism

AGATA FIJALKOWSKI
University of Lancaster, UK

Routledge
Taylor & Francis Group
LONDON AND NEW YORK

First published 2010 by Ashgate Publishing

Published 2016 by Routledge
2 Park Square, Milton Park, Abingdon, Oxon OX14 4RN
711 Third Avenue, New York, NY 10017, USA

Routledge is an imprint of the Taylor & Francis Group, an informa business

British Library Cataloguing in Publication Data
Fijalkowski, Agata.
From old times to new Europe : the Polish struggle for
democracy and constitutionalism.
1. Rule of law--Europe, Eastern. 2. Rule of law--Europe,
Central. 3. Totalitarianism.
I. Title
349.4'7-dc22

Library of Congress Cataloging-in-Publication Data
Fijalkowski, Agata.
From old times to new Europe : the Polish struggle for democracy and constitutionalism / by Agata Fijalkowski.
p. cm.
Includes bibliographical references and index.
ISBN 978-0-7546-7338-5 (hardback) -- ISBN 978-0-7546-9121-1 (ebook)
1. Constitutional history--Poland. 2. Poland--Politics and government--20th century.
I. Title.

KKP2101.F55 2010
342.43802'9--dc22

2010007087

ISBN 13: 978-0-7546-7338-5 (hbk)

Contents

Acknowledgements

I wish to thank my family, friends and colleagues, who have assisted me, through their interest in and engagement with ideas and issues, to finish this book. I am grateful to Deborah Baber-Allen, Malgosia Fitzmaurice, Wayne Kerstetter, Matthew Lippman, Sean McConville, Karen Nicholson (for introducing me to Wanda Rutkiewicz!), and Halina and Waldemar Slowinski, for commenting on different parts of this project and sharing ideas. For the same reasons, I am grateful to Alison Kirk at Ashgate, the two anonymous reviewers of the manuscript and Julie Pickard. I also would like to thank my colleagues at Lancaster University Law School, in particular, Wendy Doggett, Sharon Hinnigan, Eileen Jones, Peter Rowe, David Seymour, David Sugarman, and Janan Yakula, for support and humour. My gratitude extends to my Polish colleagues, in particular, Piotr Hofmanski, judge at the Polish Supreme Court, and Andrzej Rzeplinski, University of Warsaw, and Danuta Sadkowska at the State and Law Library of the Polish Academy of Sciences. My time at Europa-Universität Viadrina, in Frankfurt (Oder), provided much joy and inspiration, and I am especially grateful to Prof. Dr. Roland Wittmann and my colleagues in the Law Faculty who made me feel so welcome. My parents, Alicia and Alex Fijalkowski, have been a constant source of support.

Introduction

From Old Times to New Europe: The Polish Struggle for Democracy and Constitutionalism revisits pertinent questions concerning the role of the law and judges in a region where issues of democracy and constitutionalism are continually debated, and discussions are fraught. The region is Central and Eastern Europe (CEE), and the main matter concerns the success in setting up a rule-of-law state when the state has emerged from a regime that sought to control all aspects of public and private life, and where the notion of state power was one that marginalised the judicial role, aiming to eradicate independence and replace it with subservience. The year 2009 has commemorated two decades of a post-communist Europe under newly formed political structures, albeit post-totalitarian ones.[1] This is an exciting period in which to revisit questions that captivate lawyers and academics alike, as well as those who have a peculiar interest in this rich region, which continues to surprise, especially in the areas of law, history and politics.

This book is mainly about the Polish experience. The analysis focuses on the particular significance history has in the region's identity and preferences as concerns the role of the state in public and private life. Such an examination shows how tradition and a particular path of development have paved the way towards the establishment of democracy and the rule of law, revealing certain approaches, or 'sensibilities' that shape values, which, in turn, form the basis of the relation between the individual and the state.[2] Many times, the choices have led to destruction of fundamental features of the democratic state. More disturbingly, the same tensions and misunderstandings can be identified as concerns the role of the judiciary in Poland and in the wider CEE context. While attempts on the part of the executive to control the judiciary are an oft-repeated theme, the fact that lawyers' movements have time and time again proved that the judiciary reflects the 'quality of democracy in that particular country', compels us to understand the mechanisms of this effect.[3]

1 See, for example, Timothy Garton Ash, '1989!', *New York Review of Books*, 5 November 2009.

2 The pivotal works here are David Garland, *Punishment and Modern Society: A Study in Social Theory* (Oxford: Clarendon Press, 1990), and Evi Girling, 'European Identity, Penal Sensibilities, and Communities of Sentiment', in *Perspectives on Punishment: The Contours of Control*, ed. by Sarah Armstrong and Lesley McAra (Oxford: Oxford University Press, 2006), pp. 69–82.

3 Kate Malleson and Peter H. Russell, eds, *Appointing Judges in an Age of Judicial Power: Critical Perspectives from Around the World* (Toronto: University of Toronto Press, 2006).

There is much at stake. If values ensuring judicial independence and, ultimately, the rule of law are violated, the state is robbed of one of the most important guarantees ensured in a rule-of-law state. Furthermore, my focus on judicial officials is reinforced by recent developments that may be the reply to such campaigns.[4]

Methodology

My approach and presentation of findings is historical to the extent needed to appreciate contemporary developments in the region. Key events and critical developments associated with a particular time period are examined. These are then considered within the present-day context, involving an investigation of political and socio-economic as well as legal developments. The discussion in these chapters is historical; comparisons are drawn with other CEE states to support and elucidate key points. The discussion is contextual, relying on key socio-legal theories that seek to explain particular trends and general strains during the post-communist and *post-totalitarian* period.

Structure of the Book

The book is divided into five chapters. The aim is to provide readers who do not possess a specialised knowledge of the region with an examination of the key political, social and economic developments that affect legal reforms within three different time frames: interwar, communist rule, and present day. These discussions draw on research that is firmly established in the area, such as, *inter alia*, the key works by Norman Davies. My command of the Polish language has allowed access to key archival materials. This extends to the Russian language as well. Thus, in the first two chapters, while I start with a historical overview, I include material on novel features of the newly established states, in order to reinforce the contention that history has a key role to play in analysing contemporary developments.

Chapter 1 discusses events leading to national independence and particular issues that would later be the point of contention between newly established and created CEE states. It recalls the enormous significance that the re-emergence of statehood and the establishment thereof had for the respective CEE national identities that would later influence and shape relations between the state and society. The notion of nationhood was debated by intellectuals in the CEE region, and it is this group that held the key to continuity – in terms of approaches to constitutionalism and democracy – at that time. The Polish case shows that a

4 Jane Perlez, 'Detained Pakistani Seeks to Revive Judiciary Clause', *New York Times*, 8 December 2008.

strong state was, and continues to be, supported by Poles. This has consequences for the role of the judiciary, both past and present.

Chapter 2 continues to analyse the pre-war period. At this time, several newly created states were eager to introduce constitutional protections to protect the third branch of government. Pioneers of the Polish legal framework had to overcome serious obstacles in the form of the increasingly authoritarian regimes that were emerging in the region and that were not ready to recognise an independent judiciary. During this brief but tumultuous period, Polish constitutionalism shifted from individual interests to a more paternalistic stance as concerns rights protection, a stance which also demonstrated a clear tension between the state and its nascent judiciary, which was slowly being made subservient to state interests. Law and politics were inseparable. Again, the role of intellectuals, the intelligentsia, was paramount in the shaping of events. Alongside this, key Polish legal philosophers, such as Leon Petrazycki, would utilise their respective experiences gained in the respective partitions of the country, to forge ahead with new ideas about law and morality, ideas that responded to the positivist mood at that time and that would shape modern Poland to come.

Chapter 3 examines key features of German and communist rule from 1939 to 1945. Both regimes did not disguise their resentment towards the legal community, demonstrating blatant disrespect for categories of people whom they viewed as a threat to the ruling party and its values. This relatively short period was marked by the violence, corruption and repression that would be present when the communists established their rule. The chapter refers to archival material to show further how power, law and knowledge characterised communist rule and its success in perverting the law and blurring the line between the legal and the illegal. Judges served the regime and their work was controlled by the authorities; in other words, judicial independence was non-existent.

Chapter 4 is devoted to communist rule. In a regime that is characterised by constant surveillance of people in their public and private lives, the people adapt and adopt certain coping mechanisms that serve to form quite strong notions about law and justice. Archival material demonstrates specifically how the Polish administration of justice was reorganised along Soviet lines. I analyse how all judicial officials were systematically replaced by Soviet-trained officials. This was the 'war against the judiciary', but it was not waged without resistance. The prosecution services were developed outside the administration of justice, to complement surveillance and ensure compliance. Despite shows of defiance, the legal framework, under the Soviet model, revealed itself to be moribund and suffering from rigid judicial reasoning and lack of procedural guarantees. Nonetheless, Polish legal science continued to evolve and develop schools of reasoning that show innovation, remarkable insight and awareness of judicial interpretation that challenge understandings of sources of law and their normative value. Jurisprudence that illustrates this point is considered in Chapter 5. Scholars, such as Lefort, have long argued that the study of post-totalitarian law occupies an important space in the study of legal transition. 'Since the fall of the Berlin wall, a range of analysts have approached Communism with its death certificate in hand, conducting autopsies on its corpse in order to show that it had always been terminally ill, that its very birth had in some sense made it mortal.'[5] Lefort rightly asserts that communism is not dead, and that an examination of its roots and the existence of its remnants are as important as its collapse. Equally, Podgorecki's work consistently reminds us that '[i]t would be a great mistake to assume that the phenomenon of totalitarianism is an incidental digression in the process of the transformation of contemporary society.'[6]

Contemporary developments demonstrate that the much marginalised third branch of government plays a key part in the construction of the rule-of-law state. An examination of the courts and case law and the role of judges reveals that while we can see general trends and strains that are remnants of communist rule, these cannot be understood without an appreciation of the interwar period in the present-day CEE. Aspects of de-communisation and transitional justice support this point, in particular in relation to the central case of the Polish Constitutional Tribunal and Polish Supreme Court. The discussion is framed in the context of current approaches to these complex cases of de-communisation and retroactivity. The analysis is conducted within a framework of history that shows continuity with the interwar period and all its complexities and, at the same time, reveals the extent and value of exploring judicial reasoning through the lens of contemporary scholars and key Polish legal thinkers such as Leon Petrazycki and Aleksander Peczenik, as well as the regional framework embodied in the European Court of Human Rights. Tentative conclusions are put forward as concerns generalisations about post-communist legal frameworks, using the valuable, but admittedly limited, Polish case study.

The significance of this study on Poland cannot be underestimated. The country's economic, political, and cultural importance has been recognised throughout history. Its unrelenting fight to preserve its identity and language during a century of foreign rule is an incredible feat. Thus developments in the legal sphere will certainly be of interest and be followed by its neighbours, states that have also emerged from two world wars, brutal rule, and police-state regimes, notwithstanding limited experience with democracy and constitutionalism. The Polish approach to critical constitutional questions, which include the role and function of its judicial cadre, has been correctly viewed as a potential blueprint for other countries. It is therefore essential to revisit Poland's journey to the present day, and to appreciate the significance that the year 1989 holds for Poland and the wider region.

The book draws on several primary sources. Fluency in the Polish language has allowed me to use several important archival sources in Poland. I have worked

5 Claude Lefort, *Complications: Communism and the Dilemmas of Democracy*, trans. by J. Bourg (New York: Columbia University Press, 2007), p. 2.

6 Adam Podgorecki, 'Preface', *Totalitarian and Post-Totalitarian Law*, ed. by Adam Podgorecki and Vittorio Olgiati (Aldershot: Dartmouth, 1996), p. vii.

in the following archives in Warsaw, Poland: the Main Archives of New Acts (*Archiwa Akt Nowych*), the Main Archives of Old Acts (*Archiwa Akt Dawnych*) and the Parliamentary Archives (*Parlamentarne Archiwa*). My work has extended to the libraries of the University of Warsaw, the State and Law Library of the Academy of Sciences, and the library of the Polish Supreme Court. I also have had the opportunity to work in the following Russian archives as a result of a travel grant from the Central Research Fund, University of London, and the Faculty of Laws, Queen Mary and Westfield College, University of London: the Main Archives of the Communist Party, the Russian Centre for the Preservation and the Study of Records of Modern History (*Rossiiskii tsentr khranenia i izucheniia dokumentov noveishei istorii*; hereafter, RTsKhIDNI), and the State Archives of the Russian Federation (*Gosudarstvennyi archkiv Rossiiskii Federatsii*; hereafter, GARF), including work at the Library for Social Sciences (*Institut nauchnoi informatsii po obshectvenyim naukom RAN*).

I also had the opportunity to study materials on the Polish underground and its activities during the Second World War at the Archives of the Study for the Movement of the Polish Underground, in addition to the libraries of the School of Slavonic Studies (SSEES), the Institute of Legal Studies, and, in Leiden, The Netherlands, the Institute for Russian and East European Studies, University of Leiden. Finally, I conducted research at the Max-Planck-Institut, Freiburg-im-Breisgau, Germany, as the result of a scholarship.

It should be noted that while the archives of the former Soviet bloc countries had been opened to the public, much of the information was still classified while I was conducting my research; there were also many instances of materials and documents being reclassified, cutting short possible avenues of research. All in all, I am deeply indebted to the staff of each of the archives in Warsaw and Moscow for their support and assistance in procuring the necessary material. Please note the following published essay of mine adapted a small section of Chapter 4 (pp. 90–101) in 'The Abolition of the Death Penalty in Central and Eastern Europe', *Tilburg Law Review*, 9 (2001), pp. 62–83.

Chapter 1
Path to Independence

> I have never been here before, but everything in this place is etched in my memory, as though they were my own recollections.[1]

Collapse of the European Order

In an attempt to find a point of continuity between the revolutions of 1989 and the past, historians have turned to the revolutions of 1848. Garton Ash has aptly noted the role of intellectuals, ideas and ideals in the execution of the various national reform revolutions of 1989.[2] Johnson, relying on Garton Ash, also recognises that the role of intellectuals in the revolutions of 1848, in which constitutional government, civil rights, the end of serfdom, liberalism and nationalism were advocated, was identical to the aspirations of the dissidents and the intellectuals of the communist states during the 1980s.[3] Thus, a clearer understanding of the motives of these revolutionaries and the reasons for their failure is important; if the success of liberal democratic revolutions is one of the distinguishing features of the 'Western' European political experience, their relative failure has been the key attribute of most of the Central and East European ones.[4] These issues resonate to the present day, as we shall see later.

The events in France and its revolution were the catalyst for the revolutions to occur in 1848: they served as an inspiration to the peoples across Europe. In Germany, for example, there was a series of uprisings organised by students and those from other walks of life, such as artisans, workers and peasants, who demanded to be treated like citizens in a different sense, namely as citizens in a new constitutional order. But the demands in Germany and in other parts of Europe varied in their 'revolutionary' nature: not all made demands which adhered to the aims of the French Revolution, and they took on different forms.[5] In Vienna, the first step was the submission by students and the middle class of a petition for change. This resulted in a clash with imperial troops and the resignation of

---

1 Geert Mak, *In Europe: Travels Through the Twentieth Century* (London: Harvill Secker, 2007), p. 243.

2 Timothy Garton Ash, 'Eastern Europe: The Year of Truth', *New York Review of Books*, 15 February 1990, p. 17.

3 Lonnie Johnson, *Central Europe: Enemies, Neighbors, Friends* (Oxford: Oxford University Press, 1996), pp. 149–51.

4 Garton Ash, 'Eastern Europe', *supra* n. 2 and *ibid.*

5 See Philip Longworth, *The Making of Eastern Europe* (London: St. Martin's Press, 1994), pp. 96–97.

Metternich. The Austro-Hungarian emperor, Ferdinand I, acceded to the demands, one of them being the rights of his subjects as citizens to draft a new constitution. The Prussian king, Frederick Wilhelm, yielded to the same demands shortly after.

In the Central and Eastern European region (CEE), the issues raised in these revolutions were interrelated. For Poles, this 'springtime of other nations', as aptly named by Davies, was relevant.[6] But, as the term implies, it was a period during which social and constitutional reforms were gained in Prussian and Austrian Poland, but no advances towards autonomy. Instead, Poles participated in movements abroad rather than at home.[7] Further, the debates during this period also reflected the difference between Poles concerning an independent Poland.[8] It is equally important to note that neither France nor Germany was willing to make any serious commitment to the Polish question.[9] The Poles were faced with a slightly different set of problems because of the partition of their country. Moreover, the Polish uprisings of 1830, 1846 and 1863 made 1848 seem a relatively calm affair.[10] The uprising in Posen led to the short-lived existence of the Grand Duchy of Posen, but the Prussian authorities were ready to stop it from gaining momentum.[11] In the Austrian partition, the peasantry received concessions in the form of freeholds (the gentry being granted compensation from state funds), and later other rights were extended to peasants, such as access to woods, meadows and pastures. Such developments coincided with the ideals promoted in 1848. They also became the source of dispute between the peasants and the gentry. Indeed, because of the wide range of people that the revolution encompassed, it is not surprising that the sense of fraternity and equality deteriorated among the revolutionaries, thus enabling the authorities to reassert their power.[12]

It is noteworthy that the revolutionaries advocated liberal reform and that constitutions were on the agenda. For example, German revolutionaries sought to draft constitutions and participate in the creation of a unified German state. Representatives from all 40 member states of the German Confederation (including Prussia and Austria) met in Frankfurt in 1848 to draft a constitution for a unified German state. The Austrian Constituent Assembly was multinational; it included non-German-speaking representatives from the empire, namely Czechs, Poles,

---

6 Norman Davies, *God's Playground: A History of Poland, Volume II: 1795 to the Present* (New York: Columbia University Press, 1982), pp. 340–46.

7 *Ibid.*

8 *Ibid.* For example, the Manifesto of the Polish Democratic Society of 1836 was the source of strong disapproval at the Slav Congress in Prague and represented an outdated view of the Polish state.

9 *Ibid.*

10 Johnson, *Central Europe*, *supra* n. 3, pp. 151–60.

11 See, generally, R. F. Leslie, 'Triloyalism and the National Revival', in *The History of Poland Since 1863*, ed. by R. F. Leslie (Cambridge: Cambridge University Press, 1983), pp. 1–64.

12 Longworth, *The Making of Eastern Europe*, *supra* n. 5, pp. 96–97.

Ruthenes and Slovenes.[13] At the convention, the liberals hoped that the German-Austrians would volunteer to abandon the multinational Austro-Hungarian Empire in order to assume a leading role in the German state. Several terms became fashionable in the debates over the future German borders: *Anschluss* (union), *Grossdeutsch* (greater German) and *Kleindeutsch* (small German).[14]

In response to the convention, some representatives of the Slavonic nations in the Austro-Hungarian Empire revealed their interest in reforms based on confederative principles. The Czechs lobbied hard. In June 1848, Frantisek Palacký, a Czech historian, organised a 'counter-conference' for Slavs in Prague, which was attended by representatives from Slavonic national groups of the Austro-Hungarian Empire, as well as a few Polish émigrés from Russian Poland. The participants discussed the future of the Slavs in a democratic and federal transformation of the empire. Palacký was strongly opposed to the German solution, which he viewed with trepidation because he believed that a greater German state would engulf its smaller Slavonic neighbours. A similar view was taken of the Russian Empire's promotion of pan-Slavism and the creation of a Russian universal monarchy. The only solution for the smaller nations living alongside the Germans and the Russians, in his view, was to consolidate and confederate. Palacký proposed reforming the Austro-Hungarian Empire into a series of national units joined together by a form of central government and administration that would control foreign affairs, defence, finance and trade. This vision was never realised, but the conference emphasised the important task of defining the CEE region as one which excluded the Russian, Prussian and Austrians.[15] Radical democratic elements eventually took control of the Austro-Hungarian Empire and, in 1848, Franz Joseph I assumed the imperial throne upon the abdication of Emperor Ferdinand. Franz Joseph ceased work on the constitution (even though he had supported it); his advisers later prepared another document in haste, one that the people had not drafted and one that was not based on the sovereignty of the people. During the turbulent events of 1848, relations deteriorated between the Kingdom of Hungary and the Austro-Hungarian Empire, and Hungarian patriots saw their chance for independence. In April 1849, the Hungarian *Diet* revoked the crown from the Habsburgs, declared independence, and appointed Louis Kossuth, a radical democrat and fierce fighter for Hungarian independence, as the governor-president.[16] The combined forces of the Russian and Austrian powers eventually brought the revolution to an end. The Hungarians lost the revolution, but they benefited from the failure: the 1867 reorganisation of the Austro-Hungarian Empire into the Dual Monarchy of Austria–Hungary proved more beneficial.

---

13 Johnson, *Central Europe*, *supra* n. 3, pp. 152–53.

14 *Ibid.* Germany's aim of *Anschluss* was forbidden by the Treaty of Versailles.

15 *Ibid.*

16 *Ibid.* The Kingdom of Hungary enjoyed a privileged status and certain traditions, such as the Hungarian *Diet*, continued to be observed.

The notion of *Mitteleuropa*, which literally means 'middle Europe', was an important concept in CEE events during this time. The notion is a vague German concept that reflected the Germans' view of themselves as inhabiting the land in the middle, between the East and the West, or between Russia and France. The concept took on negative connotations after 1871, when it came to reflect Bismarck's aspirations (German imperial ambitions) to dominate the CEE. (The term later played a conceptual role in the occupational policies of the Third Reich.) In 1915, Friedrich Naumann published his book, *Mitteleuropa*, which was the classic formulation of the German imperial concept of Central Europe.[17] Naumann envisaged a new political and economic order for Europe, and *Mitteleuropa* represented a network of states in which Germany played a leading role. For Naumann, the borders of *Mitteleuropa* were negotiable; the minimal basis was the creation of a common market between the German and Austro-Hungarian empires, including a military alliance of the Central Powers, which would attract and indeed force neighbouring countries to seek membership.[18] This extended to a Polish state detached from Russia. Naumann's theory represented the common vision of the German army, government, and industry at the beginning of the First World War.

General Overview (1914–1919)

At the turn of the century, the population of the CEE had nearly doubled.[19] Between 1900 and 1914, the number increased by another 25 per cent.[20] Urban life underwent a serious change owing to migration; Warsaw, Prague and Budapest experienced a population increase of alarming proportions.[21] As Longworth aptly observes, the increase in the population of Vienna, from 750,000 to over 2 million, led to the rise in various movements of political and artistic nature that were based on the prevailing nationalism in the region.[22]

In the years before the war, the three empires focused their attention on the Balkans, where they had conflicting interests. Russia, for example, sought to control the Slavonic-speaking areas (Bulgaria and Serbia), while Austria had mutual economic interests with Germany in the region. By 1912, tension had mounted when Austrian authorities forced Serbia to cease its quest to conquer

17 Friedrich Naumann, *Mitteleuropa* (Berlin: Verlag Reimer, 1915).

18 *Ibid.*

19 Longworth, *The Making of Eastern Europe*, *supra* n. 5, p. 111.

20 *Ibid.*

21 *Ibid.* Between 1880 and 1910, the population of Warsaw tripled to nearly 856,000, that of Prague rose to nearly a quarter of a million, and that of Budapest doubled to nearly 900,000.

22 *Ibid.*, pp. 111–12.

further territory in Albania.[23] When Austria and Serbia entered an intense economic war,[24] Serbia was provided with the reasons for retaliation against the Austrian government; in June 1914, a small group of young nationalists from Bosnia assassinated Archduke Franz Ferdinand and his wife during an official visit in Sarajevo.

The policies of the Central Powers concerning an independent Poland vacillated greatly during the First World War. At first, the armies appealed to the Poles for war support and cooperation. Vague promises were made about Polish borders, which carried no political meaning as they were made by military forces. Almost overnight, Polish organisations were created in Cracow and Warsaw, to support the Polish cause while providing assistance to war victims.[25] In August 1914, Jozef Pilsudski formed the Polish Legions, which were subordinated to Austrian authority.[26]

In 1915, however, the direction of the war changed. The Central Powers succeeded in driving the Russian armies out of Polish territory and on 5 August Warsaw was taken over by German and Austro-Hungarian authorities, who initiated a vigorous campaign of reorganisation. The territory was divided between the two; the north was headed by the German General Hans Hartwig von Beseler; the south was headed by the Austrian General Karl von Kuk. Public appeals for a future Poland were strong, and the German-Austrian-run government had to decide whether they could offer Poles a more tangible autonomy.

As noted above, in Germany the concept of *Mitteleuropa* was prominent and the question of an independent Poland was immediately silenced in favour of German expansion eastwards. In 1915 the general outlook of the conservative and nationalist parties supported the expansion for economic necessity and general stability; this view was also supported by a powerful German lobby. Such a move would have denied freedom to German Poles and to inhabitants of the newly liberated territories.[27] The military, which also affected governmental decisions, urged expansion and the realisation of the notion of *Mitteleuropa*.

The Austrian authorities were more moderate but no less vague: they refused to clarify the position of Poland with regard to the Austro-Hungarian Empire. A compromise was reached in that Poland would be reconstituted as a monarchy under the equal control of Germany and Austria and its military headed by the

23 Serbia, with the help of Bulgaria, Greece and Montenegro, launched a successful attack against Turkish territory in 1912. The Serbs invaded Albanian territory, which paved the way for further conflict between states in the region. *Ibid.*, p. 120.

24 *Ibid.* Known as the 'pig war', because of the high tariffs and veterinary restrictions that Austrian authorities imposed on Serbian pigs, which were a major export to the empire.

25 Davies, *God's Playground*, *supra* n. 6, pp. 380–81.

26 *Ibid.*

27 Jan Karski, *The Great Powers and Poland 1919–1945: From Versailles to Yalta* (London: University Press of America, 1985), pp. 4–7.

German army. This decision was short-lived, however, and, by 1916, more liberal voices in Germany urged peace while in Austria doubts had begun to arise about a future dual monarchy. In Russia, the tendency was for a separate peace.

On 5 November 1916, the German emperor, Wilhelm II, and his Austro-Hungarian counterpart, Franz Joseph, issued a joint manifesto addressed to the Poles, in which both rulers solemnly declared that Poland would become an autonomous state and a constitutional and hereditary monarchy. The document was drawn up after the German losses at Verdun – the empire was in desperate need of military recruits and the authorities decided to play on Polish sympathies. The manifesto stressed that the state would comprise territories seized from Russia; this indicated an attack against Russia and the rejection of any peace. The issue of borders was left for future discussion. The document further stipulated the creation of a Polish army; its organisation and command was to be decided upon mutual agreement. Needless to say, the manifesto was highly criticised by all parties in the war and 'became one of the most controversial ... documents of World War I'.[28] For the Poles, however, their cause had been formally addressed by rulers, and that could only bring them closer to some form of independence.

The Declaration of 5 November sparked a debate between the 'activists' and the 'passivists'. The activists proposed taking advantage of the German defeat at Verdun by entering into negotiations with the Central Powers and, indeed, Pilsudski also saw the opportunity; the passivists categorically rejected any negotiations.[29]

When the war broke out in 1914, the Triple Entente powers of France, Russia and Great Britain pursued traditional objectives. Their aim was to fight German aggression and they sought to defeat the Central Powers of Germany and Austria–Hungary. The fact that Britain and France, the foremost representatives of Western Europe's parliamentary and republican traditions, had allied themselves with the despotic Russian Empire, did not prevent them from maintaining that they were also fighting for freedom and democracy.[30]

The Russian Empire controlled most of the territory of ethnic Poland; its policies thus were of great importance to the Poles. Events were also carefully monitored by Paris and London, where authorities were careful not to adopt any policy of their own concerning a future Polish state as Russia was a powerful ally.

Eventually the Russian authorities had to make more specific overtures to the Poles. In 1916, the Russian Tsar, Nicholas II, ordered a draft manifesto declaring the autonomy of Poland. The future Poland was to comprise Russian Poland and the German and Austrian-inhabited areas. The country would be autonomous,

28 *Ibid.*, p. 7.

29 For further details, see Henryk Wereszycki, 'Poland Under Foreign Rule', in *History of Poland*, ed. by Aleksander Gieysztor *et al.* (Warsaw: PWN, 1968), pp. 616, 619 and 624.

30 Johnson, *Central Europe*, *supra* n. 3, p. 171.

save for foreign policy, army, customs, finance and railways.[31] The future state did not differ much from the German-Austrian proposal and all activities of strategic importance would be placed under imperial control. The Russian draft was superseded by the German-Austrian manifesto and was therefore never issued. In the meantime, the Poles were consolidating their power in the Austrian partition by forming various organisations[32] and extending their activities in the Russian partition at times with encouragement on the part of the Austrian authorities. Jozef Pilsudski was one of the Poles who were active in Galicia. His alliance with the Austrian authorities was significant. His activities were tolerated until 1917, when both the German and Austro-Hungarian governments became suspicious of the Polish Legions' loyalty and Pilsudski's tactics.[33] The Poles had good reason 'to be anti-Russian, if not pro-German, and some were willing to go along with this strategy, at least at first'.[34] This outlook generally continued throughout the First World War.

Apart from weakening Germany and breaking up the German-Austro-Hungarian alliance, the Triple Entente powers had no grand designs for a new Europe. France hoped to reclaim Alsace-Lorraine, which it had lost to Germany in 1871. Russia had vaguely hoped to liberate Ukrainian minorities in the Galician parts of the Austro-Hungarian Empire. At the beginning of the war, Triple Entente generals and politicians still envisaged a post-war European order as comprising Britain, France, Germany, Austria–Hungary and Russia.

Although Austria–Hungary would be required to make major territorial sacrifices, the importance of the Habsburg dual monarchy in the European balance of power was unquestioned at the beginning of the war, and neither Britain nor France considered re-establishing an independent Poland to be one of their war aims. This view changed in 1917 with two sets of events that would change the complexion of the war: the Russian Revolution and the entry of the United States

---

31 Karski, *The Great Powers and Poland*, *supra* n. 27, p. 10.

32 The two largest minority groups in Austrian Poland were the Poles and the Ukrainians. The Austrian authorities took advantage of their traditional rivalry, and granted the Ukrainians certain concessions, using them as bargaining tools with the Poles. Following the demonstrations of 1868, the Austrian authorities yielded to Polish demands: the reinstitution of the Polish language on the same level as German in all official business (1869); Polish became the main language of instruction at the Jagiellonian University (1870); the creation of a Ministry of Galician Affairs to maintain the interests of Austrian Poland; the establishment of the *Academia Umiejetnosci* (The Academy of Learning) in Cracow (1872); and the creation of an educational board which oversaw the operation of a full-time system of primary education in the local languages (1873). It is important to note that in all of these measures, a new pool of well-educated Poles formed part of the staff, thereby increasing the chances for Poles to enter a so-called autonomous administration and obtain experience in managing Polish affairs.

33 Karski, *The Great Powers and Poland*, *supra* n. 27, p. 13.

34 Richard Blanke, *The Orphans of Versailles: The Germans in Western Poland 1918–1939* (Lexington, KY: University Press of Kentucky, 1993), p. 13.

into the conflict. It was the first time in history that the United States intervened in European affairs on such a large scale. Although Woodrow Wilson and Vladimir Lenin were two leaders with a completely different vision of Europe, they made substantial contributions to the ending of the war and articulating the conditions for peace, bringing the aim of national self-determination to the discussions.[35]

Wilson stressed the importance of a 'united, independent and autonomous Poland' in January 1917, three months prior to the United States' entry into the war. Wilson was the only Western leader to take the issue of Polish independence seriously. With the dismantling of the Russian Empire, it became a serious possibility. On 3 June 1918, France, Britain and Italy formally endorsed Poland's independence as a war aim at a meeting of the Triple Entente's Supreme War Council in Versailles. It should be remembered, however, that the Triple Entente merely sanctioned the re-establishment of the Polish state: in fact, the Polish state emerged from the vacuum created by the collapse of the Russian, German and Austro-Hungarian empires at the end of the war. The Polish situation was unique in that it was always a question of imposed rule on the part of three separate powers, in contrast, for example, to the Czechoslovak and Yugoslav situations. It should also be recalled that some 2 million Poles served as soldiers in the respective empires' forces; and the Poles on the offensive side were fighting to liberate Poland, while those on the defensive side were defending it for one of the empires. The choice of allies would not have been easy. Considering the Polish state's vulnerable geographic location and recent history, the debate over the choice of allies continued well into the interwar period. After the Peace Treaty of Brest-Litovsk, both the passivists and Pilsudski's supporters saw Germany as the enemy.

In 1918, two diametrically opposed opinions of how Poland should be restored were represented by two dynamic Polish agitators for Polish independence, Roman Dmowski and Jozef Pilsudski.[36] Dmowski and the conservatives favoured the re-establishment of the borders of the Polish–Lithuanian Republic of 1772, which included Lithuania and parts of Latvia, Belorussia and western Ukraine, whereas Pilsudski wanted a federation of countries in which Poland played a leading role, roughly coinciding with the size of the former Polish–Lithuanian Republic.

In the western provinces, for example, the National Democrats dominated Polish politics: Dmowski and his followers enjoyed much more support than did Pilsudski. Because the National Democrat position better suited Triple Entente interests, and Pilsudski controlled most of the country, Ignacy Paderewski was

35 By the end of the war, the Kingdom of Hungary had dissolved its association with Austria and proclaimed independence; the nationalists had proclaimed the Czechoslovak Republic in Prague; and the 'National Council of Slovenes, Croats, and Serbs' had constituted itself in Zagreb. By 12 November 1918, the Triple Entente had signed armistices with Germany and Austria–Hungary; Emperor Wilhelm II and Emperor Charles had abdicated and the republics of Germany and German-Austria had been proclaimed.

36 See Chapter 2 for further information.

called upon to mediate. Paderewski went to Warsaw, where he secured a compromise which recognised Pilsudski as premier of a unified government, pending national elections. Pilsudski later travelled to Poznan to speak to its inhabitants. The following day Triple Entente banners and Polish flags were torn down by local Germans, who had staged a counter-demonstration. This led to an exchange of gunfire between the Polish militia and German civilians and soldiers:[37] the Polish militia occupied Poznan and imposed martial law. The German contingent surrendered, alongside high-ranking German officers. Conflict spread throughout the province: most places surrendered after little or no resistance. No effort was made by the Polish authorities to compel Poles to give up their territorial gains. As a result of the Poznanian Insurrection, several hundred thousand Germans found themselves under Polish rule. Needless to say, the circumstances did not augur a happy beginning for this new minority.[38]

In this context it is important to recall that the application of the principle of self-determination to the new states in the CEE would prove to be a futile task. One of the guiding principles was to create states that were ethnically homogeneous, but minorities were widespread, making this task impossible. Historical frontiers, natural borders as a means of ensuring national security by establishing defendable frontiers, and whether the respective states in question had been allies or enemies of the Triple Entente also had to be considered. Moreover, all these issues had to be viewed against the larger framework of the respective national interests of the victorious powers in the region. Indeed, the problem of minorities and nationalities was one of the main sources of tensions in CEE during the pre-war period, as none of the newly created states had borders which corresponded to the notion of 'uni-nationality'.[39] Thus, 'recognition' was a key word in the Versailles settlement. In most of the countries established after the war, the duty of the national government to unify administrations of foreign powers was 'so great that the political objective fostering the nation-state soon pervaded economic life'.[40] Even in Bulgaria and Hungary, nationalism was made more extreme by the territorial losses in the Balkan War and the First World War, respectively. In this context, Polish developments during the interwar period should not be considered unique; as will be discussed shortly, the eventual and inevitable turn to an authoritarian form of government can be traced back to the underlying problems which the Versailles Treaty attempted to address in 1919.

37 Polish and German accounts differ. Blanke, *The Orphans of Versailles*, *supra* n. 34, p. 15.

38 See, generally, *ibid.*

39 M. Hauner, 'Human Resources', in *The Economic History of Eastern Europe 1919–1975*, Vol. 1, ed. by M. C. Kaser and E. A. Radice (Oxford: Clarendon Press, 1985), pp. 66–147.

40 M. C. Kaser, 'Introduction', in *The Economic History of Eastern Europe 1919–1975*, Vol. 1, ed. by M. C. Kaser and E. A. Radice (Oxford: Clarendon Press, 1985), p. 17.

Poland's position was unique in the fact that it had been wiped off the map for over a century, and it had to unify three regions which developed in separate ways during this period. Moreover, the rebirth of Poland should not be interpreted as the natural conclusion of the Polish nation's struggle during partition.[41] As Davies states, no matter how fervent Polish interests were and how alive the quest for independence was, Polish independence in 1918 had little to do with either; it was in fact a matter of coincidence and the outcome of the events which were taking place in the Russian, Prussian and Austro-Hungarian empires.

The Polish Position

The peace conference opened in Paris on 18 January 1919. The so-called 'great powers' now faced the problems of organisation and principle which had been postponed since the armistice.

The Paris peace conference was dominated by three powerful figures – French Premier Georges Clemenceau, British Prime Minister David Lloyd George and US President Woodrow Wilson. For his part, Clemenceau conducted all his policies with the thought of providing maximum security for France. Lloyd George exercised the most decisive influence, usually against the Polish interests. Wilson was undeniably for Polish interests; for him, the key to peace and security lay in the League of Nations, because he believed the United States would join it. Wilson was a good diplomat but was not able to cope with the changing stances of his European counterparts.

The discussions about the boundaries of an independent Poland were bitter and controversial. The partition meant that Poles had found themselves fighting on both sides of the war. The Central Powers and Russia had promised the Poles a certain measure of autonomy after the war. The German and Austro-Hungarian empires, however, had defeated Russia in 1917, only to collapse in 1918. This created the unique possibility of the creation of an independent CEE. The initial attitude was 'sympathetic to Polish sufferings [although] the pre-war and wartime French governments had taken a cold and realistic attitude: Russia was a vital link in French military planning, Poland was a matter of sentiment, and an independent Poland might become a German client state.'[42] This position changed with the collapse of the Russian state; Poland was then seen as the necessary substitute for Russian power on Germany's eastern border, and its re-establishment of vital importance. Clemenceau believed that Poland, Czechoslovakia, Romania and Yugoslavia would replace Russia.

Considering the number of minorities in the country, it was difficult for negotiators to reconcile the common objectives of access to the sea and a country

41 Davies, *God's Playground*, *supra* n. 6, p. 392.

42 Alan Sharp, *The Versailles Settlement: Peacemaking in Paris, 1919* (London: Macmillan, 1991), p. 119.

inhabited by an indisputably Polish population. 'The idea of a guarantee to Poland also carried with it a whole baggage train of philosophical and political assumptions about the future regulation of international relations, and stability of eastern Europe after the peace settlement.'[43] As noted by Davies, such baggage would come to haunt Poles throughout the pre-war period until the present day.[44]

Yet, while there seemed to be a similarity between the approaches of the Anglo-Americans on the Polish question, Lloyd George seemed to have different priorities than that of President Wilson. Lloyd George firmly believed that the stability of the area depended on the minimum possible number of Germans in the new state; his belief was based on the fear of creating German irredentist dissatisfaction and provoking a nationalist backlash. In contrast, Wilson was more sympathetic to the Polish cause, a view that may have been influenced by the strong Polish-American vote.

The question of the existence of a Polish state was not an issue, as at the time of the peace conference Poland was already involved in territorial disputes with all her neighbours. The question concerned rather the boundaries of the Polish state, a matter about which the Poles were adamant. Dmowski represented Polish interests at the conference. He told the Council of Ten that Poland sought her boundaries of 1772; in addition she wished to reclaim the Upper Silesian region and access to the sea via Danzig and parts of East and West Prussia.[45] The commission assigned to Poland much of the territory she sought. The proposal was accepted by the French and American delegations, but the British, who felt that it gave Poland over 2 million Germans and areas with substantial German minorities, such as Marienwerder and Danzig, wished to amend it.

The council decided that Danzig should become an autonomous state under the League of Nations but part of the Polish customs area. Warsaw became the centre of external relations, and Danzig's lines of communication were guaranteed by Poland. The second major setback for Poles was the almost last-minute revision of the draft treaty to hold a plebiscite in Upper Silesia. The draft treaty had already assigned the region to Poland, but the argument, put forth by Lloyd George, was that a plebiscite was to be held within one to two years under international supervision. In the meantime, the territory was to be governed by an inter-Allied commission and garrisoned by Allied troops. Paderewski's attempt at bargaining with the Anglo-American front was unsuccessful.

The settlement ceded the city of Danzig to the League and 260 square miles of German territory to Poland, leaving East Prussia isolated from the rest of Germany by the Polish corridor. Germany lost 3 million people, the majority of whom, however, were non-German. The plebiscites found Marienwerder voting to stay German, while Upper Silesia was divided between Poland and Germany in 1922

43 *Ibid.*, p. 120.

44 Davies, *God's Playground, supra* n. 6, pp. 393–434.

45 The Council of Ten set up a commission on Polish affairs, its key members being Jules Cambon (France), Isaiah Bowman (USA) and William Tyrrell (UK).

after a protracted dispute over the results of the plebiscite. It was difficult for Germany to come to terms with the loss of East Prussia, and it was inconceivable to have a failed nation such as Poland govern Germans. German resentment would continue during the pre-war period. Their frustration was further aggravated by the loss of the East Prussian city of Memel, which was a German city, but a natural port of Lithuania. Lithuania had seized the city in 1923 and the Allies no longer pursued the question of who would administer the city.[46]

Poland was not the only CEE nation to have her borders redrawn.[47] Even before the war Czech hopes, for example, were to gain autonomy within the Austro-Hungarian Empire. Observing the wartime developments, Czechs began to envision a new state that worked in close cooperation with Poland and Yugoslavia. Supporters had a hard task before them. During the war, which he spent in exile, the future Czech leader Masaryk sought support among his Anglo-American contacts for a proposed new state of Czech and Slovak peoples, Czechoslovakia, for which there was no historical precedent. This idea was supported by the Allies in 1918 and by November of that year the new state was formed.

The establishment of Czechoslovakia was not without its share of problems. The two most important concerned disputes over the fate of the German-speaking inhabitants of the Sudetenland,[48] with Germany, and the border of Cieszyn (Teschen), with Poland. Despite the fact that the Sudetenland comprised a majority of German-speaking inhabitants, the conference decided that the region was more useful to Czechoslovakia, as it was rich in minerals. The conference further felt that the natural mountain borders were necessary to the new state; the historic borders of Bohemia were thus retained.

The border dispute over Cieszyn raised similar points. The region was rich in coal and boosted industrial development. Although historically part of Bohemia, the majority of its inhabitants were Polish-speaking. The Czechs were supported in their claims by the Americans and the British, who sympathised with the Polish argument, but eventually sided with the Czechs. The chance for an agreement was lost when the Czechs attempted a coup in the region, provoking Polish troops and, subsequently, losing support for the claim at the conference. In an unwise move, the conference had three commissions decide the fate of the territory,[49] each of which came up with a different solution. The conference awarded Poland control over the vital railway link between Bohemia and Moravia, and granted Czechoslovakia

46 Even though it was assigned to Lithuania, depending upon the outcome of its war with Russia.

47 I concentrate on the CEE region in this section, although the treaty affected the Balkans area, Bulgaria, Romania and Yugoslavia. See Sharp, *The Versailles Settlement*, *supra* n. 42, pp. 134–46.

48 The area of the Sudetenland borderlands comprised the region between Germany and the historic kingdom of Bohemia.

49 Two commissions were Paris-based, both committees on Czech and Polish frontiers and the third commission in Cieszyn.

one-third of Cieszyn. The agreement, however, was modified once again in 1920, at the persistent lobbying of Edvard Beneš, the Czech prime minister. The Allies attempted to hold a plebiscite in the region, but owing to the tension and rivalry between the parties, it proved impossible. An attempt at arbitration, with King Albert of Belgium as mediator, proved futile. Once Poland became involved in the war with the Soviets, support for the Czech position was revived, and Beneš' proposal that the Olsa river would be the border, giving Poland Cieszyn and the Czechs the railway and most of the coal resources, was approved. The conference, needless to say, did not handle this particular dispute well. Neither party was satisfied, and any hope of future economic, political or military cooperation between Poland and Czechoslovakia was lost. The conference found it impossible to decide between the ethnic claims of the Poles and the economic needs of the Czechs and could not decide on the underlying issue: 'which of the two states should receive more consideration in the general interest of Europe'.[50]

At the peace conference, the Poles were criticised for their greediness. For Poles, however, the question of borders was a matter of territorial integrity, based on the hard lesson of partition: Polish foreign policy has always been focused on safeguarding her independence and establishing good relations with Russia and Germany.[51]

As regards Hungary, its fate was similar to that of Germany. In 1918, the Austro-Hungarian Empire quickly dissolved into chaos. The republic of Hungary was declared on 16 November, despite the fact that Emperor Charles had not abdicated but renounced his power in Hungary. Count Mihály Károlyi led the new government. Károlyi believed that Allied support could be won, and that the various nationalities would remain loyal to the newly constituted state. The situation gradually worsened when Serb, Romanian and Czech forces overran the nation, making claims to invaded areas. The Károlyi government was eventually ousted by a communist collation led by the Bolshevik, Béla Kun. Strangely enough, the Allies did not retaliate, despite having their worst fears about the communist threat in Hungary confirmed.

In contrast, the Allies did decide the fate of most of the territory disputed between Hungary and her neighbours. Hungary lost most of the Banat region to Yugoslavia and Romania, Transylvania to Romania, Slovakia and Ruthenia to Czechoslovakia, and some territory to Austria. Negotiations continued until May 1920; by then the Kun government had collapsed and the Hungarian delegation led by Count Albert Apponyi failed to argue effectively against the terms outlined in the Treaty of Trianon, which was signed on 4 June 1920. Hungary was reduced to one-third of her pre-war territory, with only 41.6 per cent of her former population.

---

50 Harold Nicolson, British diplomat, quoted in Sharp, *The Versailles Settlement*, *supra* n. 42, p. 150.

51 For an overview of Polish foreign policy at the time, see Anna M. Cienciala and Titus Komarnicki, *From Versailles to Locarno: Keys to Polish Foreign Policy 1919–1925* (Lawrence, KS: University Press of Kansas, 1984).

One-third of the Magyar population was assigned to Hungary's neighbours, a fact to which Hungary could not reconcile itself, making the country one of the most bitter throughout the interwar period.

The Baltic states were also affected by the collapse of Russia and Germany. The Allies succeeded in driving the Bolsheviks from Estonia and Latvia, and a German-led coup was staged in Latvia shortly after the Bolsheviks were ousted. In contrast to the Cieszyn dispute, the conference successfully addressed the problems of the Baltic states and carefully monitored events in Russia. The confusion was not as complex as the Polish, Czech or Hungarian cases, which in a sense raised irreconcilable ethnic issues. It should be noted that Poland retained Vilna (Wilno) after assisting the Allies in expelling the Bolsheviks.

Conclusions

In contrast to its neighbours, Poland indeed took advantage of the collapse of the Russian and German empires. Although the Poles may have been disheartened by some of the terms of the settlement, Poland had regained much of its former territory. The Poles demonstrated their firm resolve, if not stubbornness, in securing their eastern borders after the Soviet-Polish War of 1920, when the conference, more from exasperation than approval, permitted the Poles to annex the region.

The conference reflected the confusion of the CEE and the Allies' lack of knowledge about the complex historic intermingling and movements of populations in the region. The main difficulty was in determining the criteria for nationality – language, culture, race, historical precedent or geography – and which of the nationalities would have the right to self-determination. For the CEE nations, these components were considered constants in determining nationality. There was no viable alternative for the peacemakers, and this was viewed as the best way in which to control events with the collapse of the Russian, German and Austro-Hungarian empires and the results of the First World War.

In addition to the decisions concerning the Polish–German borders, the Supreme Council requested the Polish delegation (as well as the delegations of Bulgaria, Czechoslovakia, Greece, Hungary, Romania, Turkey and Yugoslavia) to sign a convention for the protection of national and religious minorities. The members of these minorities had the right to send their complaints to the League of Nations for consideration and redress. Since the convention somewhat limited the sovereignty of the countries in question, they, including Poland, reluctantly complied.

The treaty's provisions were criticised by many. Poland had access to the Baltic Sea but was denied full control of the Vistula river. Such a solution was unlikely to work, and, to Danzig's dismay, the Poles decided to build their own port, Gdynia. German–Polish relations deteriorated further in their aftermath, with Poles accusing Germans of pressuring the population during the electoral campaign, and the Germans unable to understand the partition of provinces that had been an entity for centuries. The Poles resented the obligations towards national minorities, in particular since Germany, with a considerable Polish population, was not required to assume similar responsibilities.

Finally, as mentioned earlier, the Allies had no power of enforcement of the eastern borders of Poland. This left the question to be settled between Poland and Russia, and it was, by means of war and further negotiations.

An important theme throughout this book centres on the interwar period. It is cited as evidence of success with democracy. Albeit limited, the past provides a sort of 'tangible factor' of 'harmony' and clearer issues and developments. This is a significant point. But the interwar period is far from perfect, despite arguments claiming otherwise. The valiant struggles for independence and statehood have motivated certain images of the past and present, so that 'one can tell the same story in a thousand different ways'.[52] In Elisabeth Kyle's *The Mirrors of Versailles*, the young Romanian politician muses, 'I am doing what we complain of the Magyars doing. Magnifying pin-pricks for the benefit of the impressionable stranger, instead of discussing seriously the points at issue between us.'[53] The interwar period in the CEE region features key characteristics that would come to haunt it, namely: (1) a misplaced nostalgia for harmony and clear homogeneous messages; (2) the human need for security; (3) a collective anxiety and aggressiveness that manifested itself through ressentiment; (4) the inertia of civil society. As Tismaneanu argues, 'historical legacies have become symbolic weapons used by different political actors to justify their vision not only of the past but also of the present and the future.'[54] The next chapter examines unique challenges alongside these troubling characteristics in the far-reaching and short-lived socio-political and legal frameworks of the CEE, using the Polish experience as its case study in the second part of this historical overview.

---

52 Agnes Heller, 'Between Past and Future', in *Between Past and Future: The Revolutions of 1989 and Their Aftermath*, ed. by S. Antohi and V. Tismaneanu (Budapest: Central European University Press, 2000), p. 3.

53 Elisabeth Kyle, *The Mirrors of Versailles* (London: Constable & Co., 1939), p. 146.

54 Vladimir Tismaneanu, *Fantasies of Salvation: Democracy, Nationalism, and Myth in Post-Communist Europe* (Princeton, NJ: Princeton University Press, 1998), p. 54.

Chapter 2
Independence (1918–1939)

Intellectuals are smitten by the interwar period, a period characterised by foreign policy success, relative economic prosperity, and cultural effervescence.[1]

General Background

In 1917, Polish academic life, in the form of scholarly and cultural organisations, received the support it was sorely lacking, which would eventually prove to be a key factor in promoting and maintaining Polish achievements.[2] The Poles who were part of these societies were dedicated to creating for their country an identity which all could recognise of a country which did not exist in international law. Polish writers used themes which preserved the national tradition in their writings, and their work demonstrated an awareness of economic and social questions that drew on world events and also nurtured a distinct Polish approach to problems which everyone hoped could be solved in a future independent country. These groups exhibited characteristics necessary to viable civil societies.

There were many political factions, but two are worth mentioning as they have a particular bearing on Polish politics during the interwar period. These were the *Stronnictwo Narodowo-Demokratyczne* (National Democratic Party) and the *Polska Partia Socjalistyczna* (Polish Socialist Party). The notion of Polish independence mainly involved the question of alliance with either Germany or Russia, but Polish political groups were extremely passionate in support of independence and, depending on the group, could be vehemently opposed to

1 Cosmina Tanasoiu, 'Intellectuals and Post-Communist Politics in Romania: An Analysis of Public Discourse 1900–2000', *East European Politics and Societies*, 22 (2008), p. 85.

2 The fact that these institutions were established under the partitioning powers demonstrates the perseverance and dedication of Poles in preserving their culture despite the inherent dangers. There were several main organisations created in each area. For example, the Cracow-based *Akademia Umietnosci* (Academy of Sciences and Letters), which covered all fields of learning, provided the system needed to promote Polish cultural and scientific patronage. In Poznan, the *Poznanskiw Towarzystwo Przyjaciol Nauk* (Poznanian Society of the Friends of Learning) and the *Torunskie Towarzystwo Przyjaciol Nauk* (Torun Society of the Friends of Learning), founded in 1876, promoted academic life in Prussian Poland. The Mianowski Fund financed the publication of scholarly works in Russian Poland. These academic societies and foundations succeeded in keeping Polish achievements alive, owing to the commitment shared by the Poles who founded the organisations and believed in their mission. See R. F. Leslie, 'Triloyalism and the National Revival', in *The History of Poland Since 1863*, ed. by R. F. Leslie (Cambridge: Cambridge University Press, 1983), pp. 61–64.

cooperation with either foreign power and the compromise it would entail if the opportunity presented itself. The upper and middle classes of Poland were not 'condemned' to underground activity as were the revolutionaries. Their position was based on accessibility to positions of importance, in general. Poles could become board members or technical specialists in industry, in the Russian territory, or high-ranking members of the military or public administration in the Austrian government. These classes generally knew that their passivity condoned the discriminatory legislation, and that they were the object of criticism from non-Polish nationalities and peasants. They had the support of the Catholic Church, which tended to favour the upper and middle classes, and support campaigns against the Jews and the socialists.

Growing political influence, however, came from the National Democratic Party, which appealed to the growing middle class, who shared with the party a narrow-minded philosophy. The nationalistic political platform was formulated by Roman Dmowski in his 1902 publication *Mysli Nowoczesnego Polaka* (Thoughts of a Modern Pole), in which he redefined Polish nationalism as a concept in which the 'nation' was the pinnacle of all morality. Any exhibition of sympathy for other nations was condemned as immoral, and the adherents were adamant in their views:

> A social class which might feel a sense of solidarity with the same class of another nation, a party for which an international community of principles has greater weight than the community of national traditions and interests, a social circle which enters into daily contact and social relations with circles of an enemy society ... deserves absolute condemnation from the point of view of public morality ... for putting the egoism of their own altruism above the altruism binding upon them in virtue of national egoism.[3]

The National Democrats attacked foreigners, namely Russians, and minority groups, such as the Jews, whom they condemned as a foreign element in Polish society that, owing to the circumstances of the economic crisis, competed with the Polish lower classes. Anti-Semitism was supported by various segments of the Polish population, who even encouraged the Russian pogroms of Jews in the most repressive circumstances. The success of the movement was based on the party's ability to argue along scientific and emotional lines; the common thread

3 Z. Balicki, *Egoizm narodowy wobec etyki* [National Egoism and Ethics] (Lwow-Warsaw, 1914), p. 58. Kazimierz Krzywicki, a former member of the Council of the Congress Kingdom, published *Polska i Rosja* [Poland and Russia] in 1872. In it, he argued that nations are changeable, and that history both creates and destroys them. If a nation, such as Poland, loses its independent existence, it becomes reduced to a 'nation-less' human society whose fate depends on its assimilation to the dominant nation in the state in which it has been incorporated.

that emerges is linked to the purity of origin and destiny.[4] Of course, this particular position was not peculiar to Poland.

An analysis of Dmowski's right-wing nationalism can be contrasted with the left-wing political programme of Pilsudski, the brilliant general who sought to combine military and political aspirations in a socialist platform, and who could not envision a future compromise with Russia, which, in his view, was the greater of two evils. During the First World War, the divisions which characterised the Polish groups of all three empires were exemplified by these two general trends.

The Poles entered the war with certain advantages. First, their national culture was not undermined by foreign rule. Second, their historical sense was strong. Their most severe handicap was the disunity of the political factions, which destroyed any sense of political unity.[5] The struggle between Pilsudski and Dmowski over the type of independent Polish state to be created was intense, and their inability to reach any agreement greatly undermined the Polish vision of independence in Western eyes and proved to be a source of conflict during the years of the independent Polish state.

On 12 October 1917, a rump Polish government was created in the occupied Kingdom of Poland. The *Rada Regencyjna* (Regency Council) comprised three regents, who would head the fledging ministries created by the Provisional Council of State.[6] The council's powers were very limited, as it was still very much under the control of the Germans and Austrians. Various governmental bodies were springing up throughout the provinces to rid themselves of Prussian and Austrian control,[7] but it was not until the Triple Entente that the Polish question could be addressed. As the political situation grew tense within the Polish territories, the existence of an independent Polish state increasingly grew dependent on the Triple Entente. The tension was somewhat alleviated by the famous pianist, Ignacy Paderewski, who undertook a mission to Poland in January 1918.[8] Paderewski opposed Dmowski's anti-Semitic platform and supported Pilsudski's federalist

4 Vladimir Tismaneanu, *Fantasies of Salvation: Democracy, Nationalism, and Myth in Post-Communist Europe* (Princeton, NJ: Princeton University Press, 1998), p. 66.

5 The influence of a major foreign power would have helped, but Poland was not a European question, and the Poles lacked the experience to turn the war to their advantage.

6 The three Regents were Prince Zdzislaw Lubomirski, Archbishop Aleksander Kakowski and Count Jozef Ostrowski, with Janusz Kucharzewski as head of the cabinet. The Poles who assumed high government positions were generally landowners or of aristocratic origin.

7 Some of the more important self-government bodies included the *Polska Komisja Likwidacyjna* [Polish Liquidation Committee] in Cracow.

8 The Polish National Committee was first established in 1914 in Warsaw. Dmowski and his followers created a Polish National Committee in 1917 in Lausanne. Dmowski wanted his committee to constitute a government-in-exile, but the committee merely represented Polish interests, especially in matters concerning the Polish army. Paderewski was an excellent choice as he belonged to no political party but was connected with the Polish National Committee.

plans. Internationally, this was viewed in a positive light, lending Paderewski the necessary authority and credibility.[9]

Social Background

It is within the tumultuous political context that questions of nationality are to be understood. The collapse of the Russian, German and Austro-Hungarian empires presented serious problems to the peacemakers of 1919 and their hopes of remapping Eastern Europe on the basis of nationality. This section will firstly summarise the demographic situation in pre-war Poland in the early 1920s and later 1930s, secondly describe the diverse cultural and linguistic traits of the Polish minorities, and thirdly discuss this information within the context of the Polish Minorities Treaty. The provisions of this landmark treaty were incorporated in the 1921 and 1935 Polish constitutions, signalling another step towards establishing a rule-of-law state. It will be seen that the prospects for the protection of minority rights were, after a period of short-lived hope, never fully realised.

To begin with, matters concerning minorities in pre-war Poland were hopelessly complex. There were several minority groups, each with its own language and faith.[10] Pre-war Poland was a truly multiethnic state, comprising Poles, Ukrainians, Belorussians, Germans and Jews. In 1921, 69.2 per cent of the population gave their nationality as Polish.[11] National minorities were of two kinds: those who comprised the majority in certain regions and those who were dispersed throughout the country. Ukrainians numbered 5–6 million, and resided primarily in the regions of former Austrian control. Belorussians, who numbered some 1.5 million, lived in the eastern provinces.[12] The German population numbered some 1.1 million and was spread throughout Poland, although the group continued to be an important element in the western territories.[13] There were some 3 million Jews in Poland, also widely dispersed throughout the country.[14] This situation was

---

9 In November 1918, Pilsudski was released from prison and the Regency Council handed over their power to him. Pilsudski was the one man whom all of the political parties trusted, save for the revolutionaries. Even Dmowski stated that '[i]t is certain that if we formed a government – let us assume with me at its head – we should well and truly cut the throat of Poland.' Quoted by Antony Polonsky, 'The Emergence of an Independent Polish State', in *The History of Poland Since 1863*, ed. by R. F. Leslie, *supra* n. 2, p. 131.

10 In 1921, the population was 27.4 million. By 1939, it had reached 35.1 million. Wojciech Roszkowski, 'The Reconstruction of the Government and State Apparatus in the Second Polish Republic', in *The Reconstruction of Poland 1914–1923*, ed. by Paul Latawski (London: Macmillan, 1992), pp. 158–77.

11 Antony Polonsky, 'The Breakdown of Parliamentary Government', in *The History of Poland Since 1863*, ed. by R. F. Leslie, *supra* n. 2, p. 144.

12 *Ibid.*, pp. 144–45.

13 *Ibid.*, p. 145.

14 *Ibid.*

also found in the Baltic States. Estonia, Latvia and Lithuania had various minority groups within their respective republics, mainly comprising Russian, German and Jewish minorities, who enjoyed tolerant policies that incorporated language and education rights, at least at the start of the interwar period.

The national minorities, who constituted 30 per cent of the total population, played an important role in Polish economic life during the interwar period, as already discussed.[15] The minorities also contributed to the cultural life of the country, as will be discussed later. Most Polish cities were characterised by diverse cultures. In Wilno (Vilnius), for example, one could hear spoken Polish, Yiddish, Lithuanian, Belorussian and Russian. Yet, as one Polish writer observes, language cannot be the only basis used to judge a nation state; it is a question tied to cultural 'belonging', which is usually linked to religion.[16] With regard to religion, the majority of Ukrainians were of the Uniate Christian faith, with the remainder Orthodox Christian, especially in the former Russian areas. The Belorussians were mainly Orthodox, but a sizeable group were Roman Catholic. The majority of Jews still held on to Orthodox Judaism, many declaring themselves followers of the great rabbinical courts.

As Roman Catholicism predominated in some areas, other religions took second place. Polish Roman Catholicism was distinctive, as it was influenced by the country's historical situation as a land on the edge of Roman Catholic Europe. In the nineteenth century, this translated into resistance to Prussian Protestantism and Orthodox Russia. Polish culture was affected by the Vatican; when the country disappeared from the map, the concepts of 'Pole' and 'Catholic' became synonymous, and religion was a means of preserving national identity. This was further heightened in the Russian-annexed lands, where Russification measures only enforced the Poles' sense of identity. Thus, for many of the minority groups, the issue was one of not only language but also cultural belonging. The powerful role of Roman Catholicism also meant that it was used as a political tool. For the far-eastern Polish territories, such as Lithuania, being part of Poland meant security and protection. It also meant further conflict between the two nations.

---

15 The Ukrainians, who numbered approximately 6 million, were concentrated in the eastern territories of Poland, and primarily earned their living in agriculture. By the 1900s a small circle of intellectuals had been formed by priests, teachers and managers of the cooperatives. The situation in Belorussia was similar. This group comprised approximately 1.5 million, and were concentrated in the least developed eastern regions of Poland, where they also earned their living in agriculture. The German minority (numbering 1.1 million) was dispersed throughout the community. As landlords and wealthy peasants, the German minority had an important role in shaping economic development in the northern and western regions of Poland. Their influence was seen in agricultural processing plants and textile centres, which they frequently managed. See Polonsky, 'The Breakdown of Parliamentary Government', *supra* n. 11, p. 144. See also J. Taylor, *The Economic Development of Poland 1919–1950* (Ithaca, NY: Cornell University Press, 1952), p. 103.

16 Czeslaw Milosz, *Native Realm: A Search for Self-Definition* (New York: Doubleday, 1968), pp. 54–58.

Poland was primarily an agrarian country, and nearly all of the Lithuanians were peasants. On the other hand, the contempt which Poles and Lithuanians had for each other was surpassed by the hostility which they felt towards the Orthodox Church and its followers.

It is true to say that Poland, as an ethnically heterogeneous nation, found itself involved in domestic conflicts arising out of the ever-present problem of national minorities. Pilsudski, as the 'Father of the Fatherland', failed to achieve his vision of federation. It is important to note that, for many Europeans, the division of Germany after the Second World War was unprecedented, but for the persons residing in Poland and in the east, the displacement of borders was a normal fact of life.[17]

One of the most obvious conflicts which arose was over education. For example, until the re-emergence of Poland on the map, nothing like a Belorussian state had ever existed. Polish policy on Belorussians having their own schools was straightforward: no such schools were permitted; their language was considered a dialect of the Russian language. The Belorussians never fared very well: their choice was between Russification or Polinisation. Before the Polish state could address the needs of the minorities, it was important to raise the standard of education. Illiteracy was a serious problem, especially in the former Russian and Austrian partitions. The law of 17 February 1922 concerning public primary schools began the unification of the Polish education system. This law stipulated that primary education was obligatory for all children, yet the shortage of qualified teachers, classrooms and materials made the law difficult to enforce.

No discussion about Polish minorities would be complete without mentioning the Polish Minorities Treaty (also referred to as the Minority Treaties), which ensured the rights of minorities residing in countries whose majority population was recognised to be different ethnically, nationally or religiously. The treaty provisions which ensued from the Paris peace conference were of two types: one was the provisions contained in the peace treaties signed by the enemy states; the other related to states created or enlarged by the peace conference, which were contained in separate minorities treaties.[18] The newly created Polish state was treated first, as it was considered by the peace conference to require immediate attention in order to avoid difficulties among such a diverse minority group. The provisions of the treaty served as a model for other treaties and as a basis for the

---

17 'When I started to go to school, the year the peace treaty was signed [1921], everything in my world seemed to be just as it should be. The thought that it might be strange to someone of the outside never entered my mind.' *Ibid.*, p. 53.

18 Poland, Czechoslovakia, Romania, Yugoslavia, Greece and Danzig signed such treaties. Poland: the Treaty of Versailles, 28 June 1919, 225 CTS 412; Czechoslovakia: the Treaty of St Germain-en-Laye, 10 September 1919, 226 CTS 170; Romania: the Treaty of Versailles, December 1919, (1921) 5 LNTS 335; Yugoslavia: the Treaty of St Germain-en-Laye, 10 September 1919, 226 CTS 182; Greece: the Treaty of Sèvres, 10 August 1920, (1924) 28 LNTS 244; Danzig: the Convention of Paris, 9 November 1920, (1921) 6 LNTS 189.

minorities' regime. The treaty was the result of the strong Jewish lobby, created to protect the Jewish population in the new Polish state. Other minorities were not considered; in fact, many of their needs were passed over in order to placate Polish unease at the amount of protection offered to the Jews.[19]

The Treaty of Versailles was signed by Poland on 28 June 1919. It was the first minorities' treaty of its kind. The treaty (and all subsequent treaties of this kind) sought to protect national minorities, but first and foremost to protect the fundamental rights of all inhabitants of the state, regardless of their citizenship and ethnicity.[20] All inhabitants of the states parties would be entitled to exercise their religion freely, limited only by public order or public morality. These guarantees aimed to create an overall climate of political liberalism in the belief that the rights of minorities would be secure in this kind of setting.

Citizenship was another essential element. The treaties allowed persons who were unable to accept citizenship in the new states to opt for another nationality. Individuals who chose to do so were required to move to the state of their chosen nationality within one year. One of the ideas behind this was to remove the most nationalistic of the minority groups from the new states to effect better relations between the majority and the minorities.

Articles 7, 8 and 9 of the Polish Treaty outlined the actual rights of the minorities. Article 7 of the treaty guaranteed equality before the law to every citizen of the state, without distinction of race, language or religion. Discrimination on the basis of religion in matters concerning civil and political rights was prohibited. Restrictions on the use of languages other than Polish were also prohibited, and the treaty provided for the use of languages other than Polish in the courts. Article 8 guaranteed citizens belonging to 'racial, religious or linguistic minorities' the same treatment in law as other Polish citizens. Minorities were allowed to maintain their own charitable, religious, social and educational institutions. Article 9 of the treaty obliged the state to provide primary-school education in the language of any minority that comprised a 'considerable proportion' of the population of an area. The state was obliged to provide an 'equitable share' of public funds to the minority, also when the minority constituted a considerable proportion of the population, for educational, religious or charitable aims. The provisions not only protected minorities from discrimination, but also provided the basis for a

---

19 Hungary, by comparison, entered the pre-war period with a policy that welcomed a strong Jewish role in modern Hungarian society; although loosely administered, the ruling elite encouraged assimilation and was happy to have the Jews contribute to the economic development. See J. Rothschild, *East Central Europe Between the Two World Wars*, A History of East Central Europe, IX (Seattle, WA: University of Washington Press, 1974), pp. 191, 196–99.

20 The treaties thus guaranteed full and complete protection of life and liberty to all inhabitants of the states parties without distinction of birth, nationality, language, race or religion. See Thomas Musgrave, *Self-Determination and National Minorities* (Oxford : Clarendon Press: 1997), pp. 41–44.

legal framework in which the minorities could pursue and promote their language and culture, guaranteeing no assimilation so that each minority could survive as a separate entity within the state. However, with no enforcement or sanctions against breaches, Poland was able to ignore the provisions with impunity.

The state undertook to implement the treaty provisions in national law, so that all other laws, regulations or official action which conflicted with them, whether relating to minorities or to the whole population, would be declared void. At the international level, the rights outlined in the treaties were recognised as obligations of international concern and as such were placed under the guarantee of the League of Nations. This external guarantee, however, applied only to persons belonging to racial, religious or linguistic minorities.[21] It can be said that the states which were bound by the Minorities' Treaties resented the inequality of treatment and encroachment of sovereignty which the treaties imposed on them;[22] the provisions were perceived to weigh in favour of the minorities. Not surprisingly, the issue of loyalty was a particularly sensitive area for the state; this obligation was not indicated anywhere but was implied in the citizenship provisions. The League of Nations attempted to correct this situation with the resolution of 21 September 1923, which required members of minorities to cooperate as loyal citizens with the state to which they belonged. Despite this requirement, loyalty remained a serious point of contention, and in the case of Poland, conflicts continued over the problems which the treaty had attempted to alleviate. Scholars have contended that the failure of the treaties to achieve their goals was not an intrinsic defect; the failures were rather the result of the political situation which arose in Europe, and the attack on democracy and the rule of law by fascism. Other priorities, particularly economic ones, and the gradual destruction of legality and basic liberties, weakened the implementation of norms established by the treaties. Of course, dealing with ethnic minorities *en masse* or as a whole created difficulties. The minorities in Poland differed from each other and in the way that they wished

---

21 As Musgrave points out, since the rights contained in the treaties were conferred not only on the minority groups, but also on the individuals' *locus standi* on the petitioner, it cannot be said that it amounted to the recognition of group rights. *Ibid.*, p. 44. See Natan Lerner, 'The Evolution of Minority Rights in International Law', in *Peoples and Minorities in International Law*, ed. by Catherine Brolmann *et al.* (Dordrecht: Martinus Nijhoff, 1993), pp. 77–101.

22 Ignacy Paderewski argued that any system which offered special privileges to minorities would create ill feelings towards them. For further details on the background of the discussions which took place during the peace conference, see Malcolm Evans, *Religious Liberty and International Law in Europe* (Cambridge: Cambridge University Press, 1997), pp. 104–24; K. Lundgreen-Nielsen, *The Polish Problem at the Paris Peace Conference* (Odense: Odense University Press, 1979); A. Zimmern, *The League of Nations and the Rule of Law 1918–1935* (London: Macmillan, 1936); Helmer Rosting, 'Protection of Minorities by the League of Nations', *American Journal of International Law*, 17 (1923), pp. 641–60; and Theodore Woolsey, 'The Rights of Minorities Under the Treaty with Poland', *American Journal of International Law*, 14 (1920), pp. 392–96.

to live with the Poles. Generally speaking, the Jews and Germans wished to live alongside Poles, while the Belorussians and Ukrainians in general could not come to terms with an independent Polish state.[23] Attitudes differed between the two populaces and even further between the populaces of the Belorussian and Ukrainian Soviet Republics.

Yet, educational materials continued to be subjective, compiled by persons who had a particular way of seeing the past. For example, the portrayal of Prince Jagiello (who initiated the union of the Polish–Lithuanian Commonwealth) was misconstrued: in most Polish schools, he was presented as a noble figure, in contrast to his brother, Prince Witold, who was portrayed as an unrepentant troublemaker because of his fierce desire to maintain Lithuanian autonomy; students in Lithuanian schools were taught the exact opposite.[24] Likewise, replacing the multicultural heritage with national attitudes must have laid the foundations for anti-Semitism. Literature could have played an important role in abolishing these notions, but, as one Polish writer observed, '[t]he whole country was in any case permeated by an unhealthy atmosphere.'[25] This atmosphere was also incited by the powerful Catholic Church. While the priests' behaviour could not be compared to the brutality of the Nazi regime, the lower and upper clergy, between the years 1933 and 1939, continued to spread a message of intolerance.[26] It is easy to generalise, and it is not the purpose of this book to provide a concise history of pre-war Polish–Jewish relations.[27] Such ambiguities did not exist in every institution in every Polish city. The point is that pre-war Poland was a mixture of many nationalities, who in many ways were forced to live with Poles within a newly independent country of which Poles were fiercely proud. The intense feeling of patriotism could be misconstrued as nationalistic to the point of being racist; indeed, racism did emerge among certain circles, and since it in many ways coincided with the series of events which followed in Europe in the 1930s (above all, in Germany), the result could not but influence internal tensions in Poland.[28]

---

23 For further discussion, see Yoram Dinstein, 'The Degree of Self-Rule of Minorities in Unitarian and Federal States', in *Peoples and Minorities in International Law*, *supra* n. 21, pp. 221–35.

24 Milosz, *Native Realm*, *supra* n. 16, p. 97.

25 *Ibid.*, p. 99. And '[i]f anyone mentioned Jews in their presence they took offense, at once reading racism into the remark. They tried at all costs to forget who they were, betraying a completely unjustified sense of inferiority'.

26 See, for example, Ronald E. Modras, *The Catholic Church and Antisemitism: Poland, 1933–1939* (Chur: Harwood Academic Publishers for the Vidal Sassoon International Center for the Study of Antisemitism, The Hebrew University of Jerusalem, 1994).

27 For a thoughtful account of Polish–Jewish relations, see Ewa Hoffman, *Shtetl: The History of a Small Town and an Extinguished World* (London: Vintage, 1999).

28 It must be noted that during the interwar period the Polish literary club, the PEN Club, represented part of the Polish generation of writers who opposed the growing nationalism in Europe. Thomas Mann, one of the greatest literary figures of the twentieth

This breakdown in democracy was paralleled by the situation in the Baltic States. Estonia, Latvia and Lithuania had various minority groups within their respective republics. By the 1930s, the tolerant policies towards these ethnic groups began to deteriorate, as various factions vied for the political power afforded by the electoral laws. At the start of the interwar period, all three states embraced a democratic rule that was characterised by universal, equal, secret and proportional voting; leaders were aware of competing factions. Even so, in Estonia, this meant the rise of right-wing groups. Centrist political groups were silenced, and gradually the Russian, German and Jewish segments of society felt the brunt of laws targeting language. Latvia, too, experienced instability during the interwar period. By the 1930s, right-wing groups adopting overt Nazi methods and policies had come to power. Latvia's ethnic minorities, comprising Russian, German, Belorussian, Lithuanian, Slav and Jew, became the focus of hostility. In Lithuania, the situation was no different. Having an enemy to the south, Poland, and rival political factions with communist sympathies and clearly fascist ones, resulted in serious disappointment as no stable political system could be sustained.

Legal Developments

Codification

In Poland, the unification and codification of the laws was the responsibility of the legislative *Sejm* (lower house of parliament). In its session of 3 June 1919, the Codification Commission (*Komisja Kodyfikacyjna*) was established.[29] The commission comprised 44 members, all of whom were legal experts. All branches of law were represented by its members, most of whom came from one of the three main law faculties and centres of legal thought: Warsaw, Cracow and Lwow, or were legal practitioners.

In summary, the sources of law which were in effect in 1918, according to region, are listed below.

---

century (who eventually left Germany in 1933 because of increasing attacks by the nationalist and pro-Nazi press), spoke at the PEN Club in 1927 of the need to build a Europe 'unified by one soul', where Poland for him represented the idea of 'an East–West synthesis'. Quoted in Andrzej Zawada, *Dwudziestolecie literackie* [Literary 1920s] (Wroclaw: Wydawnictwo Dolnoslaskie, 1996), p. 89.

29 *Ustawa z dnia 3 czerwca 1919r. o komisji kodyfikacyjnej* [The Law of 3 June 1919 Concerning the Codification Commission], *Dziennik Ustaw*, No. 44, item 315. The commission began its work in 1919, and continued it until the war. Discussions about the formation of a Codification Commission took place at international law conferences, usually organised in Austrian Poland, as early as 1887. See Stanislaw Grodziski, 'Komisja Kodyficacyjna Rzeczpospolitej Polskiej' [The Codification Commission of the Republic of Poland], *Czasopismo Prawno-Historyczne*, 33 (1991), p. 48.

Substantive Civil Law

1. Central area (former Kingdom of Poland) – the *Code Napoléon* was in force.
2. Eastern regions (former Russian Poland) – in force was the whole of Russian civil law from volume X of the Russian legal code.
3. Western regions (former Prussian Poland) – the main source of law was the *Bürgerliche Gesetzbuch* (BGB).
4. Southern Poland (former Austrian Poland) – the main source of law was the Austrian Code of Civil Procedure (ABGB). In the south-western regions of Spisz and Orawa, Hungarian law was in force until 1922.

Rules of Civil Procedure

1. Central and eastern regions (former Kingdom of Poland and Russian Poland) – the Russian Code of Civil Procedure from 1864 was in force.
2. Western regions (former Prussian Poland) – the main source of law was the German Code of Civil Procedure from 1877, as amended in 1898.
3. Southern Poland (former Austrian Poland) – the main source of law was the Austrian Code of Civil Procedure from 1895, in effect after 1922 in Spisz and Orawa.

Substantive Criminal Law

1. central and eastern regions – the Russian Criminal Code of 1903
2. western regions – the German Criminal Code of 1871
3. southern Poland – the Austrian Criminal Code of 1852.

Substantive Criminal Procedure

1. central and eastern regions – the Russian Code of Criminal Procedure from 1864
2. western regions – the German Code of Criminal Procedure from 1877
3. southern Poland – the Austrian Code of Criminal Procedure from 1873.

The commission, with full support from the government, decided to turn to national customs and traditions of Polish justice to form a new, Polish legal system. The systems of the three partitioning powers did not take into account Polish needs and customs, nor did they consider the social and economic requirements and general feelings of the Polish nation. As discussed above, these exigencies were often turned against the Polish nation, particularly by the Russian and Prussian authorities. Some viewed this as a brutal form of repression: '[t]he four different legal systems were the most burdensome heritage of this period of slavery.'[30] Work on the uniform legal system began at once, starting with the elimination of the most glaring differences between the provinces. For example, the existing fifth legal system of Hungarian law in the small part of southwest Poland that had belonged to Hungary before the First World War, Orawa and Spisz, was based on custom or unwritten law. In 1922, it was incorporated into the Austrian legal framework which applied in southern Poland.[31]

The creation of a wholly new Polish legal system was the task of the commission: one system for the whole country which did not neglect the needs and views of the people. The 1919 Act which created the commission outlined its functions as follows: (1) to prepare proposals for a uniform system of criminal and civil law; (2) to draft bills which had to be submitted to the parliament in cooperation with the Ministry of Justice.[32]

The commission, therefore, was a body of experts appointed by the president on the recommendation of its own chairman (with the exception of the first members) and independent of the government with respect to its organisation and its terms of reference. The commission, however, could not submit its draft proposals directly to the government, but only through the minister of justice. The government, being responsible to the legislature for the administration of national policy, decided whether or not to adopt the reports and proposals of the commission and bring them before parliament through the minister of justice. Some of the draft bills of the commission were presented to parliament without changes; others were not presented until major or minor amendments to them had been made by the government.[33]

One of the main problems was that the number of lawyers was far too small for national needs. Lawyers had to fill the posts in the newly created system of courts; in the Bar; and in the administration. The group was also required to assume the teaching in the law faculties of the universities of Warsaw, Cracow, Lwow, Poznan and Wilno (Vilnius). This made it impossible to reserve highly qualified jurists solely for work on codification. This obstacle was partly overcome by appointing

30 Zygmunt Nagorski, 'Codification of Civil Law in Poland (1918–1939)', *Studies in Polish and Comparative Law: A Symposium of 12 Articles* (London: Stevens & Sons, 1945), p. 47.

31 For further details and examples, see *ibid.*

32 Art. 2 of the Law on the Codification Commission from 3 June 1919. The first 40 members, including the chairman and the deputy chairmen, were appointed by the president of the Republic of Poland on the recommendation of the minister of justice in agreement with the speaker of parliament. The organisation of the commission, including the time and place of its sittings, and the manner of carrying out its terms of reference, was to be decided by the commission itself and set in Rules of Procedures. The minister of justice had a permanent representative on the commission, and could participate in the meetings of the commission and of its committees, or send his representative.

33 The draft bills concerning marriage presented by the commission to the minister of justice in 1926 were the only bills which the government did not present to parliament.

as members of the commission professors, judges, advocates and notaries, who generally continued with the professional activities and worked in the commission part-time. Only the chairman and the general secretary received remuneration for their work, although members were reimbursed for travel costs and were paid modest fees for their proposals.

Members of the commission were well aware that their work would take several years, an opinion voiced by the body's president: '[t]he mere mobilisation of the Codification Commission will require an enormous amount of work and energy; and then the energy will apply to the organisation of offices and necessary libraries, statistical bureaus and other resources. We cannot expect a quick result of fruitful labour, if we wish the fruit to be ripe.'[34] It was, however, guided by its purpose as dictated by law, 'to prepare a unified civil and criminal code',[35] and any other law would be determined by the *Sejm* with the approval of the ministry of justice. To do otherwise would undermine the commission's purpose and, most likely for this reason, the March Constitution makes no mention of the commission.

The 1921 Constitution

In 1917, Polish legal circles had already begun to draft a constitution and a framework of a future Polish legal system.[36] This task was the responsibility of the legislative Council of State, which was granted limited powers over the administration of justice and education. The Council of State worked in tandem with the Council of Regency, both bodies having been created after the decline of the provisional Council of State's power, but still representing the Austro-Polish solution.[37] The authorities embarked on a serious recruitment campaign and found

34 *Sejm Ustawodawczy Rzeczpospolitej Polskiej* [Legislative Parliament of the Republic of Poland], Druk No. 298.

35 *Ibid.*

36 The first signs of activity occurred in Russian Poland as early as 1915. Both German and Austrian authorities attempted to quell any initiative of Polish lawyers to practise, as exemplified in the Decree of 7 October 1915, which declared that 'Polish lawyers ... may not assume judicial functions in non-Polish courts conducted in a non-Polish language'. The only allowance made to Polish lawyers was to be defence council before courts in the occupied territories. See Artur Korobowicz, 'Ewakuacja sadow Krolestwa Polskiego i ich losy w czasie pierwszej wojny swiatowej' [The Evacuation of the Courts of the Kingdom of Poland and Their Fate During the First World War], *Czasopismo Prawno-Historyczne*, 61 (1989), pp. 87–107.

37 As regards the courts, the Council of Regency appointed officials according to Art. 20 of the 'Provisional Regulations on the arrangement of the courts', save for the investigating magistrates (*sedzia sledczych*) and justices of the peace (*sedzia pokoju*), who would be appointed by the future minister of justice. *Dekret Rady Regencyjnej o tymczasowej organizacji wladz naczelnych w Krolewstwie Polskim* [The Decree of the Council of Regency on the Provisional Organisation of the Main Leading Organs of the Kingdom of Poland], 3 January 1918, *Prezydium Rada Ministrow* [The Presidium of

many willing Polish officials who had served in lower-level government positions in the former partitioning powers and who were ready to serve in the new Polish government.[38]

In 1919, a new legislative *Sejm* was convened, and soon after the 'Little Constitution' was adopted, an interim document which remained in force until the promulgation of the 1921 Constitution.[39] During the first years of independence, the newly created *Sejm* struggled; having little experience in the practice of government, it had difficulty in passing much needed legislation on socio-economic reforms and on a solution to maintaining the different cultural standards of diverse number of nationalities and ethnic groups. Nonetheless, the Polish parliament promulgated a constitution which was viewed as one of the most progressive during the time.

Among the differing views on the structure of government, the commonly shared notion was that Poland was a democratic, capitalistic state.[40] The drafters wanted to establish a state structure which reflected those existing in Europe, namely a parliamentary democracy, basing it on the French model. Once decided, the debates turned to the nature of the parliamentary system as the underlying basis of the system: whether the parliament should consist of one or two chambers; the role of the presidency; the legal position of minorities; the freedom of conscience and religion; and the rights and liberties of citizens in general.

Ministers; hereafter, PRM], Part II, p. 32, sygnatura (hereafter, sygn.) 1, Archiwum Akt Nowych, Warsaw, Poland.

38 They were mostly Poles from the former Austrian empire, who 'were more culturally advanced than were the Poles in Prussia or Russia', E. A. Radice, 'General Characteristics of the Region between the Wars', in *The Economic History of Eastern Europe 1919–1975*, Vol. 1, ed. by M. C. Kaser and E. A. Radice (Oxford: Clarendon Press, 1985), p. 24. Letters exchanged between the PRM and other ministries indicate that highly qualified candidates did volunteer for positions of great importance for Poland. See letter from the Ministry of Internal Affairs to the PRM of 19 April 1918. PRM, Part II, p. 8, sygn. 65, Archiwum Akt Nowych, Warsaw, Poland.

39 *Dekret z dnia 8 lutego 1919r. o zwolaniu Sejmu Ustawodawczego* [Decree of 8 February 1919 Concerning the Establishment of the Legislative *Sejm*], *Dziennik Ustaw*, No. 16, item 217. The committee which was in charge of the codification of law, the Codification Commission [*Komisja Kodyficacyjna*], tackled the codification of five different legal systems. As mentioned above, Russian, Prussian and Austrian legal systems were in force, as well as the French (which was introduced by Napoleon in the Grand Duchy of Warsaw in 1807), and the Hungarian, which was in force in a small area of southern Poland. See Adam Zamoyski, *The Polish Way: A Thousand-Year History of the Poles and Their Culture* (London: John Murray, 1987); Norman Davies, *God's Playground: A History of Poland, Volume II: 1795 to the Present* (New York: Columbia University Press, 1982); and Mark Brzezinski, 'Constitutional Heritage and Renewal: The Case of Poland', *Virginia Law Review*, 77 (1991), pp. 49–112.

40 See, generally, Andrzej Ajenkiel, B. Lesnodorski and W. Rostocki, *Historia ustroju Polski* (1764–1939) [The History of the Polish Political System (1764–1939)] (Warsaw: Panstwowe Wydawnictwo Naukowe, 1974), pp. 191–210.

Without question, the role of the presidency was a controversial point. The National Democratic Party opposed a strong presidency, foreseeing that Pilsudski would assume the position, and further suggested that parliament choose the head of state. The left-wing parties supported a stronger presidency, and one that was elected by the people. As regards the position of minorities, the left-wing political parties supported their autonomy within the state structure, in contrast to the right-wing groups, which favoured the National Democratic platform advocating the elimination of constitutional guarantees which promised the preservation of the minorities' respective national institutions. Finally, the left-wing groups supported a secular state. This view, not surprisingly, was contested by the right-wing political parties, which demanded that the Roman Catholic Church hold a prominent position in the state structure.

In addition to this short summary of the parliamentary debates about the composition of the Constitution, which does not pretend to be all-encompassing, it should be mentioned that the question concerning the administration of justice was also at the forefront of discussion, as well as the establishment of a judiciary which was qualified to operate in a legal system that was in transition and to participate in creating a *Polish* legal framework out of the four existing systems.

Pilsudski, due to his defeat of the Bolshevik advance on Poland in 1920, enjoyed immense popularity, and seemed to be the most capable person to head the task of forming the new government. On 17 March 1921, a new Polish Constitution was adopted, restoring the Republic of Poland as a democratic state.[41] The document, also known as the 'March Constitution', belonged to the group of democratic constitutions that were promulgated after the First World War, modelled in this case on the French Constitution of 1875, which represented for the Polish drafters the best model of an efficient government. This Constitution also echoed the Constitution of 1791, stating in its preamble that 'the glorious tradition of the Third of May' formed an integral part of it.[42] The Constitution declared that the sovereignty of the nation belonged to the people, the nation (Article 2). In the spirit of Montesquieu, the same article outlined the separation of powers: the legislative power belonged to the *Sejm*; the executive power belonged to the president; and the judicial power belonged to an independent judiciary. A bicameral legislature, comprising the *Sejm* and the Senate, was granted more power than the executive branch (Articles 2 and 3).[43] The *Sejm* was directly elected by the people, and had responsibility for the national budget, constitutional amendments, creating an army

41 The Constitution of the Republic of Poland of 17 March 1921, *Dziennik Ustaw*, No. 44, item 267.

42 Following the Russian Revolution, the choice was between democracy and the Soviet model (as observed by the parliamentarian M. Niedzialkowski). See *Historia panstwa i prawa Polski 1918–1939, Czesc I* [The History of the Polish State and Law 1918–1939, Part I], ed. by Franciszek Ryszki (Warsaw: Panstwowe Wydawnictwo Naukowe, 1962), p. 115.

43 See Brzezinski, 'Constitutional Heritage', *supra* n. 39, pp. 72–78.

and collecting taxes. According to Article 3, no law could be passed without the authorisation of the *Sejm*. A simple majority vote of the *Sejm* could force a single minister, the whole executive cabinet, or the president to resign (Article 58). There were also important limitations placed on the presidency. As mentioned before, the main impetus came from the National Democratic Party, which feared that a strong presidency would create a precarious situation in which a strong leader, such as Pilsudski, would dominate the processes of government. Parliament elected the president to a seven-year term in office. As regards the president's competence, he was responsible for appointing and dismissing the prime minister and other ministers on the motion of the prime minister; appointing the highest civil and military officers; and assuming command of the state's armed forces, but was not granted the power to act as supreme commander of forces during war.[44]

Section 4 of the Constitution outlined the position of the courts and the judiciary. The constitutional provisions, which conformed to the 1791 document, guaranteed judicial independence (Article 77). Judges could not be removed from office, transferred to a different place of office, suspended from office, or retired against their will (Article 78), and judges were guaranteed judicial immunity (Article 79). The president of the Republic appointed judges (Article 76), while justices of the peace were elected by the populace. In political cases, or in cases entailing more serious punishment, the Constitution provided for a jury trial (Article 83). The Constitution, as in France, stopped short of granting judges the power of judicial review, a notion which was not characteristic of legal systems during the interwar period, but rather came to be incorporated later as a response to the Second World War. Courts were granted the power to review regulations and decrees made unilaterally by the executive branch, but not bills passed by the *Sejm*. According to Article 81, 'the courts of justice shall not have the right to challenge the validity of statutes legally promulgated.' Since no form of judicial review was created, the power of the *Sejm* was further strengthened. The strong position of the *Sejm* eventually crystallised in a power struggle between the legislative and executive branches of government, resulting in exactly the kind of situation that the National Democratic Party wished to avoid.

Many of the debates which took place about the draft document concerned minority rights and the freedom of conscience and religion. A catalogue of rights to be protected was provided. The Constitution protected life, freedom and property without any distinctions of ancestry, ethnicity or religion (Article 95). All citizens were entitled to access to court (Article 98), protection of private property (Article 99), protection of their dwelling (Article 101), certain protections in the workplace (Articles 102 and 103(4)), freedom of expression (Article 104), freedom of work (Article 105), the right to secret correspondence (Article 106), the right to petition (Article 107), the right to gather together (Article 108), the right to maintain nationality, language and national attributes (Articles 109 and

---

44 This limitation was the idea of the right-wing political parties, which did not trust Pilsudski's military prowess.

110), freedom of religion and faith (Article 111), freedom of education (Article 117), the right to free education in public and local schools (Article 119), and the right to compensation in the event of illegal actions by state organs (Article 121). The document also provided for a number of individual liberties, such as access to public office, the right to choose one's occupation, freedom of speech, freedom of the press, and freedom of assembly.[45] The Constitution ensured the continued recognition of civil liberties and protection against arbitrary power that sought to restrain the realisation of these liberties. There were constitutional guarantees against unlawful searches and seizures (Article 100) and ensuring the use of juries in criminal proceedings (Article 83). In this respect, it should be noted that Article 73 of the Constitution established administrative courts and the Supreme Administrative Tribunal, which ruled on the legality of administrative acts with regard to state and self-government acts, based on the French *Conseil d'Etat* model and similar to the German *Rechtsstaat* model. Finally, the underlying capitalist structure of the state was outlined in Article 99, in which private property rights were recognised as the basis for social organisation and legal order (Article 99). Article 99 and Articles 111, 114 and 120, regarding private property, provided the basis for the state structure. Article 99 declared the state's position as 'recognising that one of the fundamental principles of the social structure and the legal order was private property, as well as ensuring all residents, institutions and society the protection of their property'. Only in cases permitted by law would the abolition or limitation of property, whether personal or collective, for reasons of higher utility or for compensation, be allowed.

There was no formal separation between the Church and the state. While guaranteeing religious freedom, the 1921 Constitution stressed the primacy of the Roman Catholic religion in Polish culture. Moreover, Article 114 of the Constitution declared that the Catholic Church, 'being the religion of the preponderant majority of the nation', would be granted the chief role 'among enfranchised religions'. In this way, the Catholic Church maintained its historical link with the Polish government and constitution. Poland signed a concordat with the Vatican in 1925; this international agreement outlined the relationship between the country and the Catholic Church and the role that the latter had in the structure of the state. It should be noted that during the interwar period the Catholic Church enjoyed many privileges, comparatively unknown in other countries in the region, that were guaranteed in the concordat. The Church used its privileges not only to assert its ideological position in the country but also to participate in political life and the many political debates of this period, openly supporting the right-wing policies of the National Democratic Party. In this respect, Article 115 of the Constitution stated that the 'churches of the religious minorities and other legally organised religious communities govern themselves by their own laws, which the state may not refuse to recognise unless they contain rules contrary to the law'.

45 Arts. 96, 102, 104, 105, 108.

The 1921 document was a far-reaching one, symbolising the values which the Poles had striven for during partition, and providing a wide range of rights and liberties to the citizen. Following the basic tenets of classic liberalism, the government obtained its power from the people and, in turn, the government was obliged to ensure the people basic rights. The 1921 Constitution was rule-of-law oriented. It outlined the separation of powers, provided for the independence of the judiciary, and ensured the rights and freedoms of citizens: all essential components of a democratic rule-of-law state. Post-First World War Poland had all the elements to create such a state, and with its commitment to a capitalist system it moved towards resembling other existing 'Western-style' systems.

Unfortunately, constitutional practice dictated otherwise. The lessons of the pre-partition Polish commonwealth remained unlearned, as evidenced in the fact that the 1921 Constitution also created a political structure which was ineffective and problematic. The full extent of these problems was witnessed in 1926; by then, Poland had 92 different political parties, several of which represented national minorities. The electoral law, which embodied a strict form of political representation, did not help matters. Further, local governments pursued their own interests, creating an environment of instability and damaging fragmentation. The ideologically split Polish intelligentsia, who dominated party politics, further exacerbated the divisions of political parties, and the *Sejm* was incapable of achieving the consensus necessary to address pressing issues.[46]

Further complications arose in the actual realisation of the wide array of constitutional rights. In many instances, such as minorities' rights, the laws were not in place, so the constitutional right remained empty because right-wing political groups were able to undermine the constitutional provisions. One way that certain provisions were overruled was by calling upon the concordat, which permitted the Church to enforce religious instruction for all persons under 16 years of age in state schools. Citizens' rights were also limited by acts passed by the administrative organs, not to mention the right of the government to suspend certain rights and liberties, or to impose martial law.

Notwithstanding these shortcomings, the 1921 Constitution was a modern democratic constitution, favourably comparing with other constitutions of the period. It symbolised the most successful period of Polish liberal democracy, between 1921 and 1926. This period was the closest experience that Poland had had with democracy, and one of innovation and creativity, as also observed in economic developments and the activity of the business community, which energetically undertook the task of creating a capitalist framework. Their work was facilitated by the constitutional guarantee to private property. Further developments were obstructed in 1926, when Pilsudski, along with a selection of the army and numerous supporters, staged a coup d'état, declaring that a strong

46 Poles continued to refer to themselves as citizens of Poland and of the former partitioning power. See *A History of Poland*, ed. by Antony Polonsky and Oscar Halecki (London: Routledge & Kegan Paul, 1978).

parliament had resulted in government corruption and political lethargy. Many Poles (and the Church) supported the drastic measure, as the country was heading towards a severe economic crisis. The high degree of state intervention in the country's economic activity extended to the legal arena.[47]

Pilsudski sought to amend the 1921 Constitution substantially, and the new government set about the task of saving the economy and establishing a strong executive branch which would act effectively. Pilsudski attacked corruption, initiated his campaign of *sanacja* (purging),[48] and lobbied for the passage of legislation which would allow dismissal of legislators found by the Supreme Court to have abused their office for personal financial gain.

The declining economy, which was not immune to the difficulties faced by the wider world, provided the necessary reasons for radical political reforms that required stricter government control. By 1930, Pilsudski had consolidated power in both the executive and legislative branches. In attaining the parliamentary control which was needed, Pilsudski and his entourage passed a new Constitution (23 April 1935), which became law later in the same year.[49] While Pilsudski's political strategy was characteristic of a dictator, he has continued to be regarded as a hero by most Poles. Although he may have had noble intentions, he was nonetheless a dictator, acting very much in the spirit of the times as in other countries of Europe, such as Hungary, during the late 1930s.[50] In Hungary, the regime of Admiral Miklós (Nicolas) Horthy de Nagybánya was unmistakeably authoritarian by the mid-1930s. Both Pilsudski and Horthy had military backgrounds, but their respective visions of the future countries they were trying to build differed. Horthy embarked on his own revolutionary programme, which included destroying institutional life connected with the fallen Habsburg empire and with Jews: early on, he had allied himself with the German Nazi regime. The Treaty of Trianon may have conditioned post-war Hungarian policies; the treaty deprived Hungary of a substantial part of her population and territory. Class structures were reorganised and while Jews were permitted to participate in economic life, they were gradually being ostracised in academic life.[51] Pilsudski was authoritarian insofar as he possessed the unquestionable power to overrule any other person or institution

47 'The etatism deeply rooted in Polish soil grew like a tree with great and wide spreading branches. It had manifold sources, some inherited, some new, but every period of the short Twenty Years contributed to its development.' Ferdynand Zweig, *Poland Between Two Wars* (London: Secker & Warburg, 1944), p. 106.

48 See *ibid.*

49 *Dziennik Ustaw*, No. 30, item 227.

50 For the Hungarian context, see Istvan Pogany, *Righting Wrongs in Eastern Europe* (Manchester: Manchester University Press, 1997), in particular pp. 73–103.

51 Military detachments, better known as 'White Terror gangs', operated in Hungary in 1919, for the sole purpose of eliminating individuals suspected of communist activities. Horthy was regarded as their supreme commander, and the 'White Terror' continued during his regime. See Paul Ignotus, *Hungary*, Nations of the Modern World Series (London: Ernest Benn Limited 1972), pp. 152–73.

and to interfere in state activities; similarly, interwar Hungarian regimes could also be described as such. In contrast to Poland and Hungary, Czechoslovakia did not move towards authoritarian rule. The country was unique in that there was 'uninterrupted constitutional and civil libertarian continuity, but also … a pattern of extraordinary stability … within political parties'.[52] Czechoslovakia's pre-war experience was sharply different. This was in large part due to the pětka, or two unofficial, semi-constitutional mechanisms to handle political problems. The Czechoslovak constitutional system was one that continued facets of the Austrian, which ensured that ethnic groups, where a minimum percentage was reached, would have education in their native language and free expression supported. Political stability was evidenced in the electoral system, which meant that votes were cast not for the individual but the party. This does not mean that the state did not experience crises. When it did, the pětka provided for the backroom meetings that permitted a compromise to be reached, or 'we have agreed that we will agree.'[53]

In Poland, the main difference between the 1935 and the 1921 documents lay in the powers granted to the *Sejm* and the president. The 1935 document placed the presidency above all other state authorities, and as 'chief of the state', Pilsudski's goal that the president be elevated to a position far superior to all others was achieved. Further, constitutional guarantees of judicial independence[54] were replaced by constitutional provisions granting the executive the right to appoint and to dismiss members of the government and the judiciary.[55] The office of the justice of the peace, an institution envisaged in the 1921 Constitution, was never implemented, the main reason being the lack of lay judges with no legal qualifications. Also, as the 1921 Constitution was short-lived, there was not enough time to realise all the provisions before the 1926 coup, when Pilsudski took full control of the judiciary. He rejected the participation of judicial candidates elected by the people, rather than selected by him, ensuring that his policies would be implemented. Prior to these reforms, the judiciary had been subjected to political pressure by the executive powers, in particular after the Brzesc affair,[56] when, in an effort to introduce certain legal reforms, the

52 Rothschild, *East Central Europe Between the Two World Wars*, *supra* n. 19, p. 100.

53 R. J. Crampton, *Eastern Europe in the Twentieth Century* (London: Routledge, 1994), p. 62.

54 Art. 2, Constitution of 1921.

55 Arts. 12, 13, 65, Constitution of 1935. Pilsudski, in an attempt to strengthen, above all, the powers of the presidency, had a new Constitution drafted to reflect these changes. See Antony Polonsky, 'Pilsudski in Power, 1926–35', in *The History of Poland Since 1863*, ed. by R. F. Leslie, *supra* n. 2, pp. 159–85.

56 The Brzesc affair occurred in 1930; it was a clash between Pilsudski and his political opponents in parliament. One of these political groups, the *Centrolew*, called for Pilsudski's resignation. Arrests of the party's leaders followed, and carried on throughout the 1930 parliamentary elections. The prisoners were detained in the Brzesc fortress. This event, which showed the regime's brutality, shocked the public. See *ibid.*, pp. 171–75.

executive suspended judicial immunity and dismissed many judges who were considered to be opponents of the government.[57] The president enjoyed a seven-year term of office and unlimited re-election.

Moreover, he was supreme commander of the armed forces (a power denied to him in the 1921 Constitution) and military commanders were denied the power to act independently without the prior consent of the president. Clearly, no system of 'checks and balances' functioned, as most state power was delegated to the president. The separation of powers was no longer recognised and the judiciary was subordinated to the executive power.

As regards civil liberties, the 1935 Constitution retained the freedom of religion and of conscience, as well as freedom from unlawful searches and seizures, from the 1921 document. However, the 1935 Constitution was contradictory to the principles of classic liberalism, as reflected in the 1921 Constitution, in that common values superseded the individual's values; it was proclaimed that the individual and the nation shared the same common values.[58] Article 1 of the 1935 Constitution stated that the Polish state was the common value of all citizens, and Articles 4 and 10 redefined the relationship between the citizen and the state. The state assumed the role as 'the organiser' of public life, and the creativity of the individual was deemed the source of collective life. Article 7 provided for the balancing of the political rights of citizens against their merits and efforts for the common good.

Allegedly, in an effort to save the country from political and economic chaos, the Constitution curtailed some of the constitutional limits which had previously been placed on the government. The effort failed, primarily because of Pilsudski's premature death, three weeks after the constitution's ratification. With the executive power alienated from the legislative power, a strong, charismatic leader was needed to break through the deep antagonism which existed between both branches of government. Pilsudski possessed these qualities, and his death left a vacuum which none of his supporters could fill. The Polish political scene was once again thrown into turmoil, and Pilsudski's supporters argued over whether to return to a democratic system or to continue with an authoritarian one. The 1935 document signalled a return to authoritarianism, in line with events occurring in Europe. In Hungary, for example, constitutional developments took an alarming turn in the late 1930s, when Hungarian legislation was influenced by developments in Germany. From 1938 onwards, the Hungarian parliament adopted draconian anti-Jewish legislation, including confiscation of Jewish property, the conscription of Jews to serve in non-combatant units of the army, and the deportation of Jews

57 *Ibid.*, p. 179.

58 Brzezinski, 'Constitutional Heritage', *supra* n. 39, pp. 82–86; and Andrzej Ajenkiel, *Polskie konstytucje* [Polish Constitutions] (Warsaw: Wiedza Powszechna, 1983), pp. 315–20.

to territories controlled by the Germans (meaning their transport to concentration camps).[59]

The Polish state in 1935 was not a totalitarian regime in which the state controlled all aspects of public and private life, although it is unclear what might have developed had the war not broken out. Pilsudski's adherents attempted to implement more draconian measures, but preoccupation with the economy was at the forefront of government policies. Likewise, while constitutional developments moved in the direction of authoritarianism, the government did not adopt anti-Ukrainian and anti-Belorussian policies as a reaction to communist influence as, for example, did Hungary. This is not to say that there was no conflict with regard to this issue; there was a great deal of persecution of Ukrainians and Belorussians, in part caused by their electoral support for left-wing and 'crypto-communist' parties.[60] Some authors, such as Rothschild, argue that the German political model was highly regarded in the CEE, for its 'imposing domestic and diplomatic successes ... which contrasted vividly with the apparent stagnation and decadence of France'.[61] These factors gave the impression that an authoritarian state was, in fact, 'the wave of the future', to which the newly created or restored state looked, especially when authoritarianism was the key feature of the 'great power' during that period.[62]

Once judicial independence is tampered with, it is difficult to speak of the rule of law. After the Brzesc crisis, the undermining of the Polish judiciary can be noted, as the executive branch attained more power. Pilsudski wanted to ensure that he was surrounded by a dedicated entourage ready to serve him and carry out his policies for the good of the Polish state. He may have had noble intentions, but the fact remains that he assumed the role of a dictator; as he had rejected the 1921 Constitution from its adoption, it was clear that establishing a rule-of-law state was not part of his agenda, but just the opposite.

The *adwokatura* (Bar), to a great extent, remained a force of opposition. The Bar was divided between public and private law matters. Initially, the Polish Bar had a high representation of lawyers from the Austrian partition, whose Polish lawyers numbered three times more than those of the Russian partition, for instance.[63] The first *Zwiazek Adwokatow Polskich* (Bar Council of Polish Barristers) was organised in 1911 in Lwow and maintained an apolitical stance. This was vastly different

59 See Istvan Pogany, *Righting Wrongs in Eastern Europe*, *supra* n. 50, Chapter 2 and pp. 80–103.

60 Compare with Czechoslovakia, for example, where the rights of Slovaks, whom Czechs outnumbered by two to one, and of other minorities were guaranteed by a bill of rights. See Lloyd Cutler and Herman Schwartz, 'Constitutional Reform in Czechoslovakia: *E Duobus Unum*?', *University of Chicago Law Review*, 58 (1991), pp. 511–53.

61 Rothschild, *East Central Europe between the Two World Wars*, *supra* n. 19, p. 21.

62 *Ibid.*

63 Andrzej Kisza, Zdzislaw Krzeminski and Roman Lyczywek, *Historia adwokatury polskiej* [The History of the Polish Bar] (Warsaw: M. C. Kwadrat, 1995), p. 113.

in independent Poland, where numerous lawyers' organisations were established for specific political agendas, such as the *Kolo Adwokatow RP* (Circle of Polish Lawyers RP), which supported the presidential campaign of 'purification'. It should be noted that the Brzesc affair had a lasting effect on the Polish Bar. Among the many arrested were several Polish lawyers, an event which pushed the Main Bar Council in Warsaw into actively protesting their arrest. Some of the best lawyers in the country defended the accused in the Brzesc affair. These events (1931–32) culminated in the Supreme Council of Polish Barristers asking the *Sejm* to clarify its position towards the Polish Bar.[64] To its detriment, the Ministry of Justice, without consulting the Codification Commission, prepared a hasty draft of the law on the Bar and presented it to parliament. The law severely curtailed the ability of lawyers to fulfil their duties and the scope of the activities of the Bar. The Warsaw branch was quick to react: 'This is not a law on the Bar, this is a law of dismantling the Bar, or those who named this the law on the autonomy of the Bar either did not read the draft, or did not know what autonomy is, or are intentionally falsifying the truth.'[65] The Law on the Structure of the Bar of 1937 was the eventual compromise, dictating that the lawyer was a representative of law and order, and at the head of the Bar stood the Supreme Bar Council (*Naczelna Rada Adwokacka*).[66]

The Polish Bar did have support in parliament, as some 30 lawyers had seats in the *Sejm* and some 15 had seats in the Senate.[67] Lawyers were involved in many different political groupings during the pre-war period. Several lawyers who had left-wing sympathies served in key positions in the post-war Ministry of Justice.[68]

Legal Philosophy

At this time Polish legal science was experiencing a renaissance mainly owing to the work of Leon Petrazycki. Petrazycki was a renowned Roman law scholar, who gradually rejected what he perceived as narrow studies of legal positivism.

---

64 *Ibid.*, p. 118.

65 These were the words of the director of the Warsaw Bar Council, Jan Nowodworski, as quoted in *ibid.*, p. 118.

66 *Ustawa z dnia 4 maja 1938r. o prawo o ustroju adwokatury* [The Law of 4 May 1938 Concerning the Law Concerning the Bar], *Dziennik Ustaw*, No. 33, item 289. For further details on the notary (*notariusz*), see Piotr Jurek, *Historia panstwa i prawa polskiego: zrodla prawa, sadownictwo, zarys wykladu* [The History of the Polish State and Law: Sources of Law and Courts in the Period] (Wroclaw: Wydawnictwo Uniwersytetu Wroclawskiego, 1992), p. 141.

67 Kisza *et al.*, *Historia adwokatury polskiej*, *supra* n. 63, p. 121.

68 Such as Henryk Swiatkowski (minister of justice) and Leon Chajn, who will be mentioned in Chapter 4.

This move was most likely rooted in Polish history but also Russian legal theory.[69] The notion of a single command of the executive power was alien to the Polish 'democracy of the gentry'. Petrazycki was strongly opposed to equating law with the external coercion exercised by the state. He challenged legal positivism, calling it 'absolute legal idiotism', claiming that only a man suffering from a total inability to have legal experiences (the experience of having a legal right, or a legal obligation) could suppose that law was only a set of commands created by the powerful in their own interests to coerce the weak and defenceless, with hints of aggression in case of disobedience. Petrazycki criticised attempts to reduce legal science to analytical jurisprudence, and claimed that a break from professional jurisprudence was the first essential condition to create the scientific theory of law.[70] No one went further than Petrazycki to emphasise that law was not a system of abstract norms but a part of social reality which had to be studied causally, all the while stressing the ethical function of law, and the need to make purposeful, conscious law.[71]

Petrazycki claimed that law was to be found in inner experience and knowledge, which could be achieved by means of introspection. Law, according to him, was a psychic phenomenon, a part of our spirit. He saw it as an inner voice which tells us what our duties are in relation to others and, more importantly, what our rights are, and what we can legitimately demand from others. The only way to study law, then, was to analyse our inner experiences. Petrazycki felt, however, that the state

69 Russia was experiencing the same legal debates as in continental Europe, between legal positivism and natural law. The top Russian scholars of the legal idealism school were B. Chicherin, whose main works included *A History of Political Theories* (5 vols, 1877–1902) and V. Soloviev, *Legal Philosophy* (1902). One of the most important legal philosophers was P. I. Novgorodsteff, who supported the revival of natural law. His most important works included *The Historical School in Jurisprudence* (1896) and *Kant and Hegel* (1901). As for the legal positivism school, the writings of N. Korkunoff, *Lectures on the General Theory of Law* (1888) and *Russian Constitutional Law* profoundly affected Russian jurists and Petrazycki, who found a source of inspiration in Korkunoff's work. See W. E. Butler, 'Towards an Introduction to Russian Legal Theory', in *Russian Legal Theory*, ed. by W. E. Butler (Aldershot: Dartmouth, 1996), pp. xxxv–xxxvii.

70 See Leon Petrazycki, *0 dopelniajacych pradach kulturalnych i prawach rozwoju handlu* [On Complementary Cultural Trends and Laws of Commercial Development] (Warsaw: Nakladem Towarzystwa im. Leona Petrazyckiego, 1936). This pamphlet was based on the handwritten notes of one of Petrazycki's pupils, Jerzy Finkelkraut. See also *Prawo a Sad* [Law and the Court] (Warsaw: Nakladem Towarzystwa im. Leona Petrazyckiego, 1936).

71 During his studies, Petrazycki was sent to Berlin to participate in a seminar run by the greatest living expert in Roman law of the day, Heinrich Dernburg. This experience provided a new depth to Petrazycki's comprehension. At this time German jurists were working on the BGB, and they looked to historical and legal positivistic schools to achieve this task. Petrazycki published *Die Fruchtverteilung beim Wechsel des Nutzungsberechtigten* (1892) and *Die Lehre von Einkommen* (2 vols, 1893–95).

of the mind did not suggest the existence of a political state, or any other form of social organisation that issued commands and backed them by force.[72]

Petrazycki was best known for his emphasis on 'intuitive law', and frequently pointed out the superiority of intuitive over statutory law. He found examples in contemporary Russian history.[73] According to Petrazycki, the institution of legal expertise was underdeveloped in Russia. The excessive growth of the institution and the arbitrary explaining of existing laws were dangerous because the authority of law was not grounded, and the objective meaning of a statute law was always less important that the opinions of influential people. In addition, Russian statutes contained too many references to subjective factors, such as 'goodwill' or 'conscience', which judges were supposed to take into account in performing their duties.

Petrazycki's scholarship concerned the social order and the forces which shape its structure and substance.[74] As the distributive function of the intuitive and official law designs the social and economic system of the society, so its organisational function shapes the administrative and constitutional fabric of the social whole. The system of the official law allocates different types and volumes of power (through distribution of rights and duties) to various social agencies. The organisational function of the law is consistently engaged in the law-creation process. This organisational function of the law also 'reifies' and 'petrifies' its crucial institutions, and thus defends the whole system against internal conflicts. The law is, nevertheless, able to survive its own total destruction when new intuitive law (based on changed perceptions of the allocation of rights and duties), contradictory to the old, breaks through the binding *Grundnorm* to turn itself subsequently into official law. If the distributive and organisational functions of intuitive and official law put into operation the entire social system, then the law indeed constitutes the dominant element of basic social changes of the whole social structure.[75] This part of Petrazycki's theory relating to different kinds of legal phenomena is one of

72 After the Russian Revolution, there was an attempt to apply Petrazycki's theories. See Nicholas S. Timasheff, 'Introduction', in *Law and Morality*, by Leon Petrazycki, Twentieth Century Legal Philosophy Series, VII, trans. by Hugh W. Babb (Cambridge, MA: Harvard University Press, 1955), pp. xxxii–xxxiii.

73 Petrazycki's influence expanded with the creation of the first Russian newspaper, *Pravo*, dedicated to the struggle for legal culture in the Russian Empire. The editors were made up of members of minority groups (Jewish and Polish), who were most affected by the lack of civil liberties in the Russian Empire. See Judith Zimmerman, 'The Kadets and the Duma 1905–1907', in *Essays in Russian Liberalism*, ed. by Charles E. Timberlake (Columbia, MO: University of Missouri Press, 1972), pp. 119–38, and William Rosenberg, 'Kadets and the Politics of Ambivalence', *ibid.*, pp. 139–63.

74 Petrazycki, 'O dopelniajacych pradach', *supra* n. 70, pp. 6–7.

75 Czeslaw Znamierowski outlined the aspects of the general theory of constructing norms, namely rules which concede the new character of a given conventional act to define a human act. See *Podstawowe pojecia teorii prawa, Czesc I: Uklad prawny i norma prawna* [The Basic Concepts of the Theory of Law, Part I: The Legal System and the Legal Norm]

the most lasting, and relevant to present-day contributions, and this aspect will be revisited in Chapter 5.[76]

Petrazycki's theories offered a counter-approach to the increasingly prominent theories of Hans Kelsen, which were based on normative and positivist interpretations of the law, and which Petrazycki found to be in error.[77] In fact, Petrazycki held that the cause of revolution was the incompatibility between positive and intuitive law.[78] The theories on law and ethics of the Viennese school and the Lwow-Warsaw school were particularly influential, and offered a counter-approach to Petrazycki's theory, which was based on psychological interpretations.[79] Petrazycki's greatest opponent at the University of Warsaw was Prof. Eugeniorv Jarra, a rival who wanted to establish his own school of jurisprudence to rival Petrazycki's.

Positive law presents a uniform pattern of rules for most of society, mainly because its content can be defined by perceptions of external factors capable of being known by many people alike. In contrast, intuitive law is dynamic by nature; its content is defined by the conditions of the individuals, including their upbringing, education, social position, profession, personal relationships, etc., to name only a few factors. Intuitive law thus has a wider scope of applicability than positive law. In reality, it is positive law which plays an enormous role in individual conduct and mass, social and economic phenomena. Where positive and intuitive law meet, the development of both is defined in general terms by the

---

(Warsaw: 1924). For further information on Znamierowski, see *Polish Contributions to the Theory and Philosophy of Law*, ed. by Zygmunt Ziembinski (Amsterdam: Rodopi, 1987).

76 Timasheff, 'Introduction', *supra* n. 72, p. xvii. See Andrzej Kojder, 'Petrazycki wiecznie zywy' [Petrazycki Still Lives], *Prawo i Zycie* [Law and Life] (1991), pp. 10–11. After Petrazycki's suicide in 1931, the association created in his name and his followers (many former students) were annihilated in the Second World War. See also Anna Turska, 'Leon Petrazycki – w perspecktywie historycznej i wspolczesnej' [Leon Petrazycki – in a Historical and Contemporary Perspective], *Studia luridica*, 29 (1995), pp. 59–74, and Krzysztof Motyka, *Wplyw Leona Petrazyckiego na Polska teorie i sociologie prawa* [The influence of Leon Petrazycki on Polish Sociological Theory and Law] (Lublin: Redakcja Wydawnictwo Katolickiego Uniwersytetu Lubeiskiego, 1993).

77 Hans Kelsen, *Essays in Legal and Moral Philosophy*, ed. by Ota Weinberger (Dordrecht: D. Reidel, 1973).

78 See Leon Petrazycki, *0 nauce prawie i moralnosci: pisma wybrane* [On Teaching Law and Morality: Chosen Works] (Warsaw: Panstwowe Wydawnictwo Naukowe, 1985), pp. 276–83, and Hugh Babb, 'Petrazhitskii: Theory of Law', *Harvard Law Review*, 38 (1938), pp. 511–78. The latter work was the second of a two-part article addressing the work of Petrazycki, the first being (by the same author), 'Petrazhitskii: Science of Legal Policy and Theory of Law', *Harvard Law Review*, 37 (1937), pp. 793–829. The articles are unique in the sense that they present an excellent, comprehensive overview of Petrazycki's works in the English language.

79 See the works of Bronislaw Wroblewski, *Studia z dziedziny prawa i etyki* [Studies from the Fields of Law and Ethics] (Wilno: 1934).

operation of the same social-psychic processes acting by the same laws, though there are specific differences in intellectual composition: the greater the accord, the better laws function.[80]

Justice deals with normative experiences of principle, ethical experiences in which are present ethical imperative-attributive emotions leading to judgments as to what is due and owing according to our own personal convictions. Its scope comprises the province of distributing good and evil. This means that experiences of justice are intuitive, ethical experiences of an imperative-attributive type, or intuitive law. Justice has its projections and norms, and its rights and obligations are secured on behalf of others. Since justice is law, it exerts a more powerful pressure on conduct than does morality. Being independent of normative facts, justice is distinguished by individual distinction of content in different classes and individuals, has greater capacity of adapting to concrete circumstances than positive law, and develops gradually and unnoted without the complications characteristic of the development of positive law.[81]

The realisation of legal order and the principle of the rule of law depend, according to Petrazycki, on the formation within the society of the ideal 'citizen', possessing ideal characteristics, including skills, knowledge about the economy, energy and innovation.[82] The development of the economy is dependent on many important factors, but one of the key elements is the realisation of legality and the legal order in the economic legal framework. Thus, in order to achieve ideal moral attributes, a sense of legality must also exist; otherwise, it would be impossible to speak of 'healthy ethics'. In his writing on the subject, Petrazycki turned to the works of Lev Tolstoy to provide evidence of a society which views law as something lower than morality and not requiring respect, or even warranting a negative reaction.[83] Petrazycki considered this to stem from the absence of knowledge about the nature and meaning of the social aspects of ethics among people.[84]

Petrazycki figured prominently among the leading interwar criminological and constitutional thinkers. Waclaw Makowski, professor and speaker of the *Sejm*, observed that legal norms exist in the psyche of people, in their emotional processes, and similarly values, duties, crimes, punishment and legal order, as a grouped system of social procedure, belong to the field of psychology, reflecting the real psychological condition of the society. Makowski also created two branches of sociological and psychological functions, interpreting state power as stemming from the emotional processes of the social psyche, and adopting Petrazycki's

80 Petrazycki, *O nauce prawie i moralnosci*, *supra* n. 78, pp. 276–83.

81 *Ibid.*

82 *Ibid.*, p. 260.

83 *Ibid.*

84 See Sawa Frydman, *Uwagi podstaw skarbowosci* [The Underlying Aspects of the Monetary System] (Wilno: 1930), in Motyka, *Wplyw Leona Petrazyckiego*, *supra* n. 76, pp. 33–34.

notion of adequacy and emotional impulsions.[85] The law, in essence, not only forms clear norms for living, but is the living source of society, leading society's activities, and creating the direction of psychological life. Bad law, or law which goes against the needs of the social psyche, must in the end disappear, but before that occurs, individuals and society will suffer, and the marks will remain in the social psyche, if time does not heal the wound. Good law, supporting the needs of the social psyche, must encompass the power to evolve, and the characteristics of survival and foresight must be realised by political law.

The Polish contribution to the sociology of law is unmistakable. Its influence on the work of Timasheff, Gurvitch and Sorokin indicates the core question at the heart of this school which examines 'law in action', or Ehrlich's notion of 'living law'.[86] Undoubtedly controversial, Petrazycki's contribution to Polish legal science resulted in legal scholars of the time engaging with, for example, aspects of civil law and civil procedural law, in ways that critically revisited more established notions with a fresh perspective.[87] At a broader level, recent scholarship reveals a lacuna in the area of 'legal justice', which critiques recent claims that the state is the only official and legitimate source of law.[88] The sociology of law has successfully shown that any meaning attached to 'law' and 'justice' cannot be equated with official state law, thus identifying the importance of unofficial law, or intuitive law. Developments within the CEE seem to acknowledge the shifting notion of 'legal justice' and the manner in which it operates.

General Remarks

As mentioned previously, the *Mala Konstytucja* and the 1921 Constitution made clear that the separation of powers, between legislature, executive and judicial branches, would be guaranteed. The drafters of the Constitution, in the spirit of the Polish nation's fight for constitutional liberties, sought to implement the principles of judicial independence by guaranteeing judicial control over civil and criminal matters, judicial independence, control over judicial nominations, the capacity to assess legislative acts, and separation of the judicial position

---

85 Waclaw Makowski, *Panstwo spoleczne* [The Social State] (Warsaw: 1936).

86 Eugene Ehrlich, *Fundamental Principles of the Sociology of Law* (New Brunswick, NJ: Transaction Publishers, 2001), first published in 1922.

87 Such as Jerzy Wroblewski and Aleksander Peczenik, discussed in Chapter 5. See Adam Podgorecki, 'Unrecognized Father of Sociology of Law: Leon Petrazycki – Reflections Based on Jan Gorecki's *Sociology and Jurisprudence of Leon Petrazycki*', *Law and Society*, 15 (1980–81), pp. 183–202; see also Gorecki's book, the subject of Podgorecki's review, published by the University of Illinois Press (1975).

88 See, for example, *Social Processes and Patterns of Legal Control: European Yearbook of Sociology of Law, 2000*, ed. by Alberto Febbrajo, David Nelken and Vittorio Olgiati (Milan: Giuffre, 2001).

from state administrators.[89] Provisions made it clear that judgments could not be changed by the executive or legislative branches of government. Judges could not be dismissed, nor could they be arrested and prosecuted without the decision of a competent tribunal.

By the early 1930s, the conflict between the legislative and executive branches of government had reached its peak. Many political leaders and legal scholars argued that the executive, under Pilsudski's leadership, had over extended its power over parliament and judiciary, and was not necessarily opposed to violating the Constitution to make its power manifest.[90] The crisis that lay between both powers began when an opposition party moved to impeach Pilsudski, who retaliated by arresting its members on the grounds that the party was aiming to destroy the Polish state.[91] Oppositionists were arrested, imprisoned, and isolated from the outside world. The populace was shocked by the repressive measures of the government, which intervened in the upcoming 1928 election, invalidated electoral results, and resorted to administrative pressure to achieve the much-needed 47 per cent vote in parliament. The government became increasingly authoritarian. There was strong political opposition to authoritarianism, as expressed by the *Polskie Stronnictwo Ludowe* (Polish Peasant Party; hereafter PSL). Ethnic minorities and the political parties that expressed their views were also opposed to the Polish regime.

From March 1932, the government was granted vast powers of legislation by decree, which it used to restrict constitutional rights such as the freedom of assembly and the right to strike. Censorship became more vigorous after the elections. The government's campaign against the opposition entered the university domain. As soon as the universities lost their autonomy, 50 professors who were deemed

---

89 Andrzej Rzeplinski, 'Kolejne nowele do Rozporzadzenia Prezydenta RP z 6 II 1928r. o ustroju sadow powszechnych w Polsce Ludowej w latach 1944–1956' [Consecutive Reforms in the Presidential Decree of 6 February 1928 on the Law of the Common Courts in the Polish People's Republic in the Years 1944–1956] (1995), unpublished manuscript (on file with author).

90 The crisis affected not only the judiciary but also the entire administration of justice. The Polish state police force (*policja panstwowa*), for example, was pressured to recruit only politically reliable persons after the coup d'état of 1926. The police force became ineffective, political and more opportunistic. On the orders of Pilsudski, officers who served in the military were recruited into the state police force. During the 1930s, it became customary for military officers of lower rank to be made redundant and = to the commissariat of the state police. In practice, this meant that the police had a military connotation and, further, that Pilsudski ensured that he maintained control over the police cadre and the scope of their activities. The strict policy, which was followed from 1918 to 1926, for the police to be apolitical was abolished and in practice removed from the code of ethics. See Andrzej Musiuk, *Policja panstwowa 1919–1939: powstanie, organizacje, kierunki dzialania* [The State Police 1919–1939: Creation, Organisation, and Scope of Activities] (Warsaw: Wydawnictwo Naukowe PWN, 1996).

91 See the section '1921 Constitution' in this chapter for the details which led up to the conflict.

opponents were dismissed. The irremovability of judges was suspended for one year in 1932 in order to remove judges who were considered to be opponents of the government. During the period, Poles also witnessed the political trials of top anti-Pilsudski government leaders, trials reminiscent of the repressive tactics practised by the partitioning powers. The government's legitimacy in the eyes of the public faltered, as did the authority of the administration of justice. According to a great Polish literary figure of the time, '[t]he moral links between the government and the majority of the population were shattered. From now on all attempts to restore them, however well intentioned, were to prove vain.'[92] The chaotic state of affairs was not conducive to rapid progress in the work entrusted to the Codification Commission. By 1920, the work of the commission had expanded; members of the commission became involved in the work of newly formed sections.

We see a rapid, if not calculated, departure from these principles once the euphoria of establishing the Polish state had subsided, and political leaders (especially in Pilsudski's camp) perceived threats to their power and obstacles to putting through reforms. The 1935 Constitution reflected a complete departure from the principles enshrined in the 1921 document. For example, the drafters of the 1935 Constitution rejected Montesquieu's concept of the separation of powers, and maintained that supreme power should lie with the parliament, which represented the 'will of the people'.[93] The Supreme Court, in its role as appeals court, worked to ensure that court decisions were just and fair, a task which was not made easier by the increasing political pressures of the 1930s.[94]

This shift of power is significant in Polish history, and possibly sets out a repeated pattern of subsequent state intervention in judicial affairs, a clear deviation from the theory of the separation of powers, and an almost hypocritical stand on the constitutional principles embraced by the Polish nation. That rights are guaranteed by constitutions does not mean that they will be honoured or promulgated by a judicial system said to be committed in theory to the rule of law.[95] The fact that Polish society, in particular the intelligentsia, was aware of this may explain its reversion to previous informal mechanisms to cope with the state apparatus, which

---

92 Maria Dabrowska, quoted in Hans Roos, *A History of Modern Poland: From the Foundation of the State in the First World War to the Present Day* (London: Eyre & Spottiswoode, 1966), p. 122.

93 Despite the political vacillations, one of the most important examples of judicial independence was the decision of the Supreme Court about the elections to the *Sejm* and the Senate in 1930. Krzysztof Kauba, 'Sadownictwo w Polsce w latach 1918–1939' [The Judiciary in Poland in the Years 1918–1939] (1994), unpublished manuscript (on file with author).

94 For a detailed look at the evolution of the Polish Supreme Court, see Michal Pietrzak, 'Sad Najwyzszy w II Rzeczpospolitej' [The Supreme Court in the Second Republic], *Czasopismo Prawno-Historyczne*, 33 (1981), pp. 83–103.

95 See Carol Weisbrod, 'Minorities and Diversities: the "Remarkable Experiment" of the League of Nations', *Connecticut Journal of International Law*, 8 (1993), pp. 359–406.

was in a continued state of disarray, and slowly losing its legitimacy with the serious scandals already mentioned.[96]

The judiciary began to voice its doubts about the development of judicial practice and state intervention in important political cases.[97] Judicial officials were alarmed at the state of the administration of justice, particularly in the lower courts. They were aware of the debates about law and society that were occurring at the time, and argued that the courts played a paramount role in eliminating systems of corrupt and dishonest practices. An observation of the time arguably hints at the necessary foundations for a rule-of-law state already laid; it was not met institutionally. 'Having a well-rooted *legal consciousness* within society is dependent on an efficient court system, above all regional courts, the basic unit of the court structure.'[98] The governmental interference, which was characteristic of the partitioning powers, was occurring again in the independent Polish state, which was also beginning to mimic other developments in the region, that of governments rejecting democratic principles, and thus rejecting the principles of the rule of law, for authoritarian control. Such developments began with limiting judicial independence.[99]

Judicial officials, having had prior experience under partition, and after observing the conditions in the administration of justice in the new Polish state, urged the implementation of a vigorous educational programme, with better training of officials, who, with a solid background, 'would benefit the client … improving the language of the court and bringing the administrator closer to utilising the principles of the Code'.[100]

---

96 The Brzesc affair of 1930 is an excellent example. See Polonsky, 'Pilsudski in Power, 1926–35', *supra* n. 55, pp. 174–85.

97 'What does the court say [to real guarantees of judicial independence]? We remember that not too long ago, in complete fear within the entire court [system], the response to that question would have been: "It does not say, it remains silent." … Art. 64 of the [1921] Constitution … and Art. 65 [of the 1935 Constitution] recognise the need that the law must make separate not only the judicial position, but also [the judges'] salary.' Kazimierz Fleszynski, 'Realne gwarancje niezawislosci sedziowskiej' [Real Guarantees of Judicial Independence], *Glos sadownictwa* [The Courts' Voice], 11 (1939), p. 105. This argument is relevant to current debates about the judiciary in Poland, in which judges argue that they would be more dedicated to their work if the state showed more concern for the moribund state of the administration of justice.

98 Stanislaw Lipowski, 'Niedomagania sadow grodzkich' [The Shortcomings of the Courts of First Instance], *Glos sadownictwa*, 11 (1939), p. 677.

99 Konstanty Grzybowski, *Galicja 1848–1914: historia ustroju politycznego na tle historii ustroju Austrii, Tom XV* [Galicia 1848–1914: The History of the Political Structure Based on the History of Austria, Vol. 15], Polska Akademia Nauk, Komitet Nauk Prawnych, Studia nad Historia Panstwa i Prawa-Seria II (Cracow: Polska Akademia Nauk, 1959), p. 181.

100 *Ibid.*

Chapter 3
German and Soviet Regimes (1939–1945)

German Occupation (1939–1945)

General Overview

For Poland, September 1939 marked a fourth partition. The German–Soviet Agreement of August 1939 divided Poland into two 'zones of interest' according to the Ribbentrop–Molotov demarcation line. The area west of the Pisa, Narew, Bug and San rivers was occupied by Germany; the areas to the east were occupied by the Soviet Union. By October 1939, it was clear that neither power intended to create a rump Polish state. The German and Soviet powers wasted no time in strengthening their hold over the annexed territories by establishing administrative governments marked by severe repression and oppression. Both powers extended their regimes to include the newly acquired territories, but treated them separately.

On 8 October, Hitler annexed the northern and western regions of Poland, and created two administrative districts, the *Reichsgau Danzig* and the *Reichsgau Wartheland*, respectively. On 12 October, the remainder of the Polish territory under German control, which was west of the demarcation line, was given the name *Generalgouvernement*. The territories which were incorporated into the Third Reich were rich in resources and industry, and encompassed a population of 10.1 million, of whom 8.9 million were Poles, 603,000 Jews and 600,000 Germans.[1] The territory was targeted by Hitler for complete Germanisation, and was to serve as a German outpost in the East.

The German policy toward Poland was defined on 20 October 1939, several days prior to the official inauguration of the *Generalgouvernement* (hereafter, GG), at a conference held between Hitler and the Wehrmacht:

1. The GG was granted a quasi-independent status. Because there was no intention of its incorporation into the Third Reich, authorities were free from the Reich administration and all legal norms, and were allowed full control to do whatever was necessary to quash any oppositional forces.[2]

---

1 Jan M. Ciechanowski, 'Poland in Defeat, September 1939–July 1941', in *The History of Poland Since 1863*, ed. by R. F. Leslie (Cambridge: Cambridge University Press, 1983), p. 214.

2 Polish history was of great interest to the German occupiers. Heinrich Himmler studied nineteenth-century Polish history, and ordered SS officers to read his report about 'Polish methods of preparation and conduct of the uprising against the Russians in 1863:

2. Two key goals were generally set. First, the Polish intelligentsia[3] was to be prevented from assuming future leadership and, second, all communication lines were to be kept in good condition so that the territory could be used to mobilise the armed forces for future conquests. The administration of the GG was to assist the Reich in the goal 'to cleanse it of all Jews and Poles'.[4]

There is much literature and documentation about the various aspects of the German regime in Poland during this period.[5] Suffice it to say that the most brutal methods were used to carry out the German policy in the GG. The population was exploited in the interests of Germany. The resurgence of any nationalistic life was to be prevented at all costs, as was the reintroduction of any economic or commercial life. The only role assigned to Poles was that of cheap labour. The policy of *polnische Wirtschaft* (Polish labour)[6] was promoted at all times and the standard of living was kept appallingly low.[7] Hans Frank, the governor of the GG, declared that he simply was not interested in whether or not the Poles had enough to eat, and starving the Jews to death was, in his view, an expedient way of getting rid of them. As a result, food smuggling became a large and highly organised business. The impoverishment of the cities continued at an alarming pace, and by 1941 welfare agencies set up special soup kitchens to aid the population. Within one year after the war began, it was estimated that approximately 2.6–2.9 million people were suffering material hardship that could not be overcome without outside assistance.[8]

---

the manner of Russian defence'. The Germans did not want to repeat the errors of the Russians which had allowed the 1863 Polish Uprising. Jan Gross, *Polish Society Under the German Occupation: The Generalgouvernement, 1939–1944* (Princeton, NJ: Princeton University Press, 1979), p. 46.

3 Defined as 'Polish teachers, clergy, medical doctors, dentists, veterinarians, officers, ranking bureaucrats, big merchants, big landowners, writers, journalists' and all other individuals who possessed a high school or university education. *Ibid.*, p. 47.

4 *Ibid.*, pp. 46–47.

5 See, for example, *The German Occupation of Poland: Extract of Note Addressed to the Governments of the Allied and Neutral Powers on May 3, 1941* (London: Cornell Press Limited, 1941); Ron Rosenbaum, *Explaining Hitler: The Search for Origins of His Evil* (New York: Random House, 1998); Michael Stolleis, *The Law Under the Swastika: Studies on Legal History in Nazi Germany* (Chicago: University of Chicago Press, 1998); Wladyslaw Szpilman, *The Pianist: The Extraordinary Story of One Man's Survival in Warsaw, 1939–45*, trans. by Anthea Bell (London: Victor Gollancz, 1999).

6 A derogatory German term which denoted a 'lack of organization, clumsiness, and stupidity in the conduct of one's economic affairs'. Ciechanowski, 'Poland in Defeat', *supra* n. 1, p. 214.

7 In 1941, for example, the daily food ration of the Warsaw Jew was 184 calories; it was 669 for a Pole, and 2,613 for a German.

8 Gross, *Polish Society Under the German Occupation*, *supra* n. 2, p. 100.

The territories served as a 'dumping ground' for all 'undesirable elements' from the Reich, and from the territories which were subsequently incorporated into the Reich. The 'dumping ground' had then to be cleansed of the 'undesirable elements', leading to the German adoption of a policy of extermination of non-Germans. This would ensure the achievement of the ultimate goal: that of a racially pure German state.[9]

But before these measures were put in place, the GG was viewed as a 'gigantic labour camp, a reservoir of labour force on a huge scale', with a careful eye to the future.[10] The task of Germanisation was assumed by Heinrich Himmler, who also headed the *Schutzstaffel* (hereafter, SS) and the Gestapo. Under his plan, the population was divided into several categories, according to their suitability for Germanisation. Those who were of German descent were considered to be 'racial Germans', yet were still regarded as a lower class than the *Reichsdeutsches* (native Germans). Poles who were considered by the Germans to be a threat, or unfit for Germanisation, were deported to the other areas of the GG, to the Reich or, later, to extermination camps. Poles were considered as a source of cheap labour and stripped of all human rights. German policy on Poles who could contribute to cheap labour was more nuanced than the policies on Poles of the categories noted above. This new workforce was reduced to the status of slaves, as shown by the legal developments noted below. Certainly, the first group to suffer were the most prominent citizens and members of the intelligentsia.[11]

Social Context and Policies

The occupied territory in Poland was first subdivided into the four districts of Cracow, Warsaw, Lublin and Radom. Each of the districts was headed by a governor. This was based on the concept of the *Führerprinzip*, or the system of granting key appointments in the bureaucracy not to an office, but to a man. This ensured loyalty and the acceptance of responsibility from the appointees. Each appointee was subordinated to his superior who, in turn, was also subordinated to his superior; this continued up the ladder, to Hitler himself. While the *Führerprinzip*, on the

---

9 While the Germans were committed to this policy of *Wiedereindeutschung*, or the return to 'Germandom', it was not without its ambiguities. For example, only 3 per cent of the GG's population were considered suitable for Germanisation, while 50 per cent of the population in the occupied territory of Czechoslovakia were considered fit. It was also not uncommon for many Poles who lived in the Danzig (Gdansk) region to be considered fit for Germanisation, or for parents to be treated as 'Germans' and their children not. *Ibid.*

10 *Ibid.*, p. 76.

11 William Shirer, *The Rise and Fall of the Third Reich: A History of Nazi Germany* (London: Secker & Warburg, 1960), pp. 937–94, and Matthew Lippman, 'Fifty Years After Auschwitz: Prosecutions of Nazi Death Camp Defendants', *Connecticut Journal of International Law*, 11 (1996), pp. 199–278.

surface, appeared to be efficient and expedient, this highly centralised system in fact promoted chaos and corruption in the ranks of the GG.

Governor Frank's administration was modelled on the Reich government; to his dismay, it was not entirely autonomous. As a result, the history of the administration of the occupied Polish territory was marked by an ongoing conflict between Frank, the police and the SS. The administration, from the beginning, operated in chaos, which paved the way for corruption. The closeness of the bureaucracies allowed the Berlin authorities to bypass corresponding departments of the administration. For example, the Office of Price Setting was created even though there were five main departments already concerned with economic affairs. Some of these departments intentionally destroyed Polish enterprises, while others supported their enforcement and consolidation.

As a rule, the best-qualified German personnel were sent West. Therefore, the cadre found in the East were generally poorly qualified.[12] Those who came to the East were attracted to the riches and rewards to be reaped from the plunder, and held the hope of attaining powerful posts. This meant that corruption was present from the very beginning, paving the way for Poles to establish a black market, and other avenues for survival.[13] These factors created a framework which was firmly in place throughout the communist era. A similar pattern of establishing strategies of survival existed under Soviet occupation.

Polish cultural and educational institutions were closed, and only the most rudimentary forms of primary education were allowed. Secondary education in the GG was permitted but limited to technical and trade education. Towards the end of the war, some higher technical education was allowed to aid the German war effort. Poles were not permitted to speak Polish or to move freely throughout the territory. In 1940, the Germans looked to the countryside and sent younger peasants to Germany, to work in industry or agriculture, or deported them to other areas of the GG. This was done to make room for the resettlement of Germans in their place, to ensure a supply of cheap labour and foodstuffs for the German war effort. By the end of 1944, approximately 750,000 Germans had resettled in the newly annexed territories, while 330,000 Poles in these regions had been murdered and 860,000 deported to the GG or the Reich.[14]

---

12 This did not go unnoticed by Frank, who complained after one year about the absence of middle-level civil servants.

13 The Germans were reluctant to press charges against their fellow countrymen; instead they opted for their transfer or removal to another post if the crimes were impossible to cover up. In his book, *Kronika lat wojny i okupacji* [Chronicle of the Years of War and Occupation], Ludwik Landau reports that by September 1940 there was an unusually high turnover rate in the German administration, and suggests that the Germans were determined to plunder as much as possible. Gross, *Polish Society Under the German Occupation*, *supra* n. 2, p. 55.

14 *Ibid.*, p. 215. See Shirer, *The Rise and Fall of the Third Reich*, *supra* n. 11, p. 944, for Governor Frank's speech on this matter.

The war inevitably shattered the entire fabric of daily life in Poland. Civilians were forced to cope with the horrors of the German occupation, which led to natural decay in social organisation. The psychological terror was tremendous. Any attempt to aid others, namely Jews, risked the death penalty. According to Sorokin (1943), 'calamities generate two opposite movements in different sections of the population, one is a trend toward unreligiousness and demoralization; the other is a trend toward extreme religious, spiritual and moral exaltation.'[15]

Not surprisingly, social disorganisation resulted, the main elements being alcoholism, gradual loss of a sense of private and public property, corruption and exposure to violence. Armed assaults became commonplace against offices where documents were held for requisition of foodstuffs to the Reich, and against Gestapo agents. Interestingly, as the Polish underground became more organised and powerful, people complained to its local commanders about the violence of 'bandits', to which the local underground police responded by staging raids against banditry.[16] But the underground worked unsuccessfully against the easy availability of arms, the breakdown of order, the displacement of large numbers of people, and the deterioration of material life. At the same time, many people turned to intentional exploitation for private gain. The legitimacy of the conspiratorial organisation was used as a guise for self-interest; for example, many Jews were blackmailed in exchange for hiding them. Eventually, the Polish Underground Army established special courts which had jurisdiction over criminal offences and could sentence the offender to death for the crimes of bribery or banditry.

One of the most destructive consequences of the occupation was the breakdown of the family. In all social classes, adult authority collapsed, and children assumed economic responsibility at a very early age. Even the teachings of the Catholic Church did not apply to the young person's life. According to Martin Bormann, Hitler's secretary, Polish priests 'will preach what we want them to preach. If any priest acts differently, we shall make short work of him. The task of the priest is to keep the Poles quiet, stupid and dull-witted.'[17] It was common to find children caring for their younger siblings simply because their parents had left, disappeared, or could no longer care for them. Young people became desensitized to extreme violence, and, as they were the most valuable 'material' for labour, frequently hid from the Germans. Many joined the underground movement. With only a limited number of schools operating, young people had limited access to cultural activities. Also maintaining the German theory that the subjugated are

15 Quoted in Gross, *Polish Society Under the German Occupation*, *supra* n. 2, p. 160. See also the penetrating study of Werner Klosinski, 'Zum Phänomen der Angst' [Concerning the Phenomenon of Angst], in *Angst und Aggression* [Angst and Aggression] (Stuttgart: Ernst Klett Verlag, 1963), pp. 7–17.

16 Gross, *Polish Society Under the German Occupation*, *supra* n. 2, p. 162.

17 Shirer, *The Rise and Fall of the Third Reich*, *supra* n. 11, p. 938.

simply cheap labour was the fact that the only outlets for entertainment for Poles was the cinema showing Nazi propaganda films.[18]

Previously unacceptable forms of behaviour, such as theft, cheating, bribery or killing, were seen as 'justified' by the population because these forms of behaviour aimed to destroy the occupying power. This resulted in a situation where 'both parties not only find it profitable to break the rules that are supposed to regulate their mutual relationships, but also are able to find norms that support such behaviour.'[19]

Corruption was the social process which characterised the uncertainty in which the Polish population lived in the GG. It was the means by which both sides could achieve goals within an institutional framework which was clearly inadequate.[20] This 'trade-off' of something each party desires was promoted by the existence of conditions encouraging the development of corruption.

The active participation in corruption, albeit justified in the fight for survival, combined with the sense of alienation experienced by the Poles, resulted in the blurring of lines between the normal and abnormal, between the natural and unnatural. The line between claiming one's goods and stealing another's goods, for example, became distorted. Work failed to bring society together. The means of production, which once belonged to Poles, were in the hands of the Germans. In this respect, the economic system had a distinctly demoralising effect on society because it robbed people of a normative collective life and coexistence. The catastrophic effect of this is captured in an article from an underground Polish newspaper: 'We have lost the sense of property, and it is one of the elements of our depression, of our being tired beyond description by enslavement. It is mandatory that we acquire it anew, together with getting back our human dignity.'[21] The institutional failings and adjustment inevitably affected attitudes towards the state and law, and any notions of legal culture became questionable. What operated alongside the blatant breach of the rule of law and human rights was a highly developed Polish underground that administered laws, courts and other authorities challenging Nazi rule. This is examined in the following section.

---

18 *Ibid.*

19 See Kazimierz Wyka, *Zycie na niby* [Make-Believe Life] (Cracow: Wydawnictwo Literackie, 1984), referred to in Gross, *Polish Society Under the German Occupation, supra* n. 2.

20 Gross, *Polish Society Under the German Occupation, supra* n. 2, p. 146.

21 *Ibid.*, pp. 114–15. The topic falls outside the scope of this book. See Christopher Browning, *Ordinary Men: Reserve Battalion 101 and the Final Solution in Poland* (New York: HarperCollins, 1992).

Legal Developments

Occupied Territories

Hitler:

> detested lawyers as pen-pushers who filled whole volumes with tangled comments and prohibitions and always had their noses buried in ridiculous tomes. He once confided to a gathering of confidants that going to law school must turn every rational person into 'a complete idiot', and that for his part he would 'do everything he could … to make people despise a legal education'.[22]

Following the German occupation of Poland, the Free City of Gdansk was easily incorporated into the Reich proper, where German law was applied, effective from 1 January 1940. The transition was not so straightforward in the GG, although German authorities lost no time in establishing special courts, and German law was extended to include the occupied territories.[23] German authorities maintained that Polish law was no longer in force as of 1 September 1939. The Decree of 5 September 1939 stated that military courts and special courts could apply only German criminal law. A special system of law (*Sonderrecht*) for Poles and Jews of the annexed territories was systematically enacted by the decree of 6 June 1940, which formally introduced German penal law.[24] The German penal code was enacted with some amendments.[25]

The courts which were established in these areas had a more significant role. The courts of the Incorporated Eastern Territories rendered judgments in the name of the German people. The death penalty was to be sought in cases where anyone committed violence against a member of any German authority; instigated or incited disobedience of a decree or order issued by the German authorities;

22 Ingo Müller, *Hitler's Justice: The Courts of the Third Reich* (London: I. B. Tauris, 1991), p. 295.

23 The Poles quickly became aware of their lack of protection under the new German laws. '[B]y process of elimination one realises that the laws only apply to these groups [Poles and Jews], and offer very little by way of protection, or at the very least it is covered up very well.' 'Stan prawny ziem zachodnich w okresie okupacji niemieckiej' [The State of Law in the Eastern Territories During the German Occupation], 1944, p. 2, sygn. 203/VII-39, Armia Komendowa Glowny Odzial IV-Wydzial Informacyjny [Home Army Main Division IV-Information Department] (hereafter, AK-WI), Archiwum Akt Nowych, Warsaw, Poland.

24 German courts were already established and were applying law without legal basis. See *Trials of War Criminals Before the Nuernberg Military Tribunals Under Control Council No. 10*, Vol. III (1951), pp. 599–600.

25 See *ibid.*, pp. 602–03.

committed an act of violence against a German on account of his being German; intentionally damaged a German installation; or was in possession of a firearm.[26]

In general, the aim of the special courts was 'to combat the enemy within', and 'the member of the *Volk* forgetful of his duty', and to eliminate all forms of national resistance and destabilisation of German rule. One of the main tasks of the courts was to destroy Polish nationalism and all that was 'alien' or non-German. Summary courts were set up in the county court districts.[27] While the special courts were required to base their decisions on German law, they applied broad interpretations when the defendants were Poles.

In reality, a dual court system was created: one for the Germans, and the other for non-Germans, namely the Poles and the Jews. The jurisdiction of the latter courts, which in essence were martial or police courts, covered the following crimes: the illegal possession of firearms; food speculation; the use of railways by Jews without permission; offences against the forced labour legislation; acts committed against German civil and military authorities; acts against German individuals because of their race; and international damage done to German property. The jurisdiction of the German court covered the criminal cases of citizens of the Reich and of racial Germans; acts committed by Poles against the life, property, or honour of a German; and acts committed by Poles while in the service of the German administration.

In civil litigation, the jurisdiction covered cases where one of the parties was a German from the Reich, or a racial German, even if the other party was not German. For example, a German could sue a Pole or a Jew before a German court, which followed German law and procedure. This should not imply that the Pole's or Jew's case was heard fairly. The concept of the 'civil death' of the Jew was well under way in Germany by 1935, when the courts vigorously ruled to deprive Jews of their rights in all areas of the law, without any legal basis whatsoever.[28] The ambiguity of decisions in civil law matters which characterised the early years of the Third Reich was no more.[29] Poles and Jews were prohibited from filing private suits.

---

26 Decree of 4 December 1941 Concerning the Administration of Penal Justice Against Poles and Jews in the Incorporated Eastern Territories, reprinted in *ibid.*, pp. 632–36.

27 The courts which were set up in Gdansk and Poznan also offered law courses to candidates who wished to learn about law and practice in the Old Reich. Both cities were annexed to the Reich proper, but German authorities still needed to eliminate the 'non-German elements'. *Informacja Zachodnia* [Information about the East], 26 June 1944, p. 77, No. 25, sygn. 203/VII-35, AK-WI, Archiwum Akt Nowych, Warsaw, Poland.

28 Franz Neumann, 'The Decay of German Democracy', in *The Rule of Law Under Siege: Selected Writings of Franz L. Neumann and Otto Kirchheimer*, ed. by William E. Scheuerman (Berkeley, CA: University of California Press, 1996), pp. 29–43.

29 For example, contracts with Jews were null and void because they were 'immoral'. Müller, *Hitler's Justice*, *supra* n. 22, p. 117.

Polish courts were allowed to function, but merely for convenience. Polish law was applied unless otherwise stipulated. The courts reportedly possessed jurisdiction over civil cases and criminal cases which had no political implications. Any case could be transferred from the Polish court to the German court. The special courts were able to extend the German penal code and treated any crime as an exploitation of wartime conditions, thus ensuring that the death penalty extended to all criminal cases. Sentences were carried out immediately, and there was no right to appeal. In his letter to the Reich Chancellery, the acting minister of justice, Schlegelberger, wrote about his aim to mould the courts of the incorporated territories into institutions combating all Polish and Jewish criminals, who upon sentence of the German court were not to be allowed to appeal. The special penal code was airtight, and '[a]ny hole in the law through which a Pole or Jewish criminal might slip is also closed.'[30] The existence of Polish law alongside German law ceased in 1941, with the passage of the Decree on Criminal Justice Regarding Poles and Jews in Incorporated Eastern Territories, the basis of which was Hitler's theory that 'there can be only one master for the Poles, and that is the Germans.'[31] There was a distinction between the annexed Western territories and the GG. While the 'Polish Bar' was allowed to function, Polish and Jewish lawyers were not permitted to practise law in the GG. In the GG, the competence of the Polish courts, judges and barristers was restricted strictly to civil law cases. Only those lawyers who were racially German were permitted to practise. The Warsaw Bar Council was headed by a Warsaw lawyer of German extraction, Edward Wilhelm von Wendorff, who had been legal counsel at the German embassy in Warsaw before the war. Initially, Wendorff legally sought to block Jews from the Bar, by asking the council to vote on whether they agreed to dismiss Jews from the Bar (making it clear that if they did not agree they faced grave consequences), to which the council unanimously voted 'no'. After this act of resistance to German orders to bar all Jews from practice, the council offices were raided by the Gestapo. The entire council was suspended, and soon after, the Bar was controlled by decree only. The German authorities were well aware that an autonomous Polish Bar might become a potential centre of patriotic life, and lawyers became the target of arrests and raids during 1940. That year, the first consignment of lawyers was transported to the concentration camp of Sachsenhausen. Shortly after, some 73 lawyers were arrested and sent to Pawiak (the Warsaw jail), of whom 47 were sent to Auschwitz and exterminated.[32]

In the face of such terror, the Polish Bar demonstrated resistance by creating the *Tajny Komitet Adwokacki* (Secret Lawyers' Committee), which later was renamed the *Tajna Naczelna Rade Adwokacka* (Secret Main Bar Council) in 1941. The aim of this secret council was to organise and to supervise an autonomous underground

30 *Trials of War Criminals*, *supra* n. 24, pp. 613–14.

31 *Ibid*., p. 161.

32 Andrzej Kisza, Zdzislaw Krzeminski and Roman Lyczywek, *Historia adwokatury polskiej* [The History of the Polish Bar] (Warsaw: M. C. Kwadrat, 1995), pp. 141–43.

Bar. From its inception, the Bar represented the centre of patriotic life in that part of the legal community. It also provided legal training for law applicants under the tutorship of the 12 best-known and experienced lawyers of the Polish Bar.[33]

The Decree of 13 September 1940 permitted German lawyers from the Reich proper to practise in the occupied territories. The claim that Poles could have the privilege of a Polish defence lawyer was a farce; in undertaking the case, the defence attorney would risk death. The Decree of 3 December 1942 made it clear that German lawyers were prohibited from defending Poles in the occupied territories. On 13 October 1942, the terror was increased with the Reich Decree that Poles, Russians, Jews and Gypsies should no longer be subject to trial, but be turned over to the Gestapo for punishment.[34]

The judges in the occupied territories referred to themselves as 'heralds of German legal culture', but they clearly made a mockery of the criminal proceedings. German was the only language spoken; although many defendants spoke German, they were not permitted to cross-examine the witnesses, or have access to translated testimony. The punishment for Poles was the concentration camp or capital punishment. Although German law divided criminal acts into petty offences, misdemeanours and felonies, this did not apply to Poles and Jews, because every criminal transgression by them was viewed as a violation of the general duty that Poles and Jews obey German directives. Eventually, the courts ceased to provide a legal basis; instead judicial decisions referred to Poles as an 'inferior race', or 'the accused found guilty as a Pole'.[35] German jurists justified the implementation of the decrees in the occupied territories, and showed little sympathy with the fate of their victims.[36]

In the event of an appeal, it was heard by the Reich Supreme Court. But this also took the form of an 'extraordinary objection' against the principle of due process that all judgments are final and that persons should not be prosecuted twice for the same crime. Whenever the prosecutor had serious misgivings about a sentence, a motion for extraordinary objection was filed. Usually, sentences were changed to the penalty of death; in very few instances was the sentence reduced. In cases of an erroneous legal interpretation, the prosecutor was allowed to appeal against the final judgment (one year before its becoming final).[37] The Supreme

33 *Ibid.*, p. 143.

34 Hitler's infamous 'Night and Fog' Decree of 7 December 1941 declared that capital punishment was be used for all crimes committed by non-German civilians. Either the punishment was carried out immediately, or offenders were secretly transported to Germany. This was done to intimidate the defendant's family, and to spread terror across the occupied regions. It is still unclear how many fell victim to the decree. *Trials of War Criminals*, *supra* n. 24, p. 173.

35 *Ibid.*, p. 166.

36 In July 1941, the acting Reich Minister, Schlegelberger, expressed his severe dissatisfaction with the mild sentences he felt Poles had been receiving. *Trials of War Criminals*, *supra* n. 24, pp. 628–31.

37 Approximately three-quarters of appeals were filed by the prosecution. *Ibid.*

Court would normally refer the case back to the lower court and instruct it on how to reach the 'right' decision. Generally, it can be noted that judges proved willing to mould procedure and decisions according to Nazi ideology no matter how unjust the reasoning, as long as it was outlined in a formal agreement or decree.

It has been argued that the position of judges was undermined to such an extent that in their position as mid-level bureaucrats in the Nazi legal framework some judges were incapable of knowing right from wrong.[38] Yet this argument is not straightforward.[39] Many judges sought to ingratiate themselves with the regime, blatantly refusing to consider the implications of the law that they were applying. The timeless dictum, 'the rule of law, not of men', forces us to consider the meaning of the rule of law. How one can justify the enforcement of law that went against any notion of justice is a question which is applicable in studying courts in totalitarian regimes. In defence of their actions, German judges, following the positivist line, argued that a law is a law, and that, as judges, it was their duty to enforce it. The literature in the area has considered the debate between positive and natural law, the salient points of which have resurfaced at the present day. It can be noted here, however, in considering the role of judges and the question of judicial independence, that there are many cases of existing bad law which judges are asked to uphold. The issue becomes one of judicial reasoning, and it is clear in the context of the current discussion that the Nazi court reasoning was in reality propaganda which had nothing to do with legal interpretations; nor did the reasoning come close to meeting professional judicial standards.[40] This argument

---

38 See Hannah Arendt, *The Origins of Totalitarianism* (London: Allen & Unwin, 1958); see also, by the same author, *Eichmann in Jerusalem: A Report on the Banality of Evil* (London: Faber & Faber, 1963). See also Ron Rosenbaum, *Explaining Hitler: The Search for the Origins of His Evil* (New York: Random House, 1998).

39 Please note Carl Schmitt's contribution to constitutional law during the Weimar period and under the Third Reich. Carl Schmitt's key works can be found in English. See his *The Concept of the Political*, trans. by George Schwab (New Brunswick, NJ: Rutgers University Press, 1976); *Constitutional Theory*, trans. by Jeffrey Seitzer (Durham, NC: Duke University Press, 2008); *Legality and Legitimacy*, trans. by Jeffrey Seitzer (Durham, NC: Duke University Press, 2004); and *The Leviathan in the State Theory of Thomas Hobbes: Meaning and Failure of a Political Symbol*, trans. by George Schwab (Westport, CT: Greenwood Press, 1996). For an excellent critical analysis of Schmitt, see especially David Dyzenhaus, *Law as Politics: Carl Schmitt's Critique of Liberalism* (Durham, NC: Duke University Press, 1998). See also Otto Kirchheimer, 'Remarks on Carl Schmitt's *Legality and Legitimacy*', in *The Rule of Law Under Siege, Selected Writings of Franz L. Neumann and Otto Kirchheimer*, ed. by William E. Scheuerman (Berkeley, CA: University of California Press, 1996), pp. 63–98; Ellen Kennedy, *Constitutional Failure: Carl Schmitt in Weimar* (Durham, NC: Duke University Press, 2004); and Katalin Fuzer, *Rights and Constitutional Theory in Weimar Germany*. PhD dissertation, University of Pennsylvania (2004).

40 See Symposium, 'A Report on the Legality of Evil: The Case of Nazi Judges', *Brooklyn Law Review*, 61 (1995), pp. 1139–49, comments of David Luban.

extends to the Bar as well. Lawyers, as the most independent and influential professional group of the legal community, have a right and duty to consider the human and social costs of practising and applying the law.[41]

In time, judges observed how their tasks were gradually assumed by the police, whose chief form of abuse was preventive detention, often begun in the courtroom, where acquitted defendants would be rearrested and deported to a concentration camp. Nazi jurists viewed this practice as diminishing the authority of the courts, and they complained. Their resistance was not based on humanitarian reasons, but rather was part of the struggle for power in the conflict-ridden *Führerprinzip* type of hierarchy (as discussed above), where judges were interested in preserving control over their territory. The Reich Ministry of Justice continued to try to maintain at least the appearance of observing legal formalities[42] but they saw their efforts curtailed, and could not prevent their powers from passing into the hands of the police or SS.

Soviet Occupation (1939–1941)[43]

General Overview

On 17 September 1939, Soviet troops crossed the Polish border on the pretext of 'liberating' the Ukrainians and Belorussians, using slogans of national liberation and class emancipation from the *polskie pans* (Polish masters).[44] On 28 September, German and Soviet authorities signed a friendship treaty', which defined respective spheres of influence, territorial gains and bilateral trade measures for the immediate future.[45]

---

41 Philip Shuchman, 'Book Review: *Vichy Law and the Holocaust in France*', *Rutgers Law Review*, 50 (1998), pp. 607–43.

42 During the Nazi rule, a debate took place between the minister of justice, Franz Schlegelberger, and the new group of law practitioners about two distinct notions of law in the Third Reich. See Franciszek Ryszka, 'Spor o wprowadzenie niemieckiego prawa cywilnego na tzw. "terytoria wlaczone" (w czasie okupacji): dokumenty' [Conflict Over the Implementation of German Civil Law in the So-Called 'Occupied Territories' (During the Occupation): Documents], *Czasopismo Prawno-Historyczne*, 11 (1959), pp. 95–123.

43 The writing of this section of Chapter 3 and the whole of Chapter 4, was made possible by a Central Research Fund travel grant, from the University of London, and the Faculty of Laws, Queen Mary and Westfield College, University of London.

44 The Red Army's use of the term *pan* symbolised their rejection of bourgeois elements in society. See Jan T. Gross, 'The Sovietisation of Western Ukraine and Western Byelorussia', in *Jews in Eastern Poland and the USSR, 1939–46*, ed. by Norman Davies and Antony Polonksy (London: Macmillan, 1991), pp. 60–76.

45 The Polish government-in-exile refused to accept this arrangement of the eastern provinces, which it considered an integral part of Poland, questioning the legality of the annexation and claiming as fraudulent the elections which preceded it.

The Red Army's administration was no better than that of the GG, and policies were carried out with ruthlessness and terror. The territories were administered by Soviet officials who had little knowledge of the local conditions. At first the authorities sought to secure the cooperation and loyalty of the Ukrainian and Belorussian population by convincing them that they had come to liberate them from Polish repression. Poles were dismissed from official positions and reduced to the status of second-class citizens. A mass deportation programme ensued, the details of which will be discussed below.

Social Context and Policies

In the areas annexed by the Soviet Union were some 13 million people: over 4.5 million Ukrainians, 1.2 million Belorussians, 1.1 million Jews and other ethnic groups numbering 1 million. The Soviet authorities considered all Polish citizens of the annexed territories as Soviet subjects.

One of the consequences of the Poles being reduced to second-class citizenship was that Ukrainian and Belorussian were made official languages, while Russian became a compulsory language in schools. Religious instruction was prohibited. Once the threat to the Soviet Union from Nazi Germany was realised, Soviet policy began to change with respect to the Poles, whose support the Soviets needed. Overtones were made to the Polish Communist Party, who sent a delegation to Moscow in order to persuade Stalin to change his policy on the Polish Communist Party.[46] Under the leadership of Wanda Wasilewska and Alfred Lampe, the Polish Communist Party was re-established and operated under the wary eye of the Communist Party in Moscow.

The Polish Communist Party has not had an easy history. It was created in 1918, and supported the unification of the Polish territories with Russia. It was dedicated to the teachings of Rosa Luxemburg, but was forced to change its stand during the Polish–Soviet war in 1920. Throughout its tumultuous history, it followed the dictates of Moscow, yet despite this adherence, the Soviet Communist Party never regarded its Polish compatriots as sincere. Instead, they were viewed as burdensome, and suspect, linked to nationalism and insubordination. This notion dictated the treatment of Poles in the Soviet-occupied territory during the Second World War. In 1924, the Comintern[47] had expelled the Polish faction, accusing them of 'right-wing opportunism', and later of Pilsudskite leanings. As if the terror were not enough, charges of 'Trotskyism' caused the party to be liquidated from 1933 to 1938, costing the lives of all the Polish party leadership, including 12 members of the Central Committee, the entire section of the Comintern, most of

46 The Polish Communist Party (*Komunistyczna Partia Polska*) had been banned in 1938.

47 The Comintern, or Communist International, was the predecessor of the Cominform. See Fernando Claudin, *The Communist Movement: From Comintern to Cominform* (London: Penguin, 1970).

the party intellectuals,[48] and several hundred of its other leading functionaries.[49] In 1938, the Comintern declared the Polish Communist Party dissolved. Only after the XX Party Congress were the accusations retracted.

The Red Army launched a vigorous educational campaign, which focused on the indoctrination of the youth in Marxism–Leninism–Stalinism. The programme was geared towards de-Polonisation and aimed to destroy religious beliefs among the young, using tactics to promote the image of Stalin as 'God'.[50] These tactics of indoctrinating youth undermined the sense of social responsibility by promoting duplicity and mendaciousness. Many people were forced to speak and behave publicly in ways incompatible with their personal convictions. By ridiculing the ethical foundations of most people's beliefs, the organisers of the new order, perhaps not altogether unwittingly, were inviting licence.

The imposition of Soviet rule triggered the involuntary movement of the population in the occupied territory. In addition to the large displacement of people seeking to escape from the chaos caused by the Soviet invasion, persons were forcibly expelled from their homes to make room for incoming Soviet officials and their families. Soviet authorities inserted 'paragraph 11' in the documents issued to persons of the newly annexed territories, indicating that the bearer of the document was prohibited from residing within 100 km of major cities or of the state border. This sudden population movement resulted in tragic consequences for large sections of the population. Most residents of eastern Poland had little experience in travel and had rarely travelled outside the immediate surroundings of their village or region. The mass deportation programme was conducted in a strategic and organised manner: in synchronised fashion the Soviet authorities transported whole classes of Polish citizens to the Soviet interior. The displaced populace can be divided into the following categories: prisoners-of-war; arrestees of the *Narodny Komissariat Vnutrennikh Del* (NKVD, or the People's Commissariat for Internal Affairs, the public and secret police service of the Soviet Union);[51] and 'volunteers'. In Soviet terms, 'prisoner-of-war' was an all-encompassing category, including Polish officers who had been captured by the Red Army. The numbers

48 Anton Krajewski is but one example of the many Polish Communist Party intellectuals who was repressed in the mass purge of Polish communists. He was charged with being a spy and with anti-Soviet Trotskyite activity in the Comintern. He was tried in secret before the Military Division of the Supreme Court. 'Anton Krajewski' (1937), fond 495, opis 252, delo 1087, Rossiiskii tsentr khranenia i izucheniia dokumentov noveishei istorii [Russian Centre for the Preservation and Study of Records for Modern History, hereafter, RTsKhIDNI], Moscow, Russia.

49 George Hodos, *Show Trials: Stalinist Purges in Eastern Europe, 1948–1954* (New York: Praeger, 1987), p. 137.

50 Gross, 'The Sovietisation of Western Ukraine and Western Byelorussia', *supra* n. 44.

51 *Narodny Komissariat Vnutrennikh Del* (NKVD) was the successor of Lenin's Cheka, later GPU (*Gosudarstvennoye Politicheskoye Upravlenie*) and OGPU (*Ob'edinennoe Gosudarstvennoe Politicheskoe Upravlenie*).

provided by the Soviet Foreign Ministry most likely do not reflect the true total:[52] it is doubtful whether the number of Poles summarily executed by the Red Army were included. Of the thousands who were detained, many were released and allowed to go home, particularly those who were of Belorussian or Ukrainian origins. Those who were considered politically dangerous were detained; in addition to soldiers, many officials, priests, landowners, prison warders, military colonists, military policemen, members of the special defence corps and border guards were also detained. The fate of these groups has been one of the most significant points of contention between Poland and the Soviet Union. In the spring of 1943, the Germans uncovered a mass grave of some 4,000 Poles at the Kozielsk camp near Smolensk. The Germans were blamed for the massacre, and the West supported this theory, but Poles have always argued that the responsibility lay with the Soviets. This 'Katyn' massacre has since been the important focus of attention by many historians, and it was not until 1992 that Soviet authorities admitted Soviet responsibility for this atrocity. The consequences are significant in present-day measures of de-communisation, as we shall see in Chapter 5. The Katyn massacre is evidence of the Soviet policy on the Polish intelligentsia and proof of the lengths to which the Soviet authorities would go in order to eliminate all traces of Polish nationalism.[53]

The NKVD established control over all areas of life soon after the handover of power from the Red Army. No village, settlement or urban area was untouched. The number of arrests increased and by October 1939 mass round-ups were commonplace. The arrested included Polish officers who had made it home after successfully evading arrest, landowners, businessmen, policemen, judicial officials and local government officials. The NKVD regarded anyone who had fought in the resistance as politically dangerous, including members of pre-war organisations. Persons of important social and political standing were arrested and incarcerated. The speed and efficiency with which the NKVD made the arrests was exemplary, and the prisons were soon filled.

The third category, the 'volunteers', was not a numerically large group. It included those persons who had been pro-communist, pro-Soviet collaborators during the period of Soviet rule of West Belorussia and West Ukraine and individuals who wished to evade the advancing German army. Several persons wishing to avoid the NKVD saw no other option than to take an assumed name and apply for work in the East. The largest group were manual labourers and professionals, who volunteered for work in the Soviet Union for non-ideological reasons in order to survive (naturally, inducements were offered by the authorities). The majority of the refugees were Jews who wished to flee as far as possible from the Nazi campaign. In fact, compared to other groups, the Jews included a sizeable

---

52 Keith Sword, *Deportation and Exile: Poles in the Soviet Union, 1939–48* (London: Macmillan, 1994), pp. 2–3.

53 A powerful documentary concerning these Ukrainian events is *Ukraine – Eternal Memory: Voices from the Great Terror* (National Film Network, 1997, 81 minutes).

number of communist supporters: '[t]his circumstance … was the principal clue to the joyous atmosphere surrounding the entry of Soviet troops: where they came, Germans did not.'[54] Feeling vulnerable in the fallen Polish state in which they were not made welcome, Jews sought protection and perhaps felt some satisfaction at seeing the Poles humbled.[55]

Soviet Legal Framework

Marxism–Leninism

When the Soviet Union invaded Poland, communism had already existed for some 20 years in the former. Stalin had been in power for over a decade and Marxism–Leninism[56] had been reworked to incorporate his ideas. Little about law was written by Marx and Engels, perhaps because they foresaw that it would not play a large role in society as it progressed down the road to communism.[57] Marx's ideas were reworked into a revolutionary plan for Russia by Lenin, who argued that only a strong party could lead the working class to a successful Marxist revolution.[58]

In *What Is to Be Done?*, Lenin felt justified in the consolidation of power in the hands of such an elite group. Supporters of the cause were expected to surrender to their leaders. Later, in *The State and Revolution*, Lenin warned that coercion and terror were necessary evils of the revolution, particularly during the transition from capitalism to communism. Immediately after the Russian Revolution of 1917, Lenin initiated a campaign against class enemies, who were 'the groups and sections of workers who stubbornly cling to capitalist traditions and continue to regard the Soviet state in the old way: work as little and as badly as they can and grab as much money as possible from the state'.[59] Lenin reinterpreted the Marxist claim over the withering away of the state, and argued that the bourgeois state could not be replaced by the proletarian state (the dictatorship of the proletariat)

---

54 Gross, 'The Sovietisation of Western Ukraine and Western Byelorussia', *supra* n. 44, p. 66.

55 *Ibid.*

56 Karl Marx and Friedrich Engels, *The Communist Manifesto*, trans. by Paul M. Sweezy (New York: Monthly Review Press, 1964), in *The Communist Manifesto Including Principles of Communism and the Communist Manifesto After 100 Years*, trans. by Paul M. Sweezy (New York: Modern Reader Paperbacks, 1968), p. 5.

57 Karl Marx and Friedrich Engels, *Selected Works, Vol. 1* (Moscow: Foreign Languages Publishing House, 1955), p. 54.

58 Vladimir Lenin, *What Is to Be Done?*, 5th edn (Moscow: Foreign Languages Publishing House, 1901), p. 132.

59 See also Michael Voslensky, *Nomenklatura* (London: The Bodley Head, 1983), p. 41.

through withering away but, rather, through a violent revolution.[60] Lenin further argued that the way to fight against the class enemies was for the proletariat and the talented professional revolutionaries to come forward and become the ruling class. Lenin observed that as the party apparatus grew alongside the state, it would face rising demands to govern the country.

The idea that Lenin had in mind was a ruling class of administrators; the aim was not to abolish the bureaucracy at once.[61] This signified the gradual process of creating a new ruling elite. 'We, the workers, shall organise large-scale production on the basis of what capitalism has already created, relying on our own experience as workers, establishing strict, iron discipline backed up by the state power of armed workers.'[62] 'We' stood for the professional revolutionaries, who acted on behalf of the working class. Everything had become state property but the state itself was in the hands of the professional revolutionaries. Ironically, at the time, workers constituted less than 50 per cent of the Council of People's Commissars; workers were only occasionally permitted into the Central Committee. Purges of the bourgeoisie were regularly arranged.[63] In the end, Lenin argued against worker control, and eventually abolished it.

Lenin was forced to reject several key principles of Marxism in order to apply it to Russian conditions, especially the theory that the socialist revolution could not occur without the necessary existing preconditions, such as a developed working class and capitalist means of production. Lenin thus retained some elements of the former regime in order to achieve the realisation of his plan, and the bureaucratic nature of the Tsarist state prevailed.[64] The second reworking introduced a new class of professional revolutionaries to rule over the working class.

This ruling group of professional revolutionaries further secured their power with the creation of the All-Russian Extraordinary Commission for Combatting Counter-Revolution and Sabotage, or the *Cheka*, an autonomous quasi-legal body which became the instrument of terror. During Stalin's reign, the *Cheka* would be transformed into the NKVD. The purpose of the *Cheka* was to combat counter-revolutionaries, and to eliminate all political opponents. Revolutionary tribunals worked alongside the *Cheka*, and sentenced thousands to death. The tribunals were not guided by any legal code, and both organs managed to eliminate many of the politically inconvenient. People's courts were introduced, and judges were instructed to apply the pre-revolutionary law in the context of socialist

60 Vladimir Ilyich Lenin, *The State and Revolution*, in *Selected Works in Three Volumes*, Vol. 2, 2nd edn (Moscow: Progress Publishers, 1967), p. 282.

61 *Ibid.*, p. 303; Voslensky, *Nomenklatura, supra* n. 59, p. 42.

62 *Ibid.*, p. 303; Voslensky, *Nomenklatura, supra* n. 59, p. 39.

63 Voslensky, *Nomenklatura, supra* n. 59.

64 See Ger P. van den Berg, 'Elements of Continuity in Soviet Constitutional Law', in *Russian Law: Historical and Political Perspectives*, ed. by William E. Butler (Leyden: A. W. Sijthoff, 1977), pp. 215–34.

consciousness.[65] The use of terror was justified by Lenin, who lacked support among the population for his revolutionary policies. As observed by Trotsky, 'the dictatorship of the proletariat became the dictatorship over the proletariat.'

Marxism under Stalin

According to Medvedev, if Lenin created the organisation of professional revolutionaries, then Stalin created the *nomenklatura*.[66] Rayfield's compelling account of Stalin and his henchmen shows how this thug succeeded in carefully creating a power base that was in constant flux and fear of him.[67] Lenin had already noted after his first stroke that the idiosyncratic group of Bolsheviks had turned into corrupt careerists.[68] The Bolsheviks had always taken pride in their ability to survive in an uncertain, hostile environment. One of the reasons for this, they argued, was their solid nucleus of leaders. The Bolsheviks anticipated a need for change after Lenin's death, and the political upheavals of the mid-1920s made it all the more important. The question of who would fill the positions in the growing party was of utmost importance, simply because the number of professional revolutionaries was small. As a result, careerists sought positions in the state apparatus. Of course, the most important qualification was political, not professional – a renowned specialist was always passed over for a young, untrained party member, for example. When specialists were needed, they were found. Generally speaking, however, positions were handed to individuals with little or no qualifications for the work. Guarantees of employment in the socialist state appeared to be a right to all. In reality, however, the right to employment was a favour granted by the state, and one that could be easily withdrawn. This system of appointments and promotions was propelled by the Stalinist slogan, 'with us, no one is irreplaceable.'[69]

During his reign, Stalin relied on the NKVD, the secret police. Under his direction, the agency underwent several transformations, and at each stage

65 Legal theorists, such as the former Russian judge, Pashukanis, opposed the new policies and argued that the new interpretations of the prerevolutionary law would not change their bourgeois nature. He drafted new codes, which were never implemented because they were considered too radical.

66 His classic work, Roy Medvedev, *Let History Judge: The Origins and Consequences of Stalinism* (New York: Macmillan, 1971), was intended for the Soviet audience.

67 Donald Rayfield, *Stalin and His Hangmen: An Authoritative Portrait of a Tyrant and Those Who Served Him* (London: Penguin, 2004).

68 Robert Conquest, *The Great Terror: A Reassessment*, 3rd edn (London: Pimlico, 1990).

69 Stalin's nickname during his work at the Secretariat in the Central Committee was 'Comrade File Cabinet' (*tovarishch Kartotekov*). See Voslensky, *Nomenklatura*, *supra* n. 59, p. 47.

employed mass terror against 'socially dangerous' persons.[70] With the assistance of Vyshinsky, law was redefined as a key component of the development of socialism. In his 1930 address to the Communist Party, Stalin outlined the reasons for constructing an authoritative state. He claimed that the withering away of the state was not feasible in the near future, because the country was threatened by capitalist forces, which could be combated only by a strong state. This consolidated Stalin's power in the country and in the party, and set in motion the purges which eliminated his closest associates and top-ranking generals. Although in theory no one was safe, the careerists of the new ruling elite were best placed. It was this group which quickly discarded Marxist theory, and sought to ingratiate themselves so as to rise in the party ranks. Ironically, the 'true' communists never had a chance of survival, a phenomenon which repeated itself within communist countries throughout their existence.

An analysis of Stalin's personal letters to Molotov reveals an obsession with two very simple principles: the proper 'selection of officials' and the 'checking up on fulfilment' of policy directives.[71] When viewed against the political situation at the time, we see that in order to maintain his position, Stalin felt he had no choice but for the ruthless application of these principles. Stalin's ascent to power reveals the logic and reason behind his decision-making.[72] The motto to be followed, Stalin emphasised, was '[not to] spare individuals, no matter what position they occupy; spare only the cause, the interests of the cause.'[73] This line of thought applied not only to this agency, but all agencies, including the administration of justice, as we shall see.

At the XII Party Congress, Stalin made another speech about Lenin's demand for an improved *apparat*, and took further Lenin's desire 'to get to the point where the country contained not a single bigwig, no matter how highly placed about which the man in the street could say, "that one is above control"'.[74] This line dominated the mass media in the mid-1930s. Another speech to the Central Committee in January 1933 provided the justification for the terror which would soon follow. Stalin argued that the revolutionary transformation was coming to a close, and he called for the creation of new structures to work in a productive and efficient manner. Stalin felt that the main barrier was the 'enemy within':

> Thrown out of their groove, and scattered over the whole face of the USSR, these 'former people' [the elite disinherited by the revolution] have wormed their way into our plants and factories, into our government offices and trading

70 See Maria Los, *Communist Ideology, Law and Crime: A Comparative View of the USSR and Poland* (New York: St. Martin's Press, 1988). pp. 12–13.

71 Lars T. Lih *et al.*, *Stalin's Letters to Molotov 1925–1936*, trans. by C. Fitzpatrick (New Haven, CT: Yale University Press, 1995), p. 16.

72 *Ibid.*, p. 12.

73 *Ibid.*

74 *Ibid.*

> organizations, into our railway and water transport enterprises, and principally, into our collective and state farms. They have crept into these places and taken cover there, donning on [sic] the mask of 'workers' and 'peasants,' and some have even managed to worm their way into the party.[75]

Such a powerful speech would make one suspicious of everyone, who might or might not be a potential class enemy that exhibited a hatred of Soviet power, and was compelled to sabotage and to undermine the Soviet influence in the economy, life and culture. Such a speech also provided careerists with the basis to eliminate their colleagues, so as to assume higher positions of power. According to Stalin, 'the task is to eject these "former people" from our own enterprises and institutions and render them permanently harmless'.[76] Those who had believed the class struggle to be dying down were also viewed suspiciously, because they no longer applied the necessary revolutionary vigilance. This final statement, in essence, summarises the driving force behind Stalin's campaign of purges:

> That is the logic of all revolutions. ... Many of the people Stalin destroyed had stopped being revolutionaries by the mid-thirties. They had degenerated into officeholders and bureaucrats. They were pushing the Party and state machine not toward socialism but toward state capitalism. Stalin had to get rid of those who were interfering with the further development of the socialist Revolution; he had to push up young officials who were capable of leading the revolution forward.[77]

Stalin chose his cronies carefully, and was well aware of the true nature of appointees such as Beria[78] and Vyshinsky,[79] yet he knew that he could use these people to eliminate particular groups and colleagues effectively. His cronies would follow his directives.[80] Not surprisingly, Stalin was obsessed with the process of 'checking up on fulfilment', particularly after having appointed a man to the job. In 1930, he thought of creating a Fulfilment Commission, which would 'break through the wall of bureaucratism and [improve] the slipshod performance in

---

75 *Ibid.*

76 *Ibid.*

77 Medvedev, *Let History Judge*, *supra* n. 66, p. 313.

78 L. A. Beria was the chief of political police in Georgia. Later he became chief of the Soviet political police.

79 Vyshinsky, a former Menshevik (and an aristocrat who was disowned by his family), had ordered the arrests of Bolsheviks in 1917. It is quite likely that Stalin used this as blackmail. *Ibid.*, p. 312.

80 Stalin and Vyshinsky's relationship dates back to the early 1920s, when they were imprisoned together, and had many arguments in prison. Stalin perhaps never failed to remind Vyshinsky of his aristocratic past (Polish nobility), making Vyshinsky all the more determined to prove his loyalty. For more details, see Arkady Vaksberg, *Stalin's Prosecutor: The Life of Andrzei Vyshinsky* (New York: Grove Weidenfeld, 1990).

our bureaucracies'.[81] Without such procedures, Stalin thought that 'the center's directives will remain completely on paper'.[82] According to Stalin, directives were not followed because of class-motivated hostility. When selecting officials, competence was not a priority; rather, selection was based on loyalty, and resistance to seduction by 'bourgeois morals'. Good government was therefore a constant battle in which honourable intentions were in danger of being undermined by hostile saboteurs.

From 1928 onwards, the wheel of purges was set in motion, beginning with the 'Shakhty affair', in which engineers from the coal industry were accused 'of sabotaging the mines, wrecking, and purchasing imported equipment'.[83] The Worker-Peasant Inspection Agency embarked on a wide purge of economic bureaucracies. Their main task was to uncover any unused production reserves and to remove the bureaucrats who hid them. Engineers and other specialists were arrested and accused of 'wreckerism'. In September 1930, 48 specialists in the meat industry were executed after a secret trial found that they were guilty of 'sabotaging the meat supply'. In November, a public trial began of engineers accused of forming an industrial party devoted to wreckerism. The following spring saw a trial devoted to the 'Union Bureau' of Mensheviks. The public trials continued and, in a sense, perfected the 'show trial'. The wave of terror also reached foreign communists. As described above, the Polish Communist Party was particularly affected, and dozens of its members perished alongside Western Ukrainian and West Belorussian party leaders. In the summer of 1938, the Polish Communist Party was dissolved, accused of being wholly consumed by provocation.

With the assistance of Stalin's most trusted and ruthless jurist,[84] the role of law and the administration of justice was changed forever. Stalin's reliance on the criminal justice system did not spare the officials of these organs from terror. Many judicial officials, who had already participated in the provocation of former oppositionists and kulaks, were reluctant to apply the same policy to the best members of the party. Perhaps this was apparent to Stalin, who had decided, by 1936, 'to reform' the criminal justice organ. The NKVD and the judicial and prosecutorial organs were ruthlessly purged. Under Vyshinsky's leadership, public prosecution was catapulted to prominence, to carry out the most vicious attacks against 'counter-revolutionaries', including Stalin's closest colleagues. No other crony of Stalin's was able to gain such prestige and gain such prominence for himself and his supporters, who were 'unprincipled, cruel people'. Of course,

---

81 Lih *et al.*, *Stalin's Letters*, *supra* n. 71, p. 15.

82 *Ibid.*

83 Vyshinsky was presiding judge at the trial.

84 Andrei Ya. Vyshinsky (1883–1954), was an RSFSR public prosecutor and deputy commissar of justice from 1931, and the Soviet deputy public prosecutor from 1933 to 1939.

many individuals actively assisted the purges, and denounced citizens of their own free will.[85]

Vyshinsky succeeded in reworking the criminal law to suit Stalin's needs and provide the façade of legitimacy needed to carry out the ruthless policy on the so-called 'counter-revolutionaries'. Marxist theory about the withering away of crime was supported, but so was the increased class struggle against the enemy. The Communist Academy kept the social sciences in line with Marxist theory. Intense discussions ensued about the ideological basis for the study of criminology, led by the legal nihilists of the State Institute.[86] The end result was that criminologists were unable to defend their careers, because it was unclear what type of criminology was Marxist.[87] At this time, the study of criminology was based on its ideological utility, with the theories of Pashukanis and Krylenko at the forefront. Crime and legal institutions were in the process of disappearing, and their study would prove unnecessary and, perhaps, embarrassing. The study of criminology would inevitably change, for it did not fall into line with the regime's campaign against the kulaks and other alleged saboteurs. By 1937, the slogan 'withering away of law' had changed to the 'stability of law'; the campaign of terror continued, with jurisprudence reworked to serve its purposes.[88]

In the occupied territories, following the agreement of the Supreme Soviet of 1 and 2 November 1939 to accede to the national assemblies' requests and incorporate the occupied territories into the USSR, Soviet law was applied to the region and to its inhabitants. The kind of Soviet 'justice' which existed in the Polish territories was repressive and aimed at eliminating all persons who were considered politically dangerous. This was evidenced in the penal code which was applied to the arrestees; the Soviet, Ukrainian and Belorussian codes were similar in their provisions. Of those which were applicable to Polish detainees, Article 58 was the most relied on. Those arrested were sentenced for high treason and waging an armed struggle against the Soviet Union (paragraph 2), spying (paragraph 6), diversion and propaganda directed against the USSR (paragraph 10), historical counter-revolution (paragraph 13), and sabotage (paragraph 14). Criminal activity against historical counter-revolution was the charge most frequently employed

---

85 It is interesting to note that public confidence in Soviet courts was still intact in 1930, and that many Soviet citizens believed in the apparent 'plots'. See Medvedev, *supra* n. 66.

86 E. B. Pashukanis and his colleague, N. V. Krylenko (leading public prosecutor for the RSFSR and later its Commissar), represented the view that law and legal institutions would eventually disappear as socialism developed. For further discussion, see Peter Solomon, 'Soviet Criminology: Its Demise and Rebirth, 1928–1963', *Soviet Union* (1974), p. 122.

87 *Ibid*, pp. 124–25. See David Joravsky, *Russian Psychology: A Critical History* (Oxford: Basil Blackwell, 1989) and *Political Leadership in Eastern Europe and the Soviet Union*, ed. by R. Barry Farrell (Chicago: Aldine Publishing Company, 1970).

88 The eventual ruin of Pashukanis and Krylenko was inevitable, and at long last Vyshinsky could claim victory over criminal law and the whole body of judicial officials.

against persons who had fought in the civil war or during the Polish–Soviet War. Retroactive legislation also extended to activities of the pre-war period, which Soviet authorities regarded as fascist, corrupt and running counter to the interests of the working class; loyalty to the regime was therefore defined as criminal.

The investigative procedures of the NKVD were brutal. Interrogations were lengthy and exhausting, and threats, blackmail and violence were employed. Prisoners were often transported between prisonsin the Polish territory and in the Soviet Union before they were sent to one of the labour camps of the infamous Gulag. Sentences were varied; most defendants received from five to eight years in a correctional labour camp. Very rarely did one receive sentences of less than three years or more than 10 years. Those who did receive more than 10 years were entitled to some form of court process consisting of Soviet judges and NKVD officers[89] at which their NKVD accusers were present. Sentences were frequently handed down *in absentia* and read out in the corridor. It was not uncommon for prisoners not to learn their sentence until they were in the camp.

One of the main contradictions of this kind of Soviet justice was that, as seen above, investigations and so-called 'court processes' took place in order to establish guilt in individual cases, while at other times, in mass round-ups, innocent people were deported for merely belonging to a certain category.

With the background of the political trials which took place in the Soviet Union, the legal system which was set up in the Soviet-annexed territories during the Second World War was, above all, a political weapon used to eliminate any oppositional movement. Vyshinsky personally saw to the appointment of loyal legal officials, and ensured that the cases of defendants from underground movements were monitored. In 1941, he was particularly keen to destroy the Ukrainian underground movement, and ordered that the Military Division of the Supreme Court try their cases, and report to him. Vyshinsky wrote to Stalin: 'I report that the plenum of the Supreme Court on the 19th of June denied the appeal to the Supreme Court in the case related to the 14 defendants from the counter-revolutionary group "OUN", and ensured in the future a harder line of sentencing.'[90]

The Soviet judges who followed the Red Army to Poland had clear instructions and 'rules of conduct', established in the form of statutes and a distinctly formulated purpose of 'destroying capitalism'.[91] The annexed territories of Poland were redefined as Western Belorussia and Western Ukraine, and leaders quickly

89 These special tribunals were known as *troikas*.

90 'Soviet Ministrov Sojuza Sovetskikh Tsojalistichikh Respublik' [The Ministers of the USSR], *The Files of A. Ya. Vyshinsky*, 26 June 1941, p. 34, fond 5446, opis 81a, delo 346, Gosudarstvennyi archiv Rossiiskii Federatsii [State Archives of the Russian Federation, hereafter, GARF], Moscow, Russia. It is interesting to note that the appeal was filed. It appears that the case was closely 'directed' throughout.

91 Kazimierz Zamorski, 'Arrest and Imprisonment in the Light of Soviet Law', in *The Soviet Takeover of the Polish Eastern Provinces, 1939–41*, ed. by Keith Sword (London: Macmillan, 1991), p. 203.

organised an election, which resulted in an official annexation. From then on, all persons who resided in the areas were regarded as Soviet citizens. This move served a dual purpose, firstly as a demonstration to the West, and secondly to put Soviet justice officials in no doubt that they were now dealing with Soviet citizens. Statistics show that most of the judges were Communist Party members. In fact by 1935, 99.6 per cent of the higher judiciary, and 95.5 per cent of the lower appointments, were members.[92] Following Lenin's dictum, 'a law is a political measure, it is politics', the judge was bound to make decisions based on political rather than legal grounds. Otherwise, 'if any socially dangerous act is not directly provided for by the present Code, the basis and limits of responsibility for it shall be determined by application of those articles of the Code which provide for crimes most similar to it in nature.'[93]

The Poles were doomed from two points of view: the Soviet Penal Code permitted judges to have cases referred to the NKVD, and all the while secret decrees were being issued by Beria, Molotov and Stalin, who intended to destroy the Polish intelligentsia. This was done behind the façade of legality as well as by extra-legal measures. Reports from the Soviet-annexed territories to the provisional Polish government based in London show that Poles were well aware of the Soviet policy on the inhabitants:

> There are five different organised groups, known to people in the underground, who should be regarded as enemies to the Polish state: 1/ the Soviet partisan divisions, 2/ the Polish Workers' Party, 3/ the People's Guard of the Polish People's Workers' Party … 4/ the Polish Communist Party, 5/ official representatives from Comintern.[94]

The immediacy with which the Soviets assumed control in the cities, towns and villages, and sought to eliminate the Polish intelligentsia, suggests that the policy's purpose was to pillage and to reduce the population to subordination.[95] Poles observed how the NKVD went through the city registry to find the addresses and occupation of the residents, so as to place them on one of the five lists, the 'black list, enemy of the people, counter-revolutionary, bourgeoisie, or other insects, beyond the scope of law'.[96] The policy was enforced (against those hunted and

92 *Ibid.*, p. 204.

93 *Ibid.*

94 'Dzialalnosc Kominternu na Ziemiach Polskich' [The Comintern's Activity on Polish Territory], *Sprawozdanie Situacyine z Kraju* [Situational Account from the Country; hereafter, Sprawozdanie], No. 1/43, April 1943, p. 154, Polish Underground Movement Study Trust, London, England.

95 Keith Sword, 'Soviet Policy in the Annexed Territories', in Sword, *The Soviet Takeover of the Polish Eastern Provinces*, *supra* n. 91.

96 'Dzialalnosc wladz okupacyjnych na terytorium Rzeczpospolitej za okres 1.IX.39 do 1.XI.40' [The Activities of the Occupying Powers on the Territory of the Polish Republic

their respective families), with particular regard to the Polish judiciary, who were considered part of the intelligentsia and a threat to the future establishment of a legal system based on Marxist-Leninist-Stalinist theory. As the Soviets assumed control of the courts, groups of judicial officials disappeared, never to be heard of again. The NKVD searched for Polish legal officials with particular zeal. The following categories of people were especially tracked: '1/ Public administrators, with particular emphasis on judges [and] police officers'.[97] In the formerly Polish city of Lwow, the appellate court saw 'many of the judges taken to Russia, and there is still no information about them.... The Soviet authorities conducted a mass destruction of law books, especially those on property.'[98]

Principles were created that paved the way for practices which made a travesty of the concept of a fair trial. The court could not hope to reach absolute truth; therefore, it had to be satisfied with some degree of probability. The evaluation of evidence was based solely on inner conviction; and the law was viewed as an algebraic formula, to be corrected in the process of application by the judge.[99] Vyshinsky encouraged the belief that laws need not be applied if they were outdated. Public prosecutors were frequently reminded by their superiors of their duty. The notion of due process was ignored; instead, prisoners who declared their innocence were required to prove it. 'Scientific' justification was offered, one that 'was converted into a pseudoscientific defense of Stalinist willfulness'.[100] Any law would be passed by legislators, even if it contradicted basic societal norms. The 'rational' basis was that Stalin suggested it.

Vyshinsky crafted the Stalinist Constitution of 1936, one of the most audacious acts of doublespeak committed by Stalin. This document served as a model for the constitutions of the Soviet satellite states. While the Constitution listed a catalogue of rights, it was meaningless, and was superseded by the repressive criminal code. Vyshinsky explained the nature of the Constitution before an *aktiv*:[101]

> The Constitution does not mean the end of the class struggle. It means rather, that the class struggle must continue in other forms, and that new methods must be applied to bring people in line with the law.[102]

---

in the Period 1.IX.39 to 1.XI.40], *Sprawozdanie*, p. 182, Polish Underground Movement Study Trust, London, England.

97 *Ibid.*

98 *Sprawozdanie Departamentu Sprawiedliwosci* [Report from the Ministry of Justice] (1943), No. 5/43, p. 117, Polish Underground Movement Study Trust, London, England.

99 Medvedev, *Let History Judge*, *supra* n. 66, p. 502.

100 *Ibid.*

101 An assembly – in this case, an assembly of Communist Party judicial officials.

102 'Stenogramma doklada t. Vyshinkovo o proekte Konstitutsii SSR na obranii aktiva Sojusa rabotnikov suda i Procuraturi' [Stenogramme from Vyshinsky's Lecture on the Draft of the Constitution Before the Soviet Assembly of the Judiciary and Public Prosecution], 9 July 1936, p. 13, fond 8131, opis 13, delo 2, GARF, Moscow, Russia.

The notion of law for the Soviet state, argued Vyshinsky, had practically to serve its socialist framework, and there was no room for judicial independence, or any notions rooted in the old school of intellectuals.[103] Such talk was 'prohibited', and the fact that the new Constitution embodied a new school of revolutionary law was continually emphasised. The type of judicial official that was needed had to be politically reliable, and ideally mirrored the functionary described earlier. Any form of independence was severely criticised and reported. The following is an excerpt from a report sent to Vyshinsky by a Supreme Court judge commenting on the work of his colleagues: '[w]e need such workers here, who are able to say the following: "to judge with culture, to judge with pride, to see before me a human being"'.[104] Apparently, this type of judge did not include kulaks, for the same judge criticised a colleague 'Poliakov – a kulak's son – … These "believers" in the courts, tried at the Party meeting, to create their own work, their own opinion!'[105]

The notion of bureaucracy became twisted and corrupt during the Stalinist era, and this applied to the Soviet administration of justice as well. Inevitably, it destroyed the population's belief that they were the real masters of their country.[106] During the cult of the personality, the concept and exercise of responsibility declined among the leaders, the legitimacy of the bureaucracy was perverted, and the bureaucrat became a functionary, dependent on the leaders, not on the will and the demands of those beneath him. The ordinary feelings of people gradually came to mean nothing to administrators. But not all of the leaders during the cult period were corrupt. By the mid-1930s, there had emerged a new group of capable and dedicated officials. What halted their advancement were the conditions of the cult established by Stalin. In their place were the careerists, cruel and unprincipled people who were best adapted to Stalin's hypocrisy. The Stalinist careerist was one who 'combined arrogance and conceit with political instability and hypocrisy'. Most of these communists desired power and luxury, a marked distinction from other people. The careerists had no scruples about pillaging state property. Medvedev resists the Western definition of the Soviet bourgeoisie, but does concede that a certain caste system arose in the higher and middle levels of leadership. Tito's break with Stalin and his brand of communism provided the Soviet leader with concrete reasons to intensify and increase purges within the inner and outer communist circle,[107] with the Cominform being the most effective way to reach the

103 *Ibid.*

104 'Proverit rabotu Bostochna-Siberskovo Kraevovo Suda' [A Check on the Eastern Siberian Regional Court], 16 April 1936, p. 12, fond 8131, opis 13, delo 10, GARF, Moscow, Russia.

105 *Ibid.*

106 Medvedev, *Let History Judge*, *supra* n. 66.

107 Three elements encouraged the need for show trials in the Soviet satellite countries: the Cold War, Stalin's increasing paranoia, and the Soviet–Yugoslav split. Hodos, *Show Trials*, *supra* n. 49.

communists of the people's democracies.[108] Many scholars speculate that by this time Stalin's paranoia was increasing.[109] The Cominform provided the centralised control system that Moscow needed to keep the governments of the Eastern bloc in check. This was the Soviet Union's equivalent to the checks and balances in the United States, except that no redress was available.

The first show trial began in Albania in 1949, but it was the Rajk and Slansky trials, which took place in Hungary and Czechoslovakia, respectively, which were to serve as models for all future show trials. Representatives from Poland,[110] Czechoslovakia and East Germany came to observe the trial in Budapest.[111] The conditions for a show trial in Hungary were ideal for Stalin and Beria.[112] The Rajk case, as in all the previous show trials, began with the reinterpretation of the defendant's life (in this case a Hungarian Communist Party leader). Usually, those in his immediate circle were arrested and interrogated. The confessions were 'achieved with rubber truncheons, rifle butts, electric shocks, sleeplessness, hunger, and cold – a mixture of the most advanced and barbaric methods of physical and psychological tortures'.[113] The statements were subsequently examined by Russian and Hungarian legal officials, who pieced together the show trial, and ensured that the 'confessions' fitted into the scheme.

The selection of politically reliable judges and judicial officials was paramount. In the Rajk trial, the president and chairman of the state public prosecutor's office were puppets of the regime. The indictment, signed by them, was in fact drawn up by the leader of the Hungarian Central Committee, edited by the Soviet security police, and approved by both Beria and Stalin. Prior to the trial, the state prosecutor called in the chairman and handed over the script of the trial, including their questions and the answers of the defendants. Strict instructions were given not to deviate from the text. In the event that a defendant deviated from the text, the chairman was told to adjourn the proceedings for the day. Finally, a list of politically reliable defence attorneys was drawn up; their texts were written by the 'legal experts' as well. No witnesses were called by the defence attorneys; only the prosecution called witnesses. Witnesses were not treated any better for having provided false testimony – after the trial, they were usually sentenced in secret

108 The Cominform, or the Information Bureau of the Communist Parties, was created in September 1947. It consisted of nine countries: the Soviet Union, Poland, Czechoslovakia, Hungary, Romania, Bulgaria, Yugoslavia, France and Italy. In reality, it was a 'tool to force conformity among the Parties of the Soviet bloc'. See *ibid.* and Medvedev, *Let History Judge*, *supra* n. 66.

109 Hodos, *Show Trials*, *supra* n. 49, p. 4.

110 Several reports were sent by the Polish representative, S. Zawolszki.

111 For details which led up to the trials, see Hodos, *Show Trials*, *supra* n. 49.

112 The conditions in Poland were not so ideal. The Polish communists were reluctant to persecute their leader, but were no less bloodthirsty in finding replacements among the lower-ranking communist officials.

113 Hodos, *Show Trials*, *supra* n. 49, p. 46.

trials to long sentences on trumped-up charges. The legal experts could boast that the technique of the show trials of the 1930s was perfected in the Rajk trial.

Reports such as these offer a glimpse into what the role of law, and the legal system, signified to political leaders. Representatives from the Comintern submitted reports from the proceedings. An analysis of the Rajk trial revealed some disappointment. 'In my opinion, I do not think that the procurator … Gyula Alapi demonstrated to the court in the summations that this was a group of paid agents … The president of the court … Janko Peter, was weak in the front of the court when the defendant Rakosi showed up.'[114] The observer was also not impressed by the line of questioning, which he thought could have been more centred on the Yugoslav betrayal.

Certainly, for the upper echelon of the Communist Party, the political trial was meant as a tool to control political opponents, to purge the Communist Party ranks of any threatening elements, and at the same time to demonstrate to society the ever-present, almost omnipotent, role of the party. The press presented the political trials as a triumph over counter-revolutionaries, and many people continued to believe that the party knew best.[115] Many people had faith in the Communist Party, and even in the face of arrest and mistreatment, people were convinced that the mistake would be rectified.[116] Confidence that Stalin knew what was best prevailed: belief in the party was paramount, even in the face of death. The sheer horror of their predicament, combined with barbaric torture, drove the defendants to 'recognise' their guilt, and the righteousness of the party. What mattered was to be a 'good communist'.

Conclusions

The German and Soviet occupation of Poland destroyed any remaining notion of the rule of law, a process which had already begun to erode during the interwar period under Pilsudski's authoritarian-style regime. In the GG, German authorities wasted no time in dismantling Polish institutions and replacing them with German ones. German authorities confiscated the property of Jews and Poles in the 'public

114 'Dve Zapiski Referenta tov. Zawolshkova svezu s poezdkoj v g. Budapesht' [Two Summaries from the Report of Zawolszki in Relation to the Process in Budapest], 29 September 1949, p. 206, fond 575, opis 1, delo 95, RTsKhIDNI, Moscow, Russia.

115 Certainly public opinion was behind the courts in the political trials of the 1930s. See Medvedev, *Let History Judge*, *supra* n. 66, p. 115n.

116 See Evgenia Ginsburg, *Journey into the Whirlwind* (New York: Harcourt Brace Jovanovich, 1975). Hodos writes: 'Even I, the true believer, had some difficulty understanding and explaining the excommunication of Marshal Tito. … But I knew that the party was always correct. Stalin knew what he is doing and why he is doing it. … In May, the *Neue Zürcher Zeitung* began to serialize *Darkness at Noon* … I did not believe one word of the novel, considered it a dirty slander, and soon stopped reading the instalments'. *Show Trials*, *supra* n. 49, p. 42.

interest'. The pillage of Polish resources meant that Poles had to turn to illegal means for survival.

When the GG was established, the German authorities immediately targeted the Polish intelligentsia for elimination; this included the legal profession and, as noted above, many distinguished members were removed. The law was refashioned to fit the particular needs of the GG: the courts established in the occupied territories had a significant role, rendering judgments in the name of the German people, in cases where the law was broadly interpreted to punish Jews and Poles. The death penalty was sought in a multitude of cases which could be considered as involving an act against a German. Special courts were created to eliminate all forms of resistance. A dual court system evolved: one for Germans and another for Poles and Jews. The law was used as an instrument of terror, far from a legal code consistent with a rule-of-law state.

The kind of Soviet 'justice' which existed in the Polish territories was equally repressive and also aimed at eliminating all persons who were considered politically dangerous. Investigations were carried out by the NKVD and were brutal. Defendants were not informed of the charges until they were sentenced or had been sent to a labour camp. One of the main contradictions of this kind of Soviet justice was that investigations or so-called 'court processes' took place in order to establish guilt in individual cases, while at other times, in mass round-ups, innocent people were deported merely because they belonged to a certain category. The Soviet penal code permitted judges to refer cases to the NKVD, and all the while secret decrees were being issued by higher authorities, who were intent on eliminating the Polish intelligentsia.

According to Neumann, one of the main aspects of the rule of law is to control arbitrary governmental activities. It is true, he argues, that 'no modern theory of law and state [exists] which does not accept both force and law even if the emphasis accorded to each of these components has varied in accordance with the historical situation.'[117] This is the compromise between society and the state; society requires sovereignty to carry out its duty of safeguarding people's livelihood. This is where the predictability of laws becomes important. Recalling Weber, this provided the foundation for the developed capitalist order.[118] Thus, society expects that the state

117 Franz L. Neumann, 'The Change in the Function of Law in Modern Society', in Otto Kirchheimer and Franz Neumann, *Social Democracy and the Rule of Law*, ed. by Keith Tribe, trans. by Leena Turner and Keith Tribe (London: Allen Unwin, 1987), pp. 101–02. See also H. L. A. Hart, 'Positivism and the Separation of Law and Morals', *Harvard Law Review*, 71 (1958), pp. 593–629 and Lon F. Fuller, 'Positivism and Fidelity to Law – A Reply to Professor Hart', *Harvard Law Review*, 71 (1958), pp. 630–72.

118 Otto Kirchheimer, 'State Structure and Law in the Third Reich', in *The Rule of Law Under Siege: Selected Writings of Franz L. Neumann and Otto Kirchheimer*, ed. by William E. Scheuerman (Berkeley, CA: University of California Press, 1996), pp. 142–71.

structure and legal order are, at least in theory, treating each citizen in an equal and non-arbitrary fashion.[119]

Neither regime sought to disguise resentment towards judges and lawyers, and the regimes' respective policies were blatantly open about it. In both cases, judges served the regime and their work was controlled by the authorities; in other words, judicial independence was non-existent.[120] In both occupied territories, the new form of judicial independence that existed was noted for its unpredictability and flexibility; at any time, the law could be changed or retroactively negated by the Führer or Stalin, with complete disregard for existing legal norms or formalities. Rayfield, referring to Thomas Hobbes, succinctly argues that 'when a society loses the complex play of forces – judiciary, army, executive, public opinion, religion, culture – that keep each other in check, and both anarchy and tyranny at bay', it is difficult to speak about the existence of the rule of law.[121] Not surprisingly, Polish society's experiences during this period would affect its experience with communist rule, in both public and private lives, as we shall see in the next chapter.

119 *Ibid.*

120 *Ibid.*, p. 144.

121 Rayfield, *Stalin and His Hangmen, supra* n. 67, p. xxi.

Chapter 4
Communist Rule (1945–1989)

Four legs good. Two legs bad![1]

Circumstances Leading to the Creation of Communist Poland

At its appearance in Poland, communism was seen as foreign, brought by Russian-speaking soldiers, interrogators and officials:

> It came from abroad, and had not emerged from within the country. It was brought by alien, Russian-speaking soldiers, interrogators, and officials, so that it was difficult to say whether it was Russian or Communist, and what the difference was, if any. ... Nazi rule over Poland was experienced first and foremost as German rule, while Russian rule was above all felt as Communist.[2]

The new regime was not founded on the work of Polish socialists, who had played an important role in the political life of the Second Polish Republic. As mentioned in Chapter 3, the Polish communists were periodically suppressed by the Soviet authorities, and had suffered severe losses in 1938. Even after the party's re-establishment, Polish communists were generally regarded with suspicion. As in other CEE states, the Polish People's Republic was essentially a direct outgrowth of the Soviet organisation under Stalin's direction. On the other hand, there was clear evidence of the party's desire to forge its own brand of communism which would reverberate throughout the CEE. This will be addressed below.

The decision of the future government of Poland rested with the Yalta Conference of 4–11 February 1945, where, *inter alia*, the Polish question would be considered. It was difficult for Poles to accept the fact that the Soviet Union was one of the key decision-makers of the future political and territorial framework of the country. At the conference, it was agreed that the provisional Polish government, the *Polski Komitet Wyzwolenia Narodowego* (Polish Committee for National Liberation; hereafter, PKWN) was to be reorganised as the Polish Provisional Government of National Unity.[3] It was obliged to hold free elections

---

1 George Orwell, *Animal Farm* (London: Secker & Warburg, 1977), p. 28.

2 Jacek Kurczewski, *The Resurrection of Rights in Poland* (Oxford: Clarendon Press, 1993), p. 32.

3 The PKWN was established as a temporary executive organ in July 1944 by decree of the Committee for National Poland (*Polski Komitet Narodowy*). Under the leadership of Leon Chajn, the committee laid the plan to destroy all remnants of the pre-war structure of the judiciary, and to replace it with a politically disposed cadre of judicial personnel.

as soon as possible. As a result of the Potsdam Conference of 17 July 1945, the borders of Poland were redefined as we know them today. With these territorial adjustments, the country was literally transformed, becoming ethnically Polish and predominantly Roman Catholic. The Holocaust and subsequent migrations had reduced the Jewish population in Poland, but during the period 1945–1968 it decreased to almost zero.

Alongside these developments, the internal situation of the country was bleak.[4] Despite this, the *Polska Partia Robotnicza* (Polish Workers' Party; hereafter, PPR) sought to implement collectivisation policies with the assistance of the Red Army, but this was short-lived.[5] By May 1945, however, the Secretary of the Central Committee of the PPR, Wladyslaw Gomulka, reacted against this revolutionary programme, fearing that the scheme would further isolate the party. Gomulka argued for an independent Poland – that is, one that would not be incorporated into the Soviet Union. This was supported by many communists, who resented the fact that they had to rely on the Soviet Union for support to govern Poland. More importantly, they knew that the secret police were controlled by Soviet authorities and growing in power: most Poles regarded the communists as Soviet agents. The PPR therefore presented itself as a Polish party, and the division among party members remained hidden until Stalinism ruthlessly was enforced in the country in the late 1940s. As soon as Polish borders were fixed by the Potsdam Conference, the Soviet-backed Polish government committed itself to organising free elections. In September 1946, a new electoral law was passed. The law provided for the manipulation of votes and was especially designed to block support for other political parties, such as the PSL, which was led by Stanislaw Mikolajczyk, a protégé of Wincenty Witos, the former prime minister of Poland. Mikolajczyk was president of the Supreme Court, and a popular candidate among Poles. He was persuaded by Churchill to seek accommodation with the communists. He was viewed as a threat by the Soviet authorities.

The free elections were continually postponed and, in their place, a referendum was organised, in which the electorate was asked to vote 'three times yes', forcing the opposition either to give full support to the provisional government or fail to fulfil its promises. The PSL asked voters to say 'no' to the first two propositions concerning the abolition of the Senate in order to turn the tables on the provisional government. The elections demonstrated the total absence of ethical values and moral integrity on the part of the provisional government: votes were counted

The State National Council (KRN) was created by the Polish Workers' Party in 1944. The KRN was a pro-communist party. Definitions of the PKWN and the KRN are in *Slownik historii Polski*, Wydanie III [The Dictionary of Polish History, 3rd edn] (Warsaw: Wiedza Powszechna, 1964), pp. 264–65.

4 Jan M. Ciechanowski, 'Post-war Poland', in *The History of Poland Since 1863*, ed. by R. F. Leslie (Cambridge: Cambridge University Press, 1983), p. 283.

5 The PPR was also coping with an increase in membership from 30,000 to 300,000. A campaign to purge the party of counter-revolutionaries ensued. See *ibid.*

by government officials in secret, and in the few districts where the vote was revealed, the opposition learned that 81 per cent of the voters had followed their instructions to no avail – the government announced that 68 per cent voted in its own favour.[6]

Some 1 million voters were denied the right to vote, and candidates from the PSL Party were struck off the ballots in 10 out of 52 electoral districts.[7] On 17 January 1947, voting took place. The 'democratic bloc' – comprising the PPR, the *Polska Partia Socialistyczna* (Polish Socialist Party), and the *Wola Ludu* (Voice of the People) – took 80.1 per cent of the votes, as opposed to 10.3 per cent votes for the PSL.[8] In addition to this coercive manipulation, the Soviet authorities falsified the election results to ensure their full ascent to power. On 4 February 1947, the *Sejm* convened; the following day Boleslaw Bierut, formerly head of the provisional government, became president of the Republic.[9] The communists proved successful in eliminating opponents in the resistance and the PSL, which split and was eventually forced to amalgamate with the pro-communist wing.

The years 1947–48 were a crucial period in which Poland turned from its more moderate political and economic programmes to the Stalinist model of economic reform. This would mark the start of the one of the darkest periods of Polish post-war history, mainly characterised by purges and show trials, as discussed in Chapter 3 and below. The respective CEE 'dark' histories would overlap. It was also about this time that international developments signalled the start of the Cold War. In 1947, the Marshall Plan was established to offer economic assistance to European recovery. Poland and Czechoslovakia would readily have accepted US economic aid, but were prevented from doing so by the Soviet authorities, who were vehemently opposed to such a move, as it would have entailed accepting the conditions under which the aid was offered: this would have meant the reconstruction of the economy according to capitalistic models. In response to the potential 'disobedience' which surfaced among the communist governments of the people's democracies, the Soviet Union created the Communist Information Bureau, otherwise known as the Cominform, as an instrument of Soviet foreign policy, in the place of the Comintern. As discussed in Chapter 3 concerning the show trials, the existence of Cominform meant rigid discipline within the countries of the Soviet bloc, which in effect translated into the acceptance of

---

6 Norman Davies, *God's Playground: A History of Poland, Volume II: 1795 to the Present* (New York: Columbia University Press, 1982), p. 568.

7 A quarter of the total population resided in these districts. *Ibid.*, pp. 293–94.

8 The PSL rejected the invitation to join the democratic bloc. While the PSL was careful to make conciliatory gestures towards the Soviet Union, it promulgated civil liberties and cautioned against NKVD police terror and collectivisation programmes.

9 The newly appointed ministers mirrored the wishes of Moscow. Jozef Cyrankiewicz became prime minister; Wladyslaw Gomulka, deputy premier and minister of the regained territories; Jakub Berman, under-secretary; Hilary Minc, minister of industry; and Stanislaw Radkiewicz, minister of public security.

Soviet methods. Two political camps could now be visibly identified: the capitalist and the socialist.

The Stalinist model for Poland meant severe repression and terror. *Poles were under constant surveillance at work, and in almost all areas of daily life.* The watch was conducted by the secret police, an organ which was part of the Ministry of Public Security, and the *Urzad Bezpieczenstwa* (Security Police; hereafter, UB). The head of the UB and the minister of public security, Stanislaw Radkiewicz, as well as a number of persons who filled key positions in the organs, were members of the Central Committee of the Polish Communist Party, signifying their importance in the political system. More importantly, their functions further evidenced the dominance of the party in all spheres of Polish life.

For example, the Polish artistic community was not immune from repression and the suppression of their works. The policies of Jakub Berman, who was in charge of propaganda, played a key role in reorienting the party's course from moderate to hard line, and Berman had the intellectual capabilities and the zeal to fulfil his role successfully. The Polish Writers' Union underwent serious changes under the constant pressure to produce more socialist literature. Theatre, cinema, music, painting, sculpture and architecture were redirected to incorporate ideological themes, as social realism was considered the only correct style. Many artists conformed; most of the younger ones became true social realists, while among the older artists such a conversion was rare, unless it involved opportunistic motives. Many refused to conform in order to follow their conscience; needless to say, literature and painting suffered, as work tended to be dull, naive and crude.[10] Most periodicals and newspapers had party officials on their staff; the Association of Polish Journalists dictated the general line, which became especially anti-Western and anti-capitalist as the Cold War intensified.

Higher education, research and science were reinterpreted along lines of socialist realism. Marxism–Leninism–Stalinism dominated the scientific approach, and the curriculum was copied from the Soviet Union. Polish scholars did not welcome this change. Formerly, the policy of interpreting Marxism had been free, and this approach had long prevailed in Poland. This tradition was cut short, a change fully supported by small groups of Stalinist-Marxists, who conducted campaigns against bourgeois ideology and non-Marxists.[11] The foundation of the Academy of Sciences was one of the products of the socialist realism offensive.

The Roman Catholic Church had an enormous influence on public opinion through sermons, pastoral letters, newspapers and numerous other publications.

10 On the other hand, there was an increase in the availability of translated first-class contemporary literature and drama. In addition to this, folk culture was extensively studied and promoted.

11 Professor Adam Schaff, who was the director and chief expert in philosophy and social science of the Institute for the Training of Academic Scientific Cadres (later renamed the Institute of Social Sciences), was one of the chief designers of the campaign. Schaff would later reinterpret Marxism and be expelled from the party.

The Vatican Decree of 1949 was the turning point in Church–state relations. The decree banned Catholics from supporting or participating in communist parties and reading the communist press. The Polish government retaliated with its 1949 Decree on Liberty of Conscience and Political Opinion, which made any application of the Vatican Decree by the churches in Poland a punishable offence.[12] The second attack against the Church's influence was the mobilisation of priests who were loyal to the regime to create disunity and confusion among Polish Catholics. The government and the Church signed an agreement in 1950, whereby the Church acknowledged the supreme authority of the state in all secular matters in return for assurance of its autonomy in the religious sphere and a confirmation of its remaining privileges. The hope that the conflict between the Church and the state would be alleviated was futile. Between 1952 and 1953, priests were arrested for intelligence activities and undermining public order. In October 1952, in one of the more protested acts of repression, three bishops of the Katowice diocese were arrested. A wave of arrests followed a month later when a group of priests of the Cracow diocese were arrested and later tried before a military tribunal as spies for the CIA; they were given sentences ranging from six years' imprisonment to death. Another case involved the bishop of Kielce and three of his priests, who were tried for undermining public order by opening a centre that was considered a political threat. The bishop received a prison sentence of 12 years, notwithstanding the fact that he had already been under house arrest for several years. The final blow came when the Primate of Poland, Archbishop Stefan Wyszynski, was prohibited by the government from exercising his functions and forced to retire to a monastery. Eventually, all priests and bishops were required to take an oath of loyalty to the People's Republic. Poland was not the only people's democracy in which religious persecution was rife. In Hungary, for example, Cardinal Primate József Mindszenty was arrested for espionage; this opened the door to a wave of arrests of members of all Christian denominations and rabbis and other representatives of the Jewish community.[13]

In Poland, the expansion of the security police forces increased their importance in relation to the party, gradually replacing it as the backbone of the regime.[14] The

12 This was accompanied by the confiscation of Church property, which up to that point had enjoyed exemption from nationalisation.

13 Cardinal Mindszenty sought and obtained asylum at the US embassy after the 1956 Hungarian Revolution. He stayed at the embassy until 1971. Paul Ignotus, *Hungary*, Nations of the Modern World Series (London: Ernest Benn Limited, 1972), pp. 203–05, 254.

14 The powers of the police were increased in order to avoid possible public unrest in the face of deteriorating living standards. With its huge expansion in 1947–50, the UB created a network of secret agents who were employed as personnel officers in factories and offices. The establishment of the Tenth Department in 1952 was headed by Beria, signifying a direct link with Moscow. This department extended its powers to the activities of the Party itself, save for Bierut and Rokossovsky. It was this organ which arrested Gomulka and prepared his trial.

administration of justice was reorganised according to Soviet lines, as discussed below.

Administration of Justice

The months immediately following the end of the war saw an alarming increase in crime, such as offences against property, bribery, corruption and the continued existence of the black market.[15] Economic chaos prevailed in the region, caused by the war, and then further prolonged and complicated by the socialisation of the national economy. The introduction of a new type of ownership, combined with the absence of proper supervision and protection of property, caused further damage and devastation to the country. Traditional divisions between public and private law were rejected, and it was argued that the area of civil law should be treated as a single system which served the socio-political goals of Marxism–Leninism.

The second factor which influenced new governments like that of Poland to quickly address the area of civil law was their desire to unify the newly acquired German territory with the rest of the country. The sooner Polish law was introduced to the territories, the easier the integration of the lands with the rest of the country would be. Finally, the significant reforms within the socio-economic order, particularly in the areas of land and the nationalisation of the basic branches of the economy, called for the reform of civil law. With regard to property, various types of ownership were distinguished between three classes, depending on the identity of the holder: national ownership, or ownership by the cooperative or other socialist organisations; individual property of 'physical person' or non-socialist organisations; or personal property of physical persons.[16] In contrast to the Soviet situation, where land was nationalised, in Poland only property over and above an indicated maximum area, which varied between provinces, was taken over by the state. The situation elsewhere in the early stages of communism was bleak.[17] In Poland, the majority of the agricultural land remained in the private ownership of individual peasants; even if they joined a cooperative organisation, they still continued to own the land they brought in as their share in the venture. As observed by Grzybowski, the entire system of property rights and the gradation of the degree of legal protection under the law was the result of the social and

15 Vincent Chrypinski, 'Postwar Developments in Polish Law: A Survey of Criminal and Civil Legal Rules', in *Polish Law Throughout the Ages*, ed. by Wenceslas Wagner (Stanford, CA: Hoover Institution Press, 1970), pp. 177–214.

16 See, among other literature, Kazimierz Grzybowski, 'The Draft of the Civil Code for Poland', in *Studies for Polish Law*, ed. by Kazimierz Grzybowski *et al.*, Law in Eastern Europe Series, No. 6 (Leyden: A. W. Sijthoff, 1962), pp. 11–37. See also J. Okolski, 'Current Developments in Polish Economic Law', in *Anglo-Polish Legal Essays*, ed. by William E. Butler (New York: Transnational Publishers, 1982), pp. 117–27.

17 See Robert Conquest, *The Harvest of Sorrow: Soviet Collectivization and the Terror-Famine* (Edmonton, AB, Canada: University of Alberta Press, 1986).

economic order. The degree of protection afforded was in direct relation to the interest of the state in upholding the existing state of things. Thus, state property, being the cornerstone of the regime, and the economic platform for the transition to what were considered higher forms of social and economic organisation, required the most effective protection possible.

The work of the special commission was greatly influenced by the work of the pre-war Codification Commission.[18] Within a period of 17 months, and the passage of many subordinate regulations, the branches of civil law were unified by decrees relating to the following areas: legal and physical persons; marriage; family; guardianship and curatorship; inheritance; property; mortgages; and general principles of civil law. The unification of civil law allowed for state courts to have exclusive jurisdiction over many significant matters. The basic premise that underlay the unification, it was argued, was public interest, and the public interest was interpreted in accordance with the ruling party. This political nature of the civil law – the protection of the public interest – inevitably made its way into the courts. It was made clear that judges were to heed this interpretation and, in consequence, many judges rebelled and followed the old spirit of pre-war civil law. Vigorous judicial indoctrination followed, which required the application of the new spirit of the law, so as to shape the course of the transition between private ownership and free enterprise to a socialist system.

The PKWN was granted the crucial task of the reshaping of the future judiciary. The PKWN operated in the Soviet-occupied territories, and did not possess the legal capacity to pass and implement decrees. Nonetheless, it did so, and thus eliminated most of the pre-war judicial pool from future practice, either by passing them on to the NKVD, or by barring entry. Most of the pre-war judicial officials who passed were deemed malleable (politically reliable), or were eliminated in the future.

Because of the increasing instability, the protective measures were outlined by a Decree of 30 October 1944.[19] These measures were quite repressive in nature; the government explained that they were necessary because of the chaos caused by the war.[20] These decrees were meant to be temporary, yet many of the draconian provisions remained in force throughout the communist era.

---

18 Needless to say, the draughtsmen who were influenced by the commission's traditions were unaware of the events which were about to take place in the country and their effect on the concept of law. *Ibid.*

19 *Dekret Polskiego Komitetu Wyzwolenia Narodowego z dnia 30 pazdziernika 1944r. o ochronie Panstwa* [Decree of the Polish Committee for National Liberation from 30 October 1944 Concerning State Security], *Dziennik Ustaw*, No. 10, item 50.

20 The Decree of 30 October 1944, for example, made the distribution and publication of anti-Soviet material punishable. The decree remained in place until well after the war. Both decrees had the appropriate title of 'On Crimes Particularly Dangerous in the Period of Rebuilding the State'. *Ibid.*

The Constitutional Law of 19 February 1947 served as an interim document until a new constitution was promulgated.[21] The 1947 law was the so-called revival of the 1921 Constitution, albeit very loosely based on the principles of the democratic document of 1921. After the rigged 1947 elections, the new government was established, ceasing to be 'provisional'. With the defeat of the only political party to present serious opposition, the PSL, the new government turned its attention to eliminating political opponents from society with the help of the newly crafted legal system, as will be shown below.

The interim Constitutional Law remained in force for five years, during which time the grip of Stalinism was strengthened over all aspects of public and private life. Any chance for the establishment of the rule of law was dispelled with the promulgation of the Polish Constitution on 22 July 1952, in which the Republic of Poland was renamed the Polish People's Republic.[22] The Polish Constitution was modelled on the 1936 Soviet Constitution and, in fact, retained much of its language. The Soviet document, as mentioned above, was drafted by Vyshinsky and was one of the most blatant acts of doublespeak ever promulgated. A catalogue of provisions concerning basic political rights and civil liberties to be guaranteed was provided but with the following caveat in mind: they were not to be used against the 'will of the people' – in other words, against the state.

Article 3 of the Polish document stated that the working people were the leading class of the nation, and that the 'Polish United Workers' Party shall be the guiding political force of society in building socialism, whose leading role is recognised by all other officially recognised political bodies.' The emptiness and falsity of this cannot be stressed enough. The lie was in the assumption that the party, acting jointly with the peasant class, and with the progressive intelligentsia, represented the interests of the entire nation. The party ruled 'on behalf' of the majority, and in this hierarchical framework the state structure was controlled by the party. The party itself (allegedly) was the only true representative of the dominant social forces; therefore, no conflict could emerge between the state and the citizen. This, in effect, translated into totalitarian rule, where the possibility of working together with the working class and the peasantry never materialised, nor was there any intention on the part of the party to have it realised.

The 1952 Constitution was intentionally worded vaguely and lacked normative content on most of its provisions, as evidenced in the provisions on the relationship

---

21 *Ustawa Konstytucyjna z dnia 4 lutego 1947r. o wyborze Prezydenta Rzeczpospolitej* [Constitutional Law from 4 February 1947 Concerning the Election of the President of the Republic], *Dziennik Ustaw*, No. 9, item 43 and *Ustawa Konstytucyjna z dnia 19 lutego 1947r. o ustroju i zakresie dzialania najwyzszych organow Rzeczpospolitej Polskiej* [Constitutional Law from 19 February 1947 Concerning the Scope and Activities of the Highest State Organs of the Polish Republic], *Dziennik Ustaw*, No. 18, item 71.

22 *Konstytucja Polski Rzeczpospolitej Ludowej uchwalona przez Sejm Ustawodawczy w dniu 22 lipca 1952r.* [Constitution of the Polish People's Republic as Adopted by the Legislative *Sejm* on 22 July 1952], *Dziennik Ustaw*, No. 33, item 232.

between individual liberties and the state. The most important characteristic of the Polish Constitution, which it adopted from the Soviet document, was its malleability. There was no direct application to the life of the state or society; in fact, the Constitution was subordinated to the communist state. As observed by Frankowski, it was 'subordinate to parliamentary statutes that conclusively determine the ambit of imprecise constitutional clauses'.[23] All constitutional provisions were curtailed by Article 84, which provided that '[i]t shall be prohibited to set up and participate in an association whose objective or activities menace the socio-political system or the legal order of the Polish People's Republic.' In other words, if all constitutional provisions had to be construed according to this clause, then they, in essence, were subordinated to politics. The rule of law amounted to nothing more than one-party rule, dictating complete subordination. In this hierarchical system, there was no room for the realisation of the separation of powers, but only suppression and arbitrary rule. The underlying principles of the pre-war Polish state had disappeared, and with them the tradition of Polish constitutional history. This was facilitated first and foremost by the destruction of an independent administration of justice and the total subservience of society to the regime, two key elements of totalitarian rule.

Leon Chajn was the chief architect of the Polish legal system.[24] Under his leadership, the idea was promoted that all judicial personnel had to be screened carefully as new courts were created in the recaptured regions. The proposals which were put forward required that certain criteria be fulfilled before appointing judicial officials. For example, in the case of new courts in Rzeszow, the president judge of the appellate court, requested that certain candidates be appointed to maintain strict control over the number of judges on the bench.[25] One of the screening tools which was implemented called upon judicial officials to reapply for their positions. This process required them to reveal their work experience, placing particular emphasis on their activities during the German occupation. This was a crucial factor, for it paved the way for sentencing to death many individuals, including judges, for 'collaboration with the Nazi regime'.[26] Thus the pre-war judicial officials who were hired by the German authorities in the GG were of special interest to the

23 Stanislaw Frankowski, 'A Comment on Professor Garlicki's Article "Constitutional Developments in Poland": The Lyrics Sound Familiar, But Are They Really Playing Our Song?', *Saint Louis University Law Journal*, 32 (1988), p. 743.

24 See *supra* Chapter 2, for details on Chajn's pre-war activities and *supra* n. 3.

25 D. Adam Stawarski (appellate court judge), *Projekt: Dekret, PKWN, Resort Sprawiedliwosci* [Draft: Decree, PKWN, Department of Justice, hereafter, PKWN/RS], 1944, pp. 1–2, sygnatura (hereafter, sygn.) IX/5, Archiwum Akt Nowych, Warsaw, Poland.

26 At the time of the reapplication, many Polish judicial officials were interviewed about their or their colleagues' contacts with Germans. For example, one Polish notary public was questioned about his Ukrainian colleague, who apparently sympathised with the Nazi regime. The Polish lawyer asked that the comments be overlooked as a question of undue pressure brought on by the war. He further stated that they both were educated and worked in a free Poland, qualities which should attest to their experience and trustworthiness. Letter

PKWN, and their backgrounds were consequently marked out for investigation, as was their German 'connection'.[27] As mentioned in Chapter 3, there was no collaboration on the part of the Polish Bar with the Nazi-imposed legal regime. Thus, this policy of purging was based on false accusations: the underlying aim was to serve the Soviet authorities' goal to remove political opponents and to promote their own 'social revolution'.[28]

The Decree of 25 October 1944 created a new category of crime, economic crimes, unknown in the pre-war period.[29] The crimes which fell into this category included 'lowering the quantity or quality of production in socialised enterprises, selling on the open market of supplies intended for planned distribution, and arrogation of property left unprotected because of war'.[30] The decree also addressed the corruption of public officials, which extended the pre-war criminal code provisions to encompass a wider range of offenders, and also subjected them to much harsher penalties; the Decree of 16 November 1945, for example, extended the penalty from three years to capital punishment.[31] The series of socio-economic reforms, particularly in the area of land reform and the nationalisation of industry and commerce, was accompanied by criminal sanctions. For example, peasants who received their land had to begin cultivation immediately to produce foodstuffs. Failure to comply with this obligation warranted severe punishment: the result was that many peasants were forced to abandon their land and join collective farms.

---

from Marian Podwinski, notary public from Przemysl, to Vice-Minister of Justice Chajn, *PKWN*, 21 October 1944, p. 14, sygn. IX/5, Archiwum Akt Nowych, Warsaw, Poland.

27 See Oskar Kamienski, in a letter to the Department of Justice, *PKWN/RS*, 8 October 1944, p. 43, and also Waclaw Maciejski, *PKWN/RS*, 24 November 1944, pp. 47–48, sygn. IX/5, Archiwum Akt Nowych, Warsaw, Poland.

28 The trend of purging occurred in other communist countries. In East Germany, however, despite the fact that the Soviet authorities' move to purge the state structure of Nazi influences was undoubtedly creditable, it masked other motives, namely to eliminate ideological opponents alongside conservative elements. See Jonathan Steele, *Inside East Germany: The State That Came in from the Cold* (New York: Urizen Books, 1977).

29 *Dekret Polskiego Komitetu Wyzwolenia Narodwego z dnia 25 pazdziernika 1944r. o zwalczaniu spekulacji wojennej* [Decree of the Polish Committee for National Liberation from 25 October 1944 Concerning Combating Wartime Speculation], *Dziennik Ustaw*, No. 9, item 49. See also the amendment, *Dekret Polskiego Komitetu Wyzwolenia Narodowego z dnia 20 listopada 1944r. o zmanie dekretu o zwalczaniu spekulacji i lichwy wojennej* [Decree of the Polish Committee for National Liberation from 20 November 1944 Concerning the Amendment to the Decree Concerning Combating Wartime Speculation and Money Lending], *Dziennik Ustaw*, No. 12, item 63.

30 Art. 3, *Dziennik Ustaw*, No. 9, item 49, *ibid.*

31 *Dekret z dnia 16 listopada 1945r. o przestepstwach szczegolnie niebezpiecznych w okresie odbudowy Panstwa* [Decree from 16 November 1945 Concerning Crimes of a Dangerous Nature During the Reconstruction of the State], *Dziennik Ustaw*, No. 53, item 300.

Most of the legislation which was passed between 1944 and 1945 did not rely on normal legislative techniques, such as statutes and decrees. Instead, many critical matters were decided unofficially, not always by authorised officials, and these decisions were often unpublished. It was clear that the enactments which were passed during this period were meant to accelerate the consolidation of communist power. Yet most of the pre-war legislation remained, and the framework created by the new government was merely transitory.

Poland, apart from Yugoslavia, was the only socialist country where the new communist regime did not forbid the courts to use the pre-war criminal code. The Polish Criminal Code of 1932 remained in force, with some revisions made to keep with communist ideology. It should be mentioned that criminology at that time concentrated on juvenile crimes and Nazi crimes, the research for which was carried out by pre-war scholars and representatives of the younger generation of criminologists.[32] The first of the revisions within the criminal law was the passage of the Military Penal Code of 23 September 1944, which replaced the 1932 code.[33] The purpose of the provisions was to protect the new political structure and was not directed only at soldiers but also extended to civilians, and was very much oriented to destroy members of the underground army movement (Polish Home Army), who had placed themselves in the opposition. The Decree on State Security of 30 October 1944 was an equally repressive piece of legislation aimed at attempts to overthrow the Polish state as well as terrorist attacks, subversive activity, and sabotage.[34] Each of the crimes called for the death penalty. This decree was replaced by the Decree on Crimes of a Dangerous Nature During the Reconstruction of the State.[35] The Criminal Code of 1932 was suspended by Article 68 of the Decree of 13 June 1946, known as the 'little criminal code'. Separate 'special courts' which were to deal with so-called fascist-Nazi crimes were established in 1944.[36]

32 See Michal Fajst, 'Spor o kryminologie w Polsce w okresie stalinizmu' [Conflict over Criminology in Poland During the Stalinist Period], *Studia Iuridica* [Legal Studies], 27 (1995), pp. 43–64.

33 *Dekret Polskiego Komitetu Wyzwolenia Narodowego z dnia 23 wrzesnia 1944r. Kodeks Karny Wojska Polskiego* [Decree of the Polish Committee for National Liberation from 23 September 1944, the Military Criminal Code], *Dziennik Ustaw*, No. 6, item 27.

34 *Dziennik Ustaw*, No. 10, item 50, *supra* n. 19.

35 *Dziennik Ustaw*, No. 53, item 300, *supra* n. 31.

36 *Rozporzadzenie Kierownikow Resortu Sprawiedliwosci i Resortu Bezpieczenstwa Publicznego z dnia 3 pazdziernika 1944r. w sprawie wykonania Polskiego Komitetu Wyzwolenia Narodowego z dnia 12 wrzesnia 1944r. o specjanych sadach karnych dla spraw zbrodniarzy faszystowsko-hitlerowskich* [Order of the Leaders of the Department of Justice and the Department of Public Safety from 3 October 1944 Concerning the Implementation of the Decree of the Polish Committee for National Liberation from 12 September 1944 Concerning Special Criminal Courts for Fascist-Nazi Crimes], *Dziennik Ustaw*, No. 7, item 35. Many of the former members of the underground movement were sentenced to death or to other harsh punishment in these courts. No appeals could be made – the courts' decisions were final and binding.

The penal code also established separate military courts, which applied different military criminal and civil codes. The 'secret section' of the Appellate Court in Warsaw was established in 1949, and of the District Court in 1951. All cases, from courts throughout the country, which concerned the violation of the September Decree and other fascist-Nazi crimes, were transferred to this secret section. The secret section of the Supreme Court operated from 1950 until 1954. The initial proceedings of some 20 cases took place at the Department of Judicial Supervision of the Ministry of Justice. Later, in 1950, this section was located at the Appellate Courts and then at the Supreme Court. The Warsaw jail on Rakowiecka Street served as a location for some of the proceedings at this point. Despite the fact that these were secret, they went on with the full knowledge of most of the Warsaw residents. The proceedings were brutal, and the rights of the defendant were not given any consideration. For example, in most cases, defendants were not given the details of their official indictment, namely the charges, or the time to respond to accusations, in order to build a defence. Instead, the proceedings were limited to the reading out of the act by the court, nor were witnesses present; their testimonies were merely read out in court.[37] Between 1944 and 1946, some 670 death sentences were pronounced, most of them in September and October – some 100 during NKVD-style sham proceedings which violated all principles relating to the right to a fair trial.[38]

As mentioned above, the main purpose of establishing the secret section in the courts was to eliminate political opposition – that is, members of the Polish underground. The most flagrant example of this was the trial of General Fieldorf, one of the most valiant leaders of the Polish Home Army.[39]

A 'war against the judiciary' was initiated by the government, beginning with a series of decrees which would change the entire face of the Polish administration of justice. It should be noted that there were 7,980 practising lawyers in pre-war Poland. Of this total, 4,500, or 56 per cent, were casualties of the war, while 1,110 or 21.5 per cent of judges, procurators and judicial candidates (who once numbered 5,171) were listed as casualties.[40] After the zones of German occupation were liberated, approximately 3,500 judges and procurators who had worked during the

---

37 See Katarzyna Maria Piekarska, 'Naruszanie zasady jawnosci w "sadach tajnych"' [Violation of the Principles of Open Proceedings in the 'Secret Courts'], *Studia luridica*, 27 (1995), pp. 25–41.

38 For recent documents related to the aforementioned death sentences, see Jerzy Kochanowski, 'Zabraklo desek' [The Planks Ran Out], *Polityka*, 46 (15 November 1997), p. 80.

39 See S. Marat and J. Snopkiewicz, *Zbrodnia, sprawa generala Fieldorfa – 'Nila'* [A Crime, the Case of General Fieldorf – 'Nil'] (Warsaw: 1989), as quoted in Piekarska, 'Naruszanie zasady jawnosci', *supra* n. 37, p. 26, n. 1.

40 Several hundred lawyers fell victim to the Katyn massacre (see Chapter 4). The mass grave of 4,500 corpses, located in the Soviet Union, was discovered in April 1943 by the Germans. Also among the victims were primary school teachers, university professors, doctors and many journalists – nearly all of the Polish intelligentsia. Jan Gross, *Polish*

interwar period reapplied for work in their profession. Many of the judges had been educated in pre-war Poland, and a large number had entered the profession prior to 1932. They were viewed suspiciously by the new government, who doubted their dedication to the new political and economic order, and therefore only 1,300 candidates were allowed to return.[41]

Chajn complained bitterly about the attitude of the pre-war judges: 'I could not get any employees for the Ministry of Justice. Judges and procurators from the appellate court in Lublin expressed their desire to return to work on the bench ... yet no one wanted to work for the PKWN.'[42] There was such a deep mistrust of the pre-war judicial pool that a vigorous campaign of indoctrination in Marxism–Leninism–Stalinism was initiated.

The purpose of the 'war against the judiciary' was twofold: to destroy all pre-war tendencies in the decision-making process and the prestige of the judicial profession. The authorities set out to accomplish this by appointing judicial candidates who had not satisfied the basic requirements provided by the law up to that point and by creating special schools under the auspices of the Ministry of Justice to indoctrinate the new judges in aspects of people's justice, which was not centred in the law.[43]

During the interwar period, candidates for judgeships went through a vigorous application process. The educational requirements were high. Candidates were expected to hold a law degree, have submitted a judicial application, and have taken the judicial examination. In order to sit on a bench in the district, appellate or Supreme courts, candidates needed not only 10 years of judicial experience

---

Society Under German Occupation: The Generalgouvernement, 1939–1944 (Princeton, NJ: Princeton University Press, 1979), p. 68.

41 Andrzej Rzeplinski, *Sadownictwo w Polsce Ludowej: miedzy dyspozycyjnoscia, a niezawisloscia* [The Judiciary in People's Poland: Between Disposability and Independence] (Warsaw: Oficyna Wydawnicza Pokolenie, 1989), p. 17. Interview with Andrzej Rzeplinski, Professor of Criminal Justice and Criminal Law, Institute for Social Resocialisation and Rehabilitation (IPSiR), University of Warsaw, and of the Helsinki Foundation for Human Rights, Warsaw, 7 February 1994.

42 Chajn, in Teresa Toranska, *Oni* [Them] (Warszawa: Mysl, 1986), tells how the Red Army arrested all of the judges and public prosecutors in Kielce. Chajn appealed to Bierut (president of PKWN) and to Stalin for their release. Subsequently, 17 officials were released, but the exact number arrested remained undisclosed. See Adam Litynski, 'Obraz sadownictwa karnego pierwszej dekady Polski Ludowej: Uwagi na marginesie ksiazek Andrzeja Rzeplinskiego i Marii Turlejskiej' [Depiction of the Criminal Court in the First Decade of People's Poland: Comments on the Books of Andrzej Rzeplinski and Maria Turlejska], *Czasopismo Prawno-Historyczne* [Journal of Legal History], 63 (1991), pp. 153–70, and Anna Turska, 'Spoleczenstwo w systemie panowania totalnego' [The Society in a System of Complete Control], *Studia Iuridica*, 27 (1995), pp. 11–23.

43 Marcin Zaborski, 'Szkolenie "sedziow nowego typu" w Polsce Ludowej. Czesc I: Srednie szkoly prawnicze' [Training the 'New Type of Judge' in People's Poland. Part I: Basic Law Schools], *Palestra*, 1–2 (1998), pp. 79–92.

or to have worked in the public prosecutor's office, but also to have held the position of president in the district or appellate courts, or of public prosecutor in the Supreme Court for a minimum of three years. When it was decided that the candidate fulfilled the necessary requirements, the process of appointment began. Only after nomination by the administrative collegium, or the minister of justice, who also put forth his candidates, was final approval given by the president of the Republic of Poland.

The reforms which were initiated in 1944 significantly changed this process, with the aim of filling judicial posts with politically reliable judges. The independence of the courts or judicial independence no longer had a place. One of the earliest decrees permitted the transfer of judges to another bench, although this violated one of the basic tenets of judicial independence.[44] In another move, judges were expected to share the bench with lay judges,[45] who were granted the same powers as the professional judge in the civil and criminal courts, without the requirement of a legal education.[46] As a result, decisions were made by a bench of three judges: one professional judge and two lay judges. Lay judges were selected by the predominantly communist-led local council, from among people who were considered 'politically reliable'. Legal and educational qualifications were minimised in place of dedication to the construction of socialism. Special criminal tribunals were created to hear fascist-Nazi criminal cases,[47] and military courts were reformed to hear criminal cases outlined by the then newly created military criminal code.[48] The special criminal tribunals were composed of one judge and two lay judges, who sentenced a large number of persons that had been falsely accused because of their activity in the Polish Home Army.[49] The first

44 *Dekret Polskiego Komitetu Wyzwolenia Narodowego z dnia 4 listopada 1944r. o upwaznieniu tworzenia sadow oraz zmiany ich okregow, a pundit do przenoszenia sedziow na inne miesjsce sluzbowe* [Decree of the Polish Committee for National Liberation from 4 November 1944 Concerning the Authorisation to Create New Courts and to Change Their Jurisdiction, and the Transfer of Judges to Other Benches of Adjudication], *Dziennik Ustaw*, No. 11, item 58.

45 *Dekret Polskiego Komitetu Wyzwolenia Narodowego z dnia 12 wrzesnia 1944r. o specjanych sadach karnych dla spraw zbrodniarzy faszystowsko-hitlerowskich* [Decree of the Polish Committee for National Liberation from 12 September 1944 Concerning Special Criminal Courts for Fascist–Nazi Crimes], *Dziennik Ustaw*, No. 4, item 21.

46 Lay judges replaced the jury. The jury was abolished by law in 1938.

47 *Dziennik Ustaw*, No. 4, item 21; *ibid.*

48 *Dekret Polskiego Komitetu Wyzwolenia Narodowego z dnia 23 wrzesnia 1944r. o prawo o ustroju Sadow Wojskowych i Prokuratura Wojskowej* [Decree of the Polish Committee for National Liberation from 23 September 1944 Concerning the Structure of the Military Courts and the Public Prosecutor for the Military], *Dziennik Ustaw*, No. 6, item 29.

49 See the Decree of 31 August 1944 concerning the Administration of Punishment for Fascist-Nazi Criminals Found Guilty of Crimes and Abuses Against Civilian Persons and Soldiers, and Traitors of the Polish Nation. *Dziennik Ustaw*, No. 4, item 16. Bertrand

special criminal court took place in 1944 in Rzeszow.[50] Judicial officials and the public were frightened. In a letter of 17 December 1944 to Chajn, the Polish public prosecutor Korytkowski wrote:

> The Secret Police [*Urzad Bezpieczenstwa*] work independently in the territory, there is a lack of communication between their activities and my aims, and I continually remain uninformed of their investigations, which eventually arrive at the public prosecution with much resistance and delay. Defendants commonly are detained for weeks at a time by the Secret Police to my knowledge. This situation affects the public and brings out a lack of trust in the courts, creates panic, and the Public Prosecutor's office is left powerless to conduct any further investigations.[51]

Leon Miernik, the leader of the People's Council, a branch of the PKWN, in a letter of 16 December 1944 to the Department of Justice, wrote that

> on the territory of the [Gawroliskiego] administrative district, the Secret Police has set up its offices. This department conducts arrests of citizens without turning them over to the courts, creating a notable fear among the public of being arrested, and further, that during their detention they will not be handled through the proper court channels.[52]

The legal opinions were cautious, but clear; the quasi-judicial activities of the UB were illegal and detrimental to the establishment of a future legitimate legal system. In the opinion of Dr Szuldenfrei, Director of the Legal Bureau of the PKWN: 'I find the activities of the Secret Police illegal and their political status questionable … I consider the political activities [of this department] as unacceptable.'[53]

Russell once observed that certain situations turn people into monsters. In 1989 it was revealed that several distinguished criminal law professors had compromised themselves in the late 1940s, as judges in the special criminal courts which sentenced to death officers who had fought in the Home Army. See Litynski, 'Obraz sadownictwa', *supra* n. 42, pp. 154–55.

50 Future special criminal tribunals were slated to be heard in Cracow. For further details on the case against the 'Nazi criminal', Aleksander Miskow, see 25 November 1944, p. 5, sygn. IX/9a, *PKWN/RS*, Archiwum Akt Nowych, Warsaw, Poland.

51 Letter of 17 December 1944 from J. Korytkowski to L. Chajn, p. 17, sygn. IX/9a, *PKWN/RS*, Archiwum Akt Nowych, Warsaw, Poland.

52 Letter of 16 December 1944 from L. Miernik to the Department of Justice, p. 22, sygn. IX/9a, *PKWN/RS*, Archiwum Akt Nowych, Warsaw, Poland.

53 Communiqué of Dr Szuldenfrei from 14 October 1944, p. 9, sygn. IX/2, *PKWN/RS*, Archiwum Akt Nowych, Warsaw, Poland. See also the public prosecution's complaints against the UB's activities that 'cross ethical standards', Public Prosecutor Joel's List of Activities of the Regional Court of Bialystok in December 1944, 27 January 1945, p. 66, sygn. IX/6, *PKWN/RS*, Archiwum Akt Nowych, Warsaw, Poland.

The pre-war judges who were retained suffered a severe blow, as illustrated by a former Supreme Court justice: 'the Ministry fought fiercely against the pre-war judges. … The situation was greatly ameliorated by help from the Party in breaking down obstacles to getting in new people.'[54] The new candidates, selected from a pool of promising young, politically loyal officers or security force functionaries, were trained in Moscow. Between 1946 and 1952, approximately 400 party-selected candidates completed the special 6–15-month judicial training courses.[55] During this time, the requirements for judgeships were lowered.[56] By 1948, over 800 pre-war judges were dismissed because they were considered politically unreliable.[57] By 1949, the provisions regulating the appointment of judges had been changed and left solely to the minister of justice, with approval from the premier. It was the director of one of these special law schools that sentenced General Fieldorf to death.[58] This was later finalised by the Law of 20 July 1950, which stated that judges were appointed by the president upon nomination by the minister of justice and the premier. This law specified the qualifications of the candidate to be appointed as judge: 'he who (a) swears an oath to uphold the duty as judge in People's Poland, (b) is a Polish citizen, and has full civil and citizen rights, (c) is of excellent character, (d) has completed a law degree with written examinations, and (e) has completed the court training.' The law also allowed the minister of justice to bypass the educational requirements when considering candidates, thus creating a so-called professional judicial pool of individuals lacking a legal education, not very different from their lay judge counterparts on the bench.

A further blow was dealt to the prestige of judges when the profession was equated to that of 'a state and economic worker', who could be transferred or dismissed by the minister of justice if he did not follow the conditions and rules

54 Waclaw Barcikowski, Supreme Court Judge from 1944 and 1956, quoted in Kurczewski, *The Resurrection of Rights in Poland, supra* n. 2, p. 41.

55 Stanislaw Frankowski, 'The Independence of the Judiciary in Poland: Some Reflections on Andrzej Rzeplinski's *Sadownictwo w Polsce Ludowej* [The Judiciary in People's Poland] (1989)', *Arizona Journal of International and Comparative Law*, 8 (1991), pp. 33–52.

56 *Dekret z dnia 8 marca 1945r. o czesciowa zmiana prawa o ustroju sadow powszechnych* [Decree of 8 March 1945 Concerning the Partial Amendment to the Law Concerning the Structure of the Common Courts], *Dziennik Ustaw*, No. 11, item 54.

57 *Ibid.*

58 The first director of the Teodor Duracz Central Law School, Professor Igor Andrejew of the University of Warsaw, who was one of the three judges in the trial, went on to become a leading criminal lawyer and author of many textbooks on the subject. When questioned about the case when the details of his post-war activities were revealed, he remarked that he thought the general was 'some German'. See Marcin Zaborski, 'Szkolenie "sedziow nowego typu" w Polsce Ludowej. Czesc II: Centralna Szkola Prawnicza im. Teodora Duracza i Wyzsza Szkola Prawnicza im. Teodora Duracza' [Training the 'New Type of Judge' in People's Poland. Part II: Teodor Duracz Central Law School and Teodor Duracz Higher School of Law], *Palestra*, 3–4 (1998), pp. 105–10.

set forth in the November Decree. Three months later, judges were stripped of all guarantees of their independence. This occurred with the passage of the Decree of 8 March 1945, which shortened judicial terms in the provincial, appellate and supreme courts. Eventually, judges, public prosecutors and notaries were required to swear an oath before assuming their position. The oath required judicial officials to pledge their allegiance to the new political and economic order.

In a secret letter to the president of the People's Council, Chajn provides a progress report on filling judicial posts:

> In accordance with the Constitution of the Polish People's Republic, our judges, like other judges of the socialist type, fulfil a special function: they stand above the structure of the Polish People's Republic, protecting the working class, promoting order ... Judges ... fully educate the citizen about the spirit of the People's Republic.[59]

Chajn doubted the abilities of the new judicial pool to meet these standards. 'At this stage practice has shown that judges have bent under the influence of the class enemy ... committing acts which carry disciplinary, even criminal consequences.'[60] It was clear that the new regime would remove the last remnants of judicial practice of the pre-war period, and install a new cadre of judges who aligned themselves with the regime.

The Soviet Model: Judges, Public Prosecutors and the Bar

The competing model to Montesquieu's theory of the separation of powers was the Soviet model, which was based on Lenin's theory of the unity of state power. Vyshinsky argued that the 'will of the working people' was the source of power. The separation of powers was unnecessary, as legislature was chosen by the people, and placed no limits on its supreme power. The Communist Party, representing the will of the working class, rose above all state structures, including the legislature. The unity of power justifies the party's supreme role. As a result, the judiciary was another arm of the party apparatus. According to Lenin, courts were really class courts, and had to be told what was expected from them and what they were permitted to do. Vyshinsky took the theory further, and argued that courts must follow party directives, and to do so effectively, judges must be political activists. 'Only the Soviet court, the court of the socialist-worker peasant state, expressing the will of the entire toiling people in the Soviet Union, is truly

---

59 'Przedstawienie Ministra Sprawiedliwosci w przedmiocie sytuacji uposazeniowej sedziow' [The Minister of Justice's Speech Concerning the Situation of the Salaries of Judges], *Ministerstwo Sprawiedliwosci*, 2 May 1953, p. 2, sygn. 25, Archiwum Akt Nowych, Warsaw, Poland.

60 *Ibid.*

independent in the authentic and direct sense of the word.'[61] Stalin's jurist also wrote that the Soviet state could not abstain from violence, state force, or the throttling of dissent, methods necessary to suppress the exploiters of the people and oppressors of all kinds. The process of throttling dissent was brought about by the masses for the education of the masses. The alternative to this was coercion linked with the education of the masses, so that at one time one educates the masses for throttling dissent; at another one throttles dissent in order to educate. In perhaps his most telling statement, Vyshinsky said, 'if the law lags behind life it needs to be changed, or as Comrade Stalin has expressed it, to be put aside.'[62]

The creation of the Soviet-style prosecutorial system, the *Prokuratura*, is also important. The office of public prosecution operated independently of the administration, as did the political police. The office had broad powers, which ranged from supervision of government, the investigation of grievances made by citizens against the administration, and involvement in each stage of the judicial process. According to the 1950 law, the office of public prosecution '(1) was to be a separate branch of state power, including the Council of Ministers; (2) was to be independent from all local administrative bodies; (3) above all, its main function was to supervise the observance of law by the state administrative bodies as well as by citizens.' This was based on the Soviet model, and subsequent amendments to the law on public prosecution did not alter this basic structure. Lenin re-established the institution of the office of public prosecution true to the aims of its founder, Peter the Great, who desired an 'eye of the Tsar' to supervise and control the bureaucracy. Lenin promoted an absolutist institution, whose powers overshadowed those of a judge.

The Polish administration of justice would never again operate as it had during the interwar period. Judges were stripped of guarantees of their independence, and saw their legitimacy and authority gradually destroyed. Of course, the number of pre-war judges was low, and many of the ranks were filled with careerists. Still, Polish judges were faced with a dual dilemma, one which would plague them throughout communist rule: how to protect the rights of the defendant and remain loyal to the party. Judges, in their decision-making, were bound to the principles of Marxism–Leninism and the party directives. They were independent only when they were totally subservient to the party.[63] This requirement of 'double loyalty' is best expressed by Jakub Berman (JB), a former Politburo member under Bierut during 1944–1954, in his interview with the Polish journalist, Teresa Toranska (TT).

---

61 Andrei Vyshinsky, *The Law of the Soviet State* (Westport, CT: Greenwood Press, 1948), p. 514.

62 *Ibid.*

63 For an excellent discussion on this 'Orwellian logic', see Frankowski, 'The Independence of the Judiciary in Poland', *supra* n. 55.

JB: It's certainly true that our courts were not among the best and the problem, in my view, lay not in the trials that took place in the prison grounds, but that judges were, unfortunately, prepared for what to expect from the outset and therefore not always impartial.

TT: Those were the only kind you appointed.

JB: We didn't appoint them; the Soviet advisors did. Judges came from the security apparatus, as in the Soviet Union, because the advisors introduced their own judiciary methods over here, so our judiciary was appointed according to the Soviet model.

TT: Did they also determine sentences?

JB: Sentences were in accordance with the provisions of the criminal code and dependent on the nature and extent of the offence. We intervened only in the most serious and vital cases; for the rest penal procedure was normal.

TT: Mr. Berman!

JB: I agree, those weren't normal courts and the judges were not among the most discriminating, but you must understand that these judges also wanted conscientiously to fulfill their duties to the Party, which was the necessity of state imposed upon them. You know how it is, surely. Sometimes the interest of the individual has to be subordinated to the interest of the state, and when the state is threatened suspicions are magnified in order to render them more plausible. I don't deny that a number of sentences were incorrect, and perhaps if they had been passed by different judges we would have avoided many mistakes. But then, it wasn't all that easy to find judges who would be able at the same time to retain both their loyalty to us and their loyalty to the accused, which is essential in order to pass a just sentence.[64]

As regards the Polish Bar, it was in a struggle with the government shortly after the war, fighting to retain its pre-war autonomous position and the basic freedoms of the profession. But this was not to be realised, as the Decree of 24 May 1945 abolished the self-government of the Bar, prescribing that Bar Councils and disciplinary committees were to be appointed by the minister of justice, who also determined the number of members. As mentioned above with regard to the judiciary, members were checked to see whether they had behaved well during the

64 Teresa Toranska, *'Them': Stalin's Polish Puppets* (New York: Harper & Row, 1987), pp. 330–31. The Polish edition was cited in *supra* n. 42, as it contains more interviews (such as the one with Chajn).

German occupation and 'were worthy of belonging to the profession'.[65] Special commissions, comprising the minister of justice and representatives of the Court of Appeal and the Bar Council, were in charge of admissions. Because the Decree of 22 January 1946[66] authorised the minister to appoint as judges and public prosecutors people with no legal education, who were deemed to be qualified by their scholarly, professional, social or political activities, and were relieved of the three-year apprenticeship at the courts and the obligatory exam, he was also obliged to relieve from apprenticeship at the courts and with a practising lawyer, persons who had obtained a legal education at a Polish university and were ready to practise law based on their professional activities. As a result, the professional standing of both the bench and the Bar were significantly lowered.

In 1950, the Polish Bar was reorganised by the promulgation of the law of 27 June 1950,[67] which declared the Bar to be a 'people's democratic' institution, whose task it was 'to cooperate with the courts and other authorities for the protection of the legal system of the People's Poland and to render legal assistance in accordance with the law and with the interests of the working masses'.[68] The minister of justice was permitted to waive the requirements of a law degree, practice, or Bar examination, but the requirement of loyalty was absolute. The attorney admitted to the Bar was required to pledge an oath that 'with all his powers [he would] contribute in his work to the protection and strengthening of the People's State legality', and was not allowed to render any legal aid which was 'incompatible with the general interests of the socialized economy'.[69] Attorneys were required to keep thorough records of cases and services performed, and were monitored by the body overseeing the Bar, namely the Main Bar Council, which was concerned not only with their professional and ethical qualities, but also with their ability to adhere to the 'social' point of view. Attorneys who violated these provisions were subject to disciplinary action.

---

65 Zygmunt Nagorski, Sr, 'The Legislation of the Polish People's Republic 1958–1959: A Survey', in *Studies in Polish Law*, ed. by Kazimierz Grzybowski *et al.*, Law in Eastern Europe Series, No. 6 (Leyden: A.W. Sijthoff, 1962), p. 87.

66 *Dekret z dnia 22 stycznia 1946r. o wyjatkowym dopuszczaniu do obejmowania stanowisk sedziowskich, prokuratorskich i notarialnych oraz do wpisywania na liste adwokatow* [Decree of 22 January 1946 Concerning Extraordinary Circumstances That Would Permit Assuming the Position of a Judge, Public Prosecutor, and Notary Public, and Registering on the List of the Bar], *Dziennik Ustaw*, No. 4, item 33.

67 *Ustawa z dnia 27 czerwca 1950r. o ustroju adwokatury* [Law from 27 June 1950 Concerning the Bar], *Dziennik Ustaw*, No. 30, item 275. See also codified text, *Dziennik Ustaw*, No. 13, item 74.

68 Peter Siekanowicz, 'Poland', in *Government, Law and Courts in the Soviet Union and Eastern Europe*, ed. by Vladimir Gsovski and Kazimierz Grzybowski (London: Stevens & Stevens, 1959), p. 771.

69 *Ibid.*

Latter amendments further consolidated the hold of the authorities over the Bar.[70] The Main Bar Council resisted the new legislation, in particular the power of the minister of justice to appoint judges as members of a temporary Bar Council in case a Bar Council was dissolved. The Main Bar Council also opposed the power of the minister to determine the locality of where a lawyer might practise and to make the admission of former judges and public prosecutors dependent on the minister's consent. The Bar's complaints were not considered, despite having the minister of justice present their case at a plenary session of the Main Bar Council in 1958. Once again, the government 'forced its point of view through the communist dominated *Sejm*'.[71]

It is difficult to generalise about Polish judges. There were good and honest Polish lawyers during the communist rule who, where they could, worked around the law to see that what they felt was justice was rendered. What this indicates is that judges, despite the indoctrination they underwent (albeit less so after the 'thaw'), had a sense of judicial independence and what constituted a fair trial where the rights of the defendant were protected. Perhaps we can extrapolate that the rule of law worked at some informal level. This was certainly the case under martial law. Yet the rule of law did not exist under communist rule for the simple reason that the law was not clear or predictable; the administration was at all times was subordinated to the party.

After Stalin's death in 1954, the Polish judiciary underwent substantial changes, the most notable being the acknowledgement by the Polish authorities that abuses of the law had occurred. Some criticisms went as far as stating that the principles of judicial independence had been violated.[72] The 'thaw' continued until 1968; but, although the terror and brutality were over, the judiciary was kept in a subservient position by much more refined methods.

Because all normative acts were treated as statutes, the courts were subordinated to the executive, as this branch would promulgate generally binding rules. The judiciary yielded because, as discussed above, they were never granted the power to check the executive. Even in a specific case, the court refused to assess whether the statute presented to them was one in fact; the notion of judicial review was non-existent. All court decisions, including the judgments of the Supreme Court, could be overturned by the extraordinary appeal of the Council of State. Article 62 of the 1952 Polish Constitution provided that judges were independent and subject only to the law, but this was interpreted as prohibiting them from ruling on the

70 The codified text, which includes the amendments to the Law of 27 June 1950, is found in *Dziennik Ustaw*, No. 8, item 41.

71 Nagorski, Sr, 'The Legislation of the Polish People's Republic', *supra* n. 65, p. 90.

72 For an editorial comment, see *Panstwo i Prawo* [State and Law], 3 (1955), p. 369 and also Gustaw Auscaler and Wiktor Suchecki, 'Po XX Zjezdzie KPZR' [After the 20th Plenum of the Communist Party of the Soviet Union], *Panstwo i Prawo*, 4 (1956), pp. ii–v.

constitutionality of statutes. As concerns the Polish citizens' view of the protection of their rights against the state, very few persons perceived the public prosecutor (with whom the power was vested) as a state official ready to defend their rights.[73] Even in the case of the administrative courts (to use this example) which were created to hear disputes between the citizen and a state organ, the administrative procedure left much to be desired. The public prosecutors, who were appointed to act as the sole guardians of the 'socialist rule of law', could not act upon this role in the true sense. As aptly noted by Nagorski, the administrative courts were

> a *conditio sine qua non* of any State based on the rule of law, and of a socialist State in particular … Lenin expressed the opinion (in a letter to Stalin of the 22nd May, 1922) that a public prosecutor who opposes an administrative decision on the grounds of its illegality, should have the right to bring the case before a court of law, but that the Central Committee of the Communist Party changed this plan by giving the [public prosecutor] the right to bring the matter before the government, which is something different.[74]

Polish jurists observed that the aforementioned case applied to Poland as well, as Article 46 of the 1952 Polish Constitution empowered courts to administer justice. Thus the administrative decision also belonged to the area of administering justice; otherwise, rules which were not protected by the court could not be considered rules of law. Moreover, if judicial control did not extend to administrative acts, there could be no real development of administrative law. Therefore, 'we cannot teach the officials of administrative organs the necessity to observe the rule of law only by proclaiming *urbi et orbi* this necessity.'[75] In short, the rule of law, whether in the field of public administration or all related fields of law, can be safeguarded only if the final word in deciding the rights and the duties of citizens belongs to independent courts of law.

This investigation of Soviet communism is key in understanding the socialist experiment not only in Poland but also in CEE states. It reveals the political culture

---

73 See Stanislaw Frankowski, 'The Procuracy and the Regular Courts as the Palladium of Individual Rights and Liberties – The Case of Poland', *Tulane Law Review*, 61 (1987), pp. 1307–38. For an in-depth look at the concept of 'judge-made' law in terms of necessary defence, see William E. Butler, 'Necessary Defense, Judge-Made Law, and Soviet Man', in *Law After Revolution*, ed. by William E. Butler *et al.* (New York: Oceana Publications, 1988), pp. 99–130.

74 Bronislaw Helczynski, 'The Polish Code of Administrative Procedure' in *Studies in Polish Law*, ed. by Kazimierz Grzybowski *et al.*, Law in Eastern Europe Series, No. 6 (Leyden: A. W. Sijthoff, 1962), pp. 74–75. See also, *inter alia*, Donald D. Barry, 'Administrative Justice: The Role of Soviet Courts in Controlling Administrative Acts', in *Soviet Administrative Law: Theory and Policy*, ed. by G. Ginsburgs *et al.* (Dordrecht: Nijhoff, 1989), pp. 63–83.

75 Professor Emanuel Iserzon, one of the drafters of the Administrative Code, quoted in Helczynski, 'The Polish Code', *supra n. 74*, p. 75.

that was imposed in CEE states 'based on fear, suspicion, problematic legitimacy, spurious internationalism, populist manipulation of national symbols, unabashed personalization of power, and persecution mania'.[76] This political culture might lead us to the conclusion that socialism resulted in a huge, unmanageable bureaucratic regime, and this is not entirely incorrect. An important part of the puzzle rests with society, and the desire to reclaim society and its autonomy.[77] Hannah Arendt aptly noted that 'obedience to a movement that carries people away is not enough to explain the regulation of human conduct.'[78] Arendt, in discussing the source of authority in totalitarian regimes, argues that in going to the sources of law one discovers that communist politics were guided by fiction.[79] In this situation, laws respond to the perpetual movement of human affairs, creating a new start and division that seems to indicate the evolution of the order of the beginning and the order of permanence. In his work, Castoriadis understood history and society to be inclusive and not comprehensible without each other. He observes that the

> social-historical is the anonymous collective, the impersonal-human element that fills every given social formation but which also encompasses it, setting each society in the midst of others, inscribing them all within a continuity in which those who are no longer, those who are elsewhere, and even those yet to be born are in a certain sense present. It is, on the one hand, given structures, 'materialized' institutions and works, whether these be material or not; and, on the other hand, *that which* structures, institutes, materializes.[80]

For some, the reign of terror that characterised the Soviet legal regime (notably the quasi-judicial bodies) was a mix of violence and formalism.[81] The notorious Article 58 of the Soviet penal code was not simply a new measure of terror. In fact, it was essential to a social order, in which officials operated within a particular legal framework. According to this model, societal order was very much affected by the way guilt was constructed, so that 'conduct, arguments made in private, writings, and modes of communication were not neutral. Accordingly, one could conclude that every person became a potentially guilty party, for the *boundary between the legal and the illegal was never guaranteed.*'[82] The administration

---

76 Vladimir Tismaneanu, *Stalinism for All Seasons: A Political History of Romanian Communism* (Berkeley, CA: University of California Press, 2003), p. 5.

77 Cornelius Castoriadis, *Philosophy, Politics, Autonomy: Essays in Political Philosophy* (Oxford: Oxford University Press, 1991).

78 See Claude Lefort, *Complications: Communism and the Dilemmas of Democracy*, trans. by J. Bourg (New York: Columbia University Press, 2007), p. 148.

79 *Ibid.*, p. 151.

80 Cornelius Castoriadis, 'Marxism and Revolutionary Theory (1964–1965): Excerpts', in *The Castoriadis Reader*, ed. and trans. by David Ames Curtis (Oxford: Blackwell, 1997), p. 184.

81 Lefort, *Complications*, *supra* n. 78, p. 151.

82 Emphasis added. *Ibid.*, p. 163.

of justice has more meaning than the semblance of procedures. In a totalitarian regime, everything is likely to fall under the law, making the process of producing enemies simple. This also meant that the relationship between the accused and official was unique in that their positions could easily be reversed; we could argue that the law was perverted, but this did not mean it was personal. This is, however, further explained by Arendt's recognition of 'a tyranny of logic' that reflected the nature and propelled the regime – underlying this was a party to which everyone was fettered. Lefort is right when claiming that 'one must always return to the interweaving [*intrication*] of power, law, and knowledge in the party.'[83] Further, the party is the 'concretion of the social, the motor element of the exclusion of plurality and division. One can no more delimit what depends on ideology than one can delimit what depends on law.'[84]

The Demise of Communism

When the independent trade union movement of *Solidarnosc* (Solidarity) emerged in Poland in 1980, the prognosis for change in East–West relations was not encouraging. To recap, the strikes that began in the Gdansk shipyard in the summer of that year were caused by the increase in food prices. In fact, they were no different from the 1970 and 1976 strikes, yet this Polish workers' movement went far beyond the traditional union concerns. The support of both the Catholic Church and the majority of the peasantry provided the momentum the movement needed to obtain nationwide support from persons of all classes. Although the roots of the movement were in the revisionist movement which began in the late 1950s, it was not until the mid-1970s that it cared to champion these interests in public. The charge of Polish academics against the 'all-powerful bureaucracy' that the Polish model of socialism had evolved into resulted in the arrest and imprisonment of several academics and the expulsion of numerous others from the party in the 1960s. An analysis of the events of this period reveal that they were indeed unique, showing the ongoing discussion about socialism and the distinction which had evolved between true Marxism and pseudo-Marxism after some 20 years of the Polish 'experiment'. It was a time when Marxists, particularly university students, examined the country's experience with socialism; hardly finding any positive development, they created the movement of 'socialism with a human face'. Leszek Kolakowski, a revisionist Marxist philosopher, was perhaps one of the best-known critics of the regime.[85]

A series of initiatives assisted in bridging the traditional gap between the intellectual dissent of relatively isolated individuals and the workers' protests with their mass potential. One of the other key factors was the willingness of Polish

83 *Ibid.*, p. 171.

84 *Ibid.*

85 See his critical *Toward a Marxist Humanism: Essays on the Left Today* (New York: Grove Press, 1968).

intellectuals to overcome traditional anti-clerical tendencies and work with the Catholic Church, at least on practical issues. According to Garton Ash, 'Catholic and non-Catholic intellectuals found more and more common ground in the defence of common values, common sense and basic rights.'[86] The notion of self-defence, as in defending the people against the violence and transgressions of the state, became one of the unifying principles of action. Poles, being extremely religious, were also unified through the Church. For all the party's efforts, communism failed in creating a modern, secular society. The Church, historically, has been a popular organisation in Poland and extremely strong, serving as a haven for the Polish nation during times of occupation and repression. The relationship was further strengthened in 1978 with the election of Cardinal Karol Wojtyla, the Archbishop of Cracow, as Pope John Paul II. At this time, the coalition of workers, intellectuals and priests supplied the potential of mass protest with intellectual direction and moral authority. Economic mismanagement was the primary reason for the strike, but the ever-present anti-Russian sentiments and notions of romantic nationalism and patriotism provided a sense of national pride, endowing the Solidarity movement with a spiritual and moral aspect.

In view of the experience of several major strikes (1956, 1970, 1976), in addition to the well-known consequences of the Hungarian Revolution of 1956[87] and the 'Prague Spring' of 1968, the idea of overthrowing the regime was out of the question. At the same time, the movement dismissed the notion that the Polish Communist Party was able to reform communism. Evidence of Solidarity's success can be found in the following fact: what began as a strike in Gdansk evolved into an independent organisation of 10 million members, comprising one-third of the population.[88] One-third of the Communist Party's 3 million members were also members of Solidarity, and there was at least one member in the Politburo. Even some 40,000 of the 150,000-person police force were members. Solidarity pursued a strategy of 'self-limiting revolution', based on non-violence and constraint in order to win concessions from the party.[89] With time, the organisation increased the scope of its autonomous activities, and the Soviet authorities and other communist regimes became aware of the danger that the movement could spread.

As Solidarity's demands increased, the movement grew with it. The notion of 'self-defence' crystallised into the notion of 'self-management', whose premise

---

86 Timothy Garton Ash, *The Polish Revolution: Solidarity* (New York: Vintage, 1985), p. 21.

87 For an excellent account of the Hungarian Revolution of 1956, see Gyorgy Litvan, *The Hungarian Revolution of 1956: Reform, Revolt and Repression 1953–1963*, ed. and trans. by Janos M. Bak and Lyman H. Legters (New York: Longman, 1996).

88 For a poignant account of one man's participation in Solidarity during his youth, see Radek Sikorski, *The Polish House: An Intimate History of Poland* (London: Routledge, 1997).

89 Neal Ascherson, *The Polish August: The Self-Limiting Revolution* (New York: Penguin, 1989).

was that if Poland was indeed a workers' state as maintained by the communists, then the workers should begin to demand real rights from the Communist Party. Solidarity thus totally undermined the legitimacy of the Polish Communist Party. Its tactics were based on the idea that the state could not be reformed, but that society could. 'The government must realize that the institutionalization of conflict and compromise is the only way to base public life on the principle of social accord.'[90] This message gained Solidarity popularity all over the world. In the West, the movement was recognised by both sides of the political spectrum because everyone could find something in its programme with which they could identify. Writing from prison, Michnik argued:

> [T]he truth is that this country cannot be ruled without an agreement with the people [...] that by becoming [a] better organized, more efficient, more prosperous society that enriches Europe and the rest of the world with new values and cherishes tolerance and humanism, we will move to independence and democracy.[91]

Solidarity successfully deepened the economic crisis by its actions and challenged the party rule overtly in autumn 1981. While it is not within the scope of this chapter to provide a detailed analysis of the movement, it must be pointed out that the Communist Party did effectively lose control while Solidarity, despite its momentum and political, economic and social agenda, was not prepared to assume power, for tactical and practical reasons. On 13 December 1981, its momentum was cut short by the government when General Wojciech Jaruzelski proclaimed national emergency and martial law and at the same time assumed the positions of party secretary and prime minister. Martial law was called a necessity, a 'lesser evil' (as Jaruzelski would later argue) to save the country from Soviet invasion, the consequences of which, most Poles agreed, would have been catastrophic.[92] As the Constitution did not allow for emergency powers, to be granted to the prime minister, Jaruzelski had to impose martial law. The question of whether the general's action was constitutional was raised in 1992, and this will be the subject of discussion in the next chapter. The general public feeling about Jaruzelski

90 Adam Michnik, *Letters from Prison and Other Essays*, trans. by Maya Latynski (Berkeley, CA: University of California Press, 1985), p. 105.

91 *Ibid*., p. 107.

92 Michnik notes that Popieluszko 'personified the connection between Church and Solidarity', 'Letter from the Gdansk Prison', *New York Review of Books*, 32 (18 July 1985), at http://www.nybooks.com/articles/5402 (accessed 7 May 2008). For a general overview of events, see Tina Rosenberg, *The Haunted Land: Facing Europe's Ghosts After Communism* (New York: Vintage, 1996), pp. 125–258. For Jaruzelski's point of view, see Wojciech Jaruzelski, *Les chaînes et le refuge* [The Chains and the Refuge] (Paris: Editions Jean-Claude Lattes, 1992) and *Stan Wojenny: Dlaczego* [Martial Law: Why] (Warsaw: BGW, 1992).

has changed since 1981 from disdain to acceptance (some even hailing him as a patriot).

The Jaruzelski government detained thousands of activists, putting them in internment camps and banning Solidarity and its various sub-organisations. Most of the detainees were top leaders of Solidarity:[93] the list, prepared some months previously, contained not only their names, but also those of influential artists (such as the film director Andrzej Wajda). It is difficult to say whether Poles would have had a worse fate under the Soviets; the answer is most likely yes. While most agree that the number of casualties would have been much higher, and the tactics much more violent if the Soviets had intervened, about 100 lives were lost under Jaruzelski's martial law, through the security forces' repression of protests, through the actions of agents of the Ministry of Internal Affairs, or as a result of other causes.[94] The activists who remained in so-called freedom used civil disobedience to fight back; a million Poles returned their party cards.

The worst violence took place in December at the Wujek coal mine in Katowice when miners called a sit-in strike. Approximately 2,000 miners barricaded themselves inside, armed with petrol bombs, truncheons, dynamite and spears, threatening to blow themselves up should the government use force against them. In response, the riot police (ZOMO) arrived with 40 tanks. The police blocked off the entrance to the mine and fired rubber bullets at the strikers. The chaos escalated as the crowds retaliated, attacking the police. The ZOMO attacked persons who attempted to help the injured, including civilian doctors and ambulance drivers. By the time the violence subsided, nine protesters and four ZOMO had been killed; 41 people were wounded.

The events at the Wujek mine continue to be controversial. In May 2007, a district court in Katowice found 15 communist-era police officers guilty of firing on striking coal miners in 1981. Commander Romuald Cieslak was sentenced to 11 years in prison; 14 officers under his command received sentences of from two and one-half to three years. In a separate but related case against the communist-era general Czeslaw Kiszczak, who was accused of ordering the militia to open fire on the striking Wujek miners, Kiszczak pleaded not guilty to the charge. On 10 January, former General Wojciech Jaruzelski testified in Kiszczak's favour, stating that the latter had categorically prohibited the use of weapons to break up the strike. In February the court suspended proceedings due to Kiszczak's poor health.

Martial law also claimed Father Jerzy Popieluszko, who achieved near-cult status in Poland. The priest attracted many followers with his powerful sermons. On 20 October 1984, he did not appear for morning mass. Later that afternoon, his driver appeared and described to astonished listeners how he and Father

---

93 The conditions of detention varied greatly: some detainees were held in what could be considered self-contained apartments, and others in crowded, cold cells.

94 Human and Citizens' Rights in the Polish People's Republic (1 January–31 December 1989), Report No. 7, prepared by the Helsinki Committee in Poland (Vienna: International Helsinki Federation for Human Rights, 1989).

Popieluszko had been kidnapped by three men. The priest had been beaten, bound and forced into the boot of a car. Three policemen and their superior were soon arrested. Under pressure, one of the policemen confessed, and the priest's body was fished out of a reservoir. The four defendants received sentences ranging from 14 to 25 years. The Jaruzelski regime used the death as another argument for the imposition of martial law. When no higher officials were tried for the crime, there was speculation of a cover-up by the hard-liners, or even the KGB.

Protests from the West were loud but ineffectual, and Poles were disappointed when heads of state, such as West German Chancellor Helmut Schmidt, denounced the movement for its recklessness, calling the imposition of martial law necessary.[95] When a 400 per cent food and energy price increase was announced in February 1982, there were no protests. People went back to work and resumed what they could of a seemingly normal life. On 8 October 1982, the government officially disbanded Solidarity; it appeared that the 'self-limiting revolution' had failed and that the war on civil society had been successful.

When martial law was lifted on 22 July 1983, it was not clear whether the government had achieved its aims. True, the regime had managed to eradicate Solidarity, but not the movement of ideas and action it had set in motion. These ideas and plans for action sought to permeate communist structures with independent democratic organisations and thus transform it into some kind of democracy. In other words, socialism was equated with 'really existing socialism', namely communism, and rejected.

As regards the government, it was just as moribund as before the implementation of martial law, incapable of doing anything. The generous aid that the country had received from the West ceased once martial law was declared. The United States, for example, opposed and effectively blocked Poland's application to the International Monetary Fund. The Soviet Union, dealing with its own economic problems, no longer wanted Polish products. By 1987, Poland's debt had reached US$40bn, and more than 60 per cent of Poles were living below the poverty level.

In 1987, Jaruzelski carried out a referendum, asking Poles to vote on a 100 per cent price increase in exchange for a notable democratisation of political life; the result forced the government to acknowledge its own unpopularity. In an effort to keep control, Jaruzelski revived Solidarity and embarked on economic reform. By 1987, several things had become apparent. First, Solidarity had changed since 1980, and its leaders, finding themselves free in 1987, were different persons with opposing views. Second, the Communist Party had also changed, no longer being subservient to Moscow. Despite the fact that Jaruzelski had reformed political and legal institutions, namely introducing a Constitutional Tribunal and a Commissioner for the Protection of Citizens' Rights, as well as increasing

95 In general, the West also considered martial law the lesser of two evils. The US government was aware of the growing Soviet pressure and the plans for martial law from Ryszard Kuklinski, deputy to General Jaruzelski, who turned informer. For details, see Rosenberg, *The Haunted Land*, *supra* n. 92.

the universities' autonomy, his rule did not gain popularity owing to the dismal economic situation at the time.

The time for cooperation finally arrived in 1989. Fifty-five delegates, 29 from the party and 26 from Solidarity, including several Church delegates, gathered at Magdelenka (outside Warsaw) to hold *Porozumienie Okraglego Stolu* (Round Table Talks). The talks lasted for two months and ended on 5 April with an agreement for semi-elections in June. They were marked by a spirit of conciliation, which was, of course, not viewed in that way by everyone; accusations of 'selling out' to the communists were also prevalent. It must be recalled, however, that in April 1989 a non-communist Poland was still out of the question. The Berlin Wall and the Soviet Union were intact and seemingly indestructible. The power-sharing agreement was the best that Solidarity could hope for. The main points of contention, such as prosecution and a screening law, will be discussed later.

The 1989 elections gave Solidarity control over the Senate and allowed the *Sejm* to remain under communist control. The *Sejm* elected Jaruzelski president, and appointed Tadeusz Mazowiecki, a Catholic activist of Solidarity, prime minister (after Jaruzelski's initial appointee, General Czeslaw Kiszczak, interior minister under Jaruzelski, admitted to having too few votes). After Walesa demanded free elections, Jaruzelski resigned, with what many Poles regarded as the utmost dignity.

Conclusions

The years 1947–48 were a crucial period in the CEE. Some states, such as Poland, turned from their more moderate political and economic programmes to the Stalinist models. The retreat from milder policies was universal, following Tito's defection and Stalin's fear of something similar elsewhere. The Cold War and Germany's integration in the West contributed. Attempts to escape the straitjacket, as in Hungary in 1956 and Czechoslovakia in 1968, were brutally suppressed. This would mark the start of one of the darkest periods of CEE post-war history. The expulsion of Yugoslavia from the Cominform and the looming presence of the United States (and its Marshall Plan) forced the Soviet Union to terrify the people's democracies into servility. The creation of the Council for Mutual Economic Assistance signified to the West the unity of the Soviet satellite states. The Stalinist model applied to the respective economic systems. Despite ambitious planning, the nature of the command economy resulted in falsified reports showing that unrealistic targets had been reached. Later, well after Stalin's death and into the Stakhanovite period, the command economy would come to symbolise stagnation and decay. The Stalinist model meant severe repression and terror. As seen in the case of Poland, Poles were under constant surveillance at work, and in almost all areas of daily life. The Catholic Church was not exempt from the terror. During this period, many priests were arrested for supposed intelligence activities and put on trial. The house arrest of the popular Primate of Poland, Archbishop Stefan

Wyszynski, was clearly meant to undermine public morale. This constant watch over one's life was conducted by the secret police (UB), in a relentless, ruthless manner. *This organisation of secret police played a vital role in firmly establishing the totalitarian state.*

The administration of justice was reorganised according to Soviet lines. Soviet authorities undertook this task in 1944 by passing a series of decrees aimed at reorganising the administration of justice. These measurements permitted authorities to replace the pre-war cadre of judges with Soviet-trained judges who would follow instructions without question. In Poland, under the leadership of Chajn, the idea was promoted that all judicial personnel had to be screened carefully for the newly created courts. In essence, Chajn instigated a 'war against the judiciary'; this was not completed without problems, but it ensured that the authorities had control over the administration of justice.

Any chance for the establishment of the rule of law was finally dispelled with the promulgation of the Polish Constitution of 1952. The Constitution renamed the Republic the Polish People's Republic, and it was modelled on the 1936 Soviet Constitution. In both documents, one can find a catalogue of provisions concerning political rights and civil liberties to be guaranteed as long as they were not used against the will of the people or, in other words, the state. The 1952 Constitution established that working-class interests were represented by the party. Under communist rule, there was no conflict between the state and the citizen, and it subordinated the Constitution to politics. The notion of the division of powers or the separation of powers was non-existent, but only suppression and arbitrary rule were applied. All aspects of Poland's former constitutional history were absent from this regime.

The declaration of martial law in 1981 may have temporarily cut the movement short, but the failure of the command economy could no longer be ignored, nor could calls for legal reform. These demands led to the creation of the Constitutional Tribunal and the Office of the Commissioner for the Protection of Citizen's Rights, which some argue may have been windowdressing. Nonetheless, both have evolved into groundbreaking institutions and have served as models for other CEE countries.

The events following the Second World War with regard to constitutional developments in Europe are significant. Many countries decided to build new forms of government based on civil libertarian and democratic principles; in short, these countries were seeking to establish constitutional justice in response to the experience of unchecked state power.[96] Constitutional justice, by Cappelletti's definition, suggests the adoption of new kinds of constitutional norms, institutions and processes which limit and control political power.[97]

---

96 Mauro Cappelletti, *The Judicial Process in Comparative Perspective* (Oxford: Clarendon Press, 1989), Chapter 5.

97 *Ibid.*

Socialist legal theorists argued that 'the legislature is conceived to be the supreme expression of the will of people and beyond the reach of judicial restraint'.[98] There was no separation of powers or equal balance between powers. The legislature was recognised as the supreme power, and it was assumed that the legislative body was responsible for maintaining the constitutionality of state actions and that judicial review was reserved for internal legislative organs, such as the Presidium of the Supreme Soviet of the (former) Soviet Union or the Council of State in Poland. As concerns constitutional power, the socialist documents had a 'descriptive' rather than a 'prescriptive' role, whereby they had supreme legal force and all laws and acts of state bodies were promulgated on the basis of and in conformity with them.[99]

It is worth reiterating that socialist theory allowed citizens who believed that their constitutional rights had been violated to file a complaint with the executive branch supervising the office blamed for the violation or with the public prosecutor.[100] While this led to some satisfactory results, it should not suggest that courts were permitted to question all matters, such as those of a serious political nature.[101] Overall, however, socialist theorists argued against judicial review, following Vyshinsky's line on the subject:

> Every sort of statute (in bourgeois countries) is considered as having force until it occurs to some private person or capitalist enterprise to file a petition to have it, or a separate paragraph of it, declared unconstitutional. Naturally this right is broadly used by monopolist cliques of exploiters to obtain a declaration of 'unconstitutionality' as to laws running counter to their interests.[102]

In Poland, judicial review was also criticised as bourgeois by the country's leading socialist theorist:

> The constitutional control of statutes by extra-parliamentary bodies, particularly judicial and quasi-judicial, is a reactionary institution and because of that, there is no room for it either in a socialist state or in a state of people's democracy, which trusts people's justice and the will of the people.[103]

---

98 J. N. Hazard, W. E. Butler and P. B. Maggs, *The Soviet Legal System: The Law in the 1980s* (New York: Oceana Publications, 1984), p. 320.

99 See Mauro Cappelletti, *Judicial Review in the Contemporary World* (Indianapolis, IN: Bobbs-Merrill Company, 1971).

100 See, for example, Helczynski, 'The Polish Code of Administrative Procedure', *supra* n. 74, pp. 38–77. For the East German viewpoint, see Inga Markovits, 'Pursuing One's Rights Under Socialism', *Stanford Law Review*, 38 (1986), pp. 689–761.

101 R. Ludwikowski, 'Judicial Review in the Socialist Legal System: Current Developments', *International and Comparative Law Quarterly*, 37 (1988), pp. 89–108.

102 Vyshinsky, *The Law of the State*, *supra* n. 61, pp. 339–40.

103 Stefan Rozmaryn, 'Kontrola sprawiedliwosci ustaw' [Control of Judicial Review], *Panstwo i Prawo*, 11 (1946), pp. 36–60, and 'Kontrola sprawiedliwosci ustaw

This line of thought prevailed throughout 45 years of communist rule. While the question of judicial review was raised during periods of political relaxation,[104] these efforts were met with resistance by the majority of scholars. It was not until the mid-1970s that there was a small, but notable, breakthrough, which can be viewed as the precursor of the establishment of the Constitutional Tribunal. In February 1976, a constitutional amendment (Article 30) was passed which imposed on the Council of State the duty to 'see to the law's conformity with the Constitution'.[105] Most scholars could not agree on the meaning of the provision and whether the use of 'to see' indeed meant that there could be no law unless it was consistent with the Constitution.[106] Their caution may have reflected their fear of government retaliation should this point be pressed. The provision was in fact mere 'window dressing', but it did reflect the mood of legal scholars who were increasingly in favour of setting up a constitutional tribunal and implementing judicial review, at least in a form consistent with the ideology of the period.[107] Thus, despite being steeped in this ideology, Polish jurists were aware, or arguably had some notion, of the rule of law along more established democratic models.

(Dokonczenie)' [Control of Judicial Review (Conclusion)], *Panstwo i Prawo*, 12 (1946), pp. 3–20.

104 Feliks Siemienski was one of the scholars who advocated judicial review. See *Organy przedstawicielskie w systemie organow panstwa socjalistycznego* [Representative Bodies in the System of the Agencies of the Socialist State] (Lublin: Uniwersytet Maria Curie-Sklodowska, 1964). A similar move was made in the Soviet Union in the mid-1970s, but the concept of a socialist rule-of-law state was viewed as bourgeois and was rejected. For further details, see W. E. Butler, 'Perestroika and the Rule of Law', in *Perestroika and the Rule of Law: Anglo-American and Soviet Perspectives*, ed. by W. E. Butler (London: I. B. Tauris, 1991), pp. 7–21. See also R. R. Ludwikowski, 'Soviet Constitutional Changes of the Glastnost Era: A Historical Perspective', *New York Law School Journal of International and Comparative Law*, 10 (1989), pp. 119–50.

105 *Ustawa z dnia 10 lutego 1976r. o zmianie Konstytucji Polskiej Rzeczpospilitej Ludowej* [Law of 10 February 1976 Concernning Amendments to the Constitution of the Polish People's Republic], *Dziennik Ustaw*, No. 5, item 29.

106 See, for example, Andrzej Gwizdz, 'Trybunal Konstytucyjny' [The Constitutional Tribunal], *Panstwo i Prawo*, 12 (1983), pp. 3–15 and Kazimierz Dzialocha and Stanislaw Pawela, 'Zmiany zakresu wlasciwosci Trybunalu Konstytucyjnego de lege lata i de lege referenda' [The Changes of the Constitutional Tribunal in the Current and Future Law], *Panstwo i Prawo*, 11 (1989), pp. 3–17.

107 Zdzislaw Czeszejko-Sochacki, 'The Origins of Constitutional Review', *Saint Louis-Warsaw Transatlantic Law Journal* (1996), pp. 15–31.

Chapter 5
Rule of Law Revisited?

> I began to criticize Polish reality as I became aware that official ideas clashed with everyday practice. I quickly came to the conclusion that the revolution had been betrayed, socialism's ideas were being neglected, and that political and social democracy existed only on paper.[1]

> If you want to know how a country is doing, you need to look at the oldest people and at the youngest.[2]

Establishing a Rule-of-Law State

General Overview

The previous chapter considered developments which led to the collapse of the Polish communist state. Towards the end of communist rule, certain laws were amended to accommodate different types of economic relationships and to attract foreign investment, demonstrating a radical, clear move away from the principles of the centrally planned economy and, significantly, serving to displace the communist elites.[3] The era of popular justice also saw the emergence of thinking about rights that developed despite attempts to limit and control it. Thus, the discussion of present-day developments is strongly linked to an understanding of this experience. A seemingly bold step accompanied these changes as General Jaruzelski set out to create what would be two significant legal institutions, namely, the Constitutional Tribunal and the Commissioner for the Protection of Citizens' Rights (Ombudsman).[4]

What do these changes have to say about the law? What does the law have to say about these changes? A lawyer's typical concerns are with the abnormalities in life, rather than the normalities.[5] As has been shown, the law has a far wider scope than the norms created and applied by institutions. So the lawyer will understand

---

1 Adam Michnik, *Letters from Prison and Other Essays*, trans. by Maya Latynski (Berkeley, CA: University of California Press, 1985), p. 203.

2 Geert Mak, *In Europe: Travels Through the Twentieth Century* (London: Harvill Secker, 2007), p. 583.

3 Maria Los and Andrzej Zybertowicz, *Privatizing the Police-State: The Case of Poland* (Basingstoke: Macmillan, 2000).

4 Interview with General Wojciech Jaruzelski, 10 November 1993, Warsaw, Poland.

5 Roger Cotterrell, *The Sociology of Law: An Introduction* (London: Butterworths, 1992), p. 27.

that to embark on constitutional reform in a state emerging from totalitarianism means an attempt at achieving the 'Holy Grail' in the form of the rule of law. On the way, there might be some surprises and controversies as to what and whom the rule of law protects and serves; judges hold the key. An examination of the work of lawyers and the role of intellectuals reveals that during the pre-war period, as well as under communist rule, these groups played a vital role in setting up the Polish democratic state. 'Pockets of democracy', comprising individuals who had gained experience and knowledge of constitutional norms and values, alongside universal principles related to human rights, all of which underpin the rule of law, existed during these periods to varying degrees and resisted attempts to repress and make the judiciary subservient.[6]

The post-communist period shows that not only do remnants of communist rule manifest themselves in procedural and substantive areas, but also that the challenges concern aspects of political and legal culture that reveal a general trend towards a strong state and a reluctance to relinquish the romantic image of the interwar period in lieu of present-day developments that, to CEE societies, seem baffling and unknown. The wholesale rejection of one's life, as it was led under the totalitarian regime, does not present a constructive alternative. As Konrád aptly observes,

> Just as it made no sense to reduce a thousand years of Hungarian history to the bleak tableau of 'enslavement and servility', it would be mindless to condemn all that happened over the past few decades and all the players in a drama in which after all each of us had a role.[7]

Constitutional Developments

With the collapse of communism, post-communist regimes, emboldened by a new constitutional initiative, almost immediately embarked upon adopting new, post-communist constitutions. Yet, even in the quest to create a document which had no connection to its communist predecessor, the end result was a constitution which borrowed from both the communist and 'Western' experiences. Notably, this meant membership in the Council of Europe and being bound by universal and regional instruments, paying particular attention to instruments directly or

6 These developments were referred to as 'pockets of democracy' by the late Adam Podgorecki, at a conference in Oñati, Spain.

7 George Konrád, *The Melancholy of Rebirth: Essays from Post-Communist Central Europe, 1989–1994* (San Diego, CA: Harcourt Brace & Company, 1989), p. 36. See also Miklós Haraszti, *The Velvet Prison: Artists Under State Socialism* (London: Penguin, 1989).

indirectly involving minorities.[8] The ratification of the European Convention for the Protection of Human Rights (hereafter, European Convention) entitles individuals to bring their cases directly before the European Court of Human Rights.[9] Further, CEE states have been active participants in the Conference on Security and Cooperation in Europe (CSCE), now known as the OSCE, and adopted all the CSCE documents, most notably the 1990 Copenhagen Document, which has been considered the most definitive document adopted within the CSCE framework since the Final Act of Helsinki of 1975 (hereafter, Final Act).[10] Most CEE states ratified the International Covenant of Civil and Political Rights in the 1970s.[11] Poland entered the European Union in May 2004.

Achieving legal continuity between the communist and post-communist legal cultures is a formidable task.[12] For Poland, this discontinuity has affected the long-awaited 1997 Polish Constitution, leading some scholars to argue that a mixed constitution raises more questions than it answers, as we shall see below.[13] In contrast to the Czechoslovak and Hungarian experiences, the Polish constitutional path took time to create its identity. For Czechoslovakia, stability had been an undeniable feature of its democratic experience from the interwar period. This stability was ruptured by the unanimous rejection of the legitimacy of communist

---

8 See Charter of Paris, 'Conference and Co-operation in Europe: Charter of Paris for a New Europe and Supplementary Document to Give Effect to Certain Provisions of the Charter', *International Legal Materials*, 31 (1991), pp. 190–227, and, for example, the Europe Agreement with Poland, 'Communities and Their Member States, of the One Part, and the Republic of Poland, of the Other Part', *Official Journal*, L 348 (31 December 1993), pp. 0002–0180.

9 Protocol No. 11 of the European Convention, which restructured the control machinery of the convention, entered into force in 1998. Protocol 11 replaced the court and commission with a new, permanent court, with a right of appeal on points of law to a new appellate chamber. See also Anna Michalska, *Komitet Praw Czlowieka: kompetencje, funkcjonowanie, orzecznictwo* [The Commission of Human Rights: Its Competence, Function and Decisions] (Warsaw: EXIT, 1994), and also by the same author and Jan Sandorski, 'Remarks on the Place of International Human Rights in the Constitution of the Republic of Poland', *Polish Yearbook of International Law*, 19 (1991–92), pp. 101–31.

10 See Arie Bloed, *The Conference on Security and Co-operation in Europe: Analysis and Basic Documents, 1972–1993* (Dordrecht: Martinus Nijhoff, 1997); and Barbara Mikolajczyk, 'Polish Law and Policy Towards National Minorities', *International Journal on Group Rights*, 5 (1997), pp. 59–86, and 'Universal Protection of Minorities (Selected Problems)', *Polish Yearbook of International Law*, 20 (1993), pp. 137–50.

11 See Office of the United Nations High Commissioner for Human Rights: http://treaties.un.org/Pages/Treaties.aspx?id=4&subid=A&lang=en (last accessed 14 June 2009).

12 Maria Los, 'In the Shadow of Totalitarian Law: The Law-Making in Post-Communist Poland', working paper, Department of Criminology, Faculty of Social Sciences, University of Ottawa (1993).

13 Wojciech Sadurski, 'Rights and Freedoms Under the New Polish Constitution: Reflections of a Liberal', *Saint Louis-Warsaw Transatlantic Law Journal* (1997), pp. 91–105.

rule by the Constitutional Court in 1993. For Hungary, legal continuity existed alongside a strong and identifiable legal tradition.[14] Contemporary Polish political leaders have turned to pre-war traditions when discussing the drafting of a post-communist constitution. Where there is continuity, it can be identified with regard to statutes, such as the Polish Commercial and Criminal Codes, which date back to the pre-war period.[15] In terms of jurisprudence, this is sometimes harder to identify. As noted in Chapter 4, the Round Table Talks and subsequent legal reform possess a temporal dimension of representing the past by the attempt at rectifying it. Yet, significantly, the discussions at the Round Table Talks were about the future, rather than the past. In his work, Přibáň notes that in the post-communist transitions, the legal system 'internalizes the concept of identity and time as moral "absolutes"'.[16] This forward-looking feature of the law carries an important, paradoxical meaning, which transcends symbolic significance. The arena in which this continues to be hotly debated is that of de-communisation, as will be discussed shortly. In the end, 'knowledge' has an especially important role in what will comprise the particular normative values underpinning a certain period in the transition.[17] It is the currency that can divide and bring together respective CEE societies.

The debates concerning the new CEE political structures missed the point that a key part of the discussions concerned the future of the CEE states' 'return to Europe'.[18] This raised certain expectations on the part of the societies, later leading to disappointment and disillusionment. In view of the enduring discussions about Poland's rightful place in Europe, for example, more established democracies, capitalism and the free market were seen as the only viable choices and, in fact, no other models were seriously considered.[19] Inevitably clashes arise when crafting a constitution.

As we have seen, historically, Polish politicians and constitutionalist lawyers have not had a clear notion of the meaning of balance of powers. Pre-war and post-1989 discussions centred on the advantages and disadvantages of the parliamentarianism of the French Third Republic or the presidential supremacy of the Fifth Republic; not surprisingly, the French constitutional models were

---

14 See Bela Pokol, *The Concept of Law. The Multi-Layered Legal System* (Budapest: Rejtjel, 2001).

15 As noted by Garlicki, '[In] Poland, Hungary and Czechoslovakia all prewar regulations have remained in force after the communist revolution except for those clearly incompatible with the principles of the new system.' Leszek Garlicki, 'The Polish Legal Profession', *St Louis University Law Journal*, 24 (1980), p. 488.

16 Jiří Přibáň, *Legal Symbolism: On Law, Time and European Identity* (Aldershot: Ashgate, 2007), p. x.

17 Ruti Teitel, 'Transitional Rule of Law', in *Rethinking the Rule of Law After Communism*, ed. by Adam Czarnota, Martin Krygier and Wojciech Sadurski (Budapest: CEU Press, 2005), pp. 279–94.

18 Janine Wedel, *Collision and Collusion: The Strange Case of Western Aid to Eastern Europe 1989–1998* (New York: St. Martin's Press, 1998).

19 *Ibid.*

considered. Moreover, as aptly observed by one eminent Polish constitutionalist lawyer, 'in Poland constitutionalism was not usually understood as a limitation of democratic and parliamentary authority; Poland lacked the traditions and mechanisms of submitting parliamentary acts to constitutional review, and the traditions of administrative and constitutional courts were just as weak.'[20] The vague provisions of the 1992 Constitution echoed the uncertainty to experiment with the notion of the division of powers.[21]

Polish constitutional consciousness has been the combined experience of a strong leadership and democratic tradition.[22] The Polish tradition has been one of a fervent, patriotic and paternalistic authority with good intentions that grants favours to persons rather than an authority in which persons enjoy inalienable rights and have claims on the authorities based on those rights. The limited role of the state dates back to the failed attempt of the *liberum veto*, which eventually led to the fall of the Polish state. The *Generalgouvernement* and the communist regimes have also shaped the Polish people's need for and appreciation of a strong state, but one that is 'benevolent and democratic',[23] recalling Austin's views of the state which operates for the common good, views not necessarily consistent with modern notions of the rule of law.[24]

The constitution is also viewed as a vehicle for CEE countries in their effort to re-emerge as a Central Europe that is on par with Europe itself. The tradition is strong in Poland, the Czech Republic and Hungary, countries which always have identified with and regarded themselves as part of Europe.[25] In the pursuit of establishing the rule of law, the emphasis has been placed on the protection of human rights and the promotion of the market economy. But the caveat which must be considered when considering a legal framework for a market economy (which addresses property rights, bankruptcy law and banking law, for example) is that the 'process becomes slow and painful because fundamental constitutional (and social) issues are unresolved'.[26] This has been a particularly difficult question,

20 See Wiktor Osiatynski, 'Perspectives on the Current Constitutional Situation in Poland', in *Constitutionalism and Democracy: Transitions in the Contemporary World*, ed. by Douglas Greenberg *et al.* (Oxford: Oxford University Press, 1993), p. 313.

21 R. R. Ludwikowski, 'Constitution Making in the Countries of Former Soviet Dominance: Current Development', *Georgia Journal of International and Comparative Law*, 23 (1993), pp. 155–267.

22 *Ibid.*

23 *Ibid.*

24 John Austin, 'The Province of Jurisprudence Determined', in *The Province of Jurisprudence Determined and the Uses of the Study of Jurisprudence* (London: Weidenfeld and Nicolson, 1955), pp. 363–93.

25 Václav Havel once stated that if he lived long enough, he would love to see the day Czechs 'come home to Europe'. Václav Havel, 'Westward Ho!', *The Economist*, 18 April 1998, p. 29.

26 Andras Sajo and Vera Losonci, 'Rule of Law in East Central Europe: Is the Emperor's New Suit a Straitjacket?', in *Constitutionalism and Democracy: Transitions*

especially with regard to the kinds of rights to be included in and protected by the constitution. What is perceived by politicians and society as 'normal' requires a price which not all individuals are willing to pay.[27]

Some Polish jurists have argued that it is difficult to bring the constitution to life, because we will never understand what these principles really mean and how they interrelate.[28] This argument can be answered by the emergence of an *acquis constitutionnel* specific to the Polish Constitutional Tribunal. The term *acquis constitutionnel* does not necessarily refer to the incorporation of European law and norms. Rather, it refers to the case law built up and the reasoning peculiar to the Polish Constitutional Tribunal, in comparison with the jurisprudence pertaining to the 'invisible constitution' in Hungary.[29] The argument by post-communist courts has for the most part sought to identify and protect those values that characterise the respective nation state.

The Polish constitutional lawyer Komarnicki and his pre-war counterparts have served as an important inspiration for the post-1989 Constitutional Tribunal, in particular when interpreting the notion of the rule of law. 'The notion of law does not limit itself to formal equations, to the protection of legality, but reaches much further. It must define the substance, which results from ... the idea of the superiority of the nation, from the postulates of Christian culture, and from the idea of the autonomous individual.'[30] Yet, '[e]fforts in building in our country [Poland] the rule of law, of which the specialist and politician are aware, does not signify at all that the citizen should feel more secure in his current situation with the state structure.'[31] As Castoriadis asked us never to stop questioning our relationship with the state, the judiciary reflects the 'quality of democracy in that particular country', an exercise that should be encouraged continually and kept alive.[32]

---

in the Contemporary World, ed. by Douglas Greenberg *et al.* (Oxford: Oxford University Press, 1993), p. 321.

27 Maria Los, 'Property Rights, Market and Historical Justice: Legislative Discourses in Poland', *International Journal of the Sociology of Law*, 22 (1994), pp. 39–58.

28 Miroslaw Wyrzykowski, 'Legislacja – demokratyczne panstwo prawa – radykalne reformy polityczne i gospodarcze' [Legislation – Democratic Rule of Law State – Radical Political and Economic Reforms], *Panstwo i Prawo* [State and Law], 1 (1991), pp. 17–28.

29 Especially in the Polish judgment regarding lustration measures, as discussed below.

30 As quoted in Janina Zakrzewska, 'Trybunal Konstytucyjny – konstytucja – panstwo prawa' [The Constitutional Tribunal – the Constitution – the Rule of Law], *Panstwo i Prawo*, 1 (1992), p. 11.

31 Jerzy Szacki, 'Marzenia i rzeczywistosc polskiego demokracji' [The Hopes and Reality of Polish Democracy], *Res Publica*, 5 (1991), pp. 14–17.

32 *Appointing Judges in an Age of Judicial Power: Critical Perspectives from Around the World*, ed. by Kate Malleson and Peter H. Russell (Toronto: University of Toronto Press, 2006). See also Cornelius Castoriadis, 'Radical Imagination and the Social Instituting Imaginary (1994)', in *The Castoriadis Reader*, ed. and trans. by David Ames Curtis (Oxford: Blackwell, 1997), pp. 319–39.

Small Constitution (1992)

The first of the important steps to be taken after the collapse of communism was the Law of 7 April 1989 on Changing the Constitution of the Polish People's Republic, which abolished the Council of State and replaced it by the office of president; an interim constitutional document was passed four years later. The 1952 communist Constitution lost its force according to Article 77 of the so-called 'Small Constitution' of 17 October 1992, which served as the binding document.[33] This meant that in the event the Small Constitution could not provide for certain answers to constitutional questions before the courts, the courts were to refer to the 1952 Constitution, a document whose communist roots were painfully apparent, roots which political and legal officials desperately sought to redraft and to replace.

As regards the 1992 document, the document mainly addressed the conflict between the president (who was Lech Walesa at the time) and the *Sejm* over their respective scope of powers, about which the 1952 Constitution was no clearer after the 1989 amendments.[34] This constitutional ambiguity of the president's power dated to the Round Table Talks, when delegates (of the opposition Solidarity side) intentionally insisted on certain provisions which would curtail the powers of the executive, then headed by General Jaruzelski.[35] When Solidarity assumed power, its leaders found themselves overseeing an unbalanced government structure, a fact President Walesa realised shortly after taking up his position in 1990. While

33 *Ustawa konstytucyjna z dnia 17 pazdziernika 1992r. o wzajemnych stosunkach miedzy wladza ustawodawcza i wykonawcza Rzeczpospolitej Polskiej oraz o samorzadzie terytorialnym* [Constitutional Law of 17 October 1992 on the Mutual Relations Between the Legislative and Executive Powers of the Republic of Poland and on Local Self-Government], *Dziennik Ustaw*, No. 84, item 426. For discussion about the 1952 Polish Constitution, see Chapter 4. The term *Mala Konstytucja* ('Small Constitution') has been used several times throughout Polish constitutional history to refer to different constitutional documents, such as the 1919 and 1947 Polish Constitutions. 'Small' referred to the temporary nature of the document, which was binding until a new constitution was passed (as indicated in both preambles of the 'Small Constitutions').

34 For an excellent analysis of the Small Constitution, see Maria Kruk, 'Wstep' [Introduction], *Mala Konstytucja czyli Ustawa Konstytucyjna z dnia 17 pazdziernika 1992r. o wzajemnych stosunkach miedzy wladza ustawodawcza i wykonawcza Rzeczpospolitej Polskiej oraz samorzadzie terytorialnym wraz z pozostalymy przepisami konstytucyjnymi i ustawa z dnia 23 kwietnia 1992r. o trybie przygotowania i uchwalenia Konstytucji Rzeczpospolitej Polskiej* [The Small Constitution or the Constitutional Law of 17 October 1992 on the Relations between the Legislative and Executive Powers of the Republic of Poland and Local Government and the Remaining Constitutional Laws and the Law of 23 April 1992 on the Organisation and Enactment of the Constitution of the Republic of Poland] (Warsaw: Wydawnictwo AWA, (1992), pp. 4–37.

35 For an overview of the details, see Louisa Vinton, 'Poland's "Little Constitution" Clarifies Walesa's Powers', *RFE/RL Research Reports*, 1 (1992), pp. 19–26.

the 1992 Constitution had established the political framework, it did not address the judicial framework, leaving it to be regulated in the future constitution. The result of this was that the Polish judiciary was offered no reference point from which to define its power, apart from a vague clause in Article 1, which mentioned an independent judiciary as one of the three branches of government. The drafters of the Small Constitution instead focused on achieving a balance between two powers, solely addressing the ambiguities rather than undertaking a complete overhaul of the system.[36] Thus the executive branch was strengthened, with presidential powers limited by a system of checks and balances (Article 1). This suggested the establishment of a system of division of powers, at least with regard to the executive and legislative branches; the judicial branch was regulated by one provision only. The burden of responsibility shifted between the president and parliament in a way that the drafters hoped was balanced and would satisfy both sides of the conflict. In fact, the new procedure enhanced the president's role and required majority parliamentary support for any cabinet. The five-year presidential term was reaffirmed and the president was granted the right to veto legislation.[37] The president was also granted the right to petition the Constitutional Tribunal to rule on the constitutionality of legislation. Finally, the president remained commander-in-chief of the armed forces and retained the right to ratify international agreements, nominate the head of the National Bank, appoint judges (on the motion of the National Council for the Judiciary), grant pardons and award Polish citizenship.

The position of the *Sejm* was thus still central in the state structure, but it did not exercise supreme authority over the two remaining branches of government, following a similar framework from the pre-war period. With a weaker parliament, the position of the president was strengthened. The 1992 Constitution also provided for a part of the legislative tasks to be delegated to the authority of the executive branch. The authority of the state was very much dependent on the balance of political power in the parliament, and the ability to create a clear parliamentary majority supporting the president and/or the government was decisive. In the view of some scholars, the Small Constitution provided conditions facilitating more efficient governance, but did not and could not guarantee the utility of such conditions.[38] As concerns the framework for a constitutional democracy, there was a missing component in the absence of any mention of the role of the judiciary. As we shall see below, Polish courts were already rendering decisions which explicitly referred to the rule of law and that mentioned the court's role in shaping and reinforcing this notion.

---

36 I*bid.*

37 His veto could be overridden by a two-thirds majority in the *Sejm*.

38 See Wojciech Sokolewicz, 'Rozdzielone, lecz czy rowne? Legislatywa i egzekutywa w Malej Konstytucji 1992 roku' [Divided, But Are They Equal? Legislative and Executive Powers in the Small Constitution of 1992], *Przeglad Sejmowy* [Parliamentary Overview], 1 (1993), pp. 22–42.

In this view, while it is true that the 1992 Constitution was vague and left many unanswered questions,[39] the significance of the Small Constitution was that Poland once again experienced a 'Pilsudski-ite' era with Walesa, who clearly was preparing to base his cabinet on the pre-war Pilsudski cabinet. The enthusiasm for the new administration was short-lived, the disillusionment hastened by Walesa's open conflict with parliament. During this time, President Walesa attempted to rule with an 'iron hand' and openly opposed parliament. At the same time, various scandals were revealed within his closest circle, and the public's impatience and disillusionment with the actions of the Solidarity leaders grew.

The drafters were unwise in leaving the role of the judiciary undefined in the 1992 Constitution. It was clear that political leaders themselves were ambivalent about the role of the judiciary in the newly established democratic Polish state. The Small Constitution only *partially* reintroduced the constitutional provision of the separation of powers which replaced the one-party system of the socialist state. The so-called supremacy of parliament no longer prevailed over the other branches of government, as evidenced by the fact that the Small Constitution did not incorporate the provisions of the 1952 Constitution relating to the powers of parliament. On the other hand, it has been argued by some constitutionalist lawyers that, in fact, the drafters were not inclined to adopt any of the three main models.[40] Thus, while the 1992 Small Constitution was a bold attempt at establishing the separation of powers, it did not go far enough. As it did not address the judiciary and provide clear provisions concerning its position in relation to the executive and legislative branches, the legal framework was left in a rudimentary state. In terms of the rule of law, this was a failure, and a significant one. The rule of law is not only about the reach and competence of the branches of government. It is also an assurance that the state will not act arbitrarily, no matter which model a state chooses to adopt, and that remedies are accessible and available to address encroachments by the state upon civil liberties. Without clear rules, a bold effort on the part of lawyers or judges might succeed in addressing the gap. What is less clear is the consequence for a state that emerges from totalitarian rule with hardly any democratic tradition.

1997 Polish Constitution

The post-communist experience has once again shown how important the role of the political elites is in creating a viable legal framework which is part of a legitimate, effective government. But pluralisation has proved a more difficult

39 See Hubert Izdebski, 'Mala Konstytucja a reforma administracji publicznej' [The Small Constitution and Public Administration Reform], *Studia Iuridica* [Legal Studies], 28 (1995), pp. 57–61.

40 See R. R. Ludwikowski, '"Mixed Constitutions" – Product of an East–Central European Constitutional Melting Pot', *Boston University International Law Journal*, 16 (1998), p. 7.

exercise in democracy for CEE societies, as witnessed in the many parties to emerge during the early 1990s in response to personal conflicts and animosities (and, of course, ambition), rather than the natural process of pluralisation based on differences in political programmes. This debate between 'intellectuals' and 'interests' was a key question in which groups would be allowed to influence constitutional preparations. Here, we can, once again, return to Polish tradition. The run-up to the promulgation of the 1997 Constitution is an excellent example of such tension.

In Poland, the question during the early 1990s centred on the extent that the new constitution was to be shaped by the prevailing political arrangements; in short, it involved parliament's fear of a strong presidency led by Walesa. It was a case of whether the drafters would be able to rise above the personal conflicts and ambition which existed at the time. Such events can affect the credibility of the constitution, as Sajo has correctly observed; the chances for the draft constitution look slim when the constitution-making process itself is unauthentic.[41] According to Sajo, this authenticity is connected to the personal credibility of the drafters; that is, whether they are easily influenced by political opinion and enjoy public support.

Members of the Constitutional Committee charged with the task of drafting a new constitution originally envisaged that the document would be drafted by 1991, to coincide with the 200th anniversary of the 1791 Polish Constitution.[42] Unfortunately, this goal was not achieved, the committee's work having been disrupted by parliamentary disputes and elections, which inevitably affected the work and composition of the committee.[43] More importantly, there was a *lack of political will* to adopt a new constitution. In 1992, a new Constitutional Committee of the National Assembly, comprising the *Sejm* and the Senate, was created. This committee had to contend with further political disruption until their work was completed five years later. The new Polish Constitution was finally adopted by the National Assembly on 2 April 1997. On 25 May 1997, a nationwide referendum was

41 Andras Sajo, *Limiting Government: An Introduction to Constitutionalism* (Budapest: Central European University Press, 1999), p. 22.

42 It is beyond the scope of the work to discuss the background of the Constitutional Commission. It should be pointed out, however, that after the first non-communist government was established in 1989, with Tadeusz Mazowiecki as prime minister, parliament appointed a Constitutional Committee charged to draft a new constitution. The Senate retaliated by setting up its own committee: the move was understandable as it was the only chamber elected in the free elections. See Miroslaw Wyrzykowski, 'Introductory Note to the 1997 Constitution of the Republic of Poland', *Saint Louis-Warsaw Transatlantic Law Journal* (1997), pp. 1–4. For an insider's view, see Andrzej Rapaczynski, 'Constitutional Politics in Poland: A Report on the Constitutional Committee of the Polish Parliament', *University of Chicago Law Review*, 58 (1991), pp. 595–631.

43 For information on the composition of the Constitutional Commission, see Janina Paradowska, 'Kto to napisal' [Who Wrote It?], *Polityka* [Politics], 14 (5 April 1997), pp. 28–32.

held, in which 52 per cent voted in favour of the Constitution.[44] The Constitution came into force on 17 October 1997.

The preamble of the 1997 Constitution considered the sources and inspiration of the drafters; it referred to 'we, the Polish nation' and recalled the 'best traditions of the First and Second Republic'. The reference to the Polish 'nation' did not spark a debate, as a similar reference to the nation did, for example, in Slovakia.[45] The 1997 Constitution signified a compromise on many levels. One was between the members of the ruling coalition, the Democratic Left Alliance and the Polish Peasants' Party on the one hand, and the Union of Freedom and the Union of Labour, which represented the majority opposition, on the other hand. The document thus contains a considerable number of proposals of both parties, in addition to provisions that were found in the competing drafts prior to and after 1993 (when new parliamentary elections were held after parliament was dissolved by a vote of no confidence). The most important compromise was the acceptance of most of the demands of Solidarity and the Catholic Church, which, despite having its demands met, still opposed the document.[46] The Church's disapproval has been perceived as frustration at not being able to maintain its significant role in the political life of the nation.[47]

One notable difference between the 1997 Constitution and the 1993 drafts (of which there were seven official ones) was the presidential draft of Walesa, which contained the Charter of Rights and Freedoms. The charter, which originally was drafted by the Helsinki Foundation for Human Rights in Warsaw, was an innovative document containing a catalogue of far-reaching rights, which are of great significance when considering constitutional rights.[48] Section 8 of the 1952 Constitution also contained an exemplary catalogue of individual rights, but it was

---

44 For details on the debate surrounding the referendum, see Ewa Letowska, 'Dwie konstytucje' [Two Constitutions], *Polityka*, 9 (1 March 1997), p. 18. For general details about the referendum, see Janina Paradowska, 'Polska raz jeszcze podzielona' [Poland Is Once Again Divided], *Polityka*, 22 (31 May 1997), p. 15, and Wieslaw Wladyka, 'Trzy Polski' [Three Polands], *Polityka*, 23 (7 June 1997), pp. 20–21.

45 For an overview, see Eric Stein, 'Out of the Ashes of a Federation, Two New Constitutions', *American Journal of Comparative Law*, 45 (1997), pp. 45–69.

46 See Stanislaw Podemski, 'Konstytucja nie dekalog' [A Constitution, Not the Ten Commandments], *Polityka*, 20 (18 May 1996), p. 18.

47 Wyrzykowski, 'Introductory Note', *supra* n. 42, pp. 3–4. It should be noted that the Catholic Church was a forum for Polish people to express their views. This should not be taken to mean that all the Polish people, the majority of whom are Catholic, are 'practising Catholics'. At the same time, in an effort to maintain its control over the religious instruction of Polish society, the Polish government signed a concordat with the Vatican. See 'Konkordat miedzy Rzeczpospolita Polska i Stolica Apostolska podpisany w Warszawie 28 lipca 1993r' [Concordat Between the Republic of Poland and the Vatican Signed in Warsaw 28 July 1993], *Nowy Dziennik* [New Daily], 18 April 1997, pp. 20–21.

48 See Andrzej Rzeplinski, 'Karta praw i wolnosci: uwagi nad projektem ustawy konstytucyjnej z 12 listopada 1992 roku' [The Charter of Rights and Freedoms: Remarks

felt by the drafters that the Constitution was so steeped in the spirit of Stalinism that it would be better to draft a new document rather than transplant sections of the Stalinist Constitution to a new constitution.[49] In contrast, Hungary retained its 1948 document, while the former Czechoslovakia promulgated its Charter for Rights and Freedoms in 1993, forming a key part in its constitutional jurisprudence.

The manner in which the sections of the Polish constitution are divided, and the varying philosophical approaches to it, exemplify the three main competing trends of thought and tradition in Poland. The first is rooted in socialism, sometimes referred to as the 'socialist' view, focusing on socio-economic rights; the second is the 'Christian' view, emphasising the protection of traditional values, such as family, religion and labour, as reflected in Komarnicki's observation already mentioned; and the third is the more liberal view, seeking to control state action while promulgating political and civil rights.[50] All three perspectives are very much alive in present-day Poland and identifiable as key case law, as evidenced below. The relevant chapters of the Constitution are not as coherent and clear as its 1992 counterpart, the Charter of Rights and Freedoms, was. The problem arises with regard to social and economic rights.[51] The advantage of the charter, for example, was that it separated social and economic rights and freedoms from the economic, social and cultural tasks of public authorities; in this way the tasks were carried out by the authorities in accordance with their economic resources. This is a difficult balance to achieve – on the one hand, there is a danger that social and economic rights will be neglected not only for the aforementioned reason of the absence of economic resources, but also because of their link with 'real socialism'.[52] On the other hand, while individualism is an ideology which recognises the value and interests of the individual, the complete dominance of individualism can result in neglect of the interests of society as a whole. Sunstein, for example, argues that socio-economic rights do not belong in a constitution; he bases this argument on a negative/affirmative rights analogy. He claims that the dilemma lies in the fact that where the rights are not enforced, they undermine the protection of negative property rights.[53] Broadly speaking, the position concerning negative and positive rights has evolved differently between American and European perspectives. In

---

on the Draft of the Constitutional Law of 12 November 1992], unpublished manuscript (on file with author).

49 In contrast to Hungary, for example, which had extensively amended its 1949 Constitution in 1989 and 1990.

50 Sadurski, 'Rights and Freedoms', *supra* n. 13, pp. 91–105.

51 This problem also arises in the Russian context; see Arts. 17–64 of the Constitution of the Russian Federation. For the Hungarian context, see Andras Sajo, 'How the Rule of Law Killed Hungarian Welfare Reform', *East European Constitutional Review*, 5 (1996), pp. 31–41.

52 For discussion, see Rein Mullerson, *International Law, Rights and Politics: Developments in Eastern Europe and the CIS* (London: Routledge, 1994).

53 Cass Sunstein, 'Against Positive Right', *East European Constitutional Review*, 2 (1993), pp. 35–38.

contrast, some scholars argue that these rights do belong in a constitution, even if they are mere aspirations.[54] The conflicting aims of social and economic rights and political and civil rights have 'deprived large sectors of the population of an elementary capacity to take basic responsibility for their own livelihood in the new reality of market economy'.[55]

Indeed, Polish expectations of social justice are high, understandably so, as the people were led to believe that, as citizens, they had the right to education, employment, free health services, and housing. It did not matter that the state failed to provide these services; the fact that the state convincingly argued these rights made them part of a post-communist society's image of the state.[56] According to the Polish sociologist Jerzy Kwasniewski, in the first years of the transition the common view among members of society was that social problems were the responsibility of the state and that to change this view would mean a change in

> social consciousness involving among other things the creation of a legal sense and a sense of society's competence to take decisions concerning the state of the natural environment, the social environment, the work environment, the national environment, and so on. Members of society need to develop a sense of responsibility for the problems of collective life.[57]

In fact, the debate on the notion of a *demokratyczne panstwo prawa* (democratic rule-of-law state) has centred on the meaning of a democratic rule-of-law state as opposed to a socialist state, and the question of what, in fact, are the differences between the two.[58] This discourse, which Solidarity had initiated successfully, also challenged contemporary notions of political democracy. Indeed, discussions centred on a combination of the communist experience and 'Western-style' democracy, namely a system which combines the key components of a social and political system maintaining the advantages of both capitalism (affluence, liberty, rights) and socialism (social security, health service, full employment, comparative equality), and abolishes the disadvantages of both systems. According to Havel, a state

54 Herman Schwartz, 'In Defense of Aiming High', *East European Constitutional Review*, 3 (1992), pp. 25–28.

55 Krzysztof Drzewicki, 'Implementation of Social and Economic Rights in Central and Eastern Europe Transforming from Planned Economy to Market Economy', *Nordic Journal of International Law*, 64 (1995), pp. 373–84.

56 Maria Los, 'Legitimation, State and Law in the Central European Democracy', *Polish Sociological Bulletin*, 4 (1991), pp. 231–49.

57 Jerzy Kwasniewski, 'Social Problems in Poland', in *Social Control and the Law in Poland*, ed. by Jerzy Kwasniewski and Margaret Watson (New York: St. Martin's Press, 1991), pp. 168–69.

58 Andrzej Pullo, 'Panstwo prawne (uwagi w zwiazku z Art. 1 Konstytucji RP)' [The Rule of Law State (Remarks Relating to Art. 1 of the Constitution of RP)], *Studia Iuridica*, 28 (1995), pp. 121–29.

> based on ideas should be no more and no less than a guarantee of freedom and security for people who know that the state and its institutions can stand behind them only if they themselves take responsibility for the state – that is, if they see it as their own project and their own home, as something they need not fear, as something they can – without shame – love, because they have built it for themselves.[59]

Havel further points out, '[o]ften we ourselves are unable to appreciate fully the existential dimension of this bitter experience and all of its consequences, including those that are entirely metaphysical.'[60] Havel's statement is a succinct definition of and comment on the rule of law; it is clearly rooted in the Czechoslovak experience with communist rule, and it resonates with the CEE understanding. Reminiscent of Petrazycki's work on the relationship between law and the individual, Havel draws attention to those innate features of the concept of a rule of law that a society responds to, aspects that are substantive in nature, because they involve human dignity. This is distinct from the institutional facets of the rule of law. As mentioned previously, the introduction of new concepts, new terms of a legal code, is complicated by the fact either that the terms are non-existent, or that they have completely different meanings. But what of the concepts of 'freedom' and the 'rule of law', two terms used quite freely among laypeople, politicians and legal scholars early on in the transition?

Concepts such as 'democracy' and 'free' are also subjective, dependent on the existence of different institutions in different countries and the political experience. In established democracies, freedom has developed into a 'freedom from constraint', and even that has developed differently between the United States and the UK, for example. 'Likewise, totalitarian regimes have applied '"liberty" to the condition of individuals under a system in which they have no right other than that of obeying orders.'[61]

These perspectives are further affected by the informal relationships and networks that operated under communist rule. This was a way to access goods and services that became increasingly difficult to attain under the deteriorating command economy; this also shaped the way in which individuals represented themselves publicly and privately. Relationships which fell outside the private sphere were subject to different rules. For example, the act of lying to a public official is praiseworthy, and not viewed as immoral but as a necessary act of self-

59 Václav Havel, *Summer Meditations on Politics, Morality and Civility in a Time of Transition* (London: Faber & Faber, 1992), p. 128.

60 *Ibid.*, p. 126.

61 Bruno Leoni, *Freedom and the Law* (Los Angeles: Nash Publishing, 1961), p. 41. See also Gianmaria Ajani, 'By Chance and Prestige: Legal Transplants in Russia and Eastern Europe', *American Journal of Comparative Law*, 43 (1995), pp. 93–117.

defence.[62] Within the private sphere, however, such behaviour is not tolerated. Individuals never reveals themselves in public, and avoid showing their inner thoughts. They instead go out of their way to misrepresent themselves, or to show what Milosz has aptly described as their 'Ketman'.[63] Likewise, the notion of stealing has a dual meaning. When a person steals from 'them', or the state, then the act becomes 'taking one's share'.[64] Ironically, the state has become such an integral part of society that abolishing it will lead only to its reinvention.[65]

There is another way in which to view these informal relations and the highly bureaucratised nature of the totalitarian state. Polish legal science can assist. First, it is important to revisit Petrazycki's theory of intuitive law again, as discussed in Chapter 2. To reiterate, intuitive law (or living law) can be described as a set of norms that bind together two or more parties by their mutual acceptance; it is not based on official law. As Podgorecki notes, this distinction leads to three different possibilities: the invalidation of official law by official law, the invalidation of official law by 'reactionary' intuitive law, and the invalidation of intuitive law by 'reactionary' official law.[66] The invalidation of official law can occur in four ways, namely through 'retroactive invalidation, suspension, contradictory regulations, and denial through various kinds of rationalisations'.[67] The invalidation of official law by official law, and of official law by intuitive law, is seen in Podgorecki's example, where one of the common aspects of the totalitarian regime is its frequent use of retroactive legislation to invalidate earlier law, violating one of the oldest principles of Roman law, *lex retro non agit*. Another feature is suspension of a law for an indefinite period, such as denying citizens the exercise of their constitutional rights. In the totalitarian regime, sub-legal systems operate within the legal system; the legal system may appear valid, but, in reality, a sub-legal system operates in hidden view.

In light of the discussion of informal networks, it is important to recall that all these actors were involved in an exchange of services and commodities. These exchanges can result in a wide network of persons, as based on intuitive law. This intuitive law provides the structure for various kinds of motivation, which can, in the end, result in the corrosion or total destruction of official law.[68] The second consideration is whether a network that is accepted and reflects the

---

62 Steven Sampson, 'The Informal Sector in Eastern Europe', *Telos*, 66 (1985–86), p. 54.

63 Czeslaw Milosz, *The Captive Mind*, trans. by Jane Zielonko (New York: Alfred A. Knopf, 1953), pp. 54–82.

64 Sampson, 'The Informal Sector', *supra* n. 69, p. 56.

65 Janos Kenedi, *Do It Yourself: Hungary's Hidden Economy* (London: Pluto Press, 1982).

66 Adam Podgorecki, 'The Authorisation of Illegality', in *Social Control and the Law in Poland*, ed. by Jerzy Kwasniewski and Margaret Watson (New York: St. Martin's Press, 1991), pp. 86–99.

67 *Ibid.*, p. 87.

68 *Ibid.*, p. 94.

society's norms and attitudes operates behind a legal system that is regarded as undemocratic and unjust. This network may attain the credibility that the official system lacks, 'not on the basis of its own merits, but because it provides a convenient cover for the rampant phenomenon of "dirty togetherness"'.[69] The existence of 'dirty togetherness' implies that aspects of social control lack ethical considerations and encourage loyalties to family and friends and participation in semi-legal and illegal activities. More importantly, the participants in the networks have the firm conviction that their survival is only possible within the circle of 'dirty togetherness'; outside it, life is impossible under the repressive regime and the isolation that it inevitably encourages.[70] Everyone becomes involved in the operation of 'dirty togetherness'. It is worth quoting Podgorecki at length:

> It is clear that individuals who operate within this system will soon start to support its legal matrix, not because they accept it as a system which has normative validity or because of its own inherent virtues, but because they are familiar with it, with the rules of the game, and with who is who. Needless to say, people who constantly live in this kind of social system are gradually socialised to a pragmatic, opportunistic and instrumental life strategy.[71]

Sajo is correct in observing that instrumentalism is readily accepted, as it derives from the socialist notion of law, which comes to be considered as an instrument of social change.[72] The danger in this emerges in the area of rights, which themselves create new privileges and dependencies, and may in fact undermine both the rule-of-law system and the new rights system; this is done through the replacement of old rights structures with the new.[73]

Visitors to Poland after the June 1989 elections were surprised to find the Poles visibly unenthusiastic, even pessimistic, about the new developments. What the observers did not know was that Polish society was, and to a large extent still is, suffering from an illness. During the 1980s, a series of surveys was conducted on the 'stresses' of Polish society.[74]

From the point of view of social stress, it must be remembered that Polish society has endured at least two events which shattered the fabric of society: the

69 *Ibid.*, p. 95.

70 *Ibid.*

71 *Ibid.*, p. 96.

72 Andras Sajo, 'On Old and New Battles: Obstacles to the Rule of Law in Eastern Europe', *Journal of Law and Society*, 22 (1995), pp. 97–104.

73 *Ibid.*

74 'Stress' can be understood as a category combining three levels of our existence: physiological, psychological and social. The last of these was the focus of studies on the source of threats of stress and on the factors in our potential ability to adapt ourselves to these kinds of stress. See Anna Titkow, *Stres i zycie spoleczne: polskie doswiadczenia* [Stress and Social Life: Polish Experiences] (Warsaw: Panstwowy Instytut Wydawniczy, 1993).

Second World War and communist rule. Since the German occupation, Polish society has had a period of 'training' in maintaining control under the most horrible circumstances. After 1945, Poles turned to public institutions for answers and the realisation of equal opportunities and social justice. This dependence existed until the collapse of 'real socialism'. In the process, however, people had to adopt contradictory ways of coping with events.

According to some Polish sociologists, Polish society's identity was threatened between 1945 and 1989.[75] As rapid industrialisation and urbanisation were taking place, there was a gradual realisation of the disparity between ideology and reality. The discord translated itself into immobilisation; relations at work became ossified, dooming individuals to their place of work, and frequently undermining social roles.[76] Not only did this knowledge affect the way in which individuals and groups felt their worth, but it also affected the manner in which society viewed law and order.[77] At the same time, religion remained a strong bond. Egalitarianism became a popular ideology. Yet there was an alienation from communist structures and official ideology.

The gradual disillusionment that society felt with the regime, owing to the fact that 'several times it placed its faith in the regime – and several times it was betrayed', began to turn into a need for a change:

> In the past few years [society] slowly, inevitably, began to lose the value which was established by our society during the years of occupation and in the first few years of the rebuilding. In 1956 and 1970 twice it was pushed on the ground as something useless and unwanted. But we continued to feel the 'hunger for respect', the 'hunger for partnership', the 'hunger for democracy'.[78]

It must be recognised, however, that to a certain extent the citizen came to depend on the paternal state, despite the fact that it was unable to care for its citizenry. In 1985, 62 per cent of Poles recognised this dependence, but only 29 per cent

75 *Ibid.*, pp. 184–92.

76 *Raport o stanie Rzeczpospolitiej i drogach wiodajcych do jej naprawy* [A Report on the State of the Republic and Ways Leading to Its Correction] (Warsaw: Konserwatorium Doswiadczenie i Przyslosc, 1979), as quoted in *ibid.*, p. 203.

77 The *nomenklatura* is a list of key positions, to which appointments are made by the higher authorities of the Communist Party, and also is a list of persons appointed to those positions or held in reserve for them. Politics took precedence over qualifications, and the practice continued throughout the communist era. See, generally, *Political Leadership in Eastern Europe and the Soviet Union*, ed. by R. Barry Farrell (Chicago: Aldine Publishing Company, 1970). See also Olga Kryshtanovskaya and Stephen White, 'From Soviet *Nomenklatura* to Russian Élite', *Europe-Asia Studies*, 48 (1996), pp. 711–33.

78 *Raporto stanie Rzeczpospolitej*, as quoted in Titkow, *Stres I zycie spoleczne*, *supra* n. 74, p. 206.

would have opted for this model.[79] In 1989, 80 per cent of Poles disapproved of the possibility of less state care.[80] Understood in this way, it is not so surprising to find that the transition to democracy was characterised by a marked passivity on the part of society.[81] Alongside this lay a real danger, whereby 'sick' citizens find themselves in a purportedly healthy nation that is changing rapidly, but in which they simply cannot secure for themselves a 'healthy' condition,[82] leading to further alienation.

Havel recognised this ailment when he discussed the true nature of communist rule and its collapse. The never-ending pressure of the totalitarian system had suddenly been replaced by a spectrum of new and unknown factors:

> We knew very well how to lose and be followed – maybe that is why today we are disoriented in our victory and so surprised, that we are not being followed. We act as if we are prisoners to our individuality, that to have acquired freedom suddenly we do not know how to begin and we are scared and decided in our decision not to take any decision.[83]

In other words, the first, significant step towards breaking away from the past is to take responsibility for it and all future actions.

It would have been an opportunity to forge new and solid relations between the state and society, a chance for society to face its 'demons' head on and to attempt once again to rebuild itself – had there been a dialogue about this between the state and society. Any threat naturally creates a feeling of ambiguity about the future. The decision to draw a 'thick line' over the past threatens society's identity, as society does not take any responsibility for what happened in the past, neither placing any blame on anyone nor forgiving anyone either.[84] In short, '[w]e do not know who we were and who we are to be.'[85]

---

79 Miroslawa Marody, *Warunki trwania i zmiany ladu spolecznego w relacji do stanu swiadomosci spolecznej* [Conditions of Survival and Changes of Social Order in Relation to the State of Social Consciousness] (Warsaw: Universytet Warszawski, 1986), as quoted in Titkow, *Stres i zycie spoleczne*, *supra* n. 81, p. 203.

80 *Ibid.*

81 Andrzej Rychard, 'Zrodla leki i nadzei' [The Roots of Fears and Hopes], *Zycie Warszawy* [Warsaw Life] (1989), as quoted in Titkow, *Stres i zycie spoleczne*, *supra* n. 74, p. 230.

82 *Ibid.*

83 Václav Havel, Speech in Salzburg, 26 July 1990, *Gazeta Wyborcza* [The Voter's Gazette], p. 10.

84 W. Eichelberger, 'Odkreslamy przeszlosc gruba kreska?' [Are We Writing Off the Past with the Thick Line?], *Gazeta Wyborcza*, 27 February 1990, p. 23.

85 Titkow, *Stres*, *Stres I zycie spoleczne*, *supra* n. 74, p. 234, and Andrzej Rychard, 'Czy w Polsce jest homo sovieticus?' [Is *Homo sovieticus* in Poland?], *Zycie Gospodarcze* [Economic Life], 17 September 1995, p. 6.

New Sense of the Law

The 'search for a new sense of the law'[86] includes grounding it in the notion of rule of law, a process to which the judiciary is indispensable . More importantly, the judiciary must have constitutional guarantees protecting its independence. In this respect, the CEE constitutions provide for judicial independence, protecting the judiciary against the actions of the legislature, as well as matters regulating the structure of the courts.

The extensive list of rights mentioned above means nothing if they are not protected and enforced. This is the critical role of an independent judiciary. Throughout my study, I have discussed the role of the judiciary and judicial officials in the framework of creating a state. We have seen how critical an independent judiciary is in the establishment of a democratic rule-of-law state. The CEE's experience with totalitarian regimes has demonstrated the opposite side of the coin: how necessary a subservient judiciary is to support the unjust practices of the state. According to Article 193 of the 1997 Polish Constitution, '[a]ny court may refer a question of law to the Constitutional Tribunal … if the answer to such a question of law will determine an issue currently before such court.' Polish courts, however, have been reluctant to request preliminary rulings; as a consequence of the communist experience, Polish judges are accustomed to applying the law without raising constitutional objections.[87] This reluctance can be identified throughout the CEE.

Judicial Independence

Any discussion about the rule of law in post-communist states first addresses judicial independence and the independence of the courts, the cornerstone of a constitutional democracy, without which the rule of law has no chance of being realised. The main theory of judicial independence, or the principle of the separation of powers, first recognised by Aristotle, is attributed to Montesquieu, who argued that 'there is no freedom if one and the same body has both the legislative and the executive authority. … There is no freedom, either, unless the judicial authority is separated from the legislature and the executive.'[88] While Montesquieu is usually considered the foremost authority on the subject, it is important to remember

86 As quoted by the former Commissioner for the Protection of Citizens' Rights, Tadeusz Zielinski, in Zakrzewska, 'Trybunal Konstytucjyny', *supra* n. 30, p. 3.

87 See Mark Brzezinski, 'Constitutionalism Within Limits', *East European Constitutional Review*, 2 (1993), pp. 38–43.

88 Baron de Montesquieu, *The Spirit of Laws; a Compendium of the First English Edition*, ed. by David Wallace Carrithers (Berkeley, CA: University of California Press, 1977), text based on Thomas Nugent's translation (London: Nourse, 1750).

that in fact he believed that the judiciary is no power at all, and that of the three branches of government 'the judicial is, in a sense, null'.[89]

Locke, however, did not devote much attention to the role of the judge. He listed the three powers in the British government as the legislative, executive and federative, granting the legislative the supreme power and not mentioning the judiciary as a separate power at all.[90] Judicial independence refers both to the judiciary's independence from the other branches of government and the independence of judges when settling disputes and deciding in matters brought before them by parties. In France, for example, the separation of powers imposes effective restraint on the executive power and protects citizens against the absolutism of monarchs. In the United States, the separation of powers was a guarantee of liberty, but was also designed to protect the constitutional system against the domination of any single power. Thus, the theory put forward by Montesquieu was in fact far from the model to be adopted by the United States.

Judicial independence is, or should be, characteristic of the judge's relation to the executive authority, the court administration, political pressure groups, or political parties. In order to secure judicial independence, it is necessary to have constitutional and statutory guarantees which regulate the structure of the courts. In his discussion about judicial independence, Fiss constructed three different notions of judicial independence: party detachment; individual autonomy; and political insularity.[91] The last of the three is the most complex and gives rise to the most questions. Seeking party detachment and freedom from political influence seems a more clear-cut case in the CEE, owing to the recent experience with communism, than in the West. Of course, one could argue that guarantees to judicial independence rest with the personality of the judge. This is correct, but legal provisions should be in place as well. Aquinas, for example, in *Social Virtues Related to Justice*, wrote that a judge should live in a state of perfection and of truth, and that judges 'should be guardians of truth in courts by force of their office'.[92] Such force of office, however, does not come automatically. It must be accepted as such by the judges themselves, the government and the society.

There is no system with complete conformity of the judge's beliefs to the content of the law. The point is, however, that a law which forces various tricks

---

89 Mauro Cappelletti, 'Repudiating Montesquieu? The Expansion and Legitimacy of Constitutional Justice', *Catholic University Law Review*, 35 (1985), pp. 12–14.

90 See his *Of Civil Government: Two Treatises*, ed. Ernest Rhys (London: J.M. Dent, 1924).

91 Owen M. Fiss, 'The Limits of Judicial Independence', *Inter-American Law Review*, 25 (1993), pp. 58–59.

92 See Andrzej Rzeplinski, 'The Principles of Independence of the Judiciary and Its Statutory Application', in *Constitutionalism and Human Rights*, ed. by Andrzej Rzeplinski, Vol. 1, Papers of the International Conference, 'Human Rights and Freedoms in the New Constitutions of Central and Eastern Europe', Warsaw 24–29 April 1992 (Warsaw: Helsinki Foundation for Human Rights in Eastern Europe, 1992), pp. 121–42.

in defence of the basic conditions of professional ethos undermines the judge. Besides, a law which defines the structure of the court and the structure of the social practice should not aim at the creation of the best judges who would be prepared to sacrifice, in defence of dignity of their office, not only that office itself, but also their freedom and their lives. These debates took place during the interwar period.

> [T]he legislator has to deal with average people who are incapable of heroism and sacrifice. If they are to approximate to some extent the ideal of the judge, not jeopardising their own interest too much, it is necessary that they should not have to fear or to flatter anybody. The first and main condition here is independence of judges.[93]

This independence needed to be shielded from state intervention in judicial decision-making:

> A judge of value is one who responds with dignity to even the slightest insinuations or attempts at influencing him . . . he is, nevertheless, guided by nothing but his own conscience and the duty to serve the law in all steps he takes in a given case. A judge should be rewarded for honesty and skill, but never for submitting to the influence of others .[94]

These two views reveal the particular nature of the judge's position, especially considering Locke's somewhat cynical view of the corrupt nature of man; the judges are expected to rise above it by their strong conscience.

Dyzenhaus posits that two assumptions underlie the discussions of the judiciary in the transition from an autocratic to a democratic system.[95] The first acknowledges that the judiciary will have an important role to play in the new democratic regime, and the second is that every effort must be made to ensure the judiciary's independence.[96] The notion of 'independence' usually means the relationship of the judiciary to other institutions or agencies. Some proponents have gone further in stipulating independence from ideology. In the CEE, judges are banned from any political activity, possibly a curious notion to a judge elsewhere, but not in a country where one-party rule sought complete subservience. The

93 E. Waskowski, *System prawa cywilnego* [The Civil Law System] (Wilno: 1932), p. 43, as quoted in Rzeplinski, *ibid.*, p. 129.

94 Stanislaw Waltos, 'O potrzebie nowelizacji ustawodawstwa karnego' [The Need for a Criminal Legislation Amendment], *Nowe prawo* [New Law], 4 (1981), p. 43.

95 David Dyzenhaus, *Judging the Judges, Judging Ourselves: Truth, Reconciliation and the Apartheid Legal Order* (Oxford: Hart Publishing, 1998).

96 Rzeplinski, 'The Principles', *supra* n. 92, and Ewa Letowska, *Po co ludziom konstytucja* [Why the People Need a Constitution] (Warsaw: Agencja EXIT, 1994), pp. 116–26.

United States Constitution, for example, guarantees judicial independence; the federal courts are normally treated as the full embodiment of the ideal. Article III of the Constitution provides life tenure and protection against reduction of pay, as essential to the protection of judicial independence.[97] While judges in the United States are not allowed to engage in overtly party political activities, they generally do so and, moreover, adopt obviously political views. Until 1989, judges of the Polish Supreme Court, for example, did not enjoy these privileges, life tenure being implemented only in that year; the issue of judicial salaries continues to be a controversial matter. As we can see, the notion of judicial independence is a far more complex matter. Judges can be independent, yet can also fail to perform their most basic duties because they cannot understand the issues before them, lack courage, or are bound to an outdated philosophy.[98] Judges may also have mixed feelings about their so-called goals in the newly established state, especially if they are of the view that their work was positive under the former regime which promoted socialist legality; the manner in which to reconcile the conflicting roles of the court and the judge continues to challenge.[99] Thus the issue, in a sense, transcends the requirement to have normative law in place; in Poland, it requires a profound change in the performance by judges of their duties.

In the 1980s, a well-known professor of law, active in Solidarity and noted for his weekly commentaries, wrote:

> Taken out of the bourgeois rubbish heap and dusted was the naive theory from the eighteenth century, Montesquieuen, that three separate powers would exist: the legislative, the executive and the judiciary. The opposition took seriously the last point and began reminding everyone of it. The government treated it seriously and accepted it – if it is three branches, then it must be three branches![100]

Falandysz was an active participant at the Round Table Talks discussion that touched upon many of the arguments for the protection of judicial independence.[101]

---

97 Art. III states: 'The judges, both of the supreme and inferior courts, shall hold their offices during good behaviour, and shall, at stated times, receive for their services, a compensation, which shall not be diminished during their continuance in office', US Constitution, Art. III, para. 1. See Kate Malleson, 'Introduction', in Malleson and Russell, *Appointing Judges in an Age of Judicial Power*, *supra* n. 32, pp. 3–10.

98 Ewa Letowska, 'Dekalog dobrego sedziego' [The Ten Commandments of a Good Judge], *Gazeta Wyborcza* [Voter's Gazette], 6–7 February 1993, pp. 8–9.

99 For an insightful commentary on the East German context, see Stephen Baister, 'The Court as Educator: The Social Courts System of the German Democratic Republic', *Legal History*, 18 (1997), pp. 47–90.

100 Lech Falandysz, *Ja i moje prawo* [Me and My Law] (Warsaw: Helsinska Fundacja Praw Czlowieka, 1991), p. 191.

101 For a comparative analysis of CEE transitions to democracy negotiated by the Round Table Talks, see Jon Elster, 'Constitutionalism in Eastern Europe: An Introduction', *University of Chicago Law Review*, 58 (1991), pp. 447–82.

The Subtable on Legal and Court Reform provided a unique opportunity to discuss the actual functioning of the Polish administration of justice. Its members knew that without first addressing the long-ignored third branch of government the chance of constitutional democracy would be lost. The immediate introduction and acknowledgement of the rule of law – that is, the separation of powers – was at the forefront of the discussion. This meant that judicial independence and the independence of the courts were one of the first points to be stressed and reiterated during the discussions.[102] Solidarity representatives at the subtable observed that '[t]he independence of the courts as well as judicial independence form a basis for the legal order of the state and the protection of the rights and interests of the citizens.'[103] Moreover, the subtable recommended that several instruments relating to the administration of justice be considered for implementation, namely:

1. the introduction of a constitutional provision which guarantees judicial independence and precludes the removal or transfer of judges save for reasons of ill health or disciplinary charges;
2. the abolition of judicial terms for Supreme Court judges;
3. the abolition of the oath of office required to be taken by judges before assuming office;
4. the constitutional establishment of the National Council for the Judiciary (*Krajowa Rada Sadownictwa*), comprising members from the judicial as well as the executive and legislative branches of government, which would take decisions on future candidates to the judiciary;
5. wider discretion granted to judicial self-government to decide on, *inter alia*, nominations of judicial presidents;
6. the selection of members to the district judicial branch from the general gathering of judges from all branches;
7. the introduction of terms to the office of judicial presidents;
8. the modification of the guiding institutions of the administration of justice and the court practice as laid down by the Supreme Court in such a way that they do not violate the principles of subordination of judges only to the law;
9. the creation of judicial benches which are granted the right to directly petition the Constitutional Tribunal in matters concerning the constitutionality of constitutional acts, normative acts, or legislative acts;
10. the introduction of wider competence in the courts and the introduction of new categories of cases;
11. an increase in the range and position of lay judges as required by the appointment through direct elections;

---

102 'Sprawozdanie z posiedzen Podzespolu do sprawy reformy prawa i sadow' [Report of the Sessions of the Subtable on Legal and Court Reform], *Porozumienia Okraglego Stolu* [The Round Table Talks], Warsaw, 6 February–5 April 1989.

103 *Ibid.*, p. 59.

12. outlining in the regulations the capacity of the objective courts, the guarantee of impartial decision-making, and the substitution of principles which would be clearer to the parties;
13. the settlement of a pay scale for judges according to the social position held by the judge in society; the scale differing only in the years the judge has served on the bench.[104]

Each of these points addressed the failings of the communist system; that is, the underlying basis was what the opposition saw as unjust on the part of the regime in the administration of justice and was not placed in a wider context of more established democracies.[105] The points are also reflected in key international and regional documents, as put forward by the UN Basic Principles on the Role of Lawyers or the International Commission of Jurists.[106] With this in mind, it is essential to note that, in accordance with Prime Minister Mazowiecki's claim to draw a 'thick, black line' between the communist past and the post-communist present, the Polish judiciary applied the same principle to itself.[107] No verification of the judiciary took place; instead, it was claimed that the judiciary would 'cleanse itself'.[108] This decision has led to certain debates which continue to plague the judiciary during the post-communist period.

Recalling Přibáň's observation about temporality in the law,[109] the tension between the past and present and the limitation of law, if we accept its forward-

104 *Ibid.*, pp. 60–61.

105 In the former Soviet Union, discussions about the rule of law were not immediately initiated by Gorbachev, but *glastnost* paved the way and made it possible to discuss openly the shortcomings of the legal system, beginning with, for example, the criminal justice system. See M. D. A. Freeman, 'The Rule of Law – Conservative, Liberal, Marxist and Neo-Marxist: Wherein Lies the Attraction?', *in Perestroika and the Rule of Law: Anglo-American and Soviet Perspectives*, ed. by W. E. Butler (London: I. B. Tauris, 1991), pp. 37–59. The Russian terms for law, *zakon* (law or statute) and *pravo* (law), reflect the two very different interpretations of law, the latter (*pravo*) symbolising an ideal which has not yet been defined by its proponents. See also William Butler, 'Justice in Russia: Soviet Law and Russian History', *Emory Law Journal*, 42 (1993), pp. 433–48.

106 See, for example, International Commission of Jurists at http://www.icj.org/sommaire.php3?lang=en (last accessed 14 June 2009).

107 The *gruba, czarna kreska* ('thick, black line') was part of Solidarity's campaign to separate the past from the present. It reflects a Christian view of forgiveness and a policy that has led to much misunderstanding and a lingering need for some sort of justice, especially with regard to those persons who actively participated in the repressive regime.

108 Adam Strzembosz, 'O wymierzajacych sprawiedliwosc – sprawiedliwiej' [On Administering Justice – More Justly], *Tygodnik Solidarnosc* [Solidarity Weekly], 22 September 1989, p. 3. It should be mentioned that Adam Strzembosz was the First President of the Supreme Court and the National Council for the Judiciary until 1995 when he had to resign from his position to run as a presidential candidate. To this day, his words divide the public.

109 Přibáň, *Legal Symbolism*, *supra* n. 16.

looking element, is fully revealed when we find that most of the judges were appointed prior to 1989, a fact which raised questions about their role in the communist period and doubts about their legitimacy and right to adjudicate in a post-communist, democratic Poland. There were some efforts to rid the legal system of judges who were considered 'tainted' because of their political pliability in 1993, efforts which were supported by different factions of the government and most of the public, but not by the judiciary, which argued that the proposed legislation undermined the promise of judicial independence proposed by the Subtable of the Round Table Talks.

In 1993, the Ministry of Justice presented to parliament an amendment to the Law on the Structure of the Common Courts, in which Article 59 provided that 'the President [of the Republic], on the motion of the National Judiciary Council, dismisses a judge who has *departed* from the *principles of independence*'.[110] The amendment's wording was intentionally vague, but the underlying purpose was clear: to rid the judiciary once and for all of the judges who were politically disposed under communism. The draft law went to the Senate for consideration and shortly after the Polish ombudsman petitioned the Constitutional Tribunal to adjudicate on the constitutionality of the law. According to the ombudsman, the Small Constitution recognised the doctrine of the separation of powers, while the vaguely worded amendment would allow the executive branch to interfere in the judicial branch of affairs.[111] Moreover, the ombudsman argued that the motion resembled the former regime's limitations on the independence of the judiciary. And this was a correct observation, supported by the vague and open-textured phrasing, 'departing from the principles of judicial independence'.

The Constitutional Tribunal upheld the ombudsman's argument, declaring the proposed amendment unconstitutional.[112] The debate over Article 59 was highly controversial, causing an outcry by the judges and the public. The judges argued that the introduction of the amendment would itself interfere with judicial independence, by creating external pressure on the judiciary and their decision making. 'A judge does not function at the whim of society and politicians. ... If we want independent judges they must be free from the caprices of politicians, who, despite various lessons to be learned from the past, do not seem to realise that an independent judiciary might be needed by them one day.'[113]

---

110 Art. 59, Law of 5 February 1993 on the Amendment to the Law on the Structure of the Common Courts, Public Prosecution, Supreme Court, Constitutional Tribunal, National Council of the Judiciary and the Establishment of Appellate Courts. Emphasis added.

111 Wniosek Rzecznika Praw Obywatelskich [Motion of the Commissioner for the Protection of Citizens' Rights], RPO/127988/93/I/1/AM, 2 September 1993.

112 Judgment of 9 November 1993, K 11/93.

113 Lech Paprzycki, 'Ten, ktory jest sedzia' [He Who Is a Judge], *Palestra* [The Bar], 5–6 (1993), p. 41; Ewa Letowska, 'Dekalog dobrego sedziego', *supra* n. 104, and also by the same author, 'The Administration of Justice in Poland', *EuroCriminology*, 7 (1994), pp.

Instead of a law that provided clear and concise procedures for verification, the proposed amendment, with its vague wording, created further confusion by opening the possibility of interpretation, which could lead to potentially dangerous situations – a recurrent problem with de-communisation measures. For example, by providing the Ministry of Justice with the opportunity to influence the decision-making of a judge, and precisely by giving such a wide interpretation of the law that it affected, the amendment allowed judges to be identified and unjustifiably considered problematic.[114] Not surprisingly, the judiciary as a whole felt attacked, the draft coming at the same time that judges were fighting for a salary increase and were generally waging a battle against the state to establish the much-needed 'respect for the third branch of government'.[115] In recent developments, judges saw judicial administrative officers receiving a pay rise and obvious disparities between support staff and judges.[116]

One could argue that the move to create Article 59 was one of the consequences of leaving the judiciary unaddressed in the Small Constitution. Moreover, the fact that the question has resurfaced reflects the inability of the state to deal with this question effectively.

This conflict proved to be the first true test for the newly created National Judiciary Council.[117] The council had been struggling to maintain its position

---

97–109. See also Cass R. Sunstein, 'The Legitimacy of Constitutional Justice: Notes on Theory and Practice', *East European Constitutional Review*, 6 (1997), pp. 61–63.

114 Ireniusz Walencik, 'Kres niezawislosci?' [A Mark of Independence?], *Rzeczpospolita*, 7 September 1993, pp. 1, 9; Anna Marszalek, 'Cimoszewicz broni niezawislosci sedziow' [Cimoszewicz Protects Judicial Independence], *Rzeczpospolita*, 6–7 November 1993, p. 20; Danuta Frey, 'Weryfikacji sedziow' [The Verification of Judges], *Rzeczpospolita*, 11 March 1993 (accessed online).

115 'Prawnicy protestuja' [Lawyers Are Protesting], *Rzeczpospolita*, 5 January 1993, p. IV (prawo co dnia), and Romuald Gilewicz, 'Mit o niezawislosci' [The Myth of Independence], *Rzeczpospolita*, 10 March 1993, p. II (prawo co dnia). As regards judicial salaries, in 1991, President Walesa had signed a law increasing judicial wages. Judges never received their increase, leading many to take their cases to the courts. In the meantime, the short-lived government empathy ceased with a reshuffling. Judges had no support in their legal pursuit, which was denounced by the government (the Olszewski regime at the time) as a 'moral scandal'. For further details, see Romuald Gilewicz, 'Skandal placowy w sadownictwie' [A Payment Scandal in the Judiciary], *Rzeczpospolita*, 25 March 1993, p. II (prawo co dnia).

116 Agata Lukaszewicz, 'Sadowy urzednik dostanie wieciej niz sedzia' [Judicial Civil Servant Will Earn More Than a Judge], *Rzeczpospolita* (17 July 2008) (accessed online).

117 Law of 20 December 1989 on the National Council for the Judiciary. *Dziennik Ustaw*, No. 73, item 435. The council consists of 26 persons, *ex officio*: the first president of the Supreme Court; the president of the Supreme Court's military division; the president of the Administrative Court; the minister of justice; and, by election, 15 judges from the different types of courts; four deputies from the *Sejm*; two senators; and one person appointed by the president. The chairman is elected by the members of the council. The judicial appointment process was reformed in the following manner. Judges are appointed

during its first few years of existence. Denied a separate budget and housed in the chancellery of the president, the council did not reflect the important task with which it was entrusted, namely that of selecting judicial candidates.[118] Shortly before the proceedings, the council issued a press release concerning the composition of the post-communist judiciary.[119] According to the press release, only a few hundred judges who could be considered 'politically tainted' by their role in the former regime were on the bench.[120] Even after this official statement, not everyone was satisfied, particularly those who associated themselves with the right-wing political parties. The question was highly politicised, and detracted from the purpose of the law.

The question of judicial verification continues to plague the judiciary. A law concerning the violation of judicial independence was passed in 1998.[121] According

---

to and recalled from all positions by the president of the Republic of Poland, on the motion of the National Council of the Judiciary. Candidates are submitted to the council, usually double the number of vacancies. The candidates, with the exception of the Supreme Court, are submitted through the minister of justice, who has the option of expressing his opinion of the candidates. The minister may also submit his choice of candidates, after consultation with the board of the relevant court. The candidate for judge must be over 26 years of age, be a graduate of the faculty of law, be of unblemished character, have completed the two-year practical training in a court or prosecutor's office with the final judicial examination, and have worked a minimum of one year as an assistant judge in a court or procurator's office. The latter requirement need not be met if the person has had at least five years of experience in the legal professions, or is a professor of law. For the position of assistant judge, candidates are usually appointed to a two-year term by the minister of justice, who may grant them judicial duties in the district court. This is common because of the lack of judges, and one finds many assistant judges at the district court level.

118 Adam Zielinski, 'O statusie prawnym Krajowej Rady Sadownictwa' [About the Legal Status of the National Council of the Judiciary], *Panstwo i Prawo*, 6 (1993), pp. 84–88. See Janusz Wojciechowski, 'Dzis i jutro Krajowej Rady Sadownictwa' [Today and Tomorrow the National Council of the Judiciary], *Rzeczpospolita*, 14 February 1994, p. 12.

119 *Informacja o zmianach w polskim sadownictwie w latach 1989–1990* [Information about Changes in the Polish Judiciary 1989–1990], Krajowa Rada Sadownictwa [National Council of the Judiciary].

120 This debate was begun in the early years of post-communism. Some judges stepped forward to defend their position, claiming to have been following the law. See the debate between the following authors, a lawyer and a judge, respectively: Andrzej Litwak, 'Reforma ... bez reformy' [Reform ... Without Reform], *Wokanda* [Trial Calendar], 14 July 1991, p. 9; Waldemar Myga, 'Protest "komucha"' [Protest of a 'Commie'], *Wokanda* [Trial Calender], 18 August 1991, p. 4.

121 *Ustawa z 3 grudnia 1998r. o odpowiedzialnosci dyscyplinarnej sedziow, ktorzy w latach 1994–1989 sprzeniewierzyli sie niezawislosci sedziowskiej* [Law of 3 December 1998 Concerning the Accountability Related to Disciplinary Measures Against Judges Who Have Violated the Principles of Judicial Independence Between 1944 and 1989], *Dziennik Ustaw* (1999), No. 1, item 1.

to Article 1 of the law, judges who had adjudicated in cases between the years 1944 and 1989, in matters concerning the struggle for independence, political reasons, or the protection of human rights, or had violated the basic principles of human rights and, in doing so, had violated the principles of judicial independence, may have disciplinary measures initiated against them until 31 December 2002. Article 2 dictates that proceedings initiated before 31 December 2002 shall be followed through to the end. The 1998 law is much more specific than the controversial Article 59, in targeting a particular group of judges (in an implicit manner, however). Moreover, there is a deadline for initiating proceedings, presumably in an attempt to bring closure to this aspect of the national reconciliation question. The law came into force on 12 January 1999. At this time, there were curious ideas about judges and lawyers that reflected an authoritarian approach to controlling the judiciary, because of the political taint that seemingly prevailed in the judiciary. Somewhat ironically, the regime successfully put into place a reactionary official law, by undermining the official laws that themselves were enacted as a reaction to the 'thick, black line' policy. The quest for gaining that elusive balance between independence and accountability failed during this time owing to the nature of constitutional provisions and judicial interpretation.[122] The reactionary laws would themselves partially fail, as we shall see shortly.

The particular approach taken by the regime, or the 'Kaczynski reign', referring to the brothers who held the posts of, respectively, the president and prime minister – Lech Kaczynski and Jaroslaw Kaczynski, – also had strong religious overtones. Equating the Church with civil society can be misguided. Fine argues that the Enlightenment provided the greatest contribution to the notion of democracy and the democratic process by recognising that civil society was a middle ground between private life and the state.[123] 'The right to express our thoughts, however, means something only if we are able to have thoughts of our own.'[124] Institutional influence over values and norms reveals itself in the form of the Church. The Catholic Church in Poland, the Evangelical Church in the former East Germany, and the Protestant Church in the former Czechoslovakia have been key institutions in public and private life. As mentioned above, the Polish Church has provided a space for political dissent and association, for the articulation of political expression, during communist rule. There, issues relating to capital punishment and human rights were discussed; in 1987, a seminar on the International Peace and Helsinki Agreements was held in a small parish church in Warsaw; the

---

122 Malleson and Russell, *Appointing Judges in an Age of Judicial Power*, *supra* n. 32.

123 Robert Fine, 'Civil Society Theory, Enlightenment and Critique', in *Civil Society: Democratic Perspectives*, ed. by Robert Fine and Shirin Rai (London: Frank Cass, 1997), pp. 7–28.

124 Erich Fromm, *Escape from Freedom* (New York: Avon, 1969), p. 266. Also note the excellent BBC Radio 4 programme 'Battle for Memory: Lithuania', on *Crossing Continents*, 17 July 2008.

Church equated itself with 'freedom and peace'.[125] Human rights discourse was placed at the top of its agenda. The basis was the protection of and respect for *human dignity*. Borowik aptly notes that '[i]n [the] Polish mentality as well as the opinion of the Church, Catholicism is entirely connected with Polishness. Religious and national identity are characterised by a feeling of belonging to Polishness and Catholicism.'[126] Borowik lists the following characteristics of the Catholic Church's defence of its authority in 1992, which resonate today: a belief in its infallibility; use of 'admonition' in drawing boundaries in an increasingly multicultural society; relying on methods from the past in an effort to shape state policies; using the language of struggle as a means to continue either a 'fortress mentality' or a unified front; and unwillingness to embrace change. This reflects a clear, Eurosceptic stance, in addition to the perpetuation of xenophobic and anti-Semitic beliefs. Nowhere is this better exemplified that in the Polish Radio Maryja (Radio Maria), a radio station which advocates a return to traditional values and embraces xenophobia and anti-Semitism.[127]

Elsewhere the Church has had a positive role in participating in democratic change. The experiences of Poland and the Czech Republic could not be further apart, as far as localised concerns are discussed. Recently, the Polish prime minister warned that the country is in danger of isolating itself from Europe, along with the Czech Republic – both President Kaczynski and Czech President Klaus have been seen as Eurosceptics.[128] The Polish Church also has had to face a host of scandals revealing its collaboration with the secret intelligence services.[129] Nevertheless, its prominence in Polish life is also demonstrated in the jurisprudence of the Constitutional Tribunal.

125 Vladimir Tismaneanu, 'Unofficial Peace Activism in the Soviet Union and East Central Europe', in *In Search of Civil Society: Independent Peace Movements in the Soviet Bloc*, ed. by Vladimir Tismaneanu (London: Routledge, 1990), pp. 1–53.

126 Irena Borowik, 'The Roman Catholic Church in the Process of Democratic Transformation: The Case of Poland', *Social Compass*, 49 (2002), pp. 239–52. See also Joan Mahoney, 'The Catholic Church and Civil Society: Democratic Options in the Post-Communist Czech Republic', *Church and State in Contemporary Europe*, pp. 177–94, and Zsolt Enyedi and Joan Mahoney, 'Churches and the Consolidation of Democratic Culture: Difference and Convergence in the Czech Republic and Hungary', *Democratization*, 11 (2004), pp. 171–91.

127 See Agata Fijalkowski, 'The Paradoxical Nature of Crime Control in Post-Communist Europe', *European Journal of Crime, Criminal Law and Criminal Justice*, 15 (2007), pp. 155–72.

128 Jan Cienski, 'Poland Risks Isolation over Reform', *Financial Times*, 1 July 2008 (accessed online). Consider the debates regarding the Lisbon Treaty.

129 John L. Allen Jr, 'Polish Church Confronts Ghosts of Past', *National Catholic Reporter*, 19 January 2007, pp. 8–10.

The Constitutional Tribunal has not been embroiled in intense political battles – unlike some of its post-communist counterparts.[130] But this should not imply that the danger of intervention in judicial decision-making, whether by the executive or the legislative branches, has been removed. Recalling the point above, there has been a recent collision between the government and the tribunal over questions concerning lustration.[131]

Article 178(1) states that '[j]udges, within the exercise of their office, shall be independent and subject only to the Constitution and statutes.' Letowska aptly observes that the judiciary is naturally subordinated to statutes – in other words, subordinated to the legislature.[132] She goes on to point out that the difference rests in the fact that under the former regime this subordination extended to the executive as well, as normative acts were also statutes. The judiciary was not in a position to act as a check even when it was clear that the law was violated. Moreover, the legislature retroactively adjusted judicial decisions. However, in view of these tangible experiences and observations, Letowska finds it unfortunate, that there are no constitutional provisions stating the finality of judicial decisions. This is a significant departure from the previous provision of the 1952 Constitution, stating that judges shall be subject only to statutes. According to the 1997 Constitution, courts must apply the Constitution, statutes and binding rules of international law (Article 87(1)), making judges more aware that what matters is not so much the most specific provision to be relied upon (as previously) as a direct ground for resolution of a particular dispute, as that the Constitution is the structural and axiological basis of the entire legal system. Although Article 178 does not explicitly mention international law, there are other provisions which do.[133] As

130 For the Russian context, see Bill Bowring, 'Politics Versus the Rule of Law in the Work of the Russian Constitutional Court', in *The Rule of Law in Central Europe*, ed. by Jiří Přibáň and James Young, Socio-Legal Studies Series (Dartmouth: Ashgate, 1999), pp. 257–77. See also, by the same author, 'Human Rights in Russia: Discourse of Emancipation or Only a Mirage?', in *Human Rights in Eastern Europe*, ed. by Istvan Pogany (Aldershot: Edward Elgar, 1995), pp. 87–109.

131 Maria Los, 'Lustration and Truth Claims: Unfinished Revolutions in Central Europe', *Law and Social Inquiry*, 20 (1995), pp. 117–61. The term 'lustration' has recently emerged in legal literature. This term comes from ancient Roman religious ritual, meaning 'purification'; in this book, I will use screening law when referring to legislation concerning the bringing to justice of the former communists and police collaborators in the present CEE legal systems.

132 Ewa Letowska, 'Courts and Tribunals Under the Constitution of Poland', *Saint Louis-Warsaw Transatlantic Law Journal* (1997), pp. 69–89.

133 Article 9 mandates respect for international law binding on the Republic of Poland; Articles 87–91 incorporate international law into the legal system; Article 91(1) mandates direct application of international law. Likewise, Article 188 grants the Constitutional Tribunal the power to review domestic law with reference to international law. As mentioned in Chapters 2 and 5 of this book, concerning the 1921 Constitution (Article 49) and the 1997 Constitution (Article 15), the relationships between international law and Polish law

regards the relation between international and municipal law, the dualist approach to this question has been rejected (although not entirely) owing to the practice of the communist regime.[134] The 1997 Constitution does not afford the national legal order the widest possible regulation of norms of international law. It carefully considers international customs and resolutions of international organisations (save for regulations concerning integration into the European Union (EU)) and contains a complicated set of norms to deal with international organisations.[135] Likewise, the 1997 provision concerning the ratification of international agreements (Article 89) is based on the 1992 provision (Article 33 (2)), which, in turn, is based on the respective article of the 1921 Constitution. During communist rule, none of the people's democracies, save for the German Democratic Republic, regulated the effect of international law on their domestic law by way of a constitutional provision or general legislation; in Poland, as in the other CEE countries, practice was inconsistent or unclear, as our case study will show.[136]

The article reflects 'the goal ... to encourage judges to treat the Constitution as a source of inspiration, and as a medium of interpretation of ordinary legislation'.[137] The provision serves as a reminder to judges that the basic law inspires all kinds of interpretation, and in this way, the narrow positivistic approach has been abandoned for wider application following the principles of natural law. This is a highly significant departure from previous practice and one that has been embraced following the collapse of the communist regime in 1989.[138] This means that the courts have the duty to consider legislation according to the Constitution that is binding on all courts and that creates the possibility of different interpretation. The provision goes farther than previous documents in referring to

---

were regulated by parliament; in other words, international law provisions found in Polish municipal law were connected to the participation of parliament in the ratification process. See Wladyslaw Czaplinski, 'International Law and Polish Domestic Law', in *Constitutional Reform and International Law in Central and Eastern Europe*, ed. by Rein Mullerson, Malgosia Fitzmaurice and Mads Andenas, Studies in Law Series, Vol. 1 (The Hague: Kluwer Law International, 1998), pp. 15–36; see also by the same authors, 'International and Polish Municipal Law: Recent Jurisprudence of the Polish Supreme Judicial Organs', *Zeitschrift für ausländisches öffentliches Recht und Völkerrecht*, 53 (1993), pp. 871–81.

134 Andrzej Wasilkowski, 'Monism and Dualism at Present', in *Theory of International Law at the Threshold of the 21st Century: Essays in Honour of Krzysztof Skubiszewski*, ed. by Jerzy Makarczyk (The Hague: Kluwer Law International, 1996), pp. 323–36.

135 Andrzej Wasilkowski, 'International Law and International Relations in the New Polish Constitution of 2 April 1997', *Polish Yearbook of International Law*, 23 (1997–98), pp. 7–19.

136 Eric Stein, 'International Law and Internal Law in the New Constitutions of Central-Eastern Europe', in *Recht zwischen Umbruch und Bewahrung: Festschrift für Rudolf Bernhardt*, ed. by Ulrich Beyerlin *et al.* (Berlin: Springer, 1995), pp. 865–84.

137 Letowska, 'Courts and Tribunals', *supra* n. 132, p. 79.

138 See Maria Szyszkowska, 'Przepis na moralnosc' [A Recipe for Morality], *Polityka*, 6 (8 February 1997), pp. 68–69.

the checks and balances system, signalling another step towards establishing the courts as a real third arm of the government. Having this framework established does not mean that public confidence in the legal system is established.[139] Nor does the tension between the National Council for the Judiciary and the executive disappear. Recently, President Kaczynski once again revealed his disdain for judges in refusing to provide reasons for not approving eight of the council's recommendations for judicial posts.[140]

On this point, the Constitutional Tribunal's ruling, *inter alia*, on the constitutionality of statutes and international agreements has a leading role in the promotion of constitutional order in Poland. The tribunal's power has been further enhanced by the 1997 Constitution, in contrast to the limitations it has faced to its competence since 1982, when it was first established (but was not operating officially until 1985). At this juncture, it is useful to present a brief overview of the Constitutional Tribunal's history and competence. It was established in 1982, making it the oldest constitutional court in CEE.[141]

The Constitutional Tribunal

The notion of a 'living law' is not limited to specific courts. The renowned pre-war Polish scholar of civil law, J. Litauer, suggested a more activist court, showing a prescience of the notion of 'living law' that would become part of the case law of present-day Italian and Hungarian Constitutional Courts.[142]

> [T]he role of the judge was to be the lawmaker when he seeks to pass laws which are just, and with the goal that when the law is applied it simultaneously becomes the norm, and affects future decisions in relation to the particular law, which is its *ratio juris* within the legal framework, and legislative system and even in the binding law.[143]

139 For the Czech context, see Jiří Pehe, 'Changes in the Czech Judiciary', *RFE/RL Research Report*, 2 (17 September 1993), pp. 54–57.

140 Agata Lukaszewicz, 'Nie ma sporu na linii prezydent – KRS' [There Is No Dispute Between the President and KRS], *Rzeczpospolita* (17 July 2008) (accessed online).

141 For the Hungarian context, see László Sólyom, 'The Hungarian Constitutional Court and Social Change', *Yale Journal of International Law*, 19 (1994), pp. 223–37. See also George P. Fletcher, 'Searching for the Rule of Law in the Wake of Communism', *Brigham Young University Law Review*, 1 (1992), pp. 145–64.

142 See *Constitutional Judiciary in a New Democracy: The Hungarian Constitutional Court*, ed. by László Sólyom and Georg Brunner (Ann Arbor, MI: University of Michigan Press, 2000).

143 Jan Jakob Litauer, '0 metodzie wypelnienia luk w ustawodawstwie' [On Ways to Complete the Gaps in Legislation], *Panstwo i Prawo*, 7–8 (1947), pp. 10–11.

The existence of constitutional courts in some CEE states before 1989 was an important step towards building the body of constitutional jurisprudence that emerged in Europe, with particular reference to the progressive rulings that have been issued by certain CEE courts in the region. Nevertheless, the scope of the Polish Constitutional Tribunal's competence was limited when compared both with the older constitutional courts and with the more recent Eastern European courts.[144] In short, the authority of the Constitutional Tribunal was not wide; the *Sejm* had the power to overrule some of the court's decisions, which had no finality. Nor were there procedures for citizens to complain about the constitutionality of laws, and the tribunal was not empowered to consider issues between competing state organs.

The 1997 Polish Constitution has changed most of these elements and has established that the tribunal's judgments are of 'universally binding application and shall be final' (Article 190(1)). As regards making a constitutional complaint to the tribunal of, the filing has acquired universal nature. In other words, the complaint is one against the law. This has been criticised as being too narrow because the complaint may concern the normative basis of a decision. It is doubtful whether a petitioner may challenge the interpretation of a legal provision.[145] Likewise, the tribunal has been granted the power to decide disputes between 'central constitutional state organs', once again symbolising an important aspect of the checks and balances system and of the separation of powers.

Since the collapse of communism, the court, and indeed the entire judicial body, has been confronted with the basic question of finding a new 'sense of the law', as noted above.[146] To this end, the tribunal has based many of its decisions on the notion of the rule of law as defined in the 1992 and 1997 Constitutions, Articles 1 and 2, respectively. This new sense of law entails the basic components of ensuring that individual rights are protected during the transition – that public trust is regained, and that the process of coming to terms with the past is supported. An overview of the relevant case law will illustrate this further (see below).

Letowska has identified three factors that significantly influence the way Polish society thinks about the law: what she labels as 'text-centrism'; underestimating the value of material law regulations; and the formal approach to the question of the legitimacy of law.[147] As regards the first point, Letowska seeks to emphasise

144 For an excellent overview of the background and activities of the Constitutional Tribunal, see Mark Brzezinski, *The Struggle for Constitutionalism in Poland* (London: St. Martin's Press, 1998); by the same author, 'Constitutionalism Within Limits', *supra* n. 94, pp. 38–43; and by the same author with Leszek Garlicki, 'Judicial Review in Post-Communist Poland: The Emergence of a *Rechtsstaat*?', *Stanford Journal of International Law*, 31 (1995), pp. 13–59.

145 See Letowska, 'Courts and Tribunals', *supra* n. 132.

146 Zakrzewska, 'Trybunal Konstytucyjny', *supra* n. 30, p. 3.

147 Ewa Letowska, 'Bariery do naszego myslenia o prawie w perspekstywie integracji z Europa' [Barriers to Our Thinking About the Law in the Context of European Integration],

that the fact that there has been legal reform does not mean that that reform exists. She uses the example of consumer protection, pointing out that the civil code contains far-reaching provisions, most of which are in line with Western European provisions. Although there is a standard, it exists only theoretically; in practice, the situation is dismal, owing to the fact that the courts possess a limited grasp of the interpretation of the provisions – this is what is meant by text-centrism.[148] Letowska suggests that in the future legislators should implement two measures in order to overcome 'text-centrism': the first measure is to accept that there is more to harmonisation than bringing laws closer together – each piece of legislation should be accompanied by European standards (in this way calling upon Article 70 of the agreement for technical assistance) and by consideration of how this piece of legislation is viewed in Polish standards, namely administrative and/or judicial practice.[149] The second factor is as follows: to give meaning to substantive law, one must be inspired by the motivation for the law, such as the protection of human rights. Again, the legislature should be asked to decide whether the proposed reform should be accompanied by a longer-term plan to legitimate the law by procedures provided for in the Constitution (such as referenda) or statute.[150] Another way to consider Letowska's approach is as 'balancing jurisprudence'; in other words, more often than not, constitutional courts in the CEE have deferred to parliament. In the Polish context, the Constitutional Tribunal has created a notion of the rule-of-law state under a temporary constitutional document, a notion that reflects the trust between the citizen and the state. This is not always successful and it can result in curious, if not bad, case law. As discussed by Sadurski, the Polish Constitutional Tribunal has exercised a far-reaching deference in the series of abortion cases heard in the 1990s, culminating in a ruling that superseded all expectations, both of the supporters and of the opponents of the relevant law.[151]

Finally, the Constitutional Tribunal and the Commissioner for the Protection of Citizens' Rights (ombudsman) have played a leading role in bringing legitimacy to the law. As mentioned above, the notion of the rule-of-law state has acquired shape early on: one of the components is citizens' trust. Unless there is transparency and discussion about the law, the public will feel dissatisfied at being uninformed, possibly risking the credibility or legitimacy of the law.[152] In fact, the ombudsman has been a critical tool in the eyes of the respective officeholders as a means to ensure that an 'imprint' or impression is made and related to the official in office at

---

Panstwo i Prawo [State and Law], 4–5 (1996), p. 45.

148 *Ibid.*, p. 46.

149 *Ibid.*, p. 50. See also Krzysztof Kolakowski, 'Glos cywilisty' [The Voice of a Civil Lawyer], *Rzeczpospolita*, 6 May 1998 (accessed online).

150 Letowska, 'Bariery', *supra* n. 147, p. 52.

151 Wojciech Sadurski, *Rights Before Courts: A Study of Constitutional Courts in Postcommunist States of Central and Eastern Europe* (Dordrecht: Springer, 2008).

152 *Ibid.*, p. 58.

the time – a task that has not always been easy.[153] The creation of this institution by a regime that was soon to collapse – although this was not publicly known – could not predict its influence on the law.

The Constitutional Tribunal has concentrated on interpreting the doctrine of the rule of law since 1989. According to Article 1 of the Small Constitution (currently Article 2), 'the Republic of Poland shall be a democratic rule of law state'. This clause was modelled on the clause in the German Constitution. The most important decisions concerning constitutionalism concern the notion of the 'state ruled by law' and the 'principle of equality'.[154] In its August 1990 decision, the tribunal began to lay down jurisprudence concerning the notion of the rule-of-law state. The case concerned then President Jaruzelski's challenge to the 1990 Pension Act, which reduced pensions of former Communist Party and state officials.[155] The Act provided that former party and state officials who had not yet reached retirement age and had been awarded higher pensions would lose them, and instead receive pensions of the lowest category. The tribunal based its decision on the principles of the non-retroactivity of law, citizens' trust in the state, and the protection of vested rights. While the tribunal did not find the Act unconstitutional, it did draw important conclusions concerning vested rights, finding that the pensions granted to the party officials and state officials did not deserve protection as a vested right under the 'state ruled by law' clause. 'The vested rights came about in a manner contrary to the principles of social justice. Former party or state officials are thus able to obtain special pension privileges, on the basis of this law, although the principles of "vested right" do not apply when the right is based on law unjustly created.'[156] The tribunal's reasoning firmly established the constitutional status of the non-retroactivity of laws and the protection of vested rights.[157] It is also important to note that citizens' trust in law is an important component of the rule of law, and one that frequently appeared in the decisions of the tribunal.[158] For example, in the early 1990s the tribunal had often stressed the importance of publishing laws – the failure of such publication was criticised widely – 'the most glaring weakness of the Polish legal order in the publication of normative acts is

153 Interview with Prof. Dr Andrzej Zoll, (former) Commissioner for the Protection of Citizens' Rights (Ombudsman), 17 October 2005.

154 Brzezinski, *The Struggle for Constitutionalism in Poland*, *supra* n. 144, pp. 165–75.

155 Judgment K 7/90 of 22 August 1990, *Orzecznictwo Trybunalu Konstytucyjnego w 1990 roku* [The Decisions of the Constitutional Tribunal from 1990], pp. 42–58.

156 *Ibid.*, p. 52.

157 *Ibid.* See also Leszek Garlicki, 'Przeglad orzecznictwa Trybunalu Konstytucyjnego za 1990 rok' [An Overview of the Decisions of the Constitutional Tribunal from 1990], *Przeglad Sadowy* [Court Review], 3 (1990), pp. 58–71, and Brzezinski, *The Struggle for Constitutionalism in Poland*, *supra* n. 144, pp. 166–67.

158 Janina Zakrzewska, *Spor o konstytucji* [A Conflict over the Constitution] (Warsaw: Wydawnictwo Sejmowe, 1993), pp. 82–85.

that it permits binding legal norms despite the fact that they are not published.'[159] In 1991, parliament passed legislation amending the 1950 law on the publication of *Dziennik Ustaw* (Daily Laws) and *Monitor Polski* (Polish Monitor), in which all newly promulgated laws must appear.

The issue of vested rights was readdressed in a case concerning the protection of property of the former Communist Party. While the tribunal recognised the protection of pension rights, it was not willing to extend the rule-of-law clause (Article 1) to the property of the former Communist Party, much to the surprise of the group of deputies from the Social Democracy for the Republic of Poland Party. In 1990, the *Sejm* passed legislation on the transfer to the state treasury of all of the party's assets in existence as of 24 August 1989, save for membership dues.[160] The law provided that all legal transactions concluded after that date that were intended to reduce the party's assets were null and avoid; no compensation was provided by the law for the nationalisation of the property. The deputies argued that the law violated the rule-of-law clause (Article 1) of the Constitution by infringing vested property rights, which, they argued, were acquired in good faith by both the party and those who had purchased party assets. The tribunal rejected the claim of the petitioners, declaring that the principle of vested rights could be enforced only with regard to rights acquired in a lawful and ethical manner.[161] This approach has been criticised by scholars who point to the exceptions made to the recognition of equality in new democratic CEE states.[162]

Retroactivity and the Acquis Constitutionnel

De-communisation is complex, especially in the legal arena, where painful and paradoxical questions arise in the attempt to satisfy aspirations in setting up a rule-of-law state. It is during this process that a state wishes its foundations to be rooted in values protecting democracy and the rule of law. One of the unavoidable questions relates to addressing human rights abuses committed under former regimes. The human rights abuses need to be considered alongside the perversion of the law, collaboration with the state's security intelligence, and political crimes. As indicated in the discussion on vested rights, certain states were willing to create

159 Slawomira Wronkowska, 'O publikacji aktow normatywnych' [Concerning the Publication of Normative Acts], *Rzeczpospolita*, 30 March 1993 (accessed online). See also Zakrzewska, *supra n. 158*.

160 *Ustawa z dnia 9 listopada 1990r. o przejeciu majatku bylej Polsiej Zjednoczonej Partii Robotniczej* [Law of 9 November 1990 Concerning the Acquisition of Assets of the Former Polish United Workers' Party], *Dziennik Ustaw* (1990), No. 16, item 72.

161 Judgment K 3/91 from 25 February 1992, *Orzecznictwo Trybunalu Konstytucyjnego w 1992 – cz. I*, p. 23. See also Leszek Garlicki, 'Przeglad orzecznictwa za 1992 rok' [An Overview of the Decisions from 1992], *Przeglad Sadowy*, 10 (1993), pp. 77–78, and Brzezinski, *The Struggle for Constitutionalism in Poland*, *supra* n. 144, pp. 169–71.

162 Sadurski, *Rights Before Courts*, *supra* n. 151, p. 262.

a new category of citizens that would be denied certain rights in the developing democracy. This, in itself, is not difficult to appreciate and support, especially if the privileges were ones that were gained unfairly and unethically, in light of present-day economic considerations, but also in light of the assurances that were made to society under the socialist state.

In criminal law, the situation acquires certain complexities. The cornerstone of criminal law, namely retroactivity, is engaged when considering human rights abuses. Since the Second World War, for very good reasons, the principles of retroactivity and analogy in the criminal law have been addressed and rejected. Article 7 of the European Convention on Human Rights, for example, which incorporates the principle of legality *nullum crimen, nulla poena sine lege*, states that

> No person may be punished for an act that was not a criminal offence at the time of its commission. The article states that a criminal offence is one, under either national or international law, which would permit a party to prosecute someone for a crime which was not illegal under their domestic law at the time, so long as it was prohibited by (possibly customary) international law. The Article also prohibits a heavier penalty being imposed than was applicable at the time when the criminal act was committed.

However, the European Court of Human Rights has recognised that, in certain instances, retrospective law can be permitted to try people according to the norms and standards that had already been acknowledged internationally, before the acts were committed. In other words, there is a timeless element to values of human dignity and life. Article 7(2) has been said to endorse 'victor's justice'; however, it is important to distinguish between the procedural and substantive components of the principle.

In Poland, the principle of non-retroactivity had been challenged in 1991 by a series of cases contesting parliamentary statutes adopted to address crimes committed during the Stalinist period.[163] The question of the criminal liability of former Communist Party and state officials has been a significant political concern since 1989. In 1991, the *Sejm* amended the 1984 Law on the Main Commission for the Investigation of Nazi Crimes in Poland (*Glowna Komija Badania Zbrodnie Hitlerowskich w Polsce*), owing to the fact that the statutory period for Stalinist crimes had long expired. This law defines Stalinist crimes as 'crimes against individuals or groups of individuals, committed by authorities of the communist state, or tolerated and instigated by those authorities', providing for their prosecution if they took place before 31 December 1956. The amendment changed the law to stipulate that the statute of limitations would not apply to Stalinist crimes that were 'crimes against humanity', genocide, and 'other serious persecution' on the basis

163 For further details about this period, see Chapter 3.

of race, religion, nationality and other factors.[164] The amendment was challenged, and in September 1991, the tribunal recognised the general prohibition against retroactive criminal laws, but also found that crimes committed between 1944 and 1956 warranted a different approach. In this highly sensitive case, the tribunal noted the special nature of the political transition and argued that any departure from the principle of *lex retro non agit* requires a very precise definition.[165] This precision is important with respect to time. The tribunal maintained that the term 'Stalinist crime' (*zbrodnia stalinowska*) was not adequately defined, allowing too wide a scope to police and judicial officials. The law was eventually modified by the *Sejm* and would eventually be amended, as we shall see below.

The retroactivity of a law may not have been expressly provided for in the Constitution at the time, but quickly became one of the fundamental components of the rule of law, as interpreted by the tribunal.[166] It was not absent or inaccessible as concerns European Court of Human Rights jurisprudence. This issue has been, needless to say, a delicate one, because it not only concerns crimes committed during the Second World War and the Stalinist period, but also raises questions as to how to deal with collaborators and informants of the communist period. Of course, how does one define collaborators? Many scholars were not happy with the ruling, viewing the way in which the Polish authorities were proceeding as a violation of one of the fundamental tenets of the doctrine of the rule of law.[167] It is, however, confined to a particular period of Polish history, and one that is noted for its repression and terror, as discussed in Chapters 3 and 4.

It would have been highly questionable to retaliate against the Polish governmental leaders who participated in the agreements reached at the Round Table Talks. This was not the nature of the talks, as noted above. Moreover, the removal of all high-level administrators and judges would have created a serious administrative vacuum, and might have been detrimental, particularly in the beginning of the transition. In general, such a problem was not faced in Germany, which had the qualified persons to fill the East German posts. However, calls for

---

164 Geneva Convention of 9 September 1948, *Dziennik Ustaw* (1952), No. 2, item 9.

165 Judgment S 6/91 of 25 September 1991, *Orzecznictwo Trybunalu Konstytucyjnego w 1991 roku*, p. 294. See also Leszek Garlicki, 'Przeglad orzecznictwa Trybunalu Konstytucyjnego za 1991 rok' [An Overview of the Decisions of the Constitutional Tribunal from 1991], *Przeglad Sadowy*, 11–12 (1992), pp. 54–55. See also Brzezinski, *Struggle for Constitutionalism in Poland, supra* n. 144, pp. 167–68.

166 Judgment of 22 August 1990, K 7/90, pp. 50–51.

167 For an excellent discussion on the topic and related aspects, see Jorg Arnold and Ewa Weigend, 'Prawo karne, zmiana systemu politycznego i obrachunek z przesloscia w Polsce i w Niemczech' [Criminal Law, Changes in the Political System and Coming to Terms with the Past in Poland and Germany], in *Prawo karne a problem zmiany ustroju politycznego/Strafrecht und politischer Systemweschel* [Criminal Law and the Problems Concerning Changes in the Political Structure], ed. by Albin Eser and Andrzej Zoll (Cracow: Kantor Wydawniczy Zakamycze; Freiburg-im-Breisgau: Max-Planck-Institut, 1998), pp. 19–72.

screening have continued to be strong in Poland, if only because the public still awaits some sort of 'apology' from many of the former collaborators now in high government positions.[168] The situation was different in Czechoslovakia, where there was no negotiated transition, the tendency being more revolutionary. Many commentators argue that this led to more radical de-communisation measures.[169] Other CEE countries have had to deal with this question, and criminal liability for past transgressions was considered a viable option.[170] However, the Hungarian Constitutional Court ruled that lifting the statute of limitations with regard to crimes committed, *inter alia*, in suppressing the 1956 Revolution, was unconstitutional. In contrast to the Polish courts, the Hungarian courts ruled that any *ex post facto* attempt to extend the statute of limitations violated the principle of the rule of law, even if this meant that the worst crimes would go unpunished.[171]

Moreover, the process of de-communisation is meant to lay the foundations of democracy and the rule of law, and this entails the adoption of a new constitution and a reform of the entire legal framework.[172] One of the most important aspects of this process is that legal and political responsibility should be kept separate.[173] The rules of legal responsibility have been established by the Nuremberg trials; they have had direct relevance to criminal responsibility for past misconduct and have put forward two principles: the punitive and the due process principles.[174] A separate, parallel development is the treatment of individuals suspected of colluding or collaborating with the former security and intelligence services, and who are participating in the new state structure, in a political capacity or civil service function. Pomorski aptly observes that screening laws have a fundamental flaw in that they add political responsibility to one's past legal responsibility.[175] Screening laws, vetting laws, or lustration laws are inevitably bound by partisan politics: they can bar individuals from political life, and this, in turn, arguably deprives society of voting options, a key part of the democratic process. A critique of such

168 Los, 'Lustration and Truth Claims', *supra* n. 131.

169 See Přibáň, *Legal Symbolism*, *supra* n. 16.

170 Arnold and Weigend, 'Prawo karne', *supra* n. 167, pp. 39–44.

171 To compare the Hungarian Constitutional Court's decision with that of the famous German 'border guards' case, see Ruti Teitel, 'Paradoxes in the Revolution of the Rule of Law', *Yale Journal of International Law*, 19 (1994), pp. 239–47, and Kip Augustine Adams, 'What Is Just? The Rule of Law and Natural Law in the Trials of Former East German Border Guards', *Stanford Journal of International Law*, 29 (1993), pp. 271–314. See also Přibáň, *Legal Symbolism*, *supra* n. 16.

172 Jerzy Turowicz, 'PRL dla doroslych' [PRL for Adults], *Tygodnik Powszechny* [Common Weekly], 5 November 1995, p. 5.

173 Stanislaw Pomorski, 'Meanings of "Decommunization by Legal Means"', *Review of Central and East European Law*, 22 (1996), 331–37.

174 *Ibid.*, pp. 334–35. See also Aeyel M. Gross, 'Reinforcing the New Democracies: The European Convention on Human Rights and the Former Communist Countries – A Study of the Case Law', *European Journal of International Law*, 7 (1996), pp. 89–102.

175 *Ibid.*, p. 337.

measures in Czechoslovakia was made by the International Labour Organisation (ILO). For example, efforts have been made by several post-communist states to control the electoral process. The contention that former communists are being voted back into office should not justify the use of screening laws, no matter what the involvement of the candidate(s) entailed during the period in question. This fails to address the purpose of the measures, a point made in *Zdanoka v. Latvia*, with respect to prohibiting a former Latvian Communist Party member from standing for election. The European Court of Human Rights, referring to case law dealing with bans on fascist parties, was sensitive to the Latvian historical context, in a ruling that supported the Latvian Constitutional Court decision and one that also stressed that any preemptive measures must undergo rigorous scrutiny and are not meant to impose bans of indefinite length.[176]

In October 1998, the Polish Constitutional Tribunal passed its judgment on the constitutionality of the screening law.[177] The law concerned the disclosure of the work or activities of state security organs or the cooperation with these organs in the years 1944–1990 of persons performing public functions. The law was challenged by President Kwasniewski (1995–2005), who based his claim on, *inter alia*, the fact the law violated the right to privacy.[178] The tribunal held that the law was constitutional. Since this decision, the function of the 'screening court', or lustration court, has been transferred to the Appellate Court in Warsaw. A separate division was established to hear only cases related to screening public officials; all cases were to be reviewed first by the Office of the Ombudsman for the Public Interest.[179] This office has been replaced by the Institute of National Remembrance (*Instytut Pamieci Narodowe*; hereafter IPN).[180] These steps suggest that in Poland there is some need to address the transgressions of the former regime, yet it is not clear that the measures taken lead to demands for justice. It is equally uncertain whether the moves to create the screening court are popular; the reforms have been

176 See *X* v. *Italy* [1976] D&R 5; *Glasenapp* v. *Germany* [1986] ECHR 9; and *Vogt* v. *Germany* [1995] ECHR 29.

177 *Ustawa z 11 kwietna 1997r. o ujawnieniu pracy lub sluzby w organiach bezpieczenstwa panstwa lub wspolpracy z nimi w latach 1944–1990 osob pelniacych funkcje publiczne* [Law 816 of 11 April 1997 Concerning the Disclosure of Public Officials Who Have Worked for or Have Had Functions in State Security Organs or Cooperation with These Organs During 1944–1990], *Dziennik Ustaw* No. 70, item 443. See also *Dziennik Ustaw* (1998), No. 131, item 860.

178 Judgment K 24/98 from 21 October 1998. See http://www.trybunal.gov.pl (last accessed 14 June 2009).

179 The high case load in the criminal courts is the main reason that the competence to hear these cases was granted to the Appellate Court. Jolanta Kroner, 'Sedziowie juz sa, brakuje ustawy' [The Judges Are Here, the Law Is Absent], *Rzeczpospolita*, 7 August 1998 (accessed online).

180 See http://www.ipn.gov.pl (last accessed 14 June 2009).

supported and driven by president Lech Kaczynski, and by his brother, Jaroslaw Kaczynski, when he served as prime minister.[181]

Thus, developments in law and politics occurred in tandem and would eventually collide. Brzezinski observes that, by 1992, the tribunal had established and reaffirmed two important elements of the rule-of-law clause, namely the prohibition of retroactive laws and the protection of vested rights.[182] Moreover, the tribunal also defined certain areas not protected by the rule-of-law clause, such as rights obtained in an unjust manner and crimes committed during the Stalinist period. Since then, the tribunal has developed additional procedural and institutional components. For example, in 1993, the tribunal found that judicial independence and the independence of the judiciary are an essential aspect of the rule-of-law clause.[183] This was an important decision for the Polish judiciary. A key component concerns citizens' trust in the law, a notion frequently cited in the decisions of the tribunal.

In the former East Germany, the purge of lawyers and political officials was expedient and effective,[184] and in Czechoslovakia the 'screening' law was passed to prevent former secret police collaborators from participating in the creation of democratic institutions. In both countries, indeed in any state adopting such legislation, the screening process has raised disturbing questions about 'collaboration'.[185] The frustration on the part of the government and society is strongly linked to one of the most difficult aspects of transition: the fact that the *nomenklatura* had managed to remain in control of many important positions, and continually attempted to translate its prior political privileges into economic rights.[186] But this is not the aim of lustration laws. Albeit forward-looking, as in the Polish case, they are meant to validate a claim related to the past rather than

181 It is interesting to note that no political party has rejected the idea of a screening law. See Andrzej Rzeplinski, 'A Lesser Evil?', *East European Constitutional Review*, 1 (1992), pp. 33–35. For an excellent discussion on the screening law policies of various post-communist countries, see Stanley Cohen, 'State Crimes of Previous Regimes: Knowledge, Accountability, and the Policing of the Past', *Law and Social Inquiry*, 20 (1995), pp. 7–50.

182 Brzezinski, *The Struggle for Constitutionalism in Poland, supra* n. 144, p. 171.

183 The details of the case were discussed in the previous section.

184 For an interesting account of the purge of judicial officials from East Germany, according to West German legal principles, see Erhard Blankenburg, 'The Purge of Lawyers After the Breakdown of the East German Regime', *Law and Social Inquiry*, 20 (1995), pp. 223–43. See also Gisela Shaw, 'Courts and Judges in the New Federal States in United Germany: Has Legal Unification Worked?', *Svensk Juristtidning* (1995), pp. 32–44.

185 According to one former East German judge, there was a general feeling that the public should help in the detection of criminal acts and evidence gathering. The understanding was that every good socialist citizen kept a close watch over the actions of others. Interview with Dr Jorg Arnold, former criminal court judge, and lecturer at the Max-Planck-Institut, Freiburg-im-Breisgau, Germany, 7 May 1993.

186 'Comrades Coin It as Poles Privatise', *Guardian*, 26 July 1995, p. 9.

be used as a political weapon to prohibit participation in state activities. This has resulted in a public outcry to prosecute the former 'collaborators' and to implement radical de-communisation, including in the administration of justice.[187] But these decisions come together at the regional level, on the part of the European Court of Human Rights. While the court recognised that national states are best placed to access national matters, as in *Zdanoka* v. *Latvia*,[188] there were warnings to indicate that these measures must have a scope when dealing with a transitional period. Likewise, criticism by the ILO of the Czechoslovak law was based on grounds of discrimination that did not fully appreciate the remedies made available in the framework of administrative law.[189]

A Polish communist crime is now defined as an action of a functionary of the communist state that was carried out in the period 17 September 1939 to 31 December 1989. The action must have been repressive and have violated human rights, and can cover a variety of actions that were meant to harm or injure people. While a statute of limitations exists for communist crimes, it does not apply to crimes against humanity, war crimes, or crimes against peace, under international law. As mentioned above, these crimes are investigated by the IPN. The IPN also regulates lustration for 53 categories of people born before 1 August 1972 who hold relevant positions, such as within the state structure, legal community, the academic community or the news media.

This is where the *acquis constitutionnel* on the part of the Polish Constitutional Tribunal comes to the fore. In the tribunal's judgment of 11 May 2007, key aspects of the 2006 reform on screening were found to be unconstitutional, making the role of the IPN unclear and calling the whole process into question. Most importantly, the part of the law that would have required about 700,000 people in the above 53 categories to submit declarations on whether they had spied for the secret services has been thrown out. With this key change, the role of the IPN in the lustration process is now highly unclear. The damage that has resulted from leaks in the press has been labelled by Michnik a 'witch-hunt'.[190] Scholars and politicians alike in Poland are now declaring that, since the whole lustration process in the old format is essentially finished, the secret police archives should be made public. This is an important comment on the aspect of time limitations in a transitional period. The tribunal itself has affirmed the role of the IPN as an archive. Others oppose making it an open archive, arguing that the release of all personal and confidential information contained in the files would cause unacceptable harm to innocent

187 The outcry reached a peak in 1992, during the short-lived government of Jan Olszewski. As a rabid supporter of de-communisation, and opponent of the Mazowiecki government, Olszewski called for 'the beginning of the end of communism', invoking a moral stand against the crimes of a totalitarian government.

188 *Supra* n. 176.

189 See Přibáň, *Legal Symbolism*, *supra* n. 16, pp. 188–89.

190 Adam Michnik, 'The Polish Witch-Hunt', *New York Review of Books*, 28 June 2007, pp. 25–26.

people (yet this would be better than full disclosure, which violates informational autonomy); indeed, this risk of harm informs part of the tribunal's reasoning. What is evident, and this is something that the Constitutional Tribunal has indicated, is that the lustration aim must be clear. The judgment itself indicates an awareness of the European Court of Human Rights' approach to receiving and imparting information under Article 10 of the European Convention in Human Rights.[191] In other words, it should be a validation of a claim, *not* punishment. While the tribunal's approach reveals the maturity of the Polish court – in terms of a recognition of human rights information that demonstrates awareness of the wider human rights framework – the tension still remains between criminal prosecution and the open archive. It is worth recalling that the Hungarian courts argued along similar lines much earlier on and rejected Hungarian measures with arguments that showed the significance of continuity in the Hungarian legal order.[192] A court can be the corrective tool; it can address the faults within a policy that seeks to maintain the pernicious features of a system that continues to guide political decision-making, thus creating a situation similar to Foucault's panopticon, so reminiscent of the all-seeing eye that characterised the Soviet procuracy.[193] This, of course, cannot be entirely resolved by the constitutional courts. Both Přibáň and Sadurski recognise the problems that arise with respect to disclosure of collaborators and access to materials that are alleged to be incomplete or falsified. In the end, the need to establish the truth about the period is a compelling and indispensable part of the democratic process for CEE states.[194] The problem arises in identifying the purpose of such official bodies and how successful they are in helping society reach a consensus about the past.

The Czechoslovak court opinion on the lustration law of 4 October 1991 is often discussed as a judgment encompassing principles of natural justice and making a specific comment on the communist period.[195] For the purposes of this section, attention is paid to the part of the judgment that refers to an 'era of non-freedom' during which violations of civil liberties occurred – the court correctly viewed these as a means to control and maintain power, supporting the legislature's characterisation of the communist era. In fact, it rejected the option of a legal continuity that adhered to the principle of legal certainty – which would mean a finding of unconstitutionality on retrospective grounds – because that would have recognised the old regime as legitimate; surely such a decision, in the court's view,

191 Article 10, European Convention on Human Rights (freedom of expression).

192 See Přibáň, *supra* n. 16.

193 See Michel Foucault, *Discipline and Punish: The Birth of the Prison*, trans. by A. Sheridan (London: Penguin, 1991).

194 See Přibáň, *supra* n. 175, and Sadurski, *Rights Before Courts, supra* n. 151.

195 Constitutional Court of the Czech and Slovak Federal Republic Judgment Pl US 1/92 of 26 November 1992. See also decisions concerning extensions of provisions in judgments of 21 December 1993, 19/93 and 5 December 2001, Pl US 9/01.

would undermine all notions of substantive justice that the nascent state needed as a basic building block.[196]

The location of justice is different in these two contrasting opinions. It is almost as if the Polish leadership opted for the Czechoslovakian path, but without much regard for the meaning underlying the Round Table Talks, public opinion, or consequences, not to mention the implication that the tribunal should adopt a subservient attitude to the government's agenda.[197] Implicit in both Přibáň's and Sadurski's analyses is the significance of time and momentum. As noted above, the court can be seen as assuming a passive role in the sense that it awaits the cases to come before it. The tribunal has relied on the rule-of-law clause (Article 1) to ensure that state bodies function on the basis of justice, fairness and equity, and in nearly every decision it has invoked this notion that the clause 'democratic rule-of-law state' comprises a wide range of elements, which may not be clearly expressed in the Constitution but do derive from it.[198] The former Hungarian Constitutional Court president, László Sólyom, wrote that '[o]f all constitutional principles, the rule of law played a special, symbolic role: it represented the essence of the system change, being the watershed between the nondemocratic, nonconstitutional, socialist system and the new constitutional democracy.'[199] Still, its co-equal counterparts are expected to act or respond accordingly in policymaking areas. In the end, it takes a strong court to emerge from such pressure successfully.

The Polish Supreme Court

It is inevitable that the law will have to deal with the past in an effort to introduce the stability and consistency that a state must support in maintaining the rule of law. As we have seen, this question becomes especially salient in a state that is in the process of setting up the rule-of-law state, and all eyes (both internally and externally) will be on the way in which it considers the past. The decision to adhere to stability might have to be abandoned if the state selects the retroactive route; however, this can reflect the commitment to a higher value, or meta-value, of protecting the very core of the state's values, namely human dignity. The difficulty in reaching the heart of the discussion is the fact that these debates are largely

196 Constitutional Court of the Czech and Slovak Federal Republic Decision No. 1/92 of 26 November 1992.

197 See Roman David, 'Lustration Laws in Action: The Evaluation of Lustration Policy in the Czech Republic and Poland', *Law and Social Inquiry*, 28 (2003), 387–439.

198 Leszek Garlicki, 'Orzecznictwo w 1996 roku' [An Overview of Decisions from 1996], *Przeglad Sadowy*, 5 (1997), p. 111.

199 See Kim Lane Scheppele, 'When the Law Doesn't Count: The 2000 Election and the Failure of the Rule of Law', *University of Pennsylvania Law Review*, 149 (2000), pp. 1361–1438, and Sólyom and Brunner, *Constitutional Judiciary in a New Democracy*, *supra* n. 142.

overshadowed by politics.[200] An analysis of the discussions in this area reveals a state position that is not always supported by that state's respective constitutional court, and one that arguably means that law is much more than a system of positive laws and as such legal provisions will express certain cultural and moral values.

For the question of the past, the claim must address the aspect of time and temporality. For Přibáň, for example, the law also becomes a social symbol, and as a form of legal communication this will represent and reflect the identity of the community, and what influences its cultural and ethical position. In this context, the law also becomes a social symbol, and as a form of legal communication this will represent and reflect the identity of the community, and what influences its cultural and ethical position. Přibáň claims that the legal system internalises the notion of identity and time as moral absolutes, which can further be manipulated and fixed along the legal timeline of dealing with the past. On such issues the legal system is particularly attractive to individuals who wish to control and manipulate this identity. Because it concerns moral justice, Přibáň is correct in viewing periods of constitution-making as pertinent to legal symbolism. In other words, issues that concern moral justice require an ethical consideration if the law is to retain and reflect a symbolic value. As seen above, the process may require a further appreciation of values that are derived from universal sources, or 'meta-values'. Thus, there is a further acknowledgment of the moral and ethical aspects of constitution-making.[201]

As discussed in Chapter 3, the Hart–Fuller debate drew attention to the values that underpin the law and what our expectations are and ought to be as concerns their interpretation and application by the courts. Both positions touch upon the moral values that the judges are aware of and to a certain extent how far these should be taken into account. This is not dissimilar to the argumentation of the Czechoslovak Constitutional Court's 1991 position and its support of the parliamentary protection of substantive justice, as reflected in the depiction of communist rule, as noted above.

An analysis of legal reasoning in this area indicates that Polish judges are aware of moral values, and indeed they play a role in their reasoning. A decision might adopt a moral education argument, where there are compelling reasons for a law to be used a tool of moral education. This was the key to Petrazycki's idea about the 'active love of one's neighbour', where the claims that a legal order has on an individual can be increasing, while legal sanctions can decrease, attaining a society wherein all people would obey the law. The argument to do so would inevitably embrace majority opinion that would have acceptance as also embracing the cultural heritage of the society. If anything, the legal reasoning in this area

---

200 Sadurski, *Rights Before Courts*, *supra* n. 151.

201 See, for example, Adam Podgorecki and Vittorio Olgiati, eds, *Totalitarian and Post-Totalitarian Law* (Aldershot: Dartmouth, 1996).

does not reveal a sense of coherence, to use Peczenik's notion of truth.[202] It is impossible to assume that everyone is motivated by a moral argument, or, indeed, what its particular place in the legal framework should be, without its resulting in contradictory and further incoherence. Why this is so might be illuminated in the Supreme Court decision on the matter.

It is worth recalling that one of the points made by the subtable at the Polish Round Table Talks was that in order to promote and secure judicial independence the general courts had to petition the Constitutional Tribunal with questions relating to the constitutionality of laws. December 2007, seven months following the 2007 tribunal judgment noted above, saw the Polish Supreme Court hear a case (KZP 37/07) concerning disciplinary action to be taken against a Supreme Court judge adjudicating cases during the martial law period. The charge, brought by the IPN prosecutor, considered the retroactivity of the effect of the martial law decree, which was not published in the *Dziennik Ustaw* (Polish Official Law Gazette) until several days after it took effect. The legal question was twofold: whether the judges were breaking the criminal law maxim of *nulla poena sine lege* when convicting defendants under provisions introduced by martial law that made association with the proscribed political party Solidarity illegal. The appeal asked for clarification as to constitutional grounds or grounds relating to the date the law was said to be in force. The curious situation, as outlined above, as to the disparity in dates, namely the declaration of martial law and the official publication in the law gazette, easily fell into the category of retroactivity.

Under Article 4 of the International Covenant of Civil and Political Rights (ICCPR), no derogations from Article 15, even under martial law, are allowed. This factor, and the 1952 Polish Constitution, was considered by the Supreme Court. Poland was a party to the ICCPR since 1977. The Supreme Court began by indicating that the Law Concerning Promulgation of Laws from 1950 did not envisage such situations. According to Article 8 of the 1950 law, judges are meant to apply the law. This strict rule did not offer any clues about the application of law in instances of martial law. For the Supreme Court, it was clear that judges were not permitted constitutional review of statutes. It was the Council of State (*Rada Panstwa*) that had that competence. The court acknowledged that in the post-1989 period there was a more open-minded approach to such questions.

In a specially constituted chamber, the Supreme Court distinguished between 'date of publication' and the law taking 'effect from promulgation'. The court found in fact that this was a question of the declaration of martial law, the Polish Constitution and international law obligations. The court faced the question of whether the adjudicating bench at the time was free from statutory obligations to respect the law as from the date of publication of the law and/or the date of effect of the law. With martial law declared on 13 December 1981, if the nominal date of 14 December 1981 was recognised, then the actions of the defendants were

202 Aleksander Peczenik, 'Law Morality, Coherence and Truth', *Ratio Juris*, 7 (1994), pp. 146–76.

not criminal. The second question concerned whether the court was free from the statutory obligation of respecting the norms of Article 61 of the Decree on Martial Law. Article 61 of the decree, alongside the 1952 Constitution, does not provide for provisions prohibiting retroactive laws. In reply to the IPN prosecutor, the Supreme Court was reluctant to recognise the immunity granted to judges in question as 'clearly baseless'. It felt that such a claim of 'clearly baseless' was sound in relation to concrete cases. It was nothing of the sort. As this case concerned crimes as found in the martial law decree, the focus instead was on the state of law at the time, a situation the court characterised as one of *superfluum*. Neither Article 3 concerning publication of laws nor Article 61 of the martial law decree was incompatible with the 1952 Constitution as that document could not put into place laws that released judges from applying a range of law, even if they violated the principle of *lex retro non agit*. In an interesting twist compared to other cases, such as the border guards cases heard by the German Federal Supreme Court,[203] the Polish Supreme Court opted for a positivistic reading of the law, rather than reaching for a more creative reading and application of norms as found in the ICCPR. The Polish counterpart's decision distinguished between the 'new sense of law' found in the new constitutional period after 1997, but that as this 'new sense of law' could not apply to the period in question, it was not reasonable to ask judges to consider the questions in this light. In light of the discussion concerning judicial independence above, this is a significant comment. There is only so much that one can expect from the judge working within such strict confines of the law.

To illustrate, it is worth looking at the border guards case noted above as regards addressing retroactivity. This concerned the liability of East German border guards who had killed fugitives trying to escape over the Berlin Wall or cross the border separating East and West Germany. After 1990, the German courts were required to deal with charges of homicide against these guards. The law relevant to the crimes committed in the East German territory prior to German unification was the criminal law of East Germany, unless the law of the Federal Republic of Germany was more favourable to the defendant. The defendants called upon East German law to show that their actions were lawful.

The German State Court, of course, had a blueprint in the form of the Nuremberg trials. It applied Radbruch's formula (see below), to determine liability for the killings of the fugitives. The decision was strongly rooted in the idea of justice that was more compelling than the notion of non-retroactivity. The German court found that the action of killing fugitives, although it did not constitute a crime against humanity, was so reprehensible that it called for the actions to be criminalised. The decision further showed the importance of 'knowledge', a more difficult factor to prove as it concerns the mental state. Eventually, the decision considered the role of international law versus domestic law. The German Democratic Republic did not transform the statute into domestic law, in contrast

203 *The Shootings at the Berlin Wall Case*, BGHSt Band 39, S. 1, 5 StR 370/92, Berlin.

to Poland. Finally, the German court found that the actions were illegal even under the East German regime, and that no reading of the law would afford a defence. This position holds that there are certain situations where one would have to admit that a crime was committed under the law of that regime too. In this respect, German constitutional jurisprudence arguably is far-reaching in the application of human rights protection and the defence of it. For example, German basic law (*Grundgesetz*) also provides, in Article 20(4), for 'the right of resistance against anybody who tried to overthrow the constitutional order, if there are no other possible means'.[204] This is at times discussed as 'militant democracy' and refers specifically to resistance against dictatorship.[205] This is provided for on rare occasions by states, such as Germany, within the constitution, despite the contradictory nature of such provisions. This idea of a democracy being able to defend itself has been acknowledged and recognised in the Czechoslovak, and later the Czech, experience. According to Přibáň, this is the main basis for justifying the post-1989 Czechoslovak and German de-communisation policies.[206] The need for institutional protections far outweighs the self-contradictory feature that is attached to providing for such claims in a new constitutional framework.

The Polish court, by contrast, relied mainly on the fact that judges were subject only to the law, and that in contrast to the situation created in 1997, judges were not allowed the scope to constitutionally review statutes. This was the key to the judgment. The decision recognised the state of law at the time of martial law and the communist period. This is perhaps an indication of the Polish treatment of the past. It is also an indication of the way in which higher courts approach constitutional review. The decision, in fact, has both forward-looking and backward-looking facets, but it did not attempt to construct the 'bridge' between the two, as was done by the German courts. Of course, such a path can be criticised – *for the far-reaching scope of the role of knowledge that should be assumed by the individual*. It could be maintained that the German court went too far in expecting the East German border guards to anticipate the political changes of 1989 and the inevitable charges brought against them for violating the right to life of the fugitives. The lack of constitutional provision for the supremacy of international law, which would have guided judges during the period of martial law crimes, did not impose a responsibility on judges to recognise the principle of retroactivity. Likewise, the 1950 Law Concerning the Promulgation of Laws obliged judges to apply the law from the date of publication, as did Article 61 of the martial law

---

204 Roland Wittmann, 'Responsibility and Human Rights Protection', in *Liber Amicorum de José de Sousa e Brito*, ed. by A. Silva Dias *et al.* (Coimbra: Almedina, 2009), pp. 746–47.

205 *Zdanoka* v. *Latvia*, *supra* n. 176, and David Kommers, *The Constitutional Jurisprudence of the Federal Republic of Germany, 2nd edn* (Durham, NC: Duke University Press, 1992).

206 Přibáň, *Legal Symbolism*, *supra* n. 16, pp. 184–85.

decree, which concerned the application of laws as from the date of their effect, which would include a retroactive application.

This is not the first time that the courts had to decide on these matters. The 2007 decision recalls one slipshod move towards national reconciliation that was made in the early 1990s when an attempt was made by the Polish right-wing parties to prosecute Jaruzelski. Suffice it to say that the way in which the proceedings were conducted provided an example of the use of the courts for political means.[207] The proceedings continued in a disorganised fashion until 1995, when the charges were dropped.[208] Despite this, the political agenda as concerns lustration and dealing with past injustices, such as the inconclusive decision to impose martial law, was set with the assumption of power by Lech and Jaroslaw Kaczynski, of the Law and Justice Party (*Prawo i Sprawiedliwosc, PiS*), when for a time they were president and prime minister, respectively.

The 2007 Supreme Court decision revisited a question raised in 1992, when hearings were initiated against Jaruzelski. Imposing martial law was not a crime, as the Polish Constitution provided for martial law when the security of the state was endangered. The question was whether the state had indeed been in danger; thus the charges were based on technicalities. The first ruling found that only parliament could declare martial law, not the State Council, as had been done. The second ruling found that the decree had not been published in the Dziennik Ustaw (Polish Official Gazette) until several days after it took effect. It was this issue that the court considered in conjunction with retroactivity.

As mentioned above, the court acknowledged that Poland had several international law obligations arising from the ICCPR, which was ratified by the state in 1977.[209] As noted above, Articles 4 (emergency situations) and 15 (applicable crimes) were the key provisions. The Supreme Court, relying on

207 In September 1992, the *Sejm*'s Committee on Constitutional Responsibility opened its hearings against Jaruzelski, former minister of the interior Kiszczak, and 24 members of the Council of State in the matter of martial law. If the committee voted to proceed, the case would pass to the whole *Sejm*, which could then vote to send it to the State Tribunal. The trial of Jaruzelski served both historical and political purposes. From the legal point of view, it was a complex case. Ryszard Reiff, 'Zmarnowana szansa Jaruzelskiego' [Jaruzelski's Lost Chance], *Gazeta Wyborcza*, 24 November 1992, pp. 12–13.

208 'Szanse generalow' [The General's Chances], *Rzeczpospolita*, 7 October 1993, pp. 1, 9; Wojciech Jaruzelski, 'Rachunek sumienia' [A Bill of Conscience], *Rzeczpospolita*, 25–26 September 1993; Jan Nowak-Jazioranski, 'Rownowanie absolutne' [Balancing the Absolute], *Rzeczpospolita*, 30 October–1 November 1993, p. 11; Wojciech Jaruzelski, 'Z oddali' [From the Distance], *Rzeczpospolita*, 6–7 November 1993, p. 13; Ewa Kaszuba, 'Obrona panstwa czy ustroju' [The Protection of the State or Structure], *Rzeczpospolita*, 25 May 1994, p. 3; and Maciej Lukasiewicz, 'Nie wszystkie grzechy swiata' [Not All the Sins of the World (Interview with General Jaruzelski)], *Rzeczpospolita*, 5–6 March 1994, pp. 11, 13–14.

209 See http://treaties.un.org/Pages/Treaties.aspx?id=4&subid=A&lang=en (last accessed 14 June 2009).

research on the supremacy of international law, argued that at that time Poland did not have international law obligations (under the ICCPR), and such obligations had not been incorporated into domestic law by the Council of State, the only organ that had that competence. In the court's view, the issue of retroactivity did not exist, as supported by the 1969 Criminal Code (Article 121) and the 1952 Constitution. The court rejected the argument that judges had an obligation at that time to review the constitutionality of the provision.

The Supreme Court's 2007 decision mentioned the Constitutional Tribunal's competence of constitutional review, in particular its binding nature as from 1997. In this area, the Supreme Court took great pains to describe a situation that was far from clear, as presented by the IPN in relation to granting immunity to judges further to Article 80 of the 2001 Law Concerning Common Courts. In contrast to the Constitutional Tribunal, which has created an *acquis constitutionnel*, albeit after some time, and a normative framework that incorporated international and regional obligations, the Supreme Court provided a different answer to a long-standing question and reaffirm the state's obligations under international and regional law. Thus, the court curiously left itself open to criticism.[210] This has left some judges frustrated that in certain aspects of the court the legal thinking has not changed; for these judges, reference to natural law principles reflects the creativity and fresh air that is still craved two decades on.[211] This problem is further exacerbated by the support expressed by the European Court of Human Rights. For these judges, the rule of law does not extend to the martial law period, nor is there a recognition or appreciation of historical questions and legal questions, as expressed in the Czechoslovak approach.

Interestingly, the border guards decision considered above that reached the European Court of Human Rights reiterated the strength of legal arguments based on human dignity that outweighed other rights.[212] Přibáň's apt analysis of these decisions and the application of natural law principles to retroactivity, as well as the problems arising from imposing a legal order, are seen as upholding rule-of-law principles in lieu of the old order.[213] Despite the fact that Radbruch's

210 Interview with Prof. Dr Piotr Hofmanski, Supreme Court judge (Criminal Chamber), Warsaw, 18 October 2005 (Hofmanski interview 1).

211 Interview with Prof. Dr Piotr Hofmanski, Supreme Court judge (Criminal Chamber), Warsaw, 19 May 2008 (Hofmanski interview 2). See also Emil W. Plywaczewski, Adam Gorski and Andrzej Sakowicz, 'Wrongful Convictions in Poland: From Communist Era to the *Rechtsstaat* Experience', in *Wrongful Conviction: International Perspectives on Miscarriages of Justice*, ed. by C. Ronald Huff and Martin Killias (Philadelphia: Temple University Press, 2008), pp. 273–83.

212 See also *K.-H. W* v. *Germany* [2001] ECHR 229 and *Strzeletz, Kessler and Krenz* v. *Germany* [2001] ECHR 230.

213 Přibáň, *Legal Symbolism*, *supra* n. 16. See also P. Quint, 'The Border Guards Trial and the East German Past – Seven Arguments', *American Journal of Comparative Law*, 48 (2000), pp. 541–72; P. E. Quint, *The Imperfect Union: Constitutional Structures*

formula,[214] namely calling upon higher principles of justice, has been critiqued, certain notions of justice and values underpinning the rule of law remain timeless. Therefore, some form of retroactivity has been recognised at the constitutional level in CEE states. Furthermore, in *Strzeletz, Kessler and Krenz* v. *Germany*, the European Court of Human Rights argued that even '[i]f the GDR [German Democratic Republic] still existed, it would be responsible from the viewpoint of international law for the act concerned. It remains to be established that alongside that State responsibility the applicants individually bore criminal responsibility at the material time.'[215]

Does the Polish Supreme Court decision reveal 'an old order [that] remains valid within the framework of the amended constitution while its legitimacy rests upon the old constitution as well as the old legal order'?[216] For some, the answer is 'yes'. Nowhere are the issues more contentious than in cases dealing with retroactivity. It is this issue that is intrinsically linked to trust in the state. For some states, like Hungary, this has meant, above all, respect for the continuity of the law, in order to achieve legal stability. For other states, such as Czechoslovakia, trust in the state and law required a break with the past – a continuity in the law would undermine this. Poland never quite adopted this latter approach. Offe and Poppe point out that the 'old regime has its traces and residues within the new'.[217] In May 2008, in a Warsaw district court, a Polish judge ruled that the public prosecutors at the IPN must amend their indictment against Jaruzelski and other defendants to present a greater range of evidence. The story continues, with recent moves made to cut the pensions of former communists – the objectives of the law in question is to punish those who maintained 'an inhumane system of power'.[218]

A legal norm can be interpreted in more than one way; the interesting question concerns the intrinsic value attached to rules. Assuming that the judges are reasonable, they are free to look at sources of law when involved in legal interpretation. It is the position of source norms that reveals the boundaries of sources. A source norm or value judgment assists the judge in reasoning or judicial

of German Unification (Princeton, NJ: Princeton University Press 1997), pp. 3–6, 9–14, 22–34, 35–46, 47–55, 103–23, 166–93, 194–215.

214 Gustav Radbruch, 'Statutory Lawlessness and Supra-Statutory Law', *Oxford Journal of Legal Studies*, 26 (2006), pp. 1–11, first published in 1946, and, by the same author, 'Gesetzliches Unrecht und übergesetzliches Recht', *Süddeutsche Juristen-Zeitung*, 1 (1946), pp. 105–08.

215 *Ibid.*, para. 104.

216 *Ibid.*, p. 116.

217 Claus Offe and Ulrike Poppe, 'Transitional Justice After the Breakdown of the German Democratic Republic', in *Rethinking the Rule of Law After Communism*, ed. by Adam Czarnota, Martin Krygier and Wojciech Sadurski (Budapest: CEU Press, 2005), p. 159.

218 See Matthew Day, 'Poland Punishes Former Communist Leaders by Cutting Pensions', *Daily Telegraph*, 5 January 2010, at http://www.telegraph.co.uk/news/worldnews/europe/poland/ (accessed online).

interpretation. There are a variety of source norms that can give us the kind of knowledge that can result in further problems or puzzles, or a true knowledge of the law and the best result (that is, justice). Why do some segments of the Polish Supreme Court resist applying a particular source norm? Many norms do not contain substantive reasons. The Supreme Court did not feel compelled to create a new rule for reasons of justice. Instead it was persuaded by precedent. In the end, there are compelling reasons for maintaining continuity within a legal order. The court resisted making – recalling Peczenik – a jump in the law. For Peczenik, who was also inspired by Petrazycki, such jumps reflect the value of a just interpretation.[219] Writing about judicial reasoning in the Nordic experience, Peczenik's work explores the differences between hard and soft cases and the location of values. It can assist in this Polish context that a court's reasoning is guided by norms, which 'are principles, not rules'.[220] At times these clash, in particular, when the court has to address a particularly difficult issue such as retrospective justice, where the exact answer cannot be found within the law. Peczenik argues that this necessitates weighing and balancing, where a reasonable judicial decision is reached when based on a value judgment; this part of the decision is the deeper justification of the judicial decision, which is the 'justification of the justification', which would mean that the reasoning would be one that is 'reasonable and beneficial for legal society'.[221] In this snapshot, it could be said that the court lost an opportunity to define and support a notion of justice that is located in the source norms of international and regional instruments. It could, however, be the final comment on the 'thick, black' line policy adopted with respect to the Polish judiciary.

Conclusions

Chapter 5 examined key constitutional developments since the collapse of communism in 1989. Using Poland as a case study here, we see that the goal of the drafters to have a constitution by 1991 was overly ambitious, and it was not until 1997 that a new constitution was promulgated. In the interim, the Small Constitution, alongside certain provisions that were retained in the 1952 Constitution, functioned as a constitution. The Small Constitution thus initiated the search for the essentials of the rule of law and their realisation in the place of the aims outlined in the previous document, which, after all, embraced a wholly different ideology.[222] While the Small Constitution saw the need to regulate the

219 Aleksander Peczenik, *On Law and Reason* (Dordrecht: Kluwer, 1989).

220 *Ibid.*

221 Aulius Aarnio, 'Introduction', in Peczenik, *supra* n. 219, p. 7.

222 Wojciech Sokolewicz, 'Regulacja ustroju politycznego Polskiej Rzeczpospolitej Ludowej w Konstytucji: stan obecny i koniecznosc zmian' [The Regulation of the Political Structure of the Polish People's Republic: The Current Situation and the Need for Reform], *Studia Prawnicze* [Legal Studies], 2–3 (1989), pp. 227–44.

relation between the executive and legislative branches of government, it did not provide much guidance on the judiciary.[223] The judiciary was, in a sense, left to fend for itself. The 1997 Polish Constitution was more specific and has strengthened the position of the judiciary in relation to the executive and legislative branches of government, but it was not without problems.[224]

The 1997 Constitution also reflected the continuity of both the pre-war and communist periods. It is an interesting example of attempting to strike a balance between state restraint and state functioning for the good of all citizens. This 'common good' was a feature of the 1935 Polish Constitution, and experience has demonstrated that in an effort to carry out its many duties, the state may lose its ability to realise these goals and, in consequence, no longer protect the common good. This leads to the state protecting the interests of a limited number of persons and eventually losing legitimacy in the eyes of citizens.[225] Echoing the achievements of the pre-war period, the 1935 Polish Constitution reflects the common vision of three varying streams of thought. This is a remarkable achievement. More importantly, it contains a number of mechanisms to prevent abuses of power, as every person is able personally to address the state and its officials, already one step further since 1989, as this was permitted only via the Commissioner for the Protection of Citizens' Rights.

The attention the judiciary received early on with regard to improving their circumstances was short-lived, overshadowed by the question of national reconciliation. Not only has the judiciary itself been at the centre of measures, but recent reforms included a wide scope of society that resulted in a controversial 2007 decision on the part of the Constitutional Tribunal. This court's decision was contrasted with developments in the region and revealed the common struggle that binds CEE courts, namely independence. In the post-communist period, attempts to undermine judicial independence have occurred in various guises.

My analysis of the constitutional developments in post-communist Poland has hopefully revealed something of the intricacies of the transformation to a democratic rule-of-law state. Of course, experiences differ between CEE states. A constitution not only is an expression of the political identity of society, but is also a legal manifestation of its values and ideas, which are to be introduced in everyday life. The various democratic components must work together, but these institutions are clearly shaped and in many ways continue to be influenced by culture and values manifested and encouraged by the essential parts of society

223 Kruk, 'Wstep', *supra* n. 41.

224 Or, as Ewa Letowska has aptly formulated it, 'a Constitution for the Judge'. See Ewa Letowska, 'Poland: In Search of the "State of Law" and Its Future Constitution', in *Poland: Towards the Rule of Law*, ed. by Ewa Letowska and Janusz Letowski (Warsaw: Wydawnictwo SCHOLAR: 1996), pp. 10–22.

225 See Wiktor Osiatynski, 'A Brief History of the Constitution', *East European Constitutional Review*, 6 (1997), Nos. 2–3, 66–76, and, by the same author, 'Perspectives on the Current Constitutional Situation in Poland', *supra* n. 27, pp. 312–20.

that hold the key to hidden aspects of the democratic rule, revealing themselves in case law as further remnants of communist rule that continue to cultivate fear, ignorance and disrespect for a key feature in the rule-of-law state, judicial officials. At the same time, judicial officials continue to fight not only for further institutional resources, but also for the scope to engage in continued creativity in judicial reasoning, especially where there is blatant ignorance or absence of recognition of universal values.

For the most part, the uncritical adoption of constitutional institutions in the form of constitutional courts has resulted in unprecedented questions.[226] Scheppele shows that the cherished notions of human dignity and autonomy, underpinning the rule of law, may be shaped by CEE constitutional courts.[227] She argues that it is these bodies that respective CEE societies trust more than parliaments. Stemming from one-party rule, CEE societies crave another space within which to seek remedies for rights' violations. This may be true, where the people have knowledge of constitutional courts; in Poland, Hungary and Romania, for example, this varies and influences notions of law that shape legal consciousness and culture.[228] Such spaces are integral to redrawing the boundaries between private and public. These borders were blurred as a result of the repressive nature of the police state.[229] But the legal thinking at the constitutional level is not always reflected in the higher courts. Likewise, the respective constitutional court can only go so far in addressing significant questions related to justice. This is shown in the example of de-communisation. The rule of law might not always equate with objectives that are set out in terms of finding accountability and truth surrounding a certain event or period. This is because so many of the questions rely on developments in the political arena, an area that is so fraught in the CEE, to varying degrees.

Overall, the constitution viewed in its entirety is the starting point. Some lessons can be learned from revisiting and re-evaluating those values upon which the open society was created, when thinking about the current context within which the law and its legitimacy are discussed. Entry into the EU should not mean that this questioning ceases. This discussion has provided an overview of key developments in the post-communist period. It has identified features that comprise the link to the interwar period. The main questions have concentrated on de-communisation measures, because it is these measures that reflect the manner in which the communist state was dismantled and what features were retained.

226 Sadurski, *supra* n. 175.

227 Kim Lane Scheppele, 'A Comparative View of the Chief Justice's Role. Guardians of the Constitution: Constitutional Court Presidents and the Struggle for the Rule of Law in Post-Soviet Europe', *University of Pennsylvania Law Review*, 154 (2006), pp. 1757–1845.

228 See, for example, *Democracy in Poland 2005–2007*, ed. by Lena Kolarska-Bobinska, Jacek Kucharczyk and Jaroslaw Zbieranek (Warsaw: Institute of Public Affairs, 2007).

229 See Fijalkowski, 'The Paradoxical Nature of Crime Control in Post-Communist Europe', *supra* n. 127.

This extends to judicial reasoning and also acknowledgement of the nature of the law under communist rule, as revealed by the 2007 decision of the Polish Supreme Court. The discussion, in paring away the questions, further reveals within this contextual analysis how and why the rule of law is a challenge that is impossible to surmount in the most ideal of circumstances, let alone the experiences of CEE states such as Poland.

Chapter 6
Concluding Remarks

The poet Adam Zagajewski once wrote about the historic events of 1989 that

> [t]he changes come for me too late. Yet it is still too early for me to be able to conceive of the enormity of the changes and their significance. Citizens of the West are mere observers here .... A repugnant civilization is in decline; but it shaped me, I revolted against it, I tried to flee it, whether I liked it or not, I am certainly marked by it. It will be a while before I find out what has really happened for *me* ... I am thrilled by its fall, I am worried about the future of Europe ... I wonder about my own future.[1]

Zagajewski's observation reveals several themes that have since emerged during the transformation of Poland, namely the effects of communism on the generation that have been educated and spent a good portion of their lives under its rule, the manner in which to 'transpose' these experiences to post-communist rule, and how this generally is affected by membership in the EU. It alludes to the legacy of the past, which certainly applies but requires more than legal remedies. The communist experience was, without doubt, damaging in moral, political and economic senses.[2] These times are apparent in contemporary discussions and reflections on communism, 20 years later.

In this study, I have demonstrated that the post-communist experience in Poland is not entirely a novel experience, as present efforts have been drawing on tradition, in particular the interwar period. Indeed, Pogany has aptly questioned whether we are truly witnessing a 'return to Europe' or an unprecedented journey.[3] Based on these findings, I argue that a 'new Europe' is emerging, of which the communist past is an important part.

Since the collapse of communism, explaining the post-communist experience has been the subject of many books and articles. 'Making sense' of the current state of affairs in CEE is not an easy task: it requires an understanding of communism,

---

1 Adam Zagajewski, *Two Cities: On Exile, History, and the Imagination*, trans. by Lillian Vallee (New York: Farrar Straus Giroux, 1991), p. 223.

2 See G. Schopflin, 'The Rise of the Anti-Democratic Movements in Post-Communist Societies', in *Redefining Europe: New Patterns of Conflicted Cooperation*, ed. by H. Miall (London: Pinter Publishers, 1994), pp. 129–46.

3 Istvan Pogany, 'A New Constitutional (Dis)Order for Eastern Europe?', in *Human Rights in Eastern Europe*, ed. by Istvan Pogany (Aldershot: Edward Elgar, 1995), pp. 217–39.

and of the period prior to communist rule – in short, a working knowledge of the country's and the region's respective histories.

Chapter 1 discussed events leading to independence and particular issues that would later be the point of contention within newly established and created CEE states, namely issues of the state structure. The significance of statehood would later affect the constitutional models that would be adopted in the interwar and post-1989 periods. The preference for a stronger role of the state is a significant factor in the development of the Polish state and the manner in which societal expectations received state intervention and at times control over public and private affairs.

In Chapter 2, using the case of Poland, the discussion included new archival information on the Codification Commission, the body granted the formidable mandate of creating a legal framework out of five existing legal systems. These pioneers worked under increasingly authoritarian regimes. Nonetheless, it must be stressed that the legal community that existed in interwar Poland was a dynamic group of persons who sought to realise their vision of a Polish state, and played a critical role with respect to the way in which an increasingly authoritarian state evolved. Polish developments took place alongside similar developments in the region. Poland and, in particular the former Czechoslovakia, argued for a stronger role of the judiciary as part of the newly established democracy. Yet, with the notion of judicial review a relatively unknown concept, the emphasis was more on the way in which rights protection was minimally granted to the various minority groups that lived in Poland.

Chapter 3 discussed the gradual elimination of an independent judicial profession at the hands of German and Soviet rulers. Both regimes were characterised by complete disregard for the rule of law. The destruction of daily life owing to war and imposed rule resulted in the adoption of certain coping mechanisms and unofficial norms by society that would affect notions of justice and the role of the law. This was further influenced by show trials and the role of the secret police in everyday life. It has been argued that the position of judges was undermined to such an extent that, in their position as mid-level bureaucrats in the Nazi legal framework, some judges were incapable of distinguishing between right and wrong, in a moral sense. It is also true that many judges sought to ingratiate themselves with the regime, and refused to consider the implications of the laws that they were applying. Such was the separation between morality and the law, the issues of which have been addressed in the debate between legal philosophers, such as Hart and Fuller.[4]

The events in Soviet-occupied Poland provided insight into the communist rule which would be established in the region after the war. The Soviet authorities wasted no time in confiscating large estates and nationalising banking, heavy industry and mining. As concerns the legal framework, the NKVD established control over all areas of life. Thousands were arrested, with landowners, businessmen, policemen,

4 See Conclusions, Chapter 3.

judicial officials and local government officials particularly targeted. Under Vyshinsky, the administration of justice was forever changed. When communist rule was established, the Polish legal framework was remodelled on the Soviet one. Soviet justice comprised investigations and so-called court processes to establish guilt in individual cases; at other times, in mass round-ups, innocent people were deported. The Soviet penal code permitted Soviet-appointed judges to refer cases to the NKVD, and all the while secret decrees were being issued by Beria, Molotov and Stalin, who intended to destroy the Polish intelligentsia. This attitude prevailed until well after the end of the war. Key archival material provides insight into specific cases.

Soviet authorities did everything they could to seize control of the administration of justice. They succeeded in doing so by means of a series of decrees issued between 1944 and 1945 by the provisional government, the Polish Committee for National Liberation (PKWN). The decrees in effect abolished the pre-war framework, the most important being the decrees concerning the judiciary, which permitted the transfer of judges and changed the qualifications for the position of a judge. This enabled the Soviet authorities to fill vacancies with their own candidates. Naturally, all judges were required to undergo Marxist-Leninist-Stalinist indoctrination. This was only a part of the 'war against the judiciary' that was initiated by the provisional government. The strategy comprised two parts: first, to destroy all pre-war tendencies in the decision-making process, and second, to undermine the prestige of the judicial profession. Archival material reveals that special schools were created by the Ministry of Justice for the purpose of educating judges in 'people's justice'. Pre-war judges had to undergo a vigorous verification process intended to identify any compromising activities by them during the war. Any suspicion was used against the candidate and as a pretext for detention and punishment by the secret police. Despite this severity, the recruiting authorities detected resistance on the part of judicial candidates.

Chapter 4 addressed communist rule. Polish archival material demonstrated specifically how the administration of justice was reorganised along Soviet lines. I argue that the 'war against the judiciary' never really ended. This policy, implemented early on, came in varying degrees to affect the role of the judiciary and the scope of independence. The effects of communism on Polish society have been devastating. The early years of communism were marked by terror. The death of Stalin brought some relaxation, but the goal of 'socialist reality' was soon replaced by the Brezhnev doctrine, which basically declared that communism could not be achieved, but that *Sozialistische Realismus* should be achieved in its place. This period was marked by stagnation across communist states and unrest. The centrally planned economy did not provide strong, solid foundations, and soon workers complained about the increase in prices and the inability to make a living without basic food and services. The most serious clashes occurred in 1956, 1970, 1976 and 1981. Polish society was again forced, as it was during the war, to rely on the black market to provide goods and services. An elaborate network was set up, the inevitable result of the centrally planned economy. In short, the corruption was tolerated, as it was perceived as a necessary evil. This, alongside the moribund legal system, took a toll on CEE life and resulted in the subsequent emergence of anomie.

Chapter 5 examined present-day developments. The discussion up to this point focused on the essential role of the judiciary in setting up a rule-of-law state. The judiciary, alongside the Bar, have had to find a way to address and secure their place in a newly established democracy. Both continue to be challenged by the encroachment on their independence by the executive, inadequate guarantees of their independence, and lack of vested interest in their self-governance. The post-communist period shows that remnants of communist rule manifest themselves in various arenas, be they institutional or substantive areas, alongside support for the pre-war institutions in terms of a strong state that goes hand in hand with strong measures to ensure justice, as well as law and order. Therefore, the presidency of Walesa culminated in a conflict between the executive and the legislature, leaving the Polish judiciary dissatisfied and far from reaching its independence. This was even more apparent in the Kaczynski period, in which a strong state was promoted to achieve what the administration perceived as 'justice', succeeding in addressing issues of de-communisation and transitional justice. This, in itself, was not a bad thing. It did highlight the inability of the government to effectively address the human rights abuses committed by former communist leaders. The question of national reconciliation lingers, and in a recent, final attempt to address this issue, legislation on screening laws has been passed in Poland,; this demonstrates short-sightedness on the part of the government but signals a change in the approach and reasoning of the Constitutional Tribunal. An analysis of the Polish approach, with reference to key components of the Hungarian, former Czechoslovakian and Czech Republic's experiences, asks hard questions concerning the unresolved tension between universal human rights values and *achieving* justice (or what is perceived as justice) – and the role of the courts in striving for those universal values and playing their role as judges and prosecutors in an independent manner. Moreover, the courts have asserted themselves against attempts made to undermine their independence. In this respect, the notion of judicial independence has yet to be accepted and treated as one of the cornerstones of the *Rechtsstaat*. On the other hand, outside the constitutional court framework, we can still note a resistance in some branches of the Polish Supreme Court to acknowledge the meta-values found in regional and international human rights instruments that could redress past injustices. But this is not to say that this enquiry in itself is not a useful insight into the nature of communist legal regime and the timeless norms of criminal law and due process.

Finally, the notion of transparency and accountability are two components of the rule of law. Letowska argues that 'we are guided by the constitutional provision stating that Poland is a democratic, rule-of-law state. This provision should be highly regarded, but it also should support the view that a change in key provisions does not mean that a rule-of-law system has been implemented.… I am not at all convinced by the view that since we have provisions declaring that we are a rule-of law-state, and those institutions which are necessary to its realisation exist, this state is automatically realised.'[5] As Neumann has observed, it is the attitude of judges to the law and their position in the state which creates and concretises law.[6] But Neumann was not satisfied by this, and he further argued that judicial decision-making goes beyond formal functions – it requires the judge, in examining the incomplete legal system, to fill in the gaps; the function thus requires an element of creativity.[7] Letowska considers this element to be lacking in the current judiciary; she, too, however, recognises that it is a process, although one that is more focused on the legislative process.

The procedural and substantive aspects of the rule of law are found in key decisions and approaches taken by Polish courts. The challenge presented by de-communisation measures is an excellent example of the way that states have dealt (or, as in the Polish case, not dealt) with past human rights abuses. The nature of the Round Table Talks meant that, for countries like Poland and Hungary, stress would be placed on continuity and not retaliation, as clearly expressed by the Polish 'thick, black line' policy. The failure of this policy is evident today, and the country sees the creation of a respective truth commission that also has a mandate to prosecute. This competence, and an unclear scope as pertains to the group under investigation, has been the subject of a Constitutional Tribunal judgment. This court, an innovation for the communist world, and created during martial law, has evolved into a viable institution that has developed its own body of case law, which at times has been rightly criticised. The rulings on retroactivity are significant; it is here that the laws have undergone various reforms, not only in Poland, but in the region. While retroactivity has been analysed and redefined in light of international law, there is another interpretation that is taken by the common courts, as discussed in the Polish Supreme Court case. The Polish experience shows the continuity from the interwar period, namely politics encroaching on and in many ways shaping key legal reforms involving those vital values underpinning any democracy and rule-of-law state: dignity and life. Politics also continues to exert pressure on the judiciary.

We have already seen, however, the manner in which the transition stimulated the development of a cadre of professional officials who have the necessary knowledge to create and reform the law to make it effective. Institutional stability has for the most part been achieved owing to the resolve and vision of a society in its quest to 'return to Europe'. While the state structure has managed to overcome many obstacles, it will undoubtedly be challenged repeatedly as the CEE governments and society, along with their respective judiciaries, continue

---

5 Ewa Letowska, 'Bariery do naszego myslenia o prawie w perspekstywie integracji z Europa' [Barriers to Our Thinking About the Law in the Context of European Integration], *Panstwo i Prawo* [State and Law], 4–5 (1996), p. 45.

6 Franz Neumann, *The Rule of Law: Political Theory and the Legal System in Modern Society* (Leamington Spa: Berg, 1986), pp. 224–25.

7 *Ibid.*, p. 231.

to question and forge the meaning of the rule of law. One of the most notable qualities of the Polish judiciary of the pre-war period was its spirit and dedication: the same can be observed in the CEE, which has no less a monumental task in hand. As a Polish poet once observed,

> After each war someone must clean up. This kind of order is not created on its own. … Those who knew what happened here must make way for those who know less. And more than less. Finally almost nothing. In the grass, which has grown over the reasons and its ravages, someone must lie, with a blade between his teeth, staring at the sky.[8]

8 Wislawa Szymborska, 'Koniec i poczatek' [An End and a Beginning], in *Koniec i poczatek* (Poznan: Wydawnictwo a5, 1996), pp. 10–11.

Bibliography

Key to Translations of Foreign Journal Titles

Gazeta Bankowa
Banking Gazette

Glos Sadownictwa
Court's Voice

Polska Akademia Nauk, Komitet Nauk Prawnych, Studia nad Historia Panstwa i Prawa-Seria II
Polish Academy of Sciences, Committee of Legal Studies, Studies of History and Law, Series II

prawo co dnia
Daily Law

Prawo i Zycie
Law and Life

Prokuratura i Prawo
Public Prosecution and the Law

Przeglad Filosoficzny
Philosophical Preview

Przeglad Zachodni
Western Preview

Rzeczpospolita
The Republic

Studia luridica
Legal Studies

Svensk Juristtidning
Swedish Lawyer Newspaper

Wprost
Point-Blank

Zycie Gospodarcze
Economic Life

Books

Ackerman, Bruce, *The Future of the Liberal Revolution* (New Haven, CT: Yale University Press, 1992).

Ajenkiel, Andrzej, *Polskie konstytucje* [Polish Constitutions] (Warsaw: Wiedza Powszechna, 1983).

—— B. Lesnodorski and W. Rostocki, *Historia ustroju Polski (1764–1939)* [The History of the Polish Political System (1764–1939)] (Warsaw: Panstwowe Wydawnictwo Naukowe, 1974).

Arendt, Hannah, *The Origins of Totalitarianism* (London: Allen & Unwin, 1958).

—— *Eichmann in Jerusalem: A Report on the Banality of Evil* (London: Faber & Faber, 1963).

Ascherson, Neal, *The Polish August: The Self-Limiting Revolution* (New York: Penguin, 1989).

Austin, John, *The Province of Jurisprudence Determined and the Uses of the Study of Jurisprudence* (London: Weidenfeld and Nicolson, 1955).

Balicki, Z., *Egoizm narodowy wobec etyki* [National Egoism and Ethics] (Lwow-Warsaw: 1914).

Barber, Sotirios, A., *On What the Constitution Means* (Baltimore, MD: Johns Hopkins University Press, 1984).

Bardach, Juliusz, Boguslaw Lesnodorski and Michael Pietrzak, *Historia psanstwa i prawa polskiego* [The History of the Polish State and Law] (Warsaw: Panstwowe Wydawnictwo Naukowe, 1979).

Beyerlin, Ulrich, *et al.*, eds, *Recht zwischen Umbruch und Bewahrung: Festschrift für Rudolf Bernhardt* (Berlin: Springer, 1995).

Blanke, Richard, *Prussian Poland in the German Empire (1871–1900)* (New York: Columbia University Press, 1981).

—— *The Orphans of Versailles: The Germans in Western Poland 1918–1939* (Lexington, KY: University Press of Kentucky, 1993).

Bloed, Arie, *The Conference on Security and Co-operation in Europe: Analysis and Basic Documents, 1972–1993* (Dordrecht: Martinus Nijhoff, 1997).

Brol, Jan, *Prawo upadlosciowe w swietle praktyki sadowe* [Bankruptcy Law in Court Practice] (Warsaw: Oficyna Naukowa, 1995).

Brolmann, Catherine, *et al.*, eds, *Peoples and Minorities in International Law* (Dordrecht: Martinus Nijhoff, 1993).

Browning, Christopher, *Ordinary Men: Reserve Battalion 101 and the Final Solution in Poland* (New York: HarperCollins, 1992).

Brus, Wlodzimierz, *The Market in a Socialist Economy* (London: Routledge & Kegan Paul, 1972).
—— *The Economics and Politics of Socialism: Collected Essays* (London: Routledge & Kegan Paul, 1973).
—— and K. Laski, *From Marx to the Market* (Oxford: Clarendon Press, 1988).
Brzezinski, Mark, *The Struggle for Constitutionalism in Poland* (London: St. Martin's Press, 1998).
Butler, W. E., ed., *Anglo-Polish Essays* (New York: Transnational Publishers, 1982).
—— *Soviet Law*, 2nd edn (London: Butterworths, 1988).
—— *Perestroika and the Rule of Law: Anglo-American and Soviet Perspectives* (London: I. B. Tauris, 1991).
—— ed., *Russian Legal Theory* (Aldershot: Dartmouth, 1996).
Butler, William E., ed., *Russian Law: Historical and Political Perspectives* (Leyden: A. W. Sijthoff, 1977).
——*et al.*, eds, *Law After Revolution* (New York: Oceana Publications, 1988).
Cappelletti, Mauro, *Judicial Review in the Contemporary World* (Indianapolis, IN: Bobbs-Merrill Company, 1971).
—— *The Judicial Process in Comparative Perspective* (Oxford: Clarendon Press, 1989).
Castoriadis, Cornelius, *Philosophy, Politics, Autonomy: Essays in Political Philosophy* (Oxford: Oxford University Press, 1991).
—— *The Castoriadis Reader*, ed. and trans. by David Ames Curtis (Oxford: Blackwell, 1997).
Chicherin, Boris, *A History of Political Theories*, 5 vols (Moscow: 1877–1902).
—— *Legal Philosophy* (Moscow: 1902).
Chwalba, Andrzej, *Imperium korupcji w Rosji w Krolestwie Polskim w latach 1861–1917* [The Empire of Corruption in the Kingdom of Poland in the Years 1861–1917] (Cracow: Universitas, 1995).
Cienciala, Anna M., and Titus Komarnicki, *From Versailles to Locarno: Keys to Polish Foreign Policy 1919–1925* (Lawrence, KS: University Press of Kansas, 1984).
Cieszkowski, August, *Ojcze-Nasz* [Our Nation], 3rd edn (Poznan: Czionkam Drukarni Jaroslawa Leitgebra, 1905).
Claudin, Fernando, *The Communist Movement: From Comintern to Cominform* (London: Penguin, 1970).
Conquest, Robert, *The Harvest of Sorrow: Soviet Collectivization and the Terror-Famine* (Edmonton, AB, Canada: University of Alberta Press, 1986).
—— *The Great Terror: A Reassessment*, 3rd edn (London: Pimlico, 1990).
Cotterrell, Roger, *The Politics of Jurisprudence: A Critical Introduction to Legal Philosophy* (London: Butterworths, 1989).
—— *The Sociology of Law: An Introduction* (London: Butterworths, 1992).
Cottrell, P. L., *et al.*, eds, *Rebuilding the Financial System in Central and Eastern Europe, 1918–1994* (Aldershot: Scolar Press, 1997).

Crampton, R. J., *Eastern Europe in the Twentieth Century* (London: Routledge, 1994).
Czosnyka, Helen, *The Polish Challenge: Foundations for Dialogue in the Works of Adam Schaff and Józef Tishner* (Atlanta, GA: Scholars Press, 1995).
Czubinski, Antoni, and Jerzy Strzelczyk, *Zarys dziejow niemiec and panstw niemieckich powstalych po II wojny swiatowej* [An Overview of German Lands and States That Were Established After the Second World War] (Poznan: Wydawnictwo Poznanskie, 1986).
Dallago, B., *et al.*, *Privatisation and Entrepreneurship in Post-Socialist Countries: Economy, Law and Society* (London: St. Martin's Press, 1992).
Damaska, Mirjan, *The Faces of Justice and Authority: A Comparative Approach to the Legal Process* (New Haven, CT: Yale University Press, 1986).
Davies, Norman, *God's Playground: A History of Poland, Volume II: 1795 to the Present* (New York: Columbia University Press, 1982).
—— *Heart of Europe: A Short History of Poland* (Oxford: Oxford University Press, 1996).
—— *Europe: A History* (London: Pimlico, 1997).
—— and Antony Polonksy, eds, *Jews in Eastern Poland and the USSR, 1939–46* (London: Macmillan, 1991).
Dicey, Albert Venn, *Introduction to the Study of the Law of the Constitution*, 9th edn (London: Macmillan, 1939).
Dmowski, Roman, *Rosja, niemcy i kwestia Polska* [Russia, Germany, and the Polish Question] (Lwow, 1903).
Dunn, Seamus, and T. G. Fraser, eds, *Europe and Ethnicity: The First World War and Contemporary Ethnic Conflict* (London: Routledge, 1996).
Dyzenhaus, David, *Judging the Judges, Judging Ourselves: Truth, Reconciliation and the Apartheid Legal Order* (Oxford: Hart Publishing, 1998).
—— *Law as Politics: Carl Schmitt's Critique of Liberalism* (Durham, NC: Duke University Press, 1998).
—— *The Constitution of Law: Legality in a Time of Emergency* (Cambridge: University of Cambridge Press, 2007).
Ehrlich, Eugene, *Fundamental Principles of the Sociology of Law* (New Brunswick, NJ: Transaction Publishers, 2001), first published in 1922.
Eser, Albin, and Andrzej Zoll, eds, *Prawo karne a problemy zmiany ustroju politycznego/Strafrecht und politischer Sysytemweschel* [Criminal Law and the Problems Concerning Changes in the Political Structure] (Cracow: Kantor Wydawniczy Zakamycze; Freiburg-im-Breisgau: Max-Planck-Institut, 1998).
Evans, Malcolm, *Religious Liberty and International Law in Europe* (Cambridge: Cambridge University Press, 1997).
Falandysz, Lech, *Ja i moje prawo* [Me and My Law] (Warsaw: Helsinska Fundacja Praw Czlowieka, 1991).
Farrell, R. Barry, ed., *Political Leadership in Eastern Europe and the Soviet Union* (Chicago: Aldine Publishing Company, 1970).

Febbrajo, Alberto, David Nelken and Vittorio Olgiati, eds, *Social Processes and Patterns of Legal Control: European Yearbook of Sociology of Law, 2000* (Milan: Giuffre, 2001).

Foucault, Michel, *Discipline and Punish: The Birth of the Prison*, trans. A. Sheridan (London: Penguin, 1991).

Frankowski, Stanislaw, and Paul B. Stephen III, eds, *Legal Reform in Post-Communist Europe: The View from Within* (Dordrecht: Martinus Nijhoff, 1995).

Fromm, Eric, *Escape from Freedom* (New York: Avon Books, 1969).

Frydman, Sawa, *Uwagi podstaw skarbowosci* [The Underlying Aspects of the Monetary System] (Wilno: 1930), as quoted in Krzysztof Motyka, *Wplyw Leona Petrazyckiego na Polska teorie i sociologie prawa* [The Influence of Leon Petrazycki on Polish Sociological Theory and Law] (Lublin: Redakcja Wydawnictwo Katolickiego Uniwersytetu Lubelskiego, 1993), 33–34.

Fuller, Lon, *The Morality of Law* (New Haven, CT: Yale University Press, 1964).

Fuzer, Katalin, 'Rights and Constitutional Theory in Weimar Germany', PhD dissertation, University of Pennsylvania (2004).

Gaberle, Andrzej, *Patologia spoleczna* [Social Pathology] (Warsaw: Wydawnictwo Prawnicze, 1993).

Garewicz, Jan, and Andrzej Walicki, eds, *Prolegomena do Historiozofii* [Prologue to Historiography] (Warsaw: Panstwowe Wydawnictwo Naukowe, 1972).

Garland, David, *Punishment and Modern Society: A Study in Social Theory* (Oxford: Clarendon Press, 1990).

Garton Ash, Timothy, *The Polish Revolution: Solidarity* (New York: Vintage, 1985).

Gennep, Arnold van, *The Rites of Passage* (Chicago: University of Chicago Press, 1960).

The German Occupation of Poland: Extract of Note Addressed to the Governments of the Allied and Neutral Powers on May 3, 1941 (London: Cornell Press Limited, 1941).

Gieysztor, Aleksander, *et al.*, eds, *History of Poland* (Warsaw: PWN, 1968).

Gilas, Janusz, *Raport o sytuacji osob nalezajacych do mniejnosci narodowych i eticznych w Polsce* [Report on the Situation of Persons Belonging to National and Ethnic Minorities in Poland] (Warsaw: 1994).

Ginsburg, Evgenia, *Journey into the Whirlwind* (New York: Harcourt Brace Jovanovich, 1975).

Gogol, Nikolai, *The Inspector General: A Comedy in Five Acts* [*Revizor*], Studies in Slavic Language and Literature, Vol. 9, ed. by M. Beresford (Lewiston, NY: Edwin Mellen Press, 1996).

Gordon, Dane R., ed., *Philosophy in Post-Communist Europe*, Value Inquiry Book Series (Amsterdam: Rodopi, 1998).

Gorecki, Jan, *Sociology and Jurisprudence of Leon Petrazycki* (Champaign, IL: University of Illinois Press, 1975).

Greenburg, Douglas, *et al.*, eds, *Constitutionalism and Democracy: Transitions in the Contemporary World* (Oxford: Oxford University Press, 1993).

Gross, Jan, *Polish Society Under German Occupation: The Generalgouvernement, 1939–1944* (Princeton, NJ: Princeton University Press, 1979).

—— *Revolution from Abroad: The Soviet Conquest of Poland's Western Ukraine and Western Belorussia* (Princeton, NJ: Princeton University Press, 1988).

Grzybowski, Kazimierz, *et al.*, eds, *Studies for Polish Law*, Law in Eastern Europe Series, No. 6 (Leyden: A. W. Sijthoff, 1962).

Grzybowski, Konstanty, *Galicja 1848–1914: historia ustroju politycznego na tle historii ustroju Austrii, Tom XV* [Galicia 1848–1914: The History of Political Structure Based on the History of Austria, Vol. 15], Polska Akademia Nauk, Komitet Nauk Prawnych, Studia nad Historia Panstwa i Prawa-Seria II (Cracow: Polska Akademia Nauk, 1959).

Gsovski, Vladimir, and Kazimierz Grzybowski, eds, *Government, Law and Courts in the Soviet Union and Eastern Europe* (London: Stevens & Stevens, 1959).

Haraszti, Miklós, *The Velvet Prison: Artists Under State Socialism* (London: Penguin, 1989).

Havel, Václav, *Summer Meditations on Politics, Morality and Civility in a Time of Transition* (London: Faber & Faber, 1992).

Hazard, John N., W. E. Butler and Peter B. Maggs, *The Soviet Legal System: The Law in the 1980s* (New York: Oceana Publications, 1984).

Herzen, Alexander, *My Past and My Thoughts: The Memoirs of Alexander Herzen*, trans. by Constance Garnett (Berkeley, CA: University of California Press, 1982).

Hesse, Joachim Jens, and Nevil Johnson, eds, *Constitutional Policy and Change in Europe* (Oxford: Oxford University Press, 1995).

Hobbes, Thomas, *Leviathan*, ed. by C. B. MacPherson (London: Penguin, 1985).

Hobsbawm, E. J., *Nations and Nationalism Since 1780: Programme, Myth, Reality* (Cambridge: Cambridge University Press, 1990).

Hodos, George, *Show Trials: Stalinist Purges in Eastern Europe, 1948–1954* (New York: Praeger, 1987).

Hoffman, Ewa, *Shtetl: The History of a Small Town and an Extinguished World* (London: Vintage, 1999).

Holmes, Leslie, *The End of Communist Power* (Cambridge: Polity Press, 1993).

Human and Citizens' Rights in the Polish People's Republic (1 January–31 December 1989), Report No. 7, prepared by the Helsinki Committee in Poland (Vienna: International Helsinki Federation for Human Rights, 1989).

Ignotus, Paul, *Hungary*, Nations of the Modern World Series (London: Ernest Benn Limited, 1972).

Jacob, Herbert, Erhard Blankenburg, Herbert M. Kritzer, Doris Marie Provine and Joseph Sanders, *Courts, Law and Politics in Comparative Perspective* (New Haven, CT: Yale University Press, 1996).

Jaruzelski, Wojciech, *Les Chaînes et le refuge* [The Chains and the Refuge] (Paris: Editions Jean-Claude Lattes, 1992).

—— *Stan Wojenny: Dlaczego* [Martial Law: Why?] (Warsaw: BGW, 1992).

Jennings, Sir Robert, and Sir Arthur Watts, eds, *Oppenheim's International Law*, Vol. 1, 9th edn (London: Longman, 1992).

John, Michael, *Politics and the Law in Late Nineteenth-Century Germany: The Origins of the Civil Code* (Oxford: Clarendon Press, 1989).

Johnson, Lonnie, *Central Europe: Enemies, Neighbors, Friends* (Oxford: Oxford University Press, 1996).

Joravsky, David, *Russian Psychology: A Critical History* (Oxford: Basil Blackwell, 1989).

Jurek, Piotr, *Historia panstwa i prawa polskiego: zrodla prawa, sadownictwo zarys wykladu* [The History of the Polish State and Law: Sources of Law and Courts in the Period] (Wroclaw: Wydawnictwo Uniwersytetu Wroclawskiego, 1992).

Kadare, Ismail, *Albanian Spring: The Anatomy of Tyranny* (London: Saqi Books, 1991).

Kamenka, Eugene, and Martin Krygier, eds, *Bureaucracy: The Career of a Concept* (London: Edward Arnold, 1979).

Kamienski, Henryk, *Russia and Europe. Poland: An Introduction to the Study of Russian and the Muscovites* (Paris: 1858).

Karski, Jan, *The Great Powers and Poland 1919–1945: From Versailles to Yalta* (London: University Press America, 1985).

Kaser, M. C., and E. A. Radice, eds, *Economic History of Eastern Europe 1919–1975*, Vol. 1 (Oxford: Clarendon Press, 1985).

Kauba, Krzysztof, 'Sadownictwo w Polsce w latach 1918–1939' [The Judiciary in Poland in the Years 1918–1939], unpublished manuscript (1994) (on file with author).

Kelsen, Hans, *Pure Theory of Law*, trans. by Michael Knight (Berkeley, CA: University of California Press, 1967).

—— *Essays in Legal and Moral Philosophy*, ed. by Ota Weinberger (Dordrecht: D. Reidel, 1973).

Kenedi, Janos, *Do It Yourself: Hungary's Hidden Economy* (London: Pluto Press, 1982).

Kennedy, Ellen, *Constitutional Failure: Carl Schmitt in Weimar* (Durham, NC: Duke University Press, 2004).

Kennet, David, and Marc Lieberman, eds, *The Road to Capitalism: Economic Transformation in Eastern Europe and the Former Soviet Union* (Orlando, FL: Harcourt, Brace and Jovanovich, 1992).

Kirchheimer, Otto, and Franz Neumann, *Social Democracy and the Rule of Law*, ed. by Keith Tribe, trans. by Leena Turner and Keith Tribe (London: Allen Unwin, 1987).

Kisza, Andrzej, Zdzislaw Krzeminski and Roman Lyczywek, *Historia adwokatury polskiej* [The History of the Polish Bar] (Warsaw: M. C. Kwadrat, 1995).

Koch, H. W., *In the Name of the Volk: Political Justice in Hitler's Germany* (London: I. B. Tauris, 1989).

Kolakowski, Leszek, *Towards a Marxist Humanism: Essays on the Left Today* (New York: Grove Press, 1968).

—— *Main Currents of Marxism: Its Origin, Growth, and Dissolution*, Vol. I: *The Founders*, trans. by P. S. Falla (Oxford: Clarendon Press, 1978).

—— *Main Currents of Marxism: Its Origin, Growth, and Dissolution*, Vol. III: *The Breakdown*, trans. by P. S. Falla (Oxford: Clarendon Press, 1978).

—— ed., *Modernity on Endless Trial* (Chicago: University of Chicago Press, 1990).

Kolarska-Bobinska, Lena, Jacek Kucharczyk and Jaroslaw Zbieranek, eds, *Democracy in Poland 2005–2007* (Warsaw: Institute of Public Affairs, 2007).

Komentarz do ochronie obrotu gospodarczgo [Commentary to the Law on the Protection of Economic Transactions] (Warsaw: Wydawnictwo Przwnicze, 1995).

Konrád, George, *The Melancholy of Rebirth: Essays from Post-Communist Central Europe, 1989–1994* (San Diego, CA: Harcourt Brace & Company, 1989).

Korbel, J., *Poland Between East and West: Soviet and German Diplomacy Toward Poland, 1919–33* (Princeton, NJ: Princeton University Press, 1963).

Korkunov, N., *Lectures on the General Theory of Law* (Moscow: 1888).

—— *Russian Constitutional Law*, 2 vols (Moscow: 1883–86).

Kornai, Janos, *Contradictions and Dilemmas: Studies on the Socialist Economy and Society* (Budapest: Corvina, 1983).

—— *The Road to a Free Economy, Shifting from a Socialist System: The Example of Hungary* (New York: Norton, 1990).

Korobowicz, Artur, *Reformy ustroju sadownictwa w Krolewstwie Polskim po 1863r.* [Court Reform in the Kingdom of Poland After 1863] (Lublin: 1976).

Krawczyk, Rafal, ed., *Reforma gospodarcza: propozycje, tendencje, kierunki dyskusji* [Economic Reform: Proposals, Tendencies, Directions of Discussion] (Warsaw: Panstwowe Wydawnictwo Ekonomiczne, 1981).

Krzywicki, Kazimierz, *Polska i rosja w 1872 roku* [Poland and Russia in 1872] (Dresden: 1872).

Kucherev, Samuel, *Courts, Lawyers and Trials Under the Last Three Tsars* (New York: Praeger, 1953).

Kurczewski, Jacek, *The Resurrection of Rights in Poland* (Oxford: Clarendon Press, 1993).

Kutrzeba, Stanislaw, *Dawne polskie prawo sadowe w zarysie* (*I. Prawo karneig II. Postepek sadowy* [Polish Court Law from the Past in an Overview) (I. Criminal Law II. Court Procedure)] (Lwow: Wydawnictwo Zakladu Narodowego im. Ossolinskich, 1921).

Kwasniewski, Jerzy, and Margaret Watson, eds, *Social Control and the Law in Poland* (New York: St. Martin's Press, 1991).

Kyle, Elisabeth, *The Mirrors of Versailles* (London: Constable & Co., 1939).

Landau, Ludwik, *Kronika lat wojny i okupacji*, [Chronicle of the Years of War and Occupation], 3 vols (Warsaw: Panstwowe Wydawnictwo Naukowe, 1962–63).

Latawski, Paul, ed., *The Reconstruction of Poland 1914–23* (London: Macmillan, 1992).
Lefort, Claude, *Complications: Communism and the Dilemmas of Democracy*, trans. by J. Bourg (New York: Columbia University Press, 2007).
Lenin, Vladimir Ilyich, *What Is to Be Done?*, 5th edn (Moscow: Foreign Languages Publishing House, 1901).
—— *The State and Revolution*, in *Selected Works in Three Volumes*, Vol. 2, 2nd edn (Moscow: Progress Publishers, 1967), 263–364.
Leoni, Bruno, *Freedom and the Law* (Los Angeles: Nash Publishing, 1961).
Leslie, R. F., ed., *The History of Poland Since 1863* (Cambridge: Cambridge University Press, 1983).
Letowska, Ewa, *Po co ludziom konstytucja* [Why the People Need a Constitution] (Warsaw: Agencja EXIT, 1994).
—— and Janusz Letowski, *Poland: Towards the Rule of Law* (Warsaw: Wydawnictwo Naukowe SCHOLAR, 1996).
Liebich, *André*, trans. and ed., *Selected Writings of August Cieszkowski* (Cambridge: Cambridge University Press, 1979).
Lih, Lars T., *et al.*, *Stalin's Letters to Molotov 1925–1936*, trans. by C. Fitzpatrick (New Haven, CT: Yale University Press, 1995).
Limanowski, Boleslaw, *Patriotyzm i socjalizm* [Patriotism and Socialism], 2nd edn (Paris: 1888).
—— *Stanislaw Worcell: Zyciorys* [Stanislaw Worcell: A Biography] (Cracow: 1910 and Warsaw: 1948).
Linz, Juan J., *Totalitarian and Authoritarian Regimes* (Boulder, CO: Lynne Rienner, 2000).
Litvan, Gyorgy, *The Hungarian Revolution of 1956: Reform, Revolt and Repression 1953–1963*, ed. and trans. by Janos M. Bak and Lyman H. Legters (New York: Longman, 1996).
Locke, John, *Of Civil Government: Two Treatises*, ed. by Ernest Rhys (London: J. M. Dent & Sons, 1924).
Longworth, Philip, *The Making of Eastern Europe* (London: St. Martin's Press, 1994).
Los, Maria, *Communist Ideology, Law and Crime: A Comparative View of the USSR and Poland* (New York: St. Martin's Press, 1988).
—— ed., *The Second Economy in Marxist States* (London: Macmillan, 1990).
—— and Andrzej Zybertowicz, *Privatizing the Police-State: the Case of Poland* (Basingstoke: Macmillan, 2000).
Lundgreen-Nielsen, K., *The Polish Problem at the Paris Peace Conference* (Odense: Odense University Press, 1979).
Mace, George, *Locke, Hobbes, and the Federalist Papers: An Essay on the Genesis of the American Heritage* (Carbondale, IL: Southern Illinois University Press, 1979).
Mak, Geert, *In Europe: Travels Through the Twentieth Century* (London: Harvill Secker, 2007).

Makarczyk, Jerzy, ed., *Theory of International Law at the Threshold of the 21st Century: Essays in Honour of Krzysztof Skubiszewski* (The Hague: Kluwer Law International, 1996).

Makowski, Waclaw, *Panstwo spoleczne* [Social State] (Warsaw: 1936).

Malleson, Kate, and Peter H. Russell, eds, *Appointing Judges in an Age of Judicial Power: Critical Perspectives from Around the World* (Toronto: University of Toronto Press, 2006).

Marat, S., and J. Snopkiewicz, *Zbrodnia, sprawa generala Fieldorfa – 'Nila'* [A Crime, The Case of General Fieldorf – 'Nil'] (Warsaw: 1989), as quoted in Katarzyna Maria Piekarska, 'Naruszanie zasady jawnosci w "sadach tajnych"' [Violation of the Principles of Open Proceedings in the 'Secret Courts'], *Studia Iuridica*, 27 (1995), 25–41.

Marilena, Atanasiu Isabela, 'Institutional Analysis as an Appropriate Approach to Assessing Competition Policy during Transition – A Study of Poland, the Czech and Slovak Republics, and Hungary', PhD dissertation submitted at the European University Institute, Florence, Italy (June 1997).

Marody, Miroslawa, *Warunki trwania i zmiany ladu spolecznego w relacji do stanu swiadomosci spolecznej* [Conditions of Survival and Changes of Social Order in Relation to the State of Social Consciousness] (Warsaw: Universytet Warszawski, 1986), as quoted in Titkow, Anna, *Stres i zycie spoleczne: polskie doswiadczenia* [Stress and Social Life: Polish Experiences] (Warsaw: Panstwowy Instytut Wydawniczy, 1993), 225.

Marx, Karl, and Friedrich Engels, *Selected Works*, Vol. 1 (Moscow: Foreign Languages Publishing House, 1955).

—— *The Communist Manifesto Including Principles of Communism and the Communist Manifesto After 100 Years*, trans. by Paul M. Sweezy (New York: Modern Reader Paperbacks, 1968).

—— *Grundrisse: Foundations of the Critique of Political Economy*, ed. by M. Niclaus (Harmondsworth: Penguin, 1974).

Maryanski, Alexandra, *Narodowosci swiata* [The Nationalities of the World] (Warsaw: PWN, 1994).

Medvedev, Roy, *Let History Judge: The Origins and Consequences of Stalinism* (New York: Macmillan, 1971).

Meinecke, K., *Weltbürgertum und Nationalstaat* (Munich: 1919).

Miall, Hugh, ed., *Redefining Europe: New Patterns of Conflict and Cooperation* (London: Pinter Publishers, 1994).

Michalska, Anna, *Komitet Praw Czlowieka: kompetencje, funkcjnowanie, orzecznictwo* [The Committee of Human Rights: Its Competence, Function and Decisions] (Warsaw: EXIT, 1994).

Michnik, Adam, *Letters from Prison and Other Essays*, trans. by Maya Latynski (Berkeley, CA: University of California Press, 1985).

Milosz, Czeslaw, *The Captive Mind*, trans. by Jane Zielonko (New York: Alfred A. Knopf, 1953).

—— *Native Realm: A Search for Self-Definition* (New York: Doubleday, 1968).

Modras, Ronald E., *The Catholic Church and Antisemitism: Poland, 1933–1939* (Chur: Harwood Academic Publishers for the Vidal Sassoon International Center for the Study of Antisemitism, The Hebrew University of Jerusalem, 1994).

Montesquieu, Baron de, *The Spirit of Laws; a Compendium of the First English Edition*, ed. by David Wallace Carrithers (Berkeley, CA: University of California Press, 1977), text based on Thomas Nugent's translation (London: Nourse, 1750).

Motyka, Krzysztof, *Wplyw Leona Petrazyckiego na Polska teorie i sociologie prawa* [The Influence of Leon Petrazycki on Polish Sociological Theory and Law] (Lublin: Redakcja Wydawnictw Katolickiego Uniwersytetu Lubelskiego, 1993).

Müller, Ingo, *Hitler's Justice: The Courts of the Third Reich* (London: I. B. Tauris, 1991).

Mullerson, Rein, *International Law, Rights and Politics: Developments in Eastern Europe and the CIS* (London: Routledge, 1994).

—— Malgosia Fitzmaurice and Mads Adenas, *Constitutional Reform and International Law in Central and Eastern Europe*, Studies in Law Series, Vol. 1 (The Hague: Kluwer Law International, 1998).

Musgrave, Thomas, *Self-Determination and National Minorities* (Oxford: Clarendon, 1997).

Musiuk, Andrzej, *Policja panstwowa 1919–1939: powstanie, organizacje, kierunki dzialania* [The State Police 1919–1939: Creation, Organisation, and Scope of Activities] (Warsaw: Wydawnictwo Naukowe PWN, 1996).

Naumann, Friedrich, *Mitteleuropa* (Berlin: Verlag Reimer, 1915).

Neumann, Franz, *The Rule of Law: Political Theory and the Legal System in Modern Society* (Leamington Spa: Berg, 1986).

Nove, Alec, *Soviet Economy: An Introduction* (London: George Allen & Unwin, 1961).

—— *Stalinism and After* (London: George Allen & Unwin, 1975).

—— *et al.*, eds, *The Eastern European Economies in the 1970s* (London: Butterworths, 1982).

Novgorodstev, P. I., *The Historical School in Jurisprudence* (Moscow: 1896).

—— *Kant and Hegel* (Moscow: 1901).

Orwell, George, *Animal Farm* (London: Secker & Warburg, 1977).

Orzeszkowa, Eliza, *Patriotism and Cosmopolitanism* (Wilno: 1880).

Pavkovic, Aleksander, *et al.*, *Nationalism and Postcommunism: A Collection of Essays* (Aldershot: Dartmouth, 1995).

Peczenik, Aleksander, *On Law and Reason* (Dordrecht: Kluwer Academic Publishers, 1989).

Petrazycki, Leon, *Die Fruchtverteilung beim Wechsel des Nutzungsberechtigten* (Berlin: 1892).

—— *Die Lehre vom Einkommen*, 2 vols (Berlin: 1893–95).

—— *O dopelniajacych pradach kulturalnych i prawach rozwoju handlu* [On Complementary Cultural Trends and on Laws of Commercial Development] (Warsaw: Nakladem Towarzystwa im. Leona Petrazyckiego, 1936).

—— *Prawo a sad* [Law and the Court] (Warsaw: Nakladem Towarzystwa im. Leona Petrazyckiego, 1936).

—— *Law and Morality*, Twentieth Century Legal Philosophy Series, Vol. VII, trans. by Hugh Babb (Cambridge: Cambridge University Press, 1955).

—— *O nauce prawie i moralnosci: pisma wybrane* [On Teaching Law and Morality: Selected Works] (Warsaw: Panstwowe Wydawnictwo Naukowe, 1985).

Podgorecki, Adam, *Zalozenia polityki prawa. Metodologia pracy legislacyjnej i kodyfikcyinej* [Creating Political Law. Methodology of the Legislative Process and Codification] (Warsaw: Wydawnictwo Prawnicze, 1957).

—— 'Preface', *Totalitarian and Post-Totalitarian Law*, ed. by Adam Podgorecki and Vittorio Olgiati (Aldershot: Dartmouth, 1996), vii.

Podolski, T. M., *Socialist Banking and Monetary Control: The Experience of Poland* (Cambridge: Cambridge University Press, 1972).

Pogany, Istvan, ed., *Human Rights in Eastern Europe* (Aldershot: Edward Elgar, 1995).

—— *Righting Wrongs in Eastern Europe* (Manchester: Manchester University Press, 1997).

Poggie, J., and R. N. Lynch, *Rethinking Modernization: Anthropological Perspectives* (Westport, CT: Greenwood Press, 1975).

Pokol, Bela, *The Concept of Law. The Multi-Layered Legal System* (Budapest: Rejtjel, 2001).

Polonsky, Antony, and Oscar Halecki, eds, *A History of Poland* (London: Routledge & Kegan Paul, 1978).

Pospieszalski, Karol Marian, *Polska nad niemieckim prawem 1939–1945 (Ziemia Zachodnia)* [Poland Under German Law 1939–1945 (Western Lands)] (Poznan: Wydawnictwo Instytutu Zachodniego Poznan, 1946).

Přibáň, Jiří, *Legal Symbolism: On Law, Time and European Identity* (Aldershot: Ashgate, 2007).

Quint, P. E., *The Imperfect Union: Constitutional Structures of German Unification* (Princeton, NJ: Princeton University Press 1997).

Raport o stanie Rzeczpospolitej i drogach wiodajcych do jej naprawy [A Report on the State of the Republic and Ways Leading to Its Correction] (Warsaw: Konserwatorium Doswiadczenie i Przyslosc, 1979), as quoted in Titkow, Anna, *Stres i zycie spoleczne: polskie doswiadczenia* [Stress and Social Life: Polish Experiences] (Warsaw: Panstwowy Instytut Wydawniczy, 1993), 203.

Rayfield, Donald, *Stalin and His Hangmen: An Authoritative Portrait of a Tyrant and Those Who Served Him* (London: Penguin, 2004).

Robertson, Ritchie, and Edward Timms, eds, *National Identity in Historical Perspective*. Austrian Studies V (Edinburgh: Edinburgh University Press, 1994).

Roos, Hans, *A History of Modern Poland: From the Foundation of the State in the First World War to the Present Day* (London: Eyre & Spottiswoode, 1966).
Rosenbaum, Ron, *Explaining Hitler: The Search for Origins of His Evil* (New York: Random House, 1998).
Rosenberg, Tina, *The Haunted Land: Facing Europe's Ghosts After Communism* (New York: Vintage, 1996).
Rothschild, Joseph, *East Central Europe Between the Two World Wars*. A History of East Central Europe, Vol. IX (Seattle, WA: University of Washington Press, 1974).
Rudnicki, K., *Wspomnienia prokuratora* [Memories of a Prosecutor] (Warsaw: 1957).
Ryszki, Franciszek, ed., *Historia panstwa i prawa Polski, 1918–1939, Czesc I* [The History of the Polish State and Law 1918–1939, Part 1] (Warsaw: Panstwowe Wydawnictwo Naukowe, 1962).
Rzeplinski, Andrzej, *Sadownictwo w Polsce Ludowej: miedzy dypozycyjnoscia, a niezawisloscia* [The Judiciary in People's Poland: Between Disposability and Independence] (Warsaw: Oficyjna Wydawnicza Pokolenie, 1989).
—— 'Karta praw i wolnosci: uwagi nad projektem ustaway konstytucyjnej z 12 listopada 1992 roku' [The Charter of Rights and Freedoms: Remarks on the Draft of the Constitutional Law of 12 November 1992], unpublished manuscript (on file with author).
—— ed., *Constitutionalism and Human Rights*, Vol. 1, Papers of the International Conference on 'Human Rights and Freedoms in the New Constitutions in Central and Eastern Europe', Warsaw, 24–29 April 1992 (Warsaw: Helsinki Foundation for Human Rights in Eastern Europe, 1992).
—— 'Kolejne nowele do Rozporzadzenia Prezydenta RP z 6 II 1928r. o ustroju sadow powszechnych w Polsce Ludowej w latach 1944–1956' [Consecutive Reforms in the Presidential Decree of 6 February 1928 on the Law of the Common Courts in the Polish People's Republic in the Years 1944–1956], unpublished manuscript (1995) (on file with author).
Sachs, Jeffrey, and Katharina Pistor, eds, *The Rule of Law and Economic Reform* (New York: Westview Press, 1997).
Sadurski, Wojciech, *Giving Desert Its Due: Social Justice and Legal Theory* (Dordrecht: R. Reidel Publishing Company, 1985).
—— *Rights Before Courts: A Study of Constitutional Courts in Postcommunist States of Central and Eastern Europe* (Dordrecht: Springer, 2008).
Sajo, Andras, *Limiting Government: An Introduction to Constitutionalism* (Budapest: Central European University Press, 1999).
Sarat, Austin, and Christian Boulanger, eds, *The Cultural Lives of Capital Punishment: Comparative Perspectives* (Stanford, CA: Stanford University Press, 2005).
Schaff, Adam, *Marksizm a jednostka ludzka* [Marxism and the Human Individual] (Warsaw: Panstwowe Wydawnictwo Naukowe, 1965).

Scheuerman, William, ed., *The Rule of Law Under Siege: Selected Writings of Franz L. Neumann and Otto Kirchheimer* (Berkeley, CA: University of California Press, 1996).

Schmitt, Carl, *Die Verfassungslehre* (Munich: Duncker & Humboldt, 1931).

—— *Legalität und Legitimität* (Munich: Duncker & Humboldt, 1932).

—— *Der Begriff des Politischen* (Berlin: Duncker & Humboldt, 1963).

—— *The Concept of the Political*, trans. by George Schwab (New Brunswick, NJ: Rutgers University Press, 1976).

—— *The Leviathan in the State Theory of Thomas Hobbes: Meaning and Failure of a Political Symbol*, trans. by George Schwab (Westport, CT: Greenwood Press, 1996).

—— *Legality and Legitimacy*, trans. by Jeffrey Seitzer (Durham, NC: Duke University Press, 2004).

—— *Constitutional Theory*, trans. by Jeffrey Seitzer (Durham, NC: Duke University Press, 2008).

Service, Robert, *A History of Twentieth-Century Russia* (London: Penguin Books, 1997).

Sharp, Alan, *The Versailles Settlement: Peacemaking in Paris, 1919* (London: Macmillan, 1991).

Shirer, William, *The Rise and Fall of the Third Reich: A History of Nazi Germany* (London: Secker & Warburg, 1960).

Siemienski, Feliks, *Organy przedstawicielskie w systemie organow panstwa socialistycznego* [Representative Bodies in the System of the Agencies of the Socialist State] (Lublin: Uniwersytet Maria Curie-Sklodowska, 1964).

Sikorski, Radek, *The Polish House: An Intimate History of Poland* (London: Routledge, 1997).

Slownik historii Polski, Wydanie III [The Dictionary of Polish History], 3rd edn, (Warsaw: Wiedza Powszechna, 1964).

Sólyom, Lászlό, and Georg Brunner, eds, *Constitutional Judiciary in a New Democracy: the Hungarian Constitutional Court* (Ann Arbor, MI: University of Michigan Press, 2000).

'Sprawozdanie z posiedzien Podzespolu do sprawy reformy prawa i sadow' [Report of the Sessions of the Subtable on Legal and Court Reform], *Porozumienia Okraglego Stolu* [The Round Table Talks], Warsaw, 6 February–5 April 1989. On file with author.

Steele, Jonathan, *Inside East Germany: The State That Came in From the Cold* (New York: Urizen Books, 1977).

Stolleis, Michael, *The Law Under the Swastika: Studies on Legal History in Nazi Germany* (Chicago: University of Chicago Press, 1998).

Studies in Polish and Comparative Law: A Symposium of 12 Articles (London: Stevens & Sons, 1945).

Sugar, Peter, Peter Hanak and Tibor Frank, eds, *A History of Hungary* (Bloomington, IN: Indiana University Press, 1990).

Swietochowski, Aleksander, *Historia chlopow polskich* [The History of the Polish Peasantry] (Warsaw: Panstwowy Instytut Wydawniczy, 1949).

—— *Wspomnienia* [Recollections] (Wroclaw: Zaklad Narodowy im. Ossolinskich, 1966).

Sword, Keith, *The Soviet Takeover of the Polish Eastern Territories, 1939–1941* (London: Macmillan, 1991).

—— ed., *Deportation and Exile: Poles in the Soviet Union, 1939–1948* (London: Macmillan, 1994).

Szacki, Jerzy, *Liberalism After Communism*, trans. by Chester A. Kisiel (Budapest: Central European University Press, 1994).

Szpilman, Wladyslaw, *The Pianist: The Extraordinary Story of One Man's Survival in Warsaw, 1939–1945*, trans. by Anthea Bell (London: Victor Gollancz, 1999).

Szujski, J., *Dzieja* [History] (Cracow: 1885).

—— *Kilka prawd z dziejow naszych ku rozwazaniu w chwili obecnej* [Some Truths from Our History to Consider at the Present Moment] (Cracow: 1867), quoted in R. F. Leslie, 'Triloyalism and the National Revival', in *The History of Poland Since 1863*, ed. by R. F. Leslie (Cambridge: Cambridge University Press, 1983), 13.

Targetti, Ferdinand, ed., *Privatization in Europe: East and West Experiences* (London: Dartmouth, 1992).

Taylor, J., *The Economic Development of Poland 1919–1950* (Ithaca, NY: Cornell University Press, 1952).

Timberlake, Charles E., ed., *Essays in Russian Liberalism* (Columbia, MO: University of Missouri Press, 1972).

Tismaneanu, Vladimir, *Fantasies of Salvation: Democracy, Nationalism, and Myth in Post-Communist Europe* (Princeton, NJ: Princeton University Press, 1998).

—— *Stalinism for All Seasons: A Political History of Romanian Communism* (Berkeley, CA: University of California Press, 2003.

Titkow, Anna, *Stres i zycie spoleczne: polskie doswiadczenia* [Stress and Social Life: Polish Experiences] (Warsaw: Panstwowy Instytut Wydawniczy, 1993).

Toranska, Teresa, *Oni* [Them] (Warsaw: Mysl, 1986); in English, *'Them': Stalin's Polish Puppets* (New York: Harper & Row, 1987).

Trials of War Criminals Before the Nuernberg Military Tribunals Under Control Council No. 10, Vol. III (1951).

Vaksberg, Arkady, *Stalin's Prosecutor: The Life of Andrei Vyshinsky* (New York: Grove Weidenfeld, 1990).

Voslensky, Michael, *Nomenklatura* (London: The Bodley Head, 1983).

Vyshinsky, Andrei, *The Law of the Soviet State* (Westport, CT: Greenwood Press, 1948).

Wagner, Wenceslas, ed., *Polish Law Throughout the Ages* (Stanford, CA: Hoover Institution Press, 1970), 117–214.

Walicki, Andrzej, *Philosophy and Romantic Nationalism: The Case of Poland* (Oxford: Clarendon Press, 1982).

—— *The Enlightenment and the Birth of Modern Nationhood: Polish Political Thought from Noble Republicanism to Tadeusz Kosciuszko*, trans. by Emma Harris (Notre Dame, IN: University of Notre Dame Press, 1989).

—— *Russia, Poland and Universal Regeneration: Studies on Russian and Polish Thought of the Romantic Epoch* (Notre Dame, IN: University of Notre Dame Press, 1991).

Waltos, Stanislaw, ed., *Code of Criminal Procedure of the Polish People's Republic*, trans. by Marianna Abrahamowicz (Warsaw: Wydawnictwo Prawnicze, 1979).

Wandruszka, Adam, and Peter Urbanitsch, eds, *Die Habsburgermonarchie 1848–1918*, Vol. III, Part 1 (Vienna: Verlag Osterreichischen Akademie der Wissenschaften, 1980).

Wandycz, Piotr, *The Lands of Partitioned Poland 1795–1918* (Seattle, WA: University of Washington Press, 1974).

Waskowski, E., *System prawa cywilnego* [The Civil Law System] (Wilno: 1932), as quoted in Andrzej Rzeplinski, 'The Principles of Independence of the Judiciary and Its Statutory Application', in *Constitutionalism and Human Rights*, ed. by Andrzej Rzeplinski, Vol. 1, Papers of the International Conference, 'Human Rights and Freedoms in the New Constitutions in Central and Eastern Europe', Warsaw, 24–29 April 1992 (Warsaw: Helsinki Foundation for Human Rights in Eastern Europe, 1992), 129.

Weber, Max, *The Theory of Social and Economic Organization*, trans. by A. M. Henderson and Talcott Parsons (New York: The Free Press, 1947).

—— *Economy and Society*, 2 vols (Berkeley, CA: University of California Press, 1978).

Wedel, Janine, *Collision and Collusion: The Strange Case of Western Aid to Eastern Europe 1989–1998* (New York: St. Martin's Press, 1998).

Weinberger, Ota, ed., *Hans Kelson – Essays in Legal and Moral Philosophy* (Dordrecht: D. Reidel, 1973).

Worcell, Stanislaw, *Pisma spoleczne i polityczne* [Political and Social Writings], selection and trans. by Piotr Marciniak (Warsaw: Ksiaszka i Wiedza, 1980).

Wroblewski, Bronislaw, *Studia z dziedziny prawa i etyki* [Studies from the Fields of Law and Ethics] (Wilno: 1934).

Wyka, Kazimierz, *Zycie na niby* [Make-Believe Life] (Cracow: Wydawnictwo Literackie, 1984).

Zagajewski, Adam, *Two Cities: On Exile, History, and the Imagination*, trans. by Lillian Vallee (New York: Farrar Straus Giroux, 1991).

Zakrzewska, Janina, *Spor o konstytucji* [A Conflict over the Constitution] (Warsaw: Wydawnictwo Sejmowe, 1993).

Zamoyski, Adam, *The Polish Way: A Thousand-Year History of the Poles and Their Culture* (London: John Murray, 1987).

Zawada, Andrzej, *Dwudziestolecie literackie* [Literary 1920s] (Wroclaw: Wydawnictwo Dolnoslaskie, 1996).
Ziembinski, Zygmunt, ed., *Polish Contributions to the Theory and Philosophy of Law* (Amsterdam: Rodopi, 1987).
Zimmern, A., *The League of Nations and the Rule of Law 1918–1935* (London: Macmillan, 1936).
Znamierowski, Czeslaw, *Podstawowe pojecia teorii prawa, Czesc I: Uklad prawny i norma prawna* [The Basic Concepts of the Theory of Law, Part I: The Legal System and the Legal Norm] (Warsaw, 1924).
—— *Prolegomena do nauki o panstwie* [Prologue to the Science of the State] (Warsaw: 1930).
Zweig, Ferdynand, *Poland Between Two Wars* (London: Secker & Warburg, 1944).

Websites

Financial Times, http://www.ft.com/home/uk
Gazeta Wyborcza [The Voter's Gazette], http://wyborcza.pl/0,0.html
International Commission of Jurists at http://www.icj.org/sommaire.php3?lang=en (last accessed 14 June 2009).
Office of the United Nations High Commissioner for Human Rights, http://treaties.un.org/Pages/Treaties.aspx?id=4&subid=A&lang=en (last accessed 14 June 2009).
Rzeczpospolita, http://www.rp.pl/temat/2.html
The Warsaw Voice, http://www.warsawvoice.pl/

Documentaries/Films

'Battle for Memory: Lithuania', *Crossing Continents*, BBC Radio 4, 17 July 2008.
Katyn (Andrzej Wajda, 2007, 118 minutes).
Ukraine – Eternal Memory: Voices from the Great Terror (National Film Network, 1997, 81 minutes).

Articles and Book Chapters

Adams, Kip Augustine, 'What Is Just? The Rule of Law and Natural Law in the Trials of Former East German Border Guards', *Stanford Journal of International Law*, 29 (1993), 271–314.

Adams, Richard, 'Harnessing Technological Development', in *Rethinking Modernization: Anthropological Perspectives*, ed. by J. Poggie and R. N. Lynch (Westport, CT: Greenwood Press, 1975), 37–68.

Ajani, Gianmaria, 'By Chance and Prestige: Legal Transplants in Russia and Eastern Europe', *American Journal of Comparative Law*, 43 (1995), 93–117.

Ajenkiel, Andrzej, 'Wplywy niemieckiego i austriackiego prawa w Polsce' [The Influence of German and Austrian Law in Poland], *Czasopismo Prawno-Historyczne* [Journal of Legal History], 39 (1987), 205–09.

Allen, John L., Jr, 'Polish Church Confronts Ghosts of Past', *National Catholic Reporter*, 19 January 2007, 8–10.

Antohi, Sorin, 'Habits of the Mind: Europe's Post-1989 Symbolic Geographies', in S. Antohi and V. Tismaneanu, eds, *Between Past and Future: The Revolutions of 1989 and Their Aftermath* (Budapest: Central European University Press, 2000), 61–77.

Applebaum, Anne, 'A Movie That Matters', *New York Review of Books*, 14 February 2008, 14.

Arnold, Jorg, and Ewa Weigend, 'Prawo karne, zmiana systemu politycznego i obrachunek z przesloscia w Polsce i w Niemczech' [Criminal Law, Changes in the Political System and Coming to Terms with the Past in Poland and Germany], in *Prawo karne a problem zmiany ustroju politycznego/Strafrecht und politischer Systemweschel* [Criminal Law and the Problems Concerning Changes in the Political Structure], ed. by Albin Eser and Andrzej Zoll (Cracow: Kantor Wydawniczy Zakamycze; Freiburg-im-Breisgau: Max-Planck-Institut, 1998), 19–72.

Auscaler, Gustaw, and Wiktor Suchecki, 'Po XX Zjezdzie KPZR' [After the 20th Plenum of the Communist Party of the Soviet Union], *Panstwo i Prawo* [State and Law],4 (1956), ii–v.

Babb, Hugh, 'Petrazhitskii: Science of Legal Policy and Theory of Law', *Harvard Law Review*, 37 (1937), 793–829.

—— 'Petrazhitskii: Theory of Law', *Harvard Law Review*, 38 (1938), 511–78.

Baister, Stephen, 'Corporate Insolvency – Eastern Approaches', *Insolvency Law & Practice*, 54 (1989), 109–10.

—— 'The Court as Educator: The Social Courts System of the German Democratic Republic', *Legal History*, 18 (1997), 47–90.

Balcerowicz, Leszek, 'Dziesiec rad Balcerowicza' [Ten Suggestions of Balcerowicz], *Polityka* [Politics], 18 (3 May 1997), 80–82.

—— *et al.*, 'Economic Reform: Central Principles and Methods of Implementation', in *Reforma gospodarcza: propozycje, tendencje, kierunki dyskusji* [Economic Reform: Proposals, Tendencies, Directions of Discussion], ed. by Rafal Krawczyk (Warsaw: Panstwowe Wydawnictwo Ekonomiczne, 1981), 281–371.

Baltruszajtys, Grazyna, 'Kompanie akcyjne w Polsce w drugiej polowie XVIIIw.: z zagadnien poczatkow prawa akcyjnego' [Joint Stock Companies in Poland in the Second Half of the Eighteenth Century: On Questions of the Beginnings of the Law of Joint Stocks], *Czasopismo Prawno-Historyczne*, 11 (1959), 77–111.

Barcz, Jan, 'Membership of Poland in the European Union in Light of the Constitution of 2 April 1997. Constitutional Act on Integration', *Polish Yearbook of International Law*, 23 (1997–98), 21–34.

Barry, Donald D., 'Administrative Justice: The Role of Soviet Courts in Controlling Administrative Acts', in *Soviet Administrative Law: Theory and Policy*, ed. by G. Ginsburgs *et al.* (Dordrecht: Nijhoff, 1989), 63–83.

Batowski, Henryk von, 'Die Polen', in *Die Hapsburgmonarchie 1848–1918*, Vol. III, Part 1 (Vienna: Verlag Osterreichischen Akademie der Wissenschaften, 1980), 522–554.

Berg, Ger P. van den, 'Elements of Continuity in Soviet Constitutional Law', in *Russian Law: Historical and Political Perspectives*, ed. by William E. Butler (Leyden: A. W. Sijthoff, 1977), 215–34.

Blankenburg, Erhard, 'The Purge of Lawyers After the Breakdown of the East German Regime', *Law and Social Inquiry*, 20 (1995), 223–43.

Bonarowski, Michal, and Maciej Urbaniak, 'Syndyczny los' [The Legal Adviser's Luck], *Gazeta Bankowa* [Banking Gazette], 2 April 1995, 16–17.

Borowik, Irena, 'The Roman Catholic Church in the Process of Democratic Transformation: The Case of Poland', *Social Compass*, 49 (2002), 239–52.

Bowring, Bill, 'Human Rights in Russia: Discourse of Emancipation or Only a Mirage?', in *Human Rights in Eastern Europe*, ed. by Istvan Pogany (Aldershot: Edward Elgar, 1995), 87–109.

—— 'Politics Versus the Rule of Law in the Work of the Russian Constitutional Court', in *The Rule of Law in Central Europe*, ed. by Jiří Přibáň and James Young, Socio-Legal Studies Series (Dartmouth: Ashgate, 1999), 257–77.

Brunicki, Kaz, and Marek Czarny, 'Arrangements with Creditors Under Polish Law', *Butterworths Journal of International and Financial Law*, 8 (1993), 226–28.

Brus, Wlodzimierz, 'Aims, Methods and Political Determinants of the Economic Policy of Poland 1970–1980', in *The Eastern European Economies in the 1970s*, ed. by Alec Nove *et al.* (London: Butterworths, 1982), 91–138.

Brzezinski, Mark, 'Constitutional Heritage and Renewal: The Case of Poland', *Virginia Law Review*, 77 (1991), 49–112.

—— 'Constitutionalism Within Limits', *East European Constitutional Review*, 2 (1993), 38–43.

—— 'Constitutionalism and Post-Communist Polish Politics', *Loyola Los Angeles International and Comparative Journal*, 20 (1998), 433–53.

—— and Leszek Garlicki, 'Judicial Review in Post-Communist Poland: The Emergence of a *Rechtsstaat*?', *Stanford Journal of International Law*, 31 (1995), 13–59.

Butler, W. E., 'Perestroika and the Rule of Law', in *Perestroika and the Rule of Law: Anglo-American and Soviet Perspectives*, ed. by W. E. Butler (London: I. B. Tauris, 1991), 7–21.

—— 'The Rule of Law and the Legal System', in *Developments in Soviet and Post-Soviet Politics*, ed. by Stephen White *et al.* (London: Macmillan, 1992), 107–21.

—— 'Towards an Introduction to Russian Legal Theory', in *Russian Legal Theory*, ed. by W. E. Butler (Aldershot: Dartmouth, 1996), xi–xlv.

Butler, William, 'Civil Rights in Russian: Legal Standards in Gestation', in *Civil Rights in Imperial Russia*, ed. by Olga Crisp and Linda Edmondson (Oxford: Clarendon Press, 1989), 1–12.

—— 'Justice in Russia: Soviet Law and Russian History', *Emory Law Journal*, 42 (1993), 433–48.

Butler, William E., 'Foreign Impressions of Russian Law to 1800: Some Reflections', in *Russian Law: Historical and Political Perspectives*, ed. by William E. Butler (Leyden: A. W. Sijthoff, 1977), 65–92.

—— 'Necessary Defense, Judge-Made Law, and Soviet Man', in *Law After Revolution*, ed. by William E. Butler *et al.* (New York: Oceana Publications, 1988), 99–130.

Cappelletti, Mauro, 'Repudiating Montesquieu? The Expansion and Legitimacy of Constitutional Justice', *Catholic University Law Review*, 35 (1985), 12–14.

Castoriadis, Cornelius, 'Marxism and Revolutionary Theory (1964–1965): Excerpts', in *The Castoriadis Reader*, ed. and trans. by David Ames Curtis (Oxford: Blackwell, 1997), 139–95.

—— 'Radical Imagination and the Social Instituting Imaginary (1994)', in *The Castoriadis Reader*, ed. and trans. by David Ames Curtis (Oxford: Blackwell, 1997), 319–39.

Charter of Paris, 'Conference and Co-operation in Europe: Charter of Paris for a New Europe and Supplementary Document to Give Effect to Certain Provisions of the Charter', *International Legal Materials*, 31 (1991), pp. 190–227

Chrypinski, Vincent, 'Postwar Developments in Polish Law: A Survey of Criminal and Civil Legal Rules', in *Polish Law Throughout the Ages*, ed. by Wenceslas Wagner (Stanford, CA: Hoover Institution Press, 1970), 177–214.

Ciechanowski, Jan M., 'Poland in Defeat, September 1939–July 1941', in *The History of Poland Since 1863*, ed. by R. F. Leslie (Cambridge: Cambridge University Press, 1983), 209–26.

—— 'Post-war Poland', in *The History of Poland Since 1863*, ed. by R. F. Leslie (Cambridge: Cambridge University Press, 1983), 280–98.

Cienski, Jan, 'Poland Risks Isolation over Reform', *Financial Times*, 1 July 2008 (accessed online).

Cieslak, Tadeusz, 'Dwa projekty Niemieckego Kodeksu Cywilnego (BGB)' [Two Drafts of the German Civil Code (BGB)], *Czasopismo Prawno-Historyczne*, 7 (1955), 145–63.

Cohen, Stanley, 'State Crimes of Previous Regimes: Knowledge, Accountability, and the Policing of the Past', *Law and Social Inquiry*, 20 (1995), 7–50.

'Comrades Coin It as Poles Privatise', *The Guardian*, 26 July 1995, 9.

Cotterrell, Roger, 'Review Article', *Modern Law Review*, 51 (1988), 126–40.

Cutler, Lloyd, and Herman Schwartz, 'Constitutional Reform in Czechoslovakia: *E Duobus Unum?*', *University of Chicago Law Review*, 58 (1991), 511–53.

Czaplinski, Wladyslaw, 'International Law and Polish Domestic Law', in *Constitutional Reform and International Law in Central and Eastern Europe*, ed. by Rein Mullerson, Malgosia Fitzmaurice and Mads Adenas, Studies in Law Series, Vol. 1 (The Hague: Kluwer Law International, 1998), 15–36.

—— 'International Legal Aspects of Polish–Lithuanian Relations', *Polish Yearbook of International Law*, 19 (1992–93), 31–48.

—— 'International and Polish Municipal Law: Recent Jurisprudence of the Polish Supreme Judicial Organs', *Zeitschrift für ausländisches öffentliches Recht und Völkerrecht*, 53 (1993), 871–81.

Czarnota, Adam, 'Constitutional Nationalism, Citizenship and Hope for Civil Society in Eastern Europe', in *Nationalism and Postcommunism: A Collection of Essays*, ed. by Aleksander Pavkovic *et al.* (Aldershot: Dartmouth, 1995), 83–100.

Czarnota, Bridget, 'Biala ksiega dotyczaca przygotowania panstw stowaryszonych Europy-Srodkowo-Wshodniej do integracji z rynkiem Unii Europejskiej' [The White Paper Concerning the Preparation of CEE Countries for Integration in the Market of the European Union], *Panstwo i Prawo*, 4–5 (1996), 159–61.

Czeszejko-Sochacki, Zdzislaw, 'The Origins of Constitutional Review in Poland', *Saint Louis-Warsaw Transatlantic Law Journal* (1996), 15–31.

David, Roman, 'Lustration Laws in Action: The Evaluation of Lustration Policy in the Czech Republic and Poland', *Law and Social Inquiry*, 28 (2003), 387–439.

Day, Matthew, 'Poland Punishes Former Communist Leaders by Cutting Pensions', *Daily Telegraph*, 5 January 2010 (accessed online).

Dietl, Jerzy, 'Business Ethics in Conditions of Transformation from a Centrally Planned Economy to a Market Economy', in *Philosophy in Post-Communist Europe*, ed. by Dane R. Gordon, Value Inquiry Book Series (Amsterdam: Rodopi, 1998), 11–22.

Dinstein, Yoram, 'The Degree of Self-Rule of Minorities in Unitarian and Federal States', in *Peoples and Minorities in International Law*, ed. by Catherine Brolmann *et al.* (Dordrecht: Martinus Nijhoff, 1993), 221–35.

Domogala, Jerzy, 'Stawianie na nogi' [Putting on Legs], *Zycie Gospodarcze*, 15 March 1996, 13–16.

'Do trzech lat za zaprzeczanie zbrodniom' [Up to Three Years for Denying a Crime], *Rzeczpospolita*, 24 July 1998 (accessed online).

Drzewicki, Krzysztof, 'Implementation of Social and Economic Rights in Central and Eastern Europe Transforming from Planned Economy to Market Economy', *Nordic Journal of International Law*, 64 (1995), 373–84.

Dugan, Christopher F., and Vladimir Lechtman, 'The FCPA in Russia and Other Former Communist Countries', *American Journal of International Law*, 91 (1997), 378–88.

Dzialocha, Kazimierz, and Stanislaw Pawela, 'Zmiany zakresu wlasciwosci Trybunalu Konstytucyjnego de lege lata i de lege referenda' [The Changes of the Constitutional Tribunal in the Current and Future Law], *Panstwo i Prawo*, 11 (1989), 3–17.

Eichelberger, W., 'Odkreslamy przeszlosc gruba kreska?' [Are We Crossing Off the Past with a Thick Line?], *Gazeta Wyborcza* [The Voter's Gazette], 27 February 1990, 23.

Elster, Jon, 'Constitutionalism in Eastern Europe: An Introduction', *University of Chicago Law Review*, 58 (1991), 447–82.

Emmert, Frank, 'Administrative and Court Reform in Central and Eastern Europe', *European Law Journal*, 9 (2003), 288–315.

Enyedi, Zsolt, and Joan Mahoney, 'Churches and the Consolidation of Democratic Culture: Difference and Convergence in the Czech Republic and Hungary', *Democratization*, 11 (2004), 171–91.

Fajst, Michal, 'Spor o kryminologie w Polsce w okresie stalinizmu' [Conflict over Criminology in Poland During the Stalinist Period], *Studia luridica* [Legal Studies], 27 (1995), 43–64.

Feldbrugge, Frederick, 'Government and Shadow Economy', *Soviet Studies*, 36 (1988), 528–43.

Fijalkowski, A. 'The Paradoxical Nature of Crime Control in Post-Communist Europe', *European Journal of Crime, Criminal Law and Criminal Justice*, 15 (2007), 155–72.

Fine, Robert, 'Civil Society Theory, Enlightenment and Critique', in *Civil Society: Democratic Perspectives*, ed. by Robert Fine and Shirin Rai (London: Frank Cass, 1997), 7–28.

Fiss, Owen, 'The Limits of Judicial Independence', *Inter-American Law Review*, 25 (1993), 55–65.

Fitzmaurice, Malgosia, 'Book Review', *Netherlands International Law Review*, 36 (1989), 76–80.

Fleszynski, Kazimierz, 'Realne gwarancje niezawislosci sedziowskiej' [Real Guarantees of Judicial Independence], *Glos sadownictwa* [The Court's Voice], 11 (1939), 105–09.

Fletcher, George P., 'Searching for the Rule of Law in the Wake of Communism', *Brigham Young University Law Review*, 1 (1992), 145–64.

'Flickers of Economic Light', *The Economist*, 25–27.

Frankowski, Stanislaw, 'The Procuracy and the Regular Courts as the Palladium of Individual Rights and Liberties – The Case of Poland', *Tulane Law Review*, 61 (1987), 1307–38.

—— 'A Comment on Professor Garlicki's Article "Constitutional Developments in Poland": The Lyrics Sound Familiar, But Are They Really Playing Our Song?', *Saint Louis University Law Journal*, 32 (1988), 737–51.

—— 'The Independence of the Judiciary in Poland: Some Reflections on Andrzej Rzeplinski's *Sadownictwo w Polsce Ludowej* [The Judiciary in People's Poland

(1989)], *Arizona Journal of International and Comparative Law*, 8 (1991), 33–52.

Freeman, M. D. A., 'The Rule of Law – Conservative, Liberal, Marxist and Neo-Marxist: Wherein Lies the Attraction?', in *Perestroika and the Rule of Law: Anglo-American and Soviet Perspectives*, ed. by W. E. Butler (London: I. B. Tauris, 1991), 37–59.

Frey, Danuta, 'Weryfikacji sedziow' [The Verification of Judges], *Rzeczpospolita*, 11 March 1993 (accessed online).

Frydman, Ryszard, and Andrzej Rapaczynski, 'Mass Privatization Proposals in Eastern Europe: Ownership and the Structure of Control', in *Privatization in Europe: East and West Experiences*, ed. by Ferdinand Targetti (London: Dartmouth, 1992), 75–89.

Fukuyama, Francis, 'The End of History', *The National Interest* (Summer 1989), 3–18.

Fuller, Lon F., 'Positivism and Fidelity to Law – A Reply to Professor Hart', *Harvard Law Review*, 71 (1958), 630–72.

Gardocki, Lech, 'O ochronie obrotu gospodarczego' [The Protection of Economic Transactions], *Palestra* [The Bar], 1–2 (1995), 101–04.

Garlicki, Leszek, 'The Polish Legal Profession', *St Louis University Law Journal*, 24 (1980), 488.

—— 'Przeglad orzecznictwa Trybunalu Konstytucyjnego za 1990 rok' [An Overview of the Decisions of the Constitutional Tribunal from 1990], *Przeglad Sadowy* [Court Review], 3 (1990), 166–67.

—— 'Przeglad orzecznictwa Trybunalu Konstytucyjnego za 1991 rok' [An Overview of the Decisions of the Constitutional Tribunal from 1991], *Przeglad Sadowy*, 11–12 (1992), 54–55.

—— 'Przeglad orzecznictwa za 1992 rok' [An Overview of the Decisions from 1992], *Przeglad Sadowy*, 10 (1993), 77–78.

—— 'Orzecznictwo w 1996 roku' [An Overview of Decisions from 1996], *Przeglad Sadowy*, 5 (1997), 111.

Garlinska, Grazyna, 'Porzadkowanie upadlosci' [Cleaning Up Bankruptcy], *Zycie Gospodarcze*, 10 May 1996, 47.

Garton Ash, Timothy, 'Eastern Europe: The Year of Truth', *New York Review of Books*, 15 February 1990, 17.

—— '1989!', *New York Review of Books*, 5 November 2009.

Gazeta Sadowa Warszawska [Warsaw Court Gazette], No. 40 (1917).

Gilewicz, Romuald, 'Mit o niezawislosci' [The Myth About Independence], *Rzeczpospolita*, 10 March 1993, II (prawo co dnia).

—— 'Skandal placowy w sadownictwie' [A Payment Scandal in the Judiciary], *Rzeczpospolita*, 25 March 1993, II (prawo co dnia).

Girling, Evi, 'European Identity, Penal Sensibilities, and Communities of Sentiment', in *Perspectives on Punishment: The Contours of Control*, ed. by Sarah Armstrong and Lesley McAra (Oxford: Oxford University Press, 2006), 69–82.

—— Ian Loader and Richard Sparks, 'Crime and the Sense of One's Place: Globalization, Restructuring and Insecurity in an English Town', in *The New European Criminology: Crime and Social Order in Europe*, ed. by Vincenzo Ruggiero, Nigel Smith and Ian Taylor (London: Routledge, 1998), 304–22.

Golik, Piotr, 'No Room for Displaced Posturings', *The Warsaw Voice*, 2 August 1998 (accessed online).

Gorniok, Oktawia, 'Prawo karna ochrona obrotu gospodarczego' [Criminal Law Protection of Economic Transactions], *Przeglad Sadowy*, 9 (1993), 3–17.

—— 'Niektore problemy ustawy o ochronie obrotu gospodarczego' [Certain Problems with the Law on the Protection of Economic Transactions], *Prokuratura i Prawo*, 5 (1996), 7–18.

Gostynski, Zbigniew, and Alan Garfield, 'Taking the Other Road: Polish Legal Education During the Past Thirty Years', *Temple International and Comparative Law Journal*, 7 (1993), 243–86.

Gray, Cheryl W., and Kathryn Hendley, 'Developing Commercial Law in Transition Economies: Examples from Hungary and Russia', in *The Rule of Law and Economic Reform*, ed. by Jeffrey Sachs and Katharina Pistor (New York: Westview Press, 1997), 139–64.

Grodziski, Stanislaw, 'Zdrodla prawa w Galicji, 1772–1848' [The Sources of Law in Galicia, 1772–1848], *Czasopismo Prawno-Historyczne*, 16 (1964), 175–87.

—— 'Komisja Kodyfikacyjna Rzeczpospolitej Polskiej' [The Codification Commission of the Republic of Poland], *Czasopismo Prawno-Historyczne*, 33 (1991), 47–81.

Gross, Aeyel M., 'Reinforcing the New Democracies: The European Convention on Human Rights and the Former Communist Countries – A Study of the Case Law', *European Journal of International Law*, 7 (1996), 89–102.

Gross, Jan. T., 'The Sovietisation of Western Ukraine and Western Byelorussia', in *Jews in Eastern Poland and the USSR, 1939–46*, ed. by Norman Davies and Antony Polonksy (London: Macmillan, 1991), 60–76.

Grossman, Gregory, 'Zrodla prawa w Galicji, 1772–1848' [The Sources of Law in Galicia], *Czasopismo Prawno-Historyczne*, 16 (1964), 175–87.

—— 'The "Second Economy" of the USSR', *Problems of Communism*, 26 (1977), 25–40.

Gruszecki, Tomasz, and Jan Winiecki, 'Privatisation in East-Central Europe: A Comparative Perspective', *Aussenwirtschaft*, 46 (1991), 67–100.

Grzybowski, Kazimierz, 'The Draft of the Civil Code for Poland', in *Studies for Polish Law*, ed. by Kazimierz Grzybowski *et al.*, Law in Eastern Europe Series, No. 6 (Leyden: A. W. Sijthoff, 1962). 11–37.

Gwizdz, Andrzej, 'Trybunal Konstytucyjny' [The Constitutional Tribunal], *Panstwo i Prawo*, 12 (1983), 3–15.

Halmai, Gabor, *et al.*, 'Confronting the Past: The Hungarian Constitutional Court's Lustration Decision of 1994', *East European Human Rights Review*, 1 (1995), 111–28.

Hart, H. L. A., 'Positivism and the Separation of Law and Morals', *Harvard Law Review*, 71 (1958), 593–629.

Haselsteiner, Horst, 'Cooperation and Confrontation Between Rulers and the Noble Estates 1711–1790', in *A History of Hungary*, ed. by Peter Sugar, Peter Hanak and Tibor Frank (Bloomington, IN: Indiana University Press, 1990), 138–64.

Hauner, M., 'Human Resources', in *The Economic History of Eastern Europe 1919–1975*, Vol. 1, ed. by M. C. Kaser and E. A. Radice (Oxford: Clarendon Press, 1985), 66–147.

Hauner, Milan, 'Anti-militarism and the Independent Peace Movement in Czechoslovakia', in *The Search for Civil Society: Independent Peace Movements in the Soviet Bloc*, ed. by V. Tismaneanu (New York: Routledge, 1990), 88–117.

Havel, Václav, Speech in Salzburg, *Gazeta Wyborcza* , 26 July 1990 (accessed online).

Helczynski, Bronislaw, 'The Polish Code of Administrative Procedure', in *Studies in Polish Law*, ed. Kazimierz Grzybowski *et al.*, Law in Eastern Europe Series, No. 6 (Leyden: A. W. Sijthoff, 1962), 38–77.

Heller, Agnes, 'Between Past and Future', in *Between Past and Future: The Revolutions of 1989 and Their Aftermath*, ed. by S. Antohi and V. Tismaneanu (Budapest: Central European University Press, 2000), 3–13.

Hliwa, Renata, and Leszek Wisniewski, 'The International Covenants in Human Rights in the Decisions of the Polish Supreme Court, the Constitutional Tribunal and the Supreme Administrative Court', *German Yearbook of International Law*, 39 (1996), 468–80.

Isaievych, Iaroslav, 'Galicia and Problems of National Identity', in *The Habsburg Legacy: National Identity in Historical Perspective*, ed. by Ritchie Robertson and Edward Timms, Austrian Studies V (Edinburgh: Edinburgh University Press, 1994), 37–45.

Izdebski, Hubert, 'Mala Konstytucja a reforma administracji publicznej' [The Small Constitution and Public Administration Reform], *Studia luridica* [Juridical Studies], 28 (1995), 57–61.

Janicki, Mariusz, and Miroslaw Peczak, 'Wszystko albo nic' [All or Nothing], *Polityka*, 20 (18 May 1996), 27–29.

Jaruzelski, Wojciech, 'Rachunek sumienia' [A Bill of Conscience], *Rzeczpospolita*, 25–26 September 1993, 8–10.

—— 'Z oddali' [From the Distance], *Rzeczpospolita*, 6–7 November 1993, 13.

Jasica, Roman, 'Polish–German Treaties of 1990 and 1991 on the Confirmation of Their Mutual Border and on Good Neighbourliness and Friendly Co-operation', *Polish Yearbook of International Law*, 19 (1991–92), 71–84.

Jasinski, Jerzy, 'Polityka karna sadow w pocatku law dziewiecdziesiatych' [The Politics of Crime in the Courts in the Early 1990s], *Przeglad Sadowy*, 10 (1993), 3–22.

Kaldor, Mary, and Ivan Vejvoda, 'Democratization in Central and East European Countries', *International Affairs*, 73 (1997), 59–82.

Kaser, M. C., 'Introduction', in *Economic History of Eastern Europe 1919–1975*, Vol. 1, ed. by M. C. Kaser and E. A. Radice (Oxford: Clarendon Press, 1985), 1–22.

Kaszuba, Ewa, 'Obrona panstwa czy ustroju' [The Protection of the State or Structure], *Rzeczpospolita*, 25 May 1994, 3.

Kedziera, Mariusz, 'To tylko reorganizacja' [It's Only Reorganisation], *Rzeczpospolita*, 11 May 1998 (accessed online).

Kelsen, Hans, 'Foundations of Democracy', *Ethics*, 66 (1955), 1–101.

Kennet, David, 'The Role of Law in a Market Economy', in *The Road to Capitalism: Economic Transformation in Eastern Europe and the Former Soviet Union*, ed. by David Kennet and Marc Lieberman (Orlando, FL: Harcourt, Brace and Jovanovich, 1992), 99–109.

Kirchheimer, Otto, 'Criminal Law in National Socialist Germany', in *The Rule of Law Under Siege: Selected Writings of Franz L. Neumann and Otto Kirchheimer*, ed. by William E. Scheuerman (Berkeley, CA: University of California Press, 1996), 172–91.

—— 'Remarks on Carl Schmitt's *Legality and Legitimacy*', in *The Rule of Law Under Siege: Selected Writings of Franz L. Neumann and Otto Kirchheimer*, ed. by William E. Scheuerman (Berkeley, CA: University of California Press, 1996), 63–98.

—— 'State Structure and Law in the Third Reich', in *The Rule of Law Under Siege: Selected Writings of Franz L. Neumann and Otto Kirchheimer*, ed. by William E. Scheuerman (Berkeley, CA: University of California Press, 1996), 142–71.

Klich, Agnieszka, 'Bribery in Economies in Transition: The Foreign Corrupt Practices Act', *Stanford Journal of International Law*, 32 (1996), 121–47.

Klosinski, Werner, 'Zum *Phänomen* der Angst' [Concerning the Phenomenon of Angst], in *Angst und Aggression* [Angst and Aggression], ed. by Rolf Denker (Stuttgart: Ernst Klett Verlag, 1963), 7–17.

Kluczka, Jan, 'Comparative Study of Internal Legal Regulations of Council of Europe Member States Concerning the Protection of Minorities', *Polish Yearbook of International Law*, 21 (1993), 145–62.

Kochanowski, Jerzy, 'Zabraklo desek' [The Planks Ran Out], *Polityka*, 46 (15 November 1997), 80.

Kojder, Andrzej, 'Petrazycki wiecznie zywy' [Petrazycki Still Lives], *Prawo i Zycie* (1991), 10–11.

Kolakowski, Krzysztof, 'Glos cywilisty' [The Voice of a Civil Lawyer], *Rzeczpospolita*, 6 May 1998 (accessed online).

Kolakowski, Leszek, 'Marxism and Human Rights', in *Modernity on Endless Trial*, ed. by Leszek Kolakowski (Chicago: University of Chicago Press, 1990), 204–14.

Kommers, Donald P., and W. J. Thompson, 'Fundamentals in the Liberal Constitutional Tradition', in *Constitutional Policy and Change in Europe*, ed. by Joachim Jens Hesse and Nevil Johnson (Oxford: Oxford University Press, 1995), 23–45.

Kornai, Janos, 'The Postsocialist Transition and the State: Reflections in the Light of Hungarian Fiscal Problems', *American Sociological Review*, 82 (1992), 1–21.

Korobowicz, Artur, 'Wplyw czynnikow pozaprawnych na reforme sadowa w Krolestwie Polskim z lat 1875–1876' [Extra-Legal Factors which Affected Court Reform of the Kingdom of Poland in the Year 1875–1876], *Czasopismo Prawno-Historyczne*, 34 (1987), 69–81.

—— 'Ewakuacja sadow Krolestwa Polskiego i ich losy w czasie pierwszej wojny swiatowej' [The Evacuation of the Courts of the Kingdom of Poland and Their Fate During the First World War], *Czasopismo Prawno-Historyczne*, 61 (1989), 87–107.

Kovacs, Peter, 'Legal Protection of Minorities in Central and Eastern Europe: Hungarian Perspectives', *The Hague Yearbook of International Law*, 9 (1996), 33–42.

Krajewski, Andrzek, 'The Aliens Have Landed', *The Warsaw Voice*, 22 November 1998 (accessed online).

Kroner, Jolanta, 'Sedziowie juz sa, brakuje ustawy' [The Judges Are Here, the Law Is Absent], *Rzeczpospolita*, 7 August 1998 (accessed online).

—— 'Wniosek w Trybunale Konstytucyjnym' [Motion Before the Constitutional Tribunal], *Rzeczpospolita*, 24 July 1998 (accessed online).

Kruk, Maria, 'Wstep' [Introduction], *Mala Konstytucja czyli Ustawa Konstytucyjna z dniz 17 pazdziernika 1992r. o wzajemnych stosunkach miedzy wladza ustawodawcza i wykonawcza Rzeczpospolitej Polskiej oraz samorzadzie terytorialnym wraz z pozostalymi przespisami konstytucjynymi i ustawa z dnia 23 kwietna 1992r. o trybie przygotowania i uchwalenia Konstytucji Rzeczpospolitej Polskiej* [Small Constitution or the Constitutional Law of 17 October 1992 on the Mutual Relations Between the Legislative and Executive Powers of the Republic of Poland and Local Government and the Remaining Constitutional Laws and the Law of 23 April 1992 on the Organisation and Enactment of the Republic of Poland] (Warsaw: Wydawnictwo AWA, 1992), 4–37.

Kryshtanovskaya, Olga, and Stephen White, 'From Soviet *Nomenklatura* to Russian Élite', *Europe-Asia Studies*, 48 (1996), 711–33.

Krzeminski, Adam, 'Kresowe panstwo Europy' [The Neighbouring Country of Europe], *Polityka*, 7 (17 February 1997), 66–69.

Kurczewski, Jacek, 'Poland's Perpetually New Middle Class', *Transition*, 3 (21 March 1997), 22–25.

Kwasniewski, Jerzy, 'Social Problems in Poland', in *Social Control and the Law in Poland*, ed. by Jerzy Kwasniewski and Margaret Watson (New York: St. Martin's Press, 1991).

Landau, Zbigniew, 'The Economic Integration of Poland', in *The Reconstruction of Poland 1914–23*, ed. by Paul Latawski (London: Macmillan, 1992), 144–57.

—— 'The Relationship Between the Bank of Poland and the Government During the Interwar Period', in *Rebuilding the Financial System in Central and Eastern Europe, 1918–1994*, ed. by P. L. Cottrell *et al.* (Aldershot: Scolar Press, 1997), 75–87.

Lerner, Natan, 'The Evolution of Minority Rights in International Law', in *Peoples and Minorities in International Law*, ed. by Catherine Brolmann *et al.* (Dordrecht: Martinus Nijhoff, 1993), 77–101.

Leslie, R. F., 'Triloyalism and the National Revival', in *The History of Poland Since 1863*, ed. by R. F. Leslie (Cambridge: Cambridge University Press, 1983), 1–64.

Leszczynski, Leszek, 'A General Look at the Redefinition of the Protection of Human Rights in Eastern and Central Europe', *East European Human Rights Review*, 1 (1995), 3–10.

Letowska, Ewa, 'Dekalog dobrego sedziego' [The Ten Commandments of a Good Judge], *Gazeta Wyborcza*, 6–7 February 1993, 8–9.

—— 'The Administration of Justice in Poland', *EuroCriminology*, 7 (1994), 97–109.

—— 'Bariery do naszego myslenia o prawie w perspekstywie integracji z Europa' [Barriers to Our Thinking About the Law in the Context of European Integration], *Panstwo i Prawo*, 4–5 (1996), 44–58.

—— 'The Judge's Position in the Modern System of Government', in *Poland: Towards the Rule of Law*, ed. by Ewa Letowska and Janusz Letowski (Warsaw: Wydawnictwo Naukowe SCHOLAR, 1996), 96–116.

—— 'Poland: In Search of the "State of Law" and Its Future Constitution', in *Poland: Towards the Rule of Law*, ed. by Ewa Letowska and Janusz Letowski (Warsaw: Wydawnictwo Naukowe SCHOLAR, 1996), 10–22.

—— 'Courts and Tribunals Under the Constitution of Poland', *Saint Louis-Warsaw Transatlantic Law Journal* (1997), 69–89.

—— 'Dwie konstytucje' [Two Constitutions], *Polityka*, 9 (1 March 1997), 18.

Letowski, Janusz, 'The Polish Supreme Court on the Rule of Law and Fundamental Civil Rights', *European Review of Public Law*, 8 (1996), 283–97.

Lewandowski, Jedrzej, and Jan Szomburg, 'Property Reform as a Basis for Social and Economic Reform', *Communist Economies*, 1 (1989), as quoted in Tomasz Gruszecki and Jan Winiecki, 'Privatisation in East-Central Europe: A Comparative Perspective', *Aussenwirtschaft*, 46 (1991), 67–100.

Lipowski, Stanislaw, 'Niedomagania sadow grodzkich' [The Shortcomings of the Courts of First Instance], *Glos Sadownictwa*, 11 (1939), 677–86.

Lippman, Matthew, 'They Shoot Lawyers, Don't They?: Law in the Third Reich and the Global Threat to the Independence of the Judiciary', *California Western International Law Journal*, 23 (1993), 257–318.

—— 'Fifty Years After Auschwitz: Prosecutions of Nazi Death Camp Defendants', *Connecticut Journal of International Law*, 11 (1996), 199–278.

Lis, Maciej, 'Significant Aspects of Legal Solutions', *Polish Yearbook of International Law*, 22 (1995–96), 181–86.

Litauer, Jan Jakob, 'O metodzie wypelnienia luk w ustawodawstwie' [On Ways to Complete the Gaps in Legislation], *Panstwo i Prawo*, 7–8 (1947), 10–11.

Litwak, Andrzej, 'Reforma ... bez reformy' [Reform ... Without Reform], *Wokanda* [Trial Calendar], 14 July 1991, 4.

Litynski, Adam, 'Obraz sadownictwa karnego pierwszej dekady Polski Ludowej: Uwagi na marginesie ksiazek Andrzeja Rzeplinskiego i Marii Turlejskiej' [Depiction of the Criminal Court in the First Decade of People's Poland: Comments on the Books of Andrzej Rzeplinski and Maria Turlejska], *Czasopismo Prawno-Historyczne*, 63 (1991), 153–70.

Locke, John, Section 13, 'Book II: An Essay Concerning the True Original, Extent and End of Civil Government', in *Of Civil Government: Two Treatises*, ed. by Ernest Rhys (London: J. M. Dent, 1924), 117–242.

Los, Maria, 'Economic Crimes in Communist Countries', in *Comparative Criminology*, ed. by Israel L. Barak-Glantz and Elmer H. Johnson, Sage Research Progress Series in Criminology, Vol. 31 (Beverly Hills, CA: Sage, 1983), 41–54.

—— 'The Dynamics of the Second Economy in Poland', in *The Second Economy in Marxist States*, ed. by Maria Los (London: Macmillan, 1990), 27–49.

—— 'Legitimation, State and Law in the Central European Democracy', *Polish Sociological Bulletin*, 4 (1991), 231–49.

—— 'In the Shadow of Totalitarian Law: The Law-Making in Post-Communist Poland', working paper, Department of Criminology, Faculty of Social Sciences, University of Ottawa (1993).

—— 'Property Rights, Market and Historical Justice: Legislative Discourse in Poland', *International Journal of the Sociology of Law*, 22 (1994), 39–58.

—— 'Lustration and Truth Claims: Unfinished Revolutions in Central Europe', *Law and Social Inquiry*, 20 (1995), 117–61.

Luban, David (comments), 'Symposium: A Report on the Legality of Evil: The Case of Nazi Judges', *Brooklyn Law Review*, 61 (1995), 1139–49.

Luczka, Teresa, 'Niebezpieczne kredyty' [Dangerous Credit], *Zycie Gospodarcze*, 19 April 1996, 19.

Ludwikowski, R. R., 'Two Firsts: A Comparative Study of the American and the Polish Constitutions', *Michigan Yearbook of International Studies*, 8 (1987), 117–56.

—— 'Judicial Review in the Socialist Legal System: Current Developments', *International and Comparative Law Quarterly*, 37 (1988), 89–108.

—— 'Soviet Constitutional Changes of the Glasnost Era: A Historical Perspective', *New York Law School Journal of International and Comparative Law*, 10 (1989), 119–50.

—— 'Foreword', in *New Constitution of the Government of Poland, Established by the Revolution, The Third of May 1791, The Second Edition* (Washington, DC: Embassy of the Republic of Poland, 1991), iii–viii.

—— 'Constitution Making in the Countries of the Former Soviet Dominance: Current Development', *Georgia Journal of International and Comparative Law*, 23 (1993), 155–267.

—— '"Mixed Constitutions" – Product of an East-Central European Constitutional Melting Pot', *Boston University International Law Journal*, 16 (1998), 1–70.

Lukasiewicz, Maciej, 'Nie wszystkie grzechy swiata' [Not All the Sins of the World] (Interview with General Jaruzelski), *Rzeczpospolita*, 11 (5–6 March 1994), 13–14.

Lukaszewicz, Agata, 'Nie ma sporu na linii prezydent – KRS' [There Is No Dispute Between the President and KRS], *Rzeczpospolita*,17 July 2008 (accessed online).

—— 'Sadowy urzednik dostanie wieciej niz sedzia' [Judicial Civil Servant Will Earn More Than a Judge], *Rzeczpospolita*, 17 July 2008 (accessed online).

Lys, Gregory, 'Dluznik na indeksie' [The Debtor Is on the Index], *Gazeta Bankowa*, 11 August 1996, 9.

Mahoney, Joan, 'The Catholic Church and Civil Society: Democratic Options in the Post-Communist Czech Republic', *Church and State in Contemporary Europe*, 177–94.

Majewska, Teresa, and Anna Trebacz, 'Rozbior bloku' [Dividing the Bloc], *Polityka*, 38 (20 September 1997), 68–71.

Majewski, Michal, 'Rozmowy Polakow i Cyganow po powodzi' [Conversations Between Poles and Gypsies After the Flood], *Rzeczpospolita*, 24 June 1998 (accessed online).

Marguery, Tony, 'The "Plurality of Functions" of the Polish Minister of Justice – General Prosecutor: Paradox or Adaptation?', *European Journal of Crime, Criminal Law and Criminal Justice*, 15 (2007), 67–82.

Markiewicz, Wojciech, 'Wierzyciele uwierzyli' [The Creditors Believed], *Polityka*, 10 (16 March 1996), 59–60.

Markovits, Inga, 'Pursuing One's Rights Under Socialism', *Stanford Law Review*, 38 (1986), 689–761.

Marszalek, Anna, 'Cimoszewicz broni niezawislosci sedziow' [Cimoszewicz Protects Judicial Independence], *Rzeczpospolita*, 6–7 November 1993, 20.

Miall, Hugh, 'Wider Europe, Fortress Europe, Fragmented Europe?', in *Redefining Europe: New Patterns of Conflict and Cooperation*, ed. by Hugh Miall (London: Pinter Publishers, 1994), 1–15.

Michalska, Anna, and Jan Sandorski, 'Remarks on the Place of International Human Rights in the Constitution of the Republic of Poland', *Polish Yearbook of International Law*, 19 (1991–92), 101–31.

Michnik, Adam, '1863: Polska w oczach rosjan' [1863: Poland in Russian Eyes], in *Szanse polskiej demokracji: artykuly i eseje* [Chances for Polish Democracy: Articles and Essays], ed. by Adam Michnik (London: Aneks, 1984), 171–88.

—— 'Nowy ewolucjonizm' [New Evolution], in *Szanse polskiej demokracji: artykuly i eseje* [Chances for Polish Democracy: Articles and Essays], ed. by Adam Michnik (London: Aneks, 1984), 77–87.

—— 'Letter from the Gdansk Prison', *New York Review of Books*, 32 (18 July 1985), at http://www.nybooks.com/articles/5402 (accessed 7 May 2008).

—— 'The Polish Witch-Hunt', *New York Review of Books*, 28 June 2007, 25–26.

Mikolajczyk, Barbara, 'Universal Protection of Minorities (Selected Problems)', *Polish Yearbook of International Law*, 20 (1993), 137–50.

—— 'Polish Law and Policy Towards National Minorities', *International Journal on Group Rights*, 5 (1997), 59–86.

Murphy, Walter F., 'Constitutions, Constitutionalism, and Democracy', in *Constitutionalism and Democracy: Transitions in the Contemporary World*, ed. by Douglas Greenburg *et al.* (Oxford: Oxford University Press, 1993), 3–25.

Myga, Waldemar, 'Protest "komucha"' [Protest of a Commie], *Wokanda* [Trial Calendar], 18 August 1991, 4.

Nagorski, Zygmunt, 'Codification of Civil Law in Poland (1918–1939), *Studies in Polish and Comparative Law: A Symposium of 12 Articles* (London: Stevens & Sons, 1945), 44–69.

Nagorski, Zygmunt, Sr, 'The Legislation of the Polish People's Republic 1958–1959: A Survey', in *Studies in Polish Law*, ed. by Kazimierz Grzybowski *et al.*, Law in Eastern Europe Series, No. 6 (Leyden: A. W. Sijthoff, 1962), 78–120.

Neumann, Franz L., 'The Change in the Function of Law in Modern Society', in *Social Democracy and the Rule of Law*, by Otto Kirchheimer and Franz Neumann, ed. by Keith Tribe, trans. by Leena Turner and Keith Tribe (London: Allen Unwin, 1987), 101–41.

—— 'The Decay of German Democracy', in *The Rule of Law Under Siege: Selected Writings of Franz L. Neumann and Otto Kirchheimer*, ed. by William E. Scheuerman (Berkeley, CA: University of California Press, 1996), 29–43.

Niklewicz, Konrad, 'The (New) Official Story', *Warsaw Voice*, 29 June 1997, 16–17.

Nowak-Jazioranski, Jan, 'Rownowanie absolutne' [Balancing the Absolute], *Rzeczpospolita*, 30 October–1 November 1993, 13.

Offe, Claus and Ulrike Poppe, 'Transitional Justice After the Breakdown of the German Democratic Republic', in *Rethinking the Rule of Law After Communism*, ed. by Adam Czarnota, Martin Krygier and Wojciech Sadurski (Budapest: CEU Press, 2005), 159.

Okolski, Jan, 'Current Developments in Polish Economic Law', in *Anglo-Polish Essays*, ed. by William E. Butler (New York: Transnational Publishers, 1982), 117–27.

Oljasz, Tomasz, 'Perspectives on the Current Constitutional Situation in Poland', in *Constitutionalism and Democracy: Transitions in the Contemporary World*, ed. by Douglas Greenberg *et al.* (Oxford: Oxford University Press, 1993), 312–20.

—— 'Skinhead Provocation Sparks Unrest', *The Warsaw Voice*, 19 April 1998 (accessed online).

Opalek, Kazimierz, 'Poczatki teorii prawa w Polsce Odrodzonej' [The Beginnings of the Theories of Law in Reborn Poland], *Czasopismo Prawno-Historyczne*, 44 (1992), 107–21.

Osiatynski, Wiktor, 'A Brief History of the Constitution', *East European Constitutional Review*, 6 (1997), Nos. 2–3, 66–76.

'Panstwo bezprawa' [Illegal State], *Wprost*, 3 September 1995, 25–27.

Paprzycki, Lech, 'Ten, ktory jest sedzie' [He Who Is a Judge], *Palestra*, 5–6 (1993), 39–42.

Paradowska, Janina, 'Kto to napisal' [Who Wrote It]?, *Polityka* 14 (5 April 1997), 28–32.

—— 'Polska raz jeszcze podzielona' [Poland Is Once Again Divided], *Polityka*, 22 (31 May 1997), 15.

Peczenik, Aleksander, 'Law, Morality, Coherence and Truth', *Ratio Juris*, 7 (1994), 147–76.

Pehe, *Jiří*, 'Changes in the Czech Judiciary', *RFE/RL Research Report*, 2 (17 September 1993), 54–57.

Pelczynski, Z. A., 'The Decline of Gomulka', in *The History of Poland Since 1863*, ed. by R. F. Leslie (Cambridge: Cambridge University Press, 1983), 384–406.

Perlez, Jane, 'Detained Pakistani Seeks to Revive Judiciary Clause', *New York Times*, 8 December 2008.

Piekarska, Katarzyna Maria, 'Naruszanie zasady jawnosci w "sadach tajnych"' [Violation of the Principles of Open Proceedings in the 'Secret Courts'], *Studia luridica*, 27 (1995), 25–41.

Pietrzak, Michal, 'Sad Najwyzszy w II Rzeczpospolitej' [The Supreme Court in the Second Republic], *Czasopismo Prawno-Historyczne*, 33 (1981), 83–103.

Pippidi, Andrei, 'Historical Memory and Legislative Changes in Romania', in *Totalitarian and Authoritarian Regimes in Europe: Legacies and Lessons from the Twentieth Century*, ed. by J. W. Borejsza and K. Ziemer (New York: Berghahn Books, 2006), 465–77.

Pistor, Katharina, 'Company Law and Corporate Governance in Russia', in *The Rule of Law and Economic Reform*, ed. by Jeffrey Sachs and Katharina Pistor (New York: Westview Press, 1997), 165–87.

Plywaczewski, Emil W., Adam Gorski and Andrzej Sakowicz, 'Wrongful Convictions in Poland: From Communist Era to the Rechtsstaat Experience', in *Wrongful Conviction: International Perspectives on Miscarriages of Justice*, ed. by C. Ronald Huff and Martin Killias (Philadelphia: Temple University Press, 2008), 273–283.

Podemski, Stanislaw, 'Konstytucja nie dekalog' [A Constitution, Not the Ten Commandments], *Polityka*, 20 (18 May 1996), 18.

Podgorecki, Adam, 'Unrecognized Father of Sociology of Law: Leon Petrazycki – Reflections Based on Jan Gorecki's *Sociology and Jurisprudence of Leon Petrazycki*', *Law and Society*, 15 (1980–81), 183–202.

—— 'The Authorisation of Illegality', in *Social Control and the Law in Poland*, ed. by Jerzy Kwasniewski and Margaret Watson (New York: St. Martin's Press, 1991), 86–99.

Pogany, Istvan, 'A New Constitutional (Dis)Order for Eastern Europe?', in *Human Rights in Eastern Europe*, ed. by Istvan Pogany (Aldershot: Edward Elgar, 1995), 217–39.

—— 'Constitution Making or Constitutional Transformation in Post-Communist Societies?', *Political Studies*, 44 (1996), 568–91.

'Poland's Devolutionary Battleground', *The Economist*, 7 February 1998, 45.

'Poles of Attraction', *The Economist*, 22 November 1997.

Polonsky, Antony, 'The Breakdown of Parliamentary Government', in *The History of Poland Since 1863*, ed. by R. F. Leslie (Cambridge: Cambridge University Press, 1983), 139–58.

—— 'The Emergence of an Independent Polish State', in *The History of Poland Since 1863*, ed. by R. F. Leslie (Cambridge: Cambridge University Press, 1983), 112–38.

—— 'Pilsudski in Power, 1926–35', in *The History of Poland Since 1863*, ed. by R. F. Leslie (Cambridge: Cambridge University Press, 1983), 159–85.

Pomorski, Stanislaw, 'Meanings of "Decommunization by Legal Means"', *Review of Central and East European Law*, 22 (1996), 331–37.

'Porzadkowanie upadlosci' (Cleaning Up Bankruptcy), *Zycie Gospodarcze*, 10 May 1996, 47.

'Poslowie sedziami' [Judicial MPs], *Zycie* [Life], 11 October 1996, 2.

Pracki, Henry, 'Nowe rodzaje przestepstw gospodarczych (czesc druga)' [New Types of Economic Crime (Part Two)], *Prokuratura i Prawo*, 2 (1995), 26–40.

'Prawnicy protestuja' [Lawyers Are Protesting], *Rzeczpospolita*, 5 January 1993, IV (prawo co dnia).

Preuss, Ulrich, 'Patterns of Constitutional Evolution and Change in Eastern Europe', in *Constitutional Policy and Change in Europe*, ed. by Joachim Jens Hesse and Nevil Johnson (Oxford: Oxford University Press, 1995), 95–115.

Pullo, Andrzej, 'Panstwo prawne (uwagi w zwiazku z Art. 1 Konstytucji RP)' [The Rule-of-Law State (Remarks Relating to Art. 1 of the Constitution of RP)], *Studia Iuridica*, 28 (1995), 121–29.

Quint, P., 'The Border Guards Trial and the East German Past – Seven Arguments', *American Journal of Comparative Law*, 48 (2000), 541–72.

Radbruch, Gustav, 'Statutory Lawlessness and Supra-Statutory Law', *Oxford Journal of Legal Studies*, 26 (2006), 1–11, first published in 1946, and 'Gesetzliches Unrecht und übergesetzliches Recht', *Süddeutsche Juristen-Zeitung*, 1 (1946), 105–08.

Radice, E. A., 'General Characteristics of the Region Between the Wars', in *The Economic History of Eastern Europe 1919–1975*, Vol. 1 (Oxford: Clarendon Press, 1985), 23–65.

Raeff, Marc, 'The Russian Autocracy and Its Officials', *Harvard Slavic Studies*, 4 (1957), 77–91.

Rakowicz, Grazyna, 'Interweniowala policja i wojt' [The Police and the Chief Intervened], *Rzeczpospolita*, 27 May 1997 (accessed online).

Rapaczynski, Andrzej, 'Constitutional Politics in Poland: A Report on the Constitutional Committee of the Polish Parliament', *University of Chicago Law Review*, 58 (1991), 595–631.

Rappaport, Emile, 'Le Futur Code pénal du Troisième Reich', *Revue Internationale de droit pénal*, 11 (1934), 279–303.

Reiff, Ryszard, 'Zmarnowana szansa Jaruzelskiego' [Jaruzelski's Lost Chance], *Gazeta Wyborcza*, 24 November 1992, 12–13.

Rosenberg, William, 'Kadets and the Politics of Ambivalence', in *Essays in Russian Liberalism*, ed. by Charles E. Timberlake (Columbia, MO: University of Missouri Press, 1972), 139–63.

Rosting, Helmer, 'Protection of Minorities by the League of Nations', *American Journal of International Law*, 17 (1923), 641–60.

Roszkowski, Wojciech, 'The Reconstruction of the Government and State Apparatus in the Second Polish Republic', in *The Reconstruction of Poland 1914–23*, ed. by Paul Latawski (London: Macmillan, 1992), 158–77.

'Round Table: Redesigning the Russian Court', *East European Constitutional Review*, 3 (1994), Nos. 3–4, 72–85.

Rozmaryn, Stefan, 'Kontrola sprawiedliwosci ustaw' [Control of Judicial Review], *Panstwo i Prawo*, 11 (1946), 36–60.

—— 'Kontrola sprawiedliwosci ustaw (Dokonczenie)' [Control of Judicial Review (Conclusion)], *Panstwo i Prawo*, 12 (1946), 3–20.

Rubin, Paul H., 'Growing a Legal System in the Post-Communist Economies', *Cornell International Law Journal*, 27 (1994), 1–47.

Rychard, Andrzej, 'Zrodla leki i nadzei' [The Roots of Fears and Hopes], *Zycie Warszawy* (1989), as quoted in *Stres i zycie spoleczne: polskie doswiadczenia* [Stress and Social Life: Polish Experiences] (Warsaw: Panstwowy Instytut Wydawniczy, 1993), 230.

—— 'Czy w Polsce jest homo sovieticus?' [Is *Homo sovieticus* in Poland?], *Zycie Gospodarcze*, 27 February 1995, 6.

Ryszka, Franciszek, 'Spor o wprowadzenie niemieckiego prawa cywilnego na tzw. "terytoria wlaczone" (w czasie okupacji): dokumenty' [Conflict over the Implementation of German Civil Law in the So-Called 'Occupied Territories' (During the Occupation): Documents], *Czasopismo Prawno-Historyczne*, 11 (1959), 95–123.

Rzeplinski, Andrzej, 'A Lesser Evil?', *East European Constitutional Review*, 1 (1992) 33–35.

—— 'The Principles of Independence of the Judiciary and Its Statutory Application', in *Constitutionalism and Human Rights*, ed. by Andrzej Rzeplinski, Vol. 1, Papers of the International Conference, 'Human Rights and Freedoms in the New Constitutions in Central and Eastern Europe', Warsaw 24–29 April 1992 (Warsaw: Helsinki Foundation for Human Rights in Eastern Europe, 1992), 121–42.

Sachs, Jeffrey, 'What Is to Be Done?', *The Economist*, 13 January 1990, 23.

—— and Katharina Pistor, 'Introduction: Progress, Pitfalls, Scenarios, and Lost Opportunities', *The Rule of Law and Economic Reform in Russia*, ed. by Jeffrey Sachs and Katharina Pistor (New York: Westview Press, 1997), 1–21.

Sadurski, Wojciech, 'Rights and Freedoms Under the New Polish Constitution: Reflections of a Liberal', *Saint Louis-Warsaw Transatlantic Law Journal* (1997), 91–105.

Sajo, Andras, 'On Old and New Battles: Obstacles to the Rule of Law in Eastern Europe', *Journal of Law and Society*, 22 (1995), 97–104.

—— 'Reading the Invisible Constitution: Judicial Review in Hungary', *Oxford Journal of Legal Studies*, 15 (1995), 253–67.

—— 'How the Rule of Law Killed Hungarian Welfare Reform', *East European Constitutional Review*, 5 (1996), 31–41.

—— 'Corruption, Clientelism, and the Future of the Constitutional State in Eastern Europe', *East European Constitutional Review*, 7 (1998), 37–46.

—— and Vera Losonci, 'Rule of Law in East Central Europe: Is the Emperor's New Suit a Straitjacket?', in *Constitutionalism and Democracy: Transitions in the Contemporary World*, ed. by Douglas Greenburg *et al.* (Oxford: Oxford University Press, 1993), 321–35.

Sak, Pamela Bickford, and Henry N. Schiffman, 'Bankrupcty Law Reform in Eastern Europe', *The International Lawyer*, 28 (1994), 927–50.

Sakson, Andrzej, 'Mniejszosc niemiecka i inne mniejnosci w Polsce' [The German Minority and Other Minorities in Poland], *Przeglad Zachodni*, 1 (1991), 15–25.

Sampson, Steven, 'The Informal Sector in Eastern Europe', *Telos*, 66 (1985–86), 48–49.

Scheppele, Kim Lane, 'When the Law Doesn't Count: The 2000 Election and the Failure of the Rule of Law', *University of Pennsylvania Law Review*, 149 (2000), 1361–1438.

——'A Comparative View of the Chief Justice's Role. Guardians of the Constitution: Constitutional Court Presidents and the Struggle for the Rule of Law in Post-Soviet Europe', *University of Pennsylvania Law Review*, 154 (2006), 1757–1845.

Schmid, A. Alan, 'Legal Foundations of the Market: Implications for the Formerly Socialist Countries of Eastern Europe and Africa', *Journal of Economic Issues*, 3 (1992), 707–32.

Schopflin, George, 'The Rise of Anti-Democratic Movements in Post-Communist Societies', in *Redefining Europe: New Patterns of Conflicted Cooperation*, ed. by Hugh Miall (London: Pinter Publishers, 1994), 129–46.

Schwartz, Herman, 'In Defense of Aiming High', *East European Constitutional Review*, 3 (1992), 25–28.

'Sedziowe juz sa, brakuje ustawy' [The Judges Are Here, the Law Is Absent], *Rzeczpospolita*, 7 August 1998 (accessed online).

Semprich, Renata, 'Reforma sadownictwa' [Reform of the Judiciary], *Rzeczpospolita*, 9 April 1998 (accessed online).

Shaw, Gisela, 'Courts and Judges in the New Federal States in United Germany: Has Legal Unification Worked?', *Svensk Juristtidning* (1995), 32–44.

Shelley, Louis, 'The Second Economy in the Soviet Union', in *The Second Economy in Marxist States*, ed. by Maria Los (London: Macmillan, 1990), 11–26.

Shuchman, Philip, 'Book Review: *Vichy Law and the Holocaust in France*', *Rutgers Law Review*, 50 (1998), 607–43.

Siekanowicz, Peter, 'Poland', in *Government, Law and Courts in the Soviet Union and Eastern Europe*, ed. by Vladimir Gsovski and Kazimierz Gryzybowski, Vol. 1 (London: Stevens & Stevens, 1959), 728–80.

Skubiszewski, Krzysztof, 'Poland, Germany and Europe After 1989', in *Recht zwischen Umbruch und Bewahrung: Festschrift für Rudolf Bernhardt*, ed. by Ulrich Beyerlin *et al.* (Berlin: Springer, 1995), 1305–12.

Slay, Ben, 'The Banking Crisis and Economic Reform in Poland', *RFE/RL Research Report*, 1 (1992), 32–40.

—— 'Poland: The Rise and Fall of the Balcerowicz Plan', *RFE/RL Research Report*, 31 January 1992, 40–47.

Sokolewicz, Wojciech, 'Regulacja ustroju politycznego Polskiej Rzeczpospolitej Ludowej w Konstytucji: stan obecny i koniecznosc zmian' [The Regulation of the Political Structure of the Polish People's Republic: The Current Situation and the Need for Reform], *Studia Iuridica*, 2–3 (1989), 227–44.

—— 'Rozdzielone, lecz czy rowne? Legislatywa i egzekutywa w Malej Konstytucji 1992 roku' [Divided, But Are They Equal? Legislative and Executive Powers in the Small Constitution of 1992], *Przeglad Sejmowy* [Parliamentary Overview], 1 (1993), 22–42.

Solomon, Peter, 'Soviet Criminology: Its Demise and Rebirth, 1928–1963', *Soviet Union* (1973), 122–40.

Soltysinski, Stanislaw, 'Privatization in Poland: The Legal Framework, Practice and Political Consideration', *Forum Internationale*, 15 (1990), 1–18.

—— 'Dostosowanie praw polskiego do wymagan Ukladu Europejskiego' [The Adaption of Polish Law to the Requirements of the European Community], *Panstwo i Prawo*, 4–5 (1996), 31–43.

Sólyom, László, 'The Hungarian Constitutional Court and Social Change', *Yale Journal of International Law*, 19 (1994), 223–37.

Stein, Eric, 'International Law and Internal Law in the New Constitutions of Central-Eastern Europe', in *Recht zwischen Umbruch und Bewahrung: Festschrift für Rudolf Bernhardt*, ed. by Ulrich Beyerlin *et al.* (Berlin: Springer, 1995), 865–84.

—— 'Out of the Ashes of a Federation, Two New Constitutions', *American Journal of Comparative Law*, 45 (1997), 45–69.

Stone, Daniel, 'The Big Business Lobby in Poland in the 1920s', *Canadian Slavic Papers*, 32 (1990), 41–58.

Struminski, Juliusz, 'Rady mieskie i powiatowe w Krolestwie Polskim (1861–1863)' [Local and Town Councils in the Kingdom of Poland], *Czasopismo Prawno-Historyczne*, 4 (1952), 274–357.

Strzembosz, Adam, 'O wymierzajacych sprawiedliwosc – sprawiedliwej' [On Administering Justice – More Justly], *Tygodnik Solidarnosc* [Solidarity Weekly], 22 September 1989, 3.

Sunstein, Cass, 'Against Positive Right', *East European Constitutional Review*, 2 (1993), 35–38.

Sunstein, Cass R., 'The Legitimacy of Constitutional Justice: Notes on Theory and Practice', *East European Constitutional Review*, 6 (1997), 61–63.

Swarc, Wojciech, 'Prawo jezyka polskiego w orzecznictwie pruskiego Wyzszego Trybunalu Administracyjnego w Berlinie (1875–1914)' [The Right to the Polish Language in the Decisions of the Highest Administrative Court of Berlin (1875–1914], *Czasopismo Prawno-Historyczne*, 39 (1987), 83–102.

Szacki, Jerzy, 'Marzenia i rzeczywistosc polskiego demokracji' [The Hopes and Reality of Polish Democracy], *Res Publica*, 5 (1991), 14–17.

—— 'Korupcja: przeszlosc i przyszlosc' [Corruption: The Past and the Future], *Gazeta Bankowa*, 28 April 1996, 28.

'Szanse generalow' [The General's Chances], *Rzeczpospolita*, 7 October 1993, 1, 9.

Szawlowski, Richard, '"State Control" in Poland in the Nineteenth and Twentieth Centuries', in *Polish Law Throughout the Ages*, ed. by Wenceslas Wagner (Stanford, CA: Hoover Institution Press, 1970), 273–98.

Szostkiewicz, Adam, 'The Aliens Have Landed', *The Warsaw Voice*, 22 November 1998 (accessed online).

Szymborska, Wislawa, 'Koniec i poczatek' [An End and a Beginning], in *Koniec i poczatek* (Poznan: Wydawnictwo a5, 1996), 10–11.

Szyszkowska, Maria, 'Przepis na moralnosc' [A Recipe for Morality], *Polityka*, 6 (8 February 1997), 68–69.

Tanasoiu, Cosmina, 'Intellectuals and Post-Communist Politics in Romania: An Analysis of Public Discourse 1900–2000', *East European Politics and Societies*, 22 (2008), 80–113.

Tarkowski, Jacek, 'The Polish Crisis and Myrdal's Model of Circular Causation', *Political Studies*, 35 (1988), 463–74.

Teitel, Ruti, 'Paradoxes in the Revolution of the Rule of Law', *Yale Journal of International Law*, 19 (1994), 239–47.

—— 'Transitional Rule of Law', in *Rethinking the Rule of Law After Communism*, ed. by Adam Czarnota, Martin Krygier and Wojciech Sadurski (Budapest: CEU Press, 2005), 279–94.

Timasheff, Nicholas S., 'Introduction', in *Law and Morality*, by Leon Petrazycki, Twentieth Century Legal Philosophy Series, Vol. VII, trans. by Hugh W. Babb (Cambridge, MA: Harvard University Press, 1955), xvii–xlvi.

Tismaneanu, Vladimir, 'Unofficial Peace Activism in the Soviet Union and East Central Europe', in *In Search of Civil Society: Independent Peace Movements in the Soviet Bloc*, ed. by Vladimir Tismaneanu (London: Routledge, 1990), 1–53.

Turowicz, Jerzy, 'PRL dla doroslych' [PRL for Adults], *Tygodnik Powszechny* [Common Weekly], 5 November 1995, 5.

Turska, Anna, 'Leon Petrazycki – w perspecktywie historycznej i wspoczesnej' [Leon Petrazycki – in a Historical and Contemporary Perspective], *Studia Iuridica*, 29 (1995), 59–74.

—— 'Spoleczenstwo w systemie panowania totalnego' [The Society in a System of Complete Control], *Studia Iuridica, 27* (1995), 11–23.

'Unfair Advantage', *The Economist*, 22 November 1997, 7.

'Václav Havel, Westward Ho!', *The Economist*, 18 April 1998, 29.

Varga, Csaba, 'Transformation to the Rule of Law from No-Law: Societal Contexture of the Democratic Transition in Central and Eastern Europe', *Connecticut Journal of International Law*, 8 (1993), 487–505.

Vinton, Louisa, 'Poland's "Little Constitution" Clarifies Walesa's Powers', *RFE/RL Research Reports*, 1 (1992), 19–26.

Wade, E. C. S., 'Introduction', in *Introduction to the Study of Law of the Constitution*, ed. by Albert Venn Dicey, 9th edn (London: Macmillan, 1939), xxvii–clvi.

Walencik, Ireniusz, 'Kres niezawislosci?' [A Mark of Independence?], *Rzeczpospolita*, 7 September 1993, 19.

Waltos, Stanislaw, 'O potrzebie nowelizacji ustawodawstwa karnego' [The Need for a Criminal Legislation Amendment], *Nowe prawo* [New Law], 4 (1981), 41–47.

Wasilkowski, Andrzej, 'Monism and Dualism at Present', in *Theory of International Law at the Threshold of the 21st Century: Essays in Honour of Krzysztof Skubiszewski*, ed. by Jerzy Makarczyk (The Hague: Kluwer Law International, 1996), 323–36.

—— 'International Law and International Relations in the New Polish Constitution of 2 April 1997', *Polish Yearbook of International Law*, 23 (1997–98), 7–19.

Watts, Sir Arthur, 'The International Rule of Law', *German Yearbook of International Law*, 36 (1993), 15–45.

Weisbrod, Carol, 'Minorities and Diversities: The "Remarkable Experiment" of the League of Nations', *Connecticut Journal of International Law*, 8 (1993), 359–406.

'Wejscie syndyka' [The Entrance of the Legal Adviser], *Zycie Gospodarcze*, 12 April 1996, 13–17.

Wereszycki, Henryk, 'Poland Under Foreign Rule 1795–1918', in *History of Poland*, ed. by Aleksander Gieysztor *et al.* (Warsaw: PWN, 1968), 528–632.

Wierzycka, Lucja, and Marek Holuszko, 'Some Reflections on National Minorities in Poland: The Protection of Their Rights, Achievements and Failures', CSCE Human Dimension Seminar on Case Studies on National Minorities Issues: Positive Results, Warsaw, May 1993.

Wilson, Andrew, 'Ukraine: Between Eurasia and the West', in *Europe and Ethnicity: The First World War and Contemporay Ethnic Conflict*, ed. by Seamus Dunn and T. G. Fraser (London: Routledge, 1996), 110–37.

Wishnevsky, Julia, 'Russian Constitutional Court: A Third Branch of Government?', *RFE/RL Research Reports*, 2 (12 February 1993), 1–8.

Wladyka, Wieslaw, 'Trzy Polski' [Three Polands], *Polityka*, 23 (7 June 1997), 20–21.

Wojciechowski, Janusz, 'Dzis i jutro Krajowej Rady Sadownictwa' [Today and Tomorrow the National Council of the Judiciary], *Rzeczpospolita*, 14 February 1994, 12.

Woolsey, Theodore, 'The Rights of Minorities Under the Treaty with Poland', *American Journal of International Law*, 14 (1920), 392–96.

Wortman, Richard, 'Judicial Personnel and the Court Reform of 1864', *Canadian Slavic Studies*, 3 (1969), 224–34.

Wronkowska, Slawomira, 'O publikacji aktow normatywnuch' [Concerning the Publication of Normative Acts], *Rzeczpospolita*, 30 March 1993 (accessed online).

Wyrzykowski, Miroslaw, 'Legislacja – demokratyczne panstwo prawa – radykalne reformy polityczne i gospodarcze' [Legislation – Democratic Rule of Law State – Radical Political and Economic Reforms], *Panstwo i Prawo*, 5 (1991), 17–28.

—— 'Introductory Note to the 1997 Constitution of the Republic of Poland', *Saint Louis-Warsaw Transatlantic Law Journal* (1997), 1–4.

Yakovlev, Alexander, 'The Rule-of-Law Ideal and Russian Reality', in *Legal Reform in Post-Communist Europe: The View from Within*, ed. by Stanislaw Frankowski and Paul B. Stephan III (Dordrecht: Martinus Nijhoff, 1995), 5–19.

Zaborski, Marcin, 'Szkolenie "sedziow nowego typu" w Polsce Ludowej. Czesc I: Srednie szkoly prawnicze' [Training the 'New Type of Judge' in People's Poland. Part 1: Basic Law Schools], *Palestra*, 1–2 (1998), 79–92.

—— 'Szkolenie "sedziow nowego typu" w Polsce Ludowej. Czesc II: Centralna Szkola Przwnicza im. Teodora Duracza i Wyzsza Szkola Prawnicza im. Teodora Duracza' [Training the 'New Type of Judge' in People's Poland. Part II: Teodor Duracz Central Law School and Teodor Duracz Higher School of Law], *Palestra*, 3–4 (1998), 105–10.

Zakrzewska, Janina, 'Trybunal Konstytucyjny – konstytucja – panstwo prawa' [The Constitutional Tribunal – the Constitution – the Rule of Law], *Panstwo i Prawo*, 1 (1992), 3–12.

Zamorski, Kazimierz, 'Arrest and Imprisonment in the Light of Soviet Law', in *The Soviet Takeover of the Polish Eastern Territories, 1939–1941*, ed. by Keith Sword (London: Macmillan, 1991), 201–16.

Zbioro, Zbigniew, 'Przestepstwa na szkode wierzyciela – kontrewersje interpretacyjne' [Crimes Which Harm the Creditor – Controversy over Interpretation], *Prokuratura i Prawo*, 10 (1996), 31–44.

Zedler, Feliks, 'Recenzje: Jan Brol: *Prawo upadlosciowe w swietle praktyki sadowe*' [Insolvency Law in Light of Court Practice], *Panstwo i Prawo*, 1 (1996), 88–89.

Zielinski, Adam, 'O statusie prawnym Krajowej Rady Sadownictwa' [About the Legal Status of the National Council of the Judiciary], *Panstwo i Prawo*, 6 (1996), 84–88.

Zimmerman, Judith, 'The Kadets and the Duma 1905–1907', in *Essays in Russian Liberalism*, ed. by Charles E. Timberlake (Columbia, MO: University of Missouri Press, 1972), 119–38.

Znamierowski, Czeslaw, 'Psychologistyczna teoria prawa' [The Psychological Theories of Law], *Przeglad Filosoficzny*, 1 (1922), 1–78.

Zoethout, Carla M., 'The End of Constitutional Democracy? Challenges to the Fundamental Ideals of Contemporary Political Systems', *Netherlands International Law Review*, 44 (1997), 209–23.

Zyzniewski, Stanislaw, 'Miljutin and the Polish Question', *Harvard Slavic Studies*, 4 (1957), 237–48.

Legislative Acts and Other Documents (Chronological Order)

Decree of 7 February 1919 Concerning the Establishment of the Supreme Chamber of State Control, *Dziennik Ustaw*, No. 14, item 183.

Decree of 8 February 1919 Concerning the Supreme Court, *Dziennik Ustaw*, No. 15, item 199.

Decree of 8 February 1919 Concerning the Establishment of the Legislative *Sejm*, *Dziennik Ustaw*, No. 16, item 217.

Law of 3 June 1919 Concerning the Codification Commission, *Dziennik Ustaw*, No. 44, item 315.

The Constitution of the Republic of Poland of 17 March 1921, *Dziennik Ustaw*, No. 44, item 267.

Decree of the President of the Republic of Poland Concerning the Criminal Code, *Dziennik Ustaw*, No. 60, item 571 [1932].

Decree of the Council of Ministers of 24 March 1924 Concerning the Civil Servants Holding Positions in Category 1 in the General Public Prosecutor's Office of the Republic of Poland, *Dziennik Ustaw*, No. 32, item 321.

Decree of the President of the Republic from 11 July 1932 Concerning the Laws Implementing the Criminal Code and Offences.

Reichstag Fire Decree of 28 February 1933.

Decree of the President of the Republic of Poland of 27 June 1934 Concerning the Commercial Code, *Dziennik Ustaw*, No. 57, item 502.

Decree of the President of the Republic of Poland of 24 October 1934 Concerning Certain Crimes Against State Security, *Dziennik Ustaw*, No. 94, item 851.

Decree of the President of the Republic of Poland of 24 October 1934 Concerning Bankruptcy Law, *Dziennik Ustaw* (1991), No. 118, item 512 (unified text).

The Constitution of the Republic of Poland of 23 April 1935, *Dziennik Ustaw*, No. 30, item 227.

Law of 4 May 1938 Concerning the Bar, *Dziennik Ustaw*, No. 33, item 289.

Decree of 4 December 1941 Concerning the Administration of Penal Justice Against Poles and Jews in the Incorporated Eastern Territories.

Night and Fog Decree of 7 December 1941.

Decree of 4 July 1944 on the Authorisation to Create New Courts.

Decree of the Polish Committee for National Liberation from 31 August 1944 Concerning the Administration of Punishment for Fascist–Nazi Criminals Found Guilty of Crimes and Abuses Against Civilian Persons and Soldiers, and Traitors of the Polish Nation, *Dziennik Ustaw*, No. 4, item 16.

Decree of the Polish Committee for National Liberation from 12 September 1944 Concerning Special Criminal Courts for Fascist–Nazi Crimes, *Dziennik Ustaw*, No. 4, item 21.

Decree of the Polish Committee for National Liberation from 23 September 1944, The Military Criminal Code, *Dziennik Ustaw*, No. 6, item 27.

Decree of the Polish Committee for National Liberation from 23 September 1944 Concerning the Structure of the Military Courts and the Public Prosecutor for the Military, *Dziennik Ustaw*, No. 6, item 29.

Order of the Leaders of the Department of Justice and the Department of Public Safety from 3 October 1944 Concerning the Implementation of the Decree of the Polish Committee for National Liberation from 12 September 1944 Concerning Special Criminal Courts for Fascist–Nazi Crimes, *Dziennik Ustaw*, No. 7, item 35.

Decree of the Polish Committee for National Liberation from 25 October 1944 Concerning Combating Wartime Speculation, *Dziennik Ustaw*, No. 9, item 49.

Decree of the Polish Committee for National Liberation from 30 October 1944 Concerning State Security, *Dziennik Ustaw*, No. 10, item 50.

Decree of the Polish Committee for National Liberation from 4 November 1944 Concerning the Authorisation to Create New Courts and to Change their Jurisdiction, and the Transfer of Judges to Other Benches of Adjudication, *Dziennik Ustaw*, No. 11, item 58.

Decree of the Polish Committee for National Liberation from 20 November 1944 Concerning the Amendment to the Decree Concerning Combating Wartime Speculation and Money Lending, *Dziennik Ustaw*, No. 12, item 63.

Decree of 8 March 1945 Concerning the Partial Amendment to the Law Concerning the Structure of the Common Courts, *Dziennik Ustaw*, No. 11, item 54.

Decree of the Polish Committee for National Liberation from 16 November 1945 Concerning Crimes of a Dangerous Nature During the Reconstruction of the State, *Dziennik Ustaw*, No. 53, item 300.

Decree of 22 January 1946 Concerning Extrordinary Circumstances that would Permit Assuming the Position of a Judge, Public Prosecutor, and Notary Public, and Registering on the List of the Bar, *Dziennik Ustaw*, No. 4, item 33.

Constitutional Law from 4 February 1947 Concerning the Election of the President of the Republic, *Dziennik Ustaw*, No. 9, item 43.

Constitutional Law from 19 February 1947 Concerning the Scope and Activities of the Highest State Organs of the Polish Republic, *Dziennik Ustaw*, No. 18, item 71.

Geneva Convention of 9 September 1948, *Dziennik Ustaw* (1952), No. 2, item 9.

Law of 27 June 1950 Concerning the Bar, *Dziennik Ustaw*, No. 30, item 275; codified text, No. 8, item 41 (codified text, *Dziennik Ustaw*, No. 13, item 74).

Constitution of the Polish People's Republic as Adopted by the Legislative *Sejm* on 22 July 1952, *Dziennik Ustaw*, No. 33, item 232.

Sprawozdanie z dziesiecoletniej dzialalnosci Komisji Kodyfikacyjnej Rzeczpospolitiej za czas od 3 czerwca 1919 do 3 czerwca 1929 [An Assessment of the Ten-Year Activities of the Codification Commission of the Republic of Poland from 3 June 1919 to 3 June 1929], *Komisja Kodyfikacyjna Rzeczpospolitej Polskiej* [The Codification Commission of the Republic of Poland], Vol. 1 (1929).

Sejm Ustawodawczy Rzeczpospolitej Polskiej [Legislative Parliament of the Republic of Poland], Druk No. 298 [1919].

Law of 10 February 1976 Concerning Amendments to the Constitution of the Polish People's Republic), *Dziennik Ustaw*, No. 5, item 29.

Law of 25 September 1981 Concerning State Enterprises, *Dziennik Ustaw*, No. 24, item 122.

Law of 25 September 1981 Concerning the Self-Management of Employees of State Enterprises, *Dziennik Ustaw*, No. 24, item 123.

Decree of the Council of Ministers from 30 November 1981 Concerning the Implementation of the Law Concerning State Enterprises.

Law of 19 June 1983 Concerning the Rehabilitation and Liquidation of State Enterprises, *Dziennik Ustaw*, No. 36, item 165.

Law of 20 June 1985 on the Structure of the Common Courts, *Dziennik Ustaw*, No. 7, item 25.

Law of 20 June 1985 Concerning the Public Prosecution, *Dziennik Ustaw*, No. 31, item 138.

Law of 23 December 1988 Concerning Economic Activities with Participating Foreign Subjects, *Dziennik Ustaw*, No. 41, item 325.

Law of 20 December 1989 on the National Council for the Judiciary, *Dziennik Ustaw*, No. 73, item 435.

Informacja o zmianach w polskim sadownictwie w latach 1989–1990 (Information About Changes in the Polish Judiciary 1989–1990), Krajowa Rada Sadownictwa.

Law of 13 July 1990 Concerning the Privatisation of State Enterprises, *Dziennik Ustaw*, No. 51, item 298.

Law of 13 July 1990 Concerning the Establishment of the Ministry of Ownership, *Dziennik Ustaw*, No. 51, item 299.

Law of 9 November 1990 Concerning the Acquisition of Assets of the Former Polish United Worker's Party, *Dziennik Ustaw* (1990), No. 16, item 72.

Law of 9 November 1990 Concerning Broadening the Scope of the Law Concerning the Privatisation of State Enterprises, *Dziennik Ustaw*, No. 85, item 498.

Law on the Local Self-Government of 1990, *Dziennik Ustaw* (1990), No. 16, item 95.

Constitutional Law of 17 October 1992 on the Mutual Relations Between the Legislative and Executive Powers of the Republic of Poland, and on Local Self-Government, *Dziennik Ustaw*, No. 84, item 426.

Electoral Law of 1993, *Dziennik Ustaw* (1993), No. 45, item 205.

Law of 5 February 1993 on the Amendment to the Law on the Structure of the Common Courts, Public Prosecution, Supreme Court, Constitutional Tribunal, National Council of the Judiciary and the Establishment of Appellate Courts.

Concordat Between the Republic of Poland and the Vatican Signed in Warsaw on 28 July 1993, *Nowy Dziennik* (New Daily), 18 April 1997, 20–21.

Wniosek Rzecznika Praw Obywatelskich [Motion of the Commissioner for the Protection of Citizens' Rights], RPO/127988/93/I/1/AM, 2 September 1993.

Law Concerning Crimes Against Economic Transactions, *Dziennik Ustaw* (1994), No. 80, item 419.

Recommendation of the Council on Bribery in International Business Transactions, OECD Doc. C(94) 75/Final (24 May 1994).

White Paper, Preparation of the Associated Countries of Central and Eastern Europe for Integration into the Internal Market of the Union, Commission of the European Communities, Brussels. 3 May 1995, COM (95), 163 final.

The Constitution of the Republic of Poland as Adopted by the National Assembly on 2 April 1997, *Dziennik Ustaw*, No. 78, item 483.

The Constitution of the Republic of Poland of 6 April 1997, *Dziennik Ustaw*, No. 78, item 483.

Law 816 of 11 April 1997 Concerning the Disclosure of Public Officials Who Have Worked for or Have Had Functions in State Security Organs or Cooperation with These Organs During 1944–1990, *Dziennik Ustaw*, No. 70, item 443.

Commission Opinion on Poland's Application for Membership of the European Union, Commission of the European Communities, Brussels, 15 July 1997, COM (97) 2002 final.

Law Concerning the Criminal Code, *Dziennik Ustaw* (1998), No. 88, item 553.

Dziennik Ustaw (1998), No. 131, item 860.

Law of 3 December 1998 Concerning the Accountability Related to Disciplinary Measures Against Judges Who Have Violated the Principles of Judicial Independence Between 1944 and 1989, *Dziennik Ustaw*, No. 1, item 1.

Law of 27 July 2001 Concerning the Structure of the Common Courts, at http://www.ms.gov.pl/organizacja/usp.pdf (last accessed 14 June 2009).

Amendment to Code of Criminal Procedure, *Dziennik Ustaw* (2003), No. 17, item 155.

Treaties

The Treaty of Versailles (Poland), 28 June 1919, 225 CTS 412.

The Treaty of St Germain-en-Laye (Czechoslovakia), 10 September 1919, 226 CTS 170.

The Treaty of St Germain-en-Laye (Yugoslavia), 10 September 1919, 226 CTS 170.

The Treaty of Versailles (Romania), December 1919, (1921) 5 LNTS 335.

The Treaty of *Sèvres* (Greece), 10 August 1920, (1924) 28 LNTS 244.

The Convention of Paris (Danzig), 9 November 1920, (1921) 6 LNTS 189.

Conference on Security and Co-operation in Europe: Charter of Paris for a New Europe and Supplementary Document to Give Effect to Certain Provisions of the Charter, 31 ILM 1991, 190–227.

The Polish–German Treaty on Good Neighbourliness and Friendly Cooperation of 17 June 1991, *Dziennik Ustaw*, No. 14, items 55–57.

The Polish–Ukrainian Treaty on Good Neighbourliness and Friendly Cooperation of 18 May 1992, *Dziennik Ustaw*, No. 125, items 573–74.

The Polish–Lithuanian Treaty on Good Neighbourliness and Friendly Cooperation of 26 April 1994, *Dziennik Ustaw*, No. 15, item 72.

Europe Agreement Establishing an Association Between the European Polish–Ukraine Treaty on Good Neighbourliness, Friendly Relations and Cooperation of 18 May 1992, *Dziennik Ustaw* (1992), No. 14, items 56–57.

Communities and Their Member States, of the One Part, and the Republic of Poland, of the Other Part, *Official Journal*, L 348 (31 December 1993), 0002–0180.

Courts

Czechoslovakia

Judgment of 5 December 2001, Pl US 9/01.

Czech Republic

Judgment of 21 December 1993, 19/93.

Germany

E OVG 20 September 1877, 1 (1877).
E OVG 20 November 1903, 44 (1904).
E OVG 14 May 1907, 50 (1908).
E OVG 2 February 1914, 66 (1914).
StR 370/92, Berlin.

Hungary

Decision 23/1990 (31 October 1990).

Poland

Constitutional Tribunal
Judgment of 22 August 1990, K 7/90.
Judgment of 4 December 1990, K 12/90.
Judgment of 11 February 1991, K 14/91.
Judgment of 25 September 1991, S 6/91.
Judgment of 25 February 1992, K 3/91.
Judgment of 9 November 1993, K 11/93.
Judgment of 21 October 1998, K 24/98.
Judgment of 11 May 2007, K 2/07.
Supreme Court (Criminal Chamber)
Supreme Court Judgment of 20 December 2007 KZP 37/07.
European Court of Human Rights
Glasenapp v. *Germany* [1986] ECHR 9.
K.-H.W. v. *Germany* [2001] ECHR 229.
Strzeletz, Kessler and Krenz v. *Germany* [2001] ECHR 230.
Vogt v. *Germany* [1995] ECHR 29.
X v. *Italy* [1976] D&R 5.
Zdanoka v. *Latvia* [2006] App. 58278/00, judgment of 16 March 2006.

Archival Documents

Russia: Rossiiskii tsentr khranenia i izucheniia dokumentov noveishei istohii [Russian Centre for the Preservation and the Study of Records of Modern History, Moscow, Russia, hereafter, RTsKhIDNI].

'Anton Krajewski' (1937), fond 495, opis 252, delo 1087, RTsKhIDNI.

'Ivanok's Letter', 10 June 1944, pp. 24–25, fond 17, opis 128, delo 1161 RTsKhIDNI.

'Dve zapiski referenta tov. Zawolshkova svezu a poezdkoj v g. Budapesht' [Two Summaries from the Report of Zawolski in Relation to the Process in Budapest], 29 September 1949, p. 206, fond 575, opis 1, delo 95, RTsKhIDNI.

Informatsia zapiska o sovpemennom politicheskom i ekonomicheskom polozhenni Polshe [Informational Notes About the Contemporary Political and Economic Position of Poland], September 1947, p. 19, fond 575, opis 1, delo 32, RTsKhIDNI.

'Ob Antimarkshistitskich Ideologicheskich Ustanovleniach Rukovodstva PPR' [About the Anti-Marxist Ideology of the Polish Workers' Party], 5 April 1948, pp. 3–5, fond 17, opis 128, delo 1161, RTsKhIDNI.

Gosudarstvennyi archkiv Rossiiskii Federatsii [State Archives of the Russian Federation, Moscow, Russia; hereafter, GARF].

'Proverit rabotu Bostochna-Siberskovo Kraevovo Suda' [A Check on the Eastern Siberian Regional Court], 16 April 1936, p. 12, fond 8131, opis 13, delo 10, GARF.

'Soviet Minostrov Sojuza Sovetskikh Tsojalistichikh Respublik' [The Ministers of the USSR], *The Files of A. Ya. Vyshinsky*, 26 June 1941, p. 34, fond 5446, opis 81a, delo 346, GARF.

'Stenogramma doklada t. Vyshinskovo o proekte Konstitutsii SSR na obranii aktiva Sojusa rabotnikov suda i procuraturi' [Stenogramme from Vyshinsky's Lecture on the Draft of the Constitution Before the Soviet Assembly of the Judiciary and Public Prosecution], 9 July 1936, p. 13, fond 8131, opis 13, delo 2, GARF.

Poland: Archiwum Akt Nowych (Archive of New Acts, Warsaw, Poland).

Correspondence Between the Minister of Justice, Jerzy Lande, and the General Governor of 19 December 1917, *Prezydium Rady Ministrow* (Presidium of the Council of Ministers), Part II, pp. 17–20, sygnatura (hereafter, sygn.) 14.

Letter from Ministry of Internal Affairs to the Council of Ministers of 19 April 1918, *Prezydium Rady Ministrow* [Presidium of the Council of Ministers], Part II, p. 8, sygn. 65.

Dekret Rady Regencyjnej o tymczasowey organizacji wladz naczelnych w Krolestwie Polskim [The Decree of the Council of Regency on the Provisional Organisation of the Main Leading Organs of the Kingdom of Poland], 3 January 1918, *Prezydium Rada Ministrow* [Presidium of the Council of Ministers], p. 32, sygn. 1.

Stanislaw Wojciechowski, Minister of the Interior, Akta Wladyslawa Grabskiego, Sprawozdanie Stenograficzne z 85 posidzenia Sejmu Ustawodawczego z dnia 1-go pazdziernika 1919 roku [The Official Document of Wladylaw Grabski, Stenographic Record of the 85th Meeting of the Legislative *Sejm* of 1 October 1919], p. 11, sygn. 8.

Informacja Zachodnia [Information About the East], 26 June 1944, p. 77, sygn. 203/VII-35, Armia Komendowa Glowny Odzial IV-Wydzial Informacyjny [Home Army Main Division IV-Information Department].

Oskar Kamienski, in a letter to the PKWN/RS, 8 October 1944, p. 43 and Waclaw Maciejski, 24 November 1944, pp. 47–48, sygn. IX/5, PKWN (Polish Committee for National Liberation).

Communiqué of 14 October 1944 from Dr Szuldenfrei, Director of the Legal Bureau of the Polish Committee for National Liberation, p. 9, sygn. IX/2, PKWN/RS (Polish Committee for National Liberation/Department of Justice).

Letter from Marian Podwinski, Notary Public from Przemysl, to Vice-Minister of Justice Leon Chajn, 21 October 1944, p. 14, sygn. IX/5, PKWN/RS (Polish Committee for National Liberation/Department of Justice).

Aleksander Miskow, 25 November 1944, p. 5, sygn. IX/9a, PKWN/RS (Polish Committee for National Liberation/Department of Justice).

Letter of 16 December 1944 from L. Miernik to the Department of Justice, p. 22, sygn. IX/9a, PKWN/RS (Polish Committee for National Liberation/ Department of Justice).

Letter of 17 December 1944 from J. Korytkowski to L. Chajn, p. 17, sygn. IX/ 9a, PKWN/RS (Polish Committee for National Liberation/Department of Justice).

Public Prosecutor Joel, List of Activities of the Regional Court in Bialystok in December 1944, 27 January 1945, p. 66, sygn. IX/6, PKWN/RS (Polish Committee for National Liberation/Department of Justice).

'Stan prawny ziem zachodnich w okresie okupacji niemieckiej' [The State of Law in the Eastern Territories During the German Occupation], 1944, p. 2, sygn. 203/VII-39, Armia Komendowa Glowny Odzial IV-Wydzial Informacyjny [Home Army Main Division IV-Information Department].

D. Adam Stawarski, *Projekt: Dekret, Resort Sprawiedlowisci* [Draft: Decree, PKWN, Department of Justice], pp. 1–2, 1944, sygn. IX/5.

Informacja zachodnia [Information About the West], No. 25, sygn. 203/VII-35, AK-WI.

'Przedstawienie Ministra Sprawiedliwosci w przedmiocie sytuacji uposazeniowej sedziow' [The Minister of Justice's Speech Concerning the Situation of the Salaries of Judges], Ministerstwo Sprawiedliwosci [Ministry of Justice], 2 May 1953, p. 2, sygn. 25

United Kingdom: Polish Underground Movement Study Trust, London, England.

'Dzialalnosc wladz okupacyjnych na terytorium Rzeczpospolitej za okres 1.IX.39 do 1.XI.40' [The Activities of the Occupying Powers on the Territory of the

Polish Republic from 1.IX.39 to 1.XI.40], *Sprawozdanie Sytuacyjne z Kraju* [Situational Account from the Country], 182.

'Dzialalnosc Kominternu na Ziemach Polskich' [Comintern's Activity on Polish Territory], *Sprawozdanie Sytuacyjne z Kraju* [Situational Account from the Country], No. 1/43 (April 1943).

Sprawozdanie Departamentu Sprawiedliwosci [Report from the Ministry of Justice], No. 5/43 (1943), 117.

Interviews

Arnold, Dr Jorg, former Criminal Court Judge in East Germany, Lecturer, Max-Planck-Institut, Freiburg-im-Breisgau, Germany, 7 May 1993.

Bozek, Jolanta, presiding judge in the Bankruptcy District Court, Warsaw, 12 June 1994, Warsaw, Poland (Bozek interview 1).

Bozek, Jolanta, follow-up, 17 October 1996 (Bozek interview 2).

Hofmanski, Prof. Dr Piotr, Supreme Court Judge (Criminal Chamber), Warsaw, 18 October 2005 (Hofmanski interview 1).

Hofmanski, Prof. Dr Piotr, Supreme Court Judge (Criminal Chamber), 19 May 2008 (Hofmanski interview 2).

Jaruzelski, General Wojciech, 10 November 1993, Warsaw, Poland.

Rzeplinski, Andrzej, Professor of Criminal Justice and Criminal Law, Institute for Social Resocialisation and Rehabilitation (IPSiR), University of Warsaw, and of the Helsinki Foundation for Human Rights, Warsaw, 7 February 1994, Warsaw, Poland.

Zoll, Prof. Dr Andrzej, (former) Commissioner for the Protection of Citizens' Rights (Ombudsman), Warsaw, 17 October 2005.

Index

For Product Safety Concerns and Information please contact our EU representative GPSR@taylorandfrancis.com
Taylor & Francis Verlag GmbH, Kaufingerstraße 24, 80331 München, Germany

www.ingramcontent.com/pod-product-compliance
Ingram Content Group UK Ltd.
Pitfield, Milton Keynes, MK11 3LW, UK
UKHW020159200926
475702UK00004B/525
* 9 7 8 0 7 5 4 6 7 3 3 8 5 *